L.

133.072   Baker, Robert A.

BAKER   **Missing pieces.**

$23.95

DATE			

BAKER & TAYLOR BOOKS

MISSING PIECES

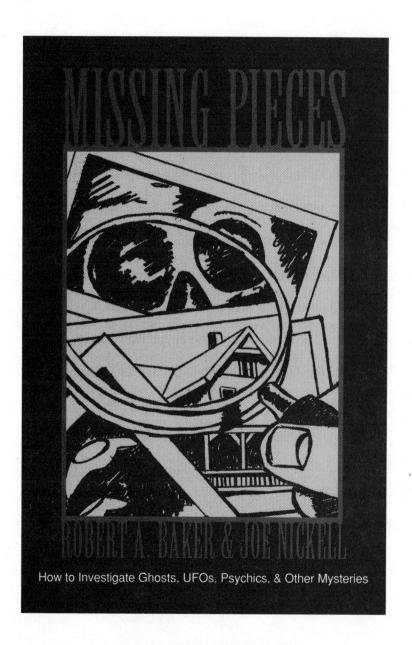

MISSING PIECES

How to Investigate Ghosts, UFOs, Psychics, & Other Mysteries

ROBERT A. BAKER & JOE NICKELL

Prometheus Books ▪ Buffalo, New York

Published 1992 by Prometheus Books.

Missing Pieces: How to Investigate Ghosts, UFOs, Psychics, and Other Mysteries.
Copyright © 1992 by Robert A. Baker and Joe Nickell. All rights reserved. No
part of this publication may be reproduced, stored in a retrieval system, or transmitted in any form or by any means, electronic, mechanical, photocopying, recording, or otherwise, without prior written permission of the publisher, except
in the case of brief quotations embodied in critical articles and reviews. Inquiries
should be addressed to Prometheus Books, 59 John Glenn Drive, Buffalo, New
York 14228, 716-837-2475 (FAX: 716-835-6901).

96 95 94 93 92   5 4 3 2 1

Library of Congress Cataloging-in-Publication Data

Baker, Robert A.
    Missing pieces : how to investigate ghosts, UFOs, psychics, and other mysteries /
by Robert A. Baker and Joe Nickell.
        p.   cm.
    Includes bibliographical references and index.
    ISBN 0-87975-729-9
    1. Parapsychology—Investigation—Handbooks, manuals, etc. 2. Occultism—
Investigation—Handbooks, manuals, etc. I. Nickell, Joe. II. Title.
BF1040.N48   1992
133'.072—dc20   92-3439
                                                                                  CIP

Printed in the United States of America on acid-free paper.

Contents

Part 2: Specific Applications

Part 3: Dealing with Others

Foreword

The following book is a "how-to manual" for anyone who would like to become a qualified investigator of paranormal claims or who is interested in knowing more about the secrets of the alleged supernatural. The authors, both Fellows of the *Committee for the Scientific Investigation of Claims of the Paranormal* (*CSICOP*), collectively have over fifty years of experience in studying and investigating bizarre claims and unusual events. In studying these phenomena the two P.I.s (Paranormal Investigators) developed tactics and techniques which they have put together in this step-by-step textbook showing how to investigate ghosts and haunted houses, UFO sightings and claimed abductions, psychics and psychic healers, prophets and astrologers, miracle workers, crop circles, spontaneous human combustion, and numerous other such incredible claims. If you have ever wondered about such things and are interested in knowing why people believe in the supernatural and how trained investigators go about tracking down and solving these alleged paranormal mysteries, then this is a book you must read.

Invariably, whenever one sets out to investigate a paranormal or supernatural claim, one immediately discovers that vital pieces of information are missing. Like a detective entering the apartment of a murder suspect and stumbling over the suspect's corpse, the paranormal investigator also finds himself or herself in the position of having to search for clues—for the missing pieces of the puzzle, for evidence that once uncovered will enable the detective to complete the jigsawed pattern and see the total picture, i.e., the who, what, when, where, how, and why—and, therefore, come up with the solution to the mystery.

We have chosen the title *Missing Pieces* for our study of how to go about scientifically and systematically investigating paranormal claims because it is axiomatic that every case one encounters, whether simple or complex—be it a claim of a UFO abduction or the presence of a pesky poltergeist—will require that the investigator carefully determine *what* is supposed to have happened, *who* is making the claim, *when* was the event purported to have happened, *where* did the event occur, *how* did it supposedly happen, and, if it *did* happen, *why* did it happen?

In some instances, like the famous (or infamous) haunted Hannah House in Indianapolis, the investigators discovered to their surprise that none of the claimed supernatural events ever occurred in the first place. Similarly, the nationally touted crash of a UFO in Kecksburg, Pennsylvania, featured prominently on the TV show "Unsolved Mysteries," also proved to be a nonevent. There was no crash, only rumors of a crash that quickly ballooned into a UFO *cause celebré*. In both these instances the "missing pieces" were the facts that, like the Amityville Horror, proved all the claims were false.

For most supernatural claims, however, finding the pieces necessary to complete the picture and/or to disclose the truth is not so simple or so easy. One may find oneself spending days, months, or even years searching in the darkest and most remote corners of both the human mind and the human habitat to bring forth the one essential fact that clarifies the mystery. To help you carry out your own successful search for the various missing pieces of the endless paranormal puzzles is the authors' purpose in the pages that follow. To assist in this endeavor we have divided the book into three parts. Part 1 is concerned with general principles of science, the scientific method, human psychology, the art of interrogation, investigatory tools and techniques, and the world of the paranormal. In Part 2 these general principles are demonstrated in specific application to the investigation of ghosts, claims of amazing powers, UFOs and UFO abductions, and where other claims of mysterious marvels and supernatural powers are made. Providing both general principles and their application in specific areas of investigatory concern we believe will maximize their usefulness to the beginning investigator. Part 3 is concerned with public relations.

While it is theoretically possible that some or even many paranormal claims and odd, unusual, or even "supernatural" events will continue to defy or resist natural or scientific explanation, it is becoming daily more difficult to find the miraculous or truly otherworldly event that is beyond the natural pale. Certainly, before one embraces the transcendental or supernatural view, one should first rule out any and all natural possibilities. That this is rarely done—particularly by the antiscientific or unscientific paranormalist—makes your task considerably easier. Too many of the true believers, when they look at the world, see only what they want to see and expect to see. Those who look for and expect to find a miracle at every turn are seldom disappointed. For the transcendentalists there are no mysteries, no puzzles, no missing pieces—only evidence of a divine manifestation. Consequently there is no need to look any further and they accept what they are told as confirmation of their pre-existing belief. Their picture of the world is perfect and complete; there are no missing pieces and, thus, no puzzle to solve. What they see is what they get—a miracle, proof of reincarnation, an extraterrestrial spaceship, mind-reading, and a return to life of one long dead. For the true believer the mysteries are to be protected and maintained. The last thing on earth they want is an answer in natural or scientific terms, and no amount of evidence one could amass would change their point of view.

It may well be true that those who harbor a scientific or skeptical point of view are equally biased and even more difficult to persuade or convince that some experiences and events defy the laws of nature. The difference between the transcendentalist and the skeptic, however, is profound. The skeptic carries out an empirical investigation whenever possible and tries to explain the event in natural, human, and scientific terms. What is truly extraordinary is that whenever such efforts are made by dedicated and determined investigators, nearly every mysterious, strange, paranormal event turns out to be something easily understood by those familiar with the natural and social sciences. This is not to say that science has solved all of the mysteries of the universe nor that we know all there is to know about the powers of the human mind. We are, however, inalterably convinced that these mysteries will only be solved by the combined efforts of scientifically trained citizens using the tools and techniques of modern science and attacking systematically the illogic, the unreason, and the superstitious beliefs of a naive and credulous minority who accept as the gospel truth whatever the media tells them. For those who are interested in fighting the war against superstition, we hope this book will be of some assistance in helping you to discover the missing pieces in the paranormalists' claims, to put the pieces together and complete the picture, and to solve the mystery. Happy hunting!

Robert A. Baker and Joe Nickell

Introduction

Some skeptical investigators refer to themselves as "debunkers," which is unfortunate. Although thorough investigation may often result in the debunking of fanciful claims, to call oneself a debunker implies bias, suggesting—rightly or wrongly—that the results are known prior to investigation and will always be negative. This not only lessens the investigator's credibility, but can lead to a habit of mind that too readily accepts a dubious fact simply because it supports a negative position.

Between the two extremes functions the true investigator. To him, or her, mysterious phenomena are not to be critically heralded as proof of transcendent realms; neither are they annoyances to be dismissed or debunked at all cost. Instead, to the investigator, mysteries are meant to be *solved*.

—Joe Nickell, *Secrets of the Supernatural*

The primary purpose of this book is to provide the beginning investigator of alleged paranormal phenomena with a handy and concise manual of procedures and techniques for investigating unusual phenomena and paranormal claims. A secondary purpose is to provide alternative explanations for many "unsolved mysteries" and supposedly "supernatural and occult" events. Though it is impossible to be encyclopedic in this small volume, we will, nevertheless, cover a fairly wide range of paranormal and parapsychological topics. Because of the large number of irrational beliefs and their ever-increasing popularity we are forced to emphasize breadth at the expense of depth. Although the mysterious and sensational have ever been popular, such popularity has, unfortunately, been aided and abetted by

13

the media who are, increasingly it seems, more concerned with the size of their audience than with either scientific truth or accurate reporting.

A nagging and irksome question in the minds of most skeptics today is the following: Why in this modern scientific age is belief in the supernatural and the occult so prevalent? Shades of the Middle Ages! National polls regarding ghosts, UFOs, Bigfoot, demon possession, and so forth invariably show widespread acceptance of and allegiance to these and other superstitious beliefs. A recent Gallup poll carried out in June 1990 and reported in the Winter 1991 issue of *The Skeptical Inquirer* revealed that 1 out of every 4 Americans believes in ghosts; 1 out of every 4 believes he/she has had a telepathic experience and has communicated extrasensorily with another person; 1 in 6 believes he/she has been in touch with someone who has died; 1 in 10 claims to have seen or been in the presence of a ghost or apparition; more than half believe in the Devil and 1 in 10 claims to have talked to Satan; 1 in 7 reports he/she has personally seen a UFO; and 3 in 4 state that at least occasionally they read their horoscopes in the newspaper, and 1 in 4 states that he/she does indeed believe in the tenets of astrology. In fact, Gallup and Newport report that, "All in all, only 7 percent of Americans deny believing in any of a list of 18 paranormal experiences (e.g., *déjà vu,* the Devil, ESP, demon possession, psychic or spiritual healing, telepathy, haunted houses, extraterrestrial visitations, clairvoyance, astrology, ghosts, reincarnation, communication with the dead, telekinesis, witches, channeling and spirit possession, pyramid power and the healing power of crystals)." Almost one-half said they believe in five or more on the list, and even though actual experience is much less frequent than belief, 3 of 4 reported experiencing at least one such occurrence, with about half claiming experience with more than three on the list. Most interesting is the fact that belief in "paranormal" experiences also cuts across conventional religious lines; i.e., almost as many deeply religious Americans as those who are not religious professed belief in and experience with the paranormal. Sadly enough, a comparison of beliefs held in 1990 with those held in 1978 shows that, with the exception of astrology and ESP, which showed slight declines, belief in ghosts, witches, devils, clairvoyance, and *déjà vu* showed significant gains.

For skeptics, the $64 question remains: Why do people who encounter strange and unusual events immediately jump to a supernatural or paranormal explanation rather than to a scientific or naturalistic one? To answer this question we need to look a little more closely at the essence of human nature and, particulalry, the psychology of human belief.

The Nature of Human Nature

Whenever we attempt to answer questions about human behavior we must, perforce, look at human motivation, i.e., the reasons why people do the things they do and believe the things they believe. Over the past two hundred years psychologists, sociologists, and other students of human behavior, while they have not developed laws and principles as fixed and firm as those we find in physics and chemistry, have, nevertheless, learned a great deal about human beings and have amassed a fund of knowledge that is both reliable and valid. Once gained, this knowledge can be most useful in helping us to understand even the most bizarre and outlandish of human actions and even behavior which is clearly irrational or "crazy," i.e., psychotic. Just as there is no physical action without a physical cause, there is also no human action without a human cause. These causes are, in psychological terms, referred to as *motives*. To understand human behavior we need to understand its causes, i.e., human motivation.

The Hierarchy of Motives

A number of years ago the psychologist Abraham Maslow, in the process of developing his theory of personality, outlined his now famous theory of human motivation or action. Human needs, Maslow claims, are arranged in a series like a ladder. At the bottom or on the level of the first rung, we find that the *physiological needs* are predominant. We must have air, water, food, rest, and sex. These are the most powerful for all human beings. Their satisfaction is necessary for the survival of the individual and the race. Once these needs are satisfied, they are no longer needs and other needs can and do come into play and dominate the field of our attention. Once the physiological needs are taken care of, we can then move to the second rung of the ladder.

At this level we find the *safety needs* are dominant. The human being needs to feel secure, safe, free from anxiety and fear. We need to feel that the world is dependable and reliable, that something in the way of order exists in the universe. Nothing is so unpleasant as uncertainty, never knowing from one moment to the next whether one will live or die. We need to be sure that tomorrow will come. We want protection for our future and for our loved ones. Thus, we buy life insurance, demand job security, buy stocks and bonds, and open savings accounts. Security and stability are also important human needs.

After the physiological needs are met and a certain measure of personal safety and security have been achieved, we move up to the third rung of the ladder where *love and affection* and the *belongingness needs* become paramount. These we satisfy by falling in love and creating an intimate, personal relationship of love and trust with another person or several persons. We find it necessary and important to both give and receive love and affection and to find a place in the world where we belong. We seek an end to our feelings of loneliness, isolation, and alienation through seeking out other human beings and joining them in work and play activities. We join clubs, groups, and other types of social organizations because we have these needs for other people. We need companionship, human attachments, and social reinforcement.

Another important aspect of the need hierarchy is that the higher level needs do not come into play unless all of the needs lower in the series have been satisfied first. This does not, however, mean that various needs may not operate simultaneously. They often do. If, however, the individual is fortunate enough to have all of his biological needs met, his safety and security needs taken care of, as well as his needs for love and belongingness, then and only then will the need for satisfying his *self-esteem needs* become dominant. This need at the fourth rung of the ladder is actually two separate needs—esteem from others and self-esteem. The esteem in the eyes of others is the most important of the two since it is difficult for us to feel good about ourselves unless we know that others think we are good and important. Our social status, prestige, reputation, etc., as well as our needs for power and control and our efforts to raise these things, are representative of these types of needs. Our feelings of confidence and self-worth are also important to us, and without a measure of self-esteem we feel depressed, inadequte, helpless, inferior, and incapable of dealing or coping with life itself.

Even if all the needs previously mentioned have been met, there is still a measure of discontent—the next rung of the ladder. Something in human life seems to be missing unless we have used our skills and abilities to the maximum and are living our lives to the fullest possible extent. Even if all the other needs are met, discontent and restlessness will occur unless the poet is writing poetry, the artist is painting pictures, and the inventor is creating new things of value. What a person *can* become— they *must* become—if they are to be happy and satisfied. We must achieve *self-realization.*

Finally, at the top of the hierarchy we find the need to serve others, to do something for the good of mankind, or to reach some sort of union with higher powers or principles. There seems to be a need to leave our personal egos behind and to become one with something bigger than ourselves. This need for "transcendence," or religious yearnings, or union with something greater than ourselves also seems to be a built-in human need that can be satisfied in a number of ways. This is the need that great spiritual or religious leaders, as well as the less great psychics, channels, mediums, and charlatans cater to by promising to provide what the yearners are aching to have. Here we also find the powerful "need to believe."

In those afflicted with this "need to believe" we also find as dominant themes the need for certainty, surety, and security; the need for control and power; the need for social feedback and reinforcement; the need for assurance and reassurance; the need for simple and "easy answers," i.e., intellectual simplicity; the need for safe and vicarious excitement, for novelty and the new; the need to attach oneself to and identify with something large and powerful and thereby indirectly gain a measure of status, importance, and significance. There is always a strong need to feel important, special, and significant in the vast and awesome scheme of things. For example, how nice and comforting it is to believe that "Jesus is coming all the way down from heaven just to save little, old, unimportant me." Or, "From all of the millions of people on earth the Virgin Mary selected me to appear before and give me a message for all of mankind!" Only a veritable saint could be so favored! Therefore, since the virgin has favored me, I must be someone of tremendous importance indeed! Moreover, she has given me a mission! Such a missionary spirit and its accompanying motivation is easily understood. Consider all of the human motives that are so neatly satisfied by this one transcendent vision: power, status, security, self-esteem, and respect and deference from fellow believers. These are wonderful rewards indeed for a little belief!

Human Perception

Another aspect of human nature we must consider is that of human perception of our awareness of the world we live in. Human beings are not merely passive receivers of sensory information from the physical and social environment. Indeed, we take this information and interpret it according to our past experience and prior knowledge. What we make of it depends upon what we have learned about it in the past. Based upon our prior experience we make assumptions about the world, and we act not upon the raw information but upon our *assumptions* and *expectations* about this information. For this reason many of our perceptions are flawed, and people receiving the same information interpret it differently. Our expectations, furthermore, pretty much determine what we see and don't see, and just how we interpret what we do see. Magicians take full advantage of such expectations to fool us. Because of our faulty human perception, we are not very accurate observers or eyewitnesses. The unreliability of eyewitness testimony is legendary and the fact that you saw it with your own eyes is no proof that what you saw was what transpired. Not only do our eyes and ears often deceive us, but our mind-set and our expectations also cause us to hear and see events as we assumed them to be, not as they actually were. We must also be painfully aware of the fact that not only do human beings lie—they lie *unintentionally* as well as intentionally because of their misperceptions. And as for deliberate lying, this is so commonplace we take it for granted in our daily dealings with others. Obtaining the truth about any event is far from easy, and the more extraordinary the event, the more difficult it is to determine exactly what did or did not occur. Obtaining an accurate and truthful account of any happening—as policemen, detectives, insurance investigators, lawyers, judges, and parents of children well know—is hard to come by. Psychologists are also painfully aware of another set of obstacles standing in the way of the truth: the large number of so-called *ego-defense mechanisms* that we all use to protect ourselves and to preserve our self-esteem and public image.

The Psychological Defense Mechanisms

Whenever people encounter something that is too anxiety-arousing or stressful for them to deal with, they either *suppress* it by willfully and consciously refusing to think about it or they *repress* it, that is, they unconsciously reject it and push it down into the subconscious where it is hidden out of sight and out of mind. If these defense strategies don't work or are not available, then one may retreat into a world of *fantasy* and thus escape from the unpleasant facts of reality. If we retreat too fast and too far, then we may enter a *psychosis*—a mental state wherein we are unable to discriminate reality from fantasy. If we are able to keep our hold on reality most of the time but still begin to believe some particular things that everyone else knows to be untrue, then we suffer from a *delusion,* or false belief. Another way in which we react to mental stresses and anxieties is to develop *hallucinations,* or false perceptions. Under certain conditions, hallucinatory phenomena may occur in normal, healthy individuals (Assad 1990). A number of surveys carried out both in Europe and the United States have shown that between 10 percent and 27 percent of the general population has reported some type of hallucinatory experience, often in the visual modality, that involves the sensory perception of the presence of another person when, in fact, no one is physically present. While such vague hallucinatory perceptions may occur under normal circumstances, more elaborate and definite hallucinations can occur in people who are subjected to abnormal environmental conditions such as prolonged sensory deprivation, sleep deprivation, starvation, and severe stress, as well as fatigue and grief.

We may also develop *phobias* of various sorts which are other ways of protecting ourselves from our fears. Some of the more common phobias are claustrophobia—fear of closed places; pyrophobia—fear of fire; agoraphobia—fear of open spaces; misophobia—fear of dirt; astrophobia —fear of lightning; brontephobia—fear of thunder; and hundreds of others. We can also become *fixated* at a certain period within the normal stages of growth and development and stop growing and developing altogether. We can even *regress,* or go backwards, to a simpler and more primitive stage of thinking, feeling, and acting. We may also engage in *displacement* by shifting onto others our own feelings, attitudes, and values through *projection,* i.e., endowing others with our own deficiencies, needs, wants, and attitudes. We *project* our own weaknesses and fears onto others.

Another very common ego-defense mechanism is *identification,* a situation wherein we become one with or identify with the other person. We admire them so much we *become* them. Fan club members—the "fanatics"—are classic examples. By becoming the person you admire, you also share his/her strength, beauty, glory, and fame. Along with these mechanisms we also have a number of *character defenses*—psychological attitudes and beliefs built up over time to control our feelings of loss, failure, and insecurity. One of the most common character defenses is *narcissism,* or extreme love of self, of one's body, one's ego, one's creations, etc. The narcissist is always seeking admiration from others and finds it impossible to live without the admiration of others. Narcissists must have status and prestige and they are always in the process of building a facade of strength. Another defense given particular emphasis in the work of Alfred Adler is *compensation.* Here we bend over backwards to cover our weaknesses and develop compensatory strengths in other directions or areas of life. The frail child minus athletic skills becomes an "A" student and master of the violin as *compensation.* We also find *masochism,* or an overt love of humility, as a prominent trait in many people. Masochists love to abase themselves and denigrate their skills or talents. Such individuals dread self-assertion and set up, unconsciously and unwittingly, this sort of defense against hostility. In extreme cases it shows up as a love of pain, punishment, and sexual degradation. Perfectionism is another trait, another mechanism through which we manage to escape criticism by leaving nothing undone which might attract criticism. No one would dare criticize something which is perfect! Then we have the very common act of *rationalization* in which we provide socially acceptable reasons for the ego-damaging truth. Thus, our true feelings and impulses are masked or disguised. *Sublimation* is yet another common defense whereby we make the socially unacceptable acceptable. Our prurient interest in naked bodies is sublimated by our taking up art and photography where such interests are socially permissible. *Reaction formation* is yet another defense against our rampant and dangerous aggressiveness. Since our true impulses are so evil and dangerous, we go to the opposite behavior extremes to protect ourselves from them. Our original hostility becomes impeccable good manners and an extreme and excessive politeness. Whenever death is mentioned, we tell a joke about it and thus defuse and divert the anxiety and fear. Other forms our worries and anxieties take are that of *obsessions* and *compulsions.* At times we are unable to stop thinking of certain things or we must continue to engage in repetitive behaviors—behaviors that make no sense. Phobias and repetitive behaviors or compulsions are common examples of additional defenses against overwhelming fear and anxiety. Finally, because of the psychological mechanism called *introjection,* we take onto ourselves the feelings, attitudes, standards, and values (and sometimes even the physical mannerisms) of our parents and authority figures. If such figures are overly strict or authoritarian, we may develop guilt and even engage in self-punishment or we may become overly dependent and submissive. It is essential that every investigator understand that people become very astute at defending their egos and selves against all such psychological threats and the subsequent anxiety that all such threats arouse. In order to solve the mystery of strange and deviant human behavior, to understand why people do the things they do and believe the things they believe, it is imperative that we look beyond the overt and superficial behavior and delve into the underlying motivational causes. In no other area of human behavior is this more important than in the matter of human belief and the appeal of the transcendent vision or salvation from above and beyond this earthly pale.

The Psychology of Belief and Transcendence

Only a moment's reflection will make it clear that our lives are surrounded on every side by mystery. We do not know where the human race came from or where it is going. The very purpose of human existence is also unknown and is even, perhaps, unknowable. We find it difficult to answer even the simplest of questions: Why were we born? Why must we die? Are we alone in the universe? What does the future hold? Is there life beyond the grave—or is this all there is? To answer such questions thoughtful men have developed philosophies and religions, i.e., systems of belief designed to answer such questions and to attenuate and relieve the basic human anxieties surrounding all such existential and eschatological questions. If the answers are not readily available, then it is better to believe something rather than to continue trembling in the dark. For many—too many—belief is just about all they have.

For the majority of men and women on the planet earth today life is short, mean, cruel, and brutal. War continues to ravage the planet daily and hunger and starvation are facts of life on half of the continents. For many, disease and death are common and constant companions. For such individuals who struggle day and night merely to survive, their understanding of themselves and the world they live in is minimal and has a very low priority. Illiterate, ignorant, and fearful, their only hope, their only solace lies in their belief in a good, forgiving, and loving deity—a deity who will provide another and better place than this horrible, pain-filled sink of suffering and despair. For them there is little more than the hope of a spiritual paradise, a world beyond the senses, a place where all human needs are met, and where no one suffers and dies. For the wretched of the earth their religious belief—their dreams of a better world to come— is all they have. No one with an ounce of humanity in his being would deny or think of depriving these suffering masses of their only solace— their vision of another life and a better world beyond this present horror.

Well-educated, scientifically trained, and enlightened scholars who have read and understood human history, cultural anthropology, sociology, and psychology not only comprehend but perhaps clearly understand the superstitions of primitive men and the whys and wherefores of their animistic beliefs. Gods and goddesses, spirits and demons, ghosts and ghouls, witches and warlocks, medicine men and shamans, and priests and priestesses control and govern the world that primitive man inhabits. To survive and prosper, all these spiritual forces and the middle men who attend them must be courted and propitiated. Surrounding the universe of primitive man is a superordinate, ever-present, and ominous world of the gods— spirits who are quixotic, jealous, vengeful, and all-powerful, who strike without warning and at random. They must be pleased and placated if one is to survive. This is particularly true of the dead—those restless souls who leave their graves and wander over the land, besieging and haunting the living. Little wonder that the need to believe in controlling forces above and beyond our own feeble and futile efforts is such a powerful demand. When such human needs and fears are reinforced and then supported and strengthened by those other human beings in his social group, as well as by the spiritual middle men—the priests and the shamans— a deep and passionate religious commitment is the only possible outcome. In this way the needs of primitive man are met and the institutionalized answers are available for each and every existential question he is able to raise.

The greatest error that contemporary scientists and skeptics can make is to assume that the sociopsychological mechanisms underlying the primitive's belief systems are applicable only to those earlier times. On the contrary, the belief psychology of the caveman and that of modern man are fundamentally the same. While it is true that most modern men do not attribute thunder to Thor throwing his hammer, nor do most believe that the world is flat or that "bad air" causes disease or that witches ride broomsticks through the air, there are many modern men who do belong to the Flat Earth Society, who believe that quartz crystals can be programmed like a computer and that wearing them around your neck can prevent (or cure) cancer, and that it is possible to use a radio to listen to the dead talk to one another. It is also important to note that most of these modern people who hold such strange beliefs are in no way psychotic or mentally ill. Neither do they need to be institutionalized, placed under the care of a psychiatrist, or placed upon a strict regimen of medication. They offer no danger to themselves or others and, for the most part, all other aspects of their daily behavior is indiscriminable from yours and mine. They do, however, hold one or more unusual or irrational beliefs. Merely believing that God talked to you last night and told you to love everyone and give all your money away is insufficient grounds for putting you away. Even if you act on this delusion and stand on the corner passing out $100 bills, no one has the right to arrest you and put you in an institution. If, on the other hand, God told you to kill all your neighbors and you proceeded to buy an AK-47 and carry out his request, then you most definitely should have your belief system challenged, your actions restrained, and your body institutionalized. While psychologically there is little difference, i.e., God talked to you in both instances, socially the content of the messages is vital and fundamentally different. Calling ourselves scientists—or even being scientists—does not give us the right to decide what people shall or shall not believe. Science has a mighty—not an almighty—mission! As long as a man's beliefs and his belief systems do not interfere with the rights of others, we have no God-given right to decide what he/she can or cannot believe. While we may disagree fundamentally and have libraries of data and empirical fact on our side—we may even understand how they came to their erroneous conclusions, and we may know more than they will ever know about the phenomena in question— we still have no right to force our convictions upon them. We may know they are wrong and be able to prove it on moral, legal, empirical, scientific, and every other conceivable logical ground—yet such knowledge does not endow us with either the right or the power to force our convictions upon others. If we are to change their beliefs and opinions, we must use persuasion, not force. The difference is more than critical; it is crucial.

On May 21, 1991 "The Oprah Winfrey Show" topic was "Ghosts: Fact or Fancy." Among Oprah's guests were Ben and Jean Williams, authors of *The Black Hope Horror* (William Morrow & Co., 1991), a book describing in detail their encounters with ghosts and evil spirits in their home in the Newport subdivision of Houston, Texas. The Williamses were unalterably convinced that evil spirits—ghosts of the dead—killed their thirty-year-old daughter Tina Lynn Howard, who died of a massive heart attack. Other guests on the show were Loyd Auerbach, a noted parapsychologist and ghost hunter, as well as Paul Kurtz, the noted humanist, skeptic, and head of CSICOP. Every effort on the part of Auerbach and Kurtz to introduce a note of reason or any element of skepticism about the existence of ghosts or any doubt as to the ability of the dead to cause heart attacks in the living was met by a barrage of emotional invective and furious shouts of denial, with glares of hatred directed at both Auerbach and Kurtz. It is important to know that, with one exception, none of the other neighbors in the subdivision whose homes were atop the graves in the Black Hope Cemetery ever encountered any evil spirits or apparitions, or saw or heard any indication of ghostly goings-on. In their neighbors' collective opinion, the Williamses and their neighbor Haney were haunted only by overactive imaginations. With the Williamses' strong emotional investment in their experience and their public commitment to their published beliefs, nothing on earth could now convince them that these experiences were, perhaps, due to the operation of psychological forces they not only were unaware of, but would quickly dismiss even if they were told about their presence and mode of operation. In all such instances of vested psychological interests and total emotional commitment, the wisest and safest course for the investigator to take is that of nonconfrontation. By this we mean hear the believer out, investigate his claims and beliefs carefully and dispassionately, and reserve judgment until all facts are at hand. Then you can calmly present the believer with your findings and hope that he will be sane enough to accept them. If your results show he is in error and that a simpler, more rational, and more natural explanation exists for his experience, again you cannot force him to accept your logic. If he makes this decision, he must do it on his own.

For some reason many people are not very well informed about the nature of neuroses and psychoses. People who are in touch with consensual reality but who have one or more various types of "mental problems" are labeled *neurotic.* These same individuals, however, who lose contact with reality and who have *hallucinations,* i.e., false perceptions, and/or *delusions,* i.e., false beliefs, are termed *psychotic.* All human mental disorders, however, lie upon a continuum and the differences are differences in degree. Psychotics are not "crazy all over" or "crazy all the time." They are crazy only in spots and only some of the time. People do not actively hallucinate all day and all night, day in and day out, night in and night out; they only hallucinate some of the time. As for delusions or false beliefs, you would not know you were talking to someone who is disturbed as long as you avoided the topic of the person's delusion. In fact, the world is filled with people with some very, very strange beliefs and people who do some very, very strange things. The Breatharians, for example, believe that eating is merely an acquired habit and that one can live, lichen-like, off of nothing but light and air. Another deranged group of people believe that aluminum is poisonous and they sell "polarity pillows" to negate its deadly effects. Another group sells "time cameras" and "anti-gravity devices." Many other groups believe that the earth is hollow and spews forth demons and, despite all evidence to the contrary, that the earth is, indeed, flat as a pancake! Hundreds of other individuals and small groups of madmen are described in Ivan Stang's *High Weirdness By Mail* (Simon & Schuster, 1988) and the periodical *Fact Sheet Five,* published eight times a year by Mike Gunderloy of Rensselaer, N.Y. Each issue of *Factsheet Five* contains descriptions of literally two to three hundred privately published magazines extolling exotic, unusual, strange, and weird belief systems and odd points of view ranging in content from the totally bizarre and psychotic to the mildly strange journals devoted to music, hobbies, and comic book characters. Many of the publications are blatantly obscene and are designed to be *maximally* offensive. What is truly remarkable is the range of human beliefs and belief-systems that these unusual publications are able to span. Book reviews and record reviews are also included in each issue. Despite the strangeness of the beliefs and practices, it must be remembered that none of these people are psychotic or so dangerous they need to be put away for either their own safety or the safety of others. Strange as their beliefs may be these persons are, in no way, dangerous. The mere fact that a person possesses one or more strange and bizarre beliefs does not give anyone the right to deprive such an individual of personal freedom or the right to publish and promote his or her odd convictions. We still have the right to be different as long as this right does not infringe upon or restrict the rights of others. In our eagerness to solve the occult enigmas we must remember not to become so fanatical that we lose our own sense of proportion or fair play and contact with consensual reality.

We must recognize that in our society only a relatively few people are scientifically trained. Scientific illiteracy is the norm and even among the well educated in the nonscientific disciplines, we find gross misunderstanding and misconceptions about the nature of the scientific enterprise.*

---

*Scientific illiteracy extends to science itself: scientists often know little or nothing about fields of science outside their own (Pool 1991).

Intelligent and articulate journalists, newspaper editors, and other media personnel seldom understand the rules of logic, the principles of experimentation and experimental design, or the requirement of scientific proof. We must also be very clear about the fact that there is no way that one can escape the "human element" in any investigation: you are nearly always dealing with unreliable data—data collected by fallible and biased individuals; you are always dealing with phenomena poorly or fleetingly observed; you will always encounter inadequate descriptions, emotionally colored and distortedly reported. While the old Missouri stance "show me" is not always feasible or inevitably the wisest course with regard to matters paranormal, it is usually the "best" of possible choices. Truth, i.e., validity, in such an area as this is very hard to come by for a number of reasons: (1) human perception is unreliable; (2) human communication and reporting are faulty; (3) human motivation is complex and often hidden —even from those experiencing it; (4) human emotion is inescapable and usually interferes with logic and reason; (5) human beings prevaricate, i.e., lie—knowingly and often unknowingly—and they also perpetrate hoaxes; (6) human beings are exceedingly credulous and the range of what humans will believe is awe-inspiring; (7) normal, ordinary, everyday run-of-the-mill human beings occasionally hallucinate (have false perceptions) and many maintain daily delusions and illusions (false beliefs) which complicate truth-getting operations; and (8) most human beings are suggestible and many human beings are highly suggestible—even fantasy-prone—having as their creed "reality is a nice place to visit but I wouldn't want to live there."

Moreover, if we examine the "whys" of human belief and take a careful look at "believer" psychology, we also find that, as we noted earlier: (1) human beings have strong needs for control and for power over their physical environment and their social world; (2) human beings have strong needs for certainty, surety, security, and stability—assurance as an antidote to fear and panic; (3) human beings have strong social needs, i.e., the need for companionship, human attachments, and social reinforcement, as well as and in addition to powerful sexual needs; (4) human beings have strong needs for "new" things, for novelty and excitement—we want and expect to be amused and entertained—we want the thrill of danger, but most of us want to be safe and to experience the power vicariously; (5) human beings have strong needs for simplicity, for facile, easily understood answers to complex questions—they can only tolerate so much frustration— they want quick solutions to all the "unsolved mysteries"; (6) human beings have strong needs for "something more," i.e., the need to attach oneself to, or identify with, something bigger and more powerful than oneself and one's ego—religions, psychics, prophets, et al., often supply the material that meets these "transcendent" needs; (7) human beings have strong needs to feel important, special, significant, and "different" in the universal scheme of things. For example, "Out of all the people on the planet Earth the aliens abducted *me* and asked *me* to save the world."

Whenever we encounter human behavior that is odd, strange, or different—behavior that does not follow ordinary human routes—we can look to the above motives and needs as plausible and possible clues to understanding.

Before leaving the topic of *belief,* perhaps it would be useful to define the term and also to distinguish it from *fact.* A belief can be defined quite usefully as Nickerson (1986) does: "confidence that a particular thing is true, as evidenced by a willingness to act as though it were." Facts, on the other hand, can be viewed as beliefs that are well supported by evidence and, therefore, as justifying a high degree of confidence. Facts are capable of verification; beliefs may not be. We also might distinguish here between beliefs and opinions. *Beliefs* are statements that, in principle, can be shown to be true or false, whereas with an *opinion,* it does not make sense to consider it as true or false because people differ in their preferences and opinions. Opinions are closer to a *point of view* but differ in that those expressing a point of view usually make statements in a manner that solicits critical review. Not only can views be examined because they are clearly stated, but people with a point of view are usually open to clarifying their statements when asked. Those with an opinion, however, may not be able to further clarify or state the reasons for their preference. We must also remember that reason alone does not necessarily yield the truth; reasoning can be good or bad, as well as correct or flawed. Plausible reasons for seemingly paranormal or supernatural events are much more likely to be arrived at if we discriminate between facts, beliefs, and opinions.

The Ideal Investigator

The competent paranormal investigator should, first of all, be a "good thinker," which is to say he or she should be able to think clearly and make and evaluate arguments, form and test hypotheses, make judgments and draw conclusions, and solve problems. The terms reasoning, problem-solving, thinking, and decision-making are closely related, and the tasks they involve overlap. As for the good thinker or competent investigator, Nickerson (1987) described and characterized him and her as follows. One who:

Uses evidence skillfully and impartially;

Organizes thoughts and articulates them concisely and coherently;

Suspends judgment in the absence of sufficient evidence to support a decision;

Understands the difference between reasoning and rationalizing;

Attempts to anticipate the probable consequences of alternative actions before choosing among them;

Understands the idea of degrees of belief;

Has a sense of the value and the cost of information, knows how to seek information, and does so when it makes sense;

Seeks similarities and analogies that are not superficially apparent;

Can learn independently and . . . has an interest in doing so;

Applies problem-solving techniques appropriately in domains other than those in which they were learned;

Can structure informally represented problems in such a way that formal techniques (for example, mathematics) can be used to solve them;

Listens carefully to other people's ideas;

Understands the difference between winning an argument and being right;

Recognizes that most real-world problems have more than one possible solution and that those solutions may differ in numerous respects and may be difficult to compare in terms of a single figure of merit;

Looks for unusual approaches to complex problems;

Can represent differing viewpoints without distortion, exaggeration, or caricaturization;

Is aware of the fact that one's understanding is always limited;

Recognizes the fallibility of one's own opinions, the probability of bias in these opinions, and the danger of differentially weighing evidence according to personal preferences;

Can strip a verbal argument of irrelevancies and phrase it in terms of its essentials;

Understands the differences among conclusions, assumptions, and hypotheses;

Habitually questions one's own views and attempts to understand both the assumptions that are critical to those views and the implications of the views;

Is sensitive to the difference between the validity of a belief and the intensity with which it is held.

In addition to being a good thinker, the paranormal investigator should also be a good scientist. We do not mean by this that it is necessary that one have a Ph.D. degree in one of the physical or natural sciences, but it does mean that the ideal investigator should be familiar with the scientific method and in possession of a *scientific attitude*. The scientific method consists of observations, classifying and organizing the observations, developing hypotheses, experimentally testing these hypotheses, repeating and verifying the results, and reporting the results to the general public. Science is, in general, public rather than private knowledge. As for the scientific "attitude," a truly excellent summary of what makes up the common sense of science and the components of the attitudes of science was published recently by the *Kansas School Naturalist* of Emporia State University (1989). Taken from works published by Bronowski (1978), Diederich (1967), and Whaley and Surratt (1967), it expresses in Table 1 (headed "Twenty 'Scientific Attitudes'") those attributes that every paranormal investigator should have.

Table 1

Twenty "Scientific Attitudes"
Modified from Bronowski (1978), Diedrich (1967),
and Whaley & Surratt (1967)

1. Empiricism

Simply said, a scientist prefers to "look and see." You do not argue about whether it is raining outside—just stick a hand out the window. Underlying this is the belief that there is one real world following constant rules of nature, and that we can probe that real world and build our understanding—it will not change on us. Nor does the real world depend on our understanding—we do not "vote" on science.

2. Determinism

"Cause-and-effect" underlie everything. In simple mechanisms, an action causes a reaction, and effects do not occur without causes. This does not mean that some processes are not random or chaotic. But a causative agent does not produce one effect today and another effect tomorrow.

3. A Belief that Problems have Solutions

Major problems have been tackled in the past, from the Manhattan Project to sending a man to the moon. Other problems such as pollution, war, poverty, and ignorance are seen as having real causes and are therefore solvable—perhaps not easily, but possible.

4. Parsimony

Prefer the simple explanation to the complex; when both the complex earth-centered system with epicycles and the simple Copernican sun-centered system explain apparent planetary motion, we chose the simpler.

5. Scientific Manipulation

Any idea, even though it may be simple and conform to apparent observations, must usually be confirmed by work that teases out the possibility that the effects are caused by other factors.

6. Skepticism

Nearly all statements make assumptions about prior conditions. A scientist often reaches a dead end in research and has to go back and determine if all of the assumptions made are true to how the world operates.

7. Precision

Scientists are impatient with vague statements: A virus causes disease? How many viruses are needed to infect? Are any hosts immune to the virus? Scientists are very exact and very "picky."

8. Respect for Paradigms

A paradigm is our overall understanding about how the world works. Does a new concept "fit" with our overall understanding or does it fail to weave in with our broad knowledge of the world? If it doesn't fit, it is "bothersome" and the scientist goes to work to find out if the new concept is flawed or if the paradigm must now be altered.

9. A Respect for Power of Theoretical Structure

Diederich describes how a scientist is unlikely to adopt the attitude: "That's all right in theory but it won't work in practice." He notes that the theory is "all right" only if it works in practice. Indeed the rightness of a theory is in the end what the scientist is working toward; no science facts are accumulated at random. (This is an understanding that many science fair students must learn!)

10. Willingness to Change an Opinion

When Harold Urey, author of one textbook theory on the origin of the moon's surface, examined the moon rocks brought back from the Apollo mission, he immediately recognized his theory did not fit with the hard facts before him. "I've been wrong!" he proclaimed without any thought of defending the theory he had supported for decades.

11. Loyalty to Reality

Dr. Urey did not convert to just any new idea, but accepted a model that matched reality better. He would never have considered holding to an old conclusion just because his name was associated with it.

12. Aversion to Superstition and an Automatic Preference for Scientific Explanation

No scientist can know all of the experimental evidence underlying current science concepts and therefore must adopt some views without understanding their basis. A scientist rejects superstition and prefers science paradigms out of an appreciation for the power of reality-based knowledge.

13. A Thirst for Knowledge, an "Intellectual Drive"

Scientists are addicted puzzle-solvers. The little piece of the puzzle that doesn't fit is the most interesting. However, as Diederich notes, scientists are willing to live with incompleteness rather than "fill the gaps with off-hand explanations."

14. Suspended Judgment

Again Diederich describes: "A scientist tries hard not to form an opinion on a given issue until he has investigated it, because it is so hard to give up opinions already formed, and they tend to make us find the facts that support the opinions. . . . There must be, however, a willingness to act upon the best hypothesis that one has the time or opportunity to form."

15. Awareness of Assumptions

Diederich describes how a good scientist starts by defining terms, making all assumptions very clear, and reducing necessary assumptions to the smallest number possible. Often we want scientists to make broad statements about a complex world. But usually scientists are very specific about what they "know" or will say with some certainty: "When these conditions hold true, the usual outcome is such-and-such."

16. Ability to Separate Fundamental Concepts from the Irrelevant or Unimportant

Some young scientists get bogged down in observations and data that are of little importance to the concept they want to investigate.

17. Respect for Quantification and Appreciation of Mathematics as a Language of Science

Many of nature's relationships are best revealed by patterns and mathematical relationships when reality is counted or measured; and this beauty often remains hidden without this tool.

18. An Appreciation of Probabilities and Statistics

Correlations do not prove cause-and-effect, but some pseudoscience arises when a chance occurrence is taken as "proof." Individuals who insist on an all-or-nothing world and who have little experience with statistics will have difficulty understanding the concept of an event occurring by chance.

19. An Understanding That All Knowledge Has Tolerance Limits

All careful analyses of the world reveal values that scatter at least slightly around an average point; a human's core body temperature is about so many degrees and objects fall at a certain rate of acceleration, but there is some variation. There is no absolute certainty.

20. Empathy for the Human Condition

Contrary to popular belief, there is a value system in science and it is based on humans being the only organisms that can "imagine" things that are not triggered by stimuli present at the immediate time in their environment; we are, therefore, the only creatures to "look" back at our past and plan forward to our future. This is why when you are reading a moving book, you imagine yourself in the position of another person and you think "I know what the author means and feels." Practices that ignore this empathy and resultant values for human life produce inaccurate science. (See Bronowski for more examples of this controversial "scientiific attitude.")

Reprinted from *The Kansas School Naturalist,* Emporia State University, Vol. 35, No. 4, April 1989, by the Great Lakes Skeptics

---

In addition to these attitudes the ideal investigator should also beware of what has been called "scientific immoralities." The good investigator, for example, avoids carelessness in making his observations—he eschews "sloppy work," he never generalizes beyond his data, nor does he confuse his opinions with his knowledge. Neither does he allow his egoism or pride to cause him to cling to theories that are outmoded or to invent new ones for the sake of selling them in books, articles, or lectures. Neither would he adjust his theories to reflect popular likes and dislikes or oppose the proof of another theory because of jealousy, or worse, because of ignorance and stupidity. He also refrains from sarcasm, ridicule, and resorting to authorities when confronted with data, logical argument, and verification. He is also careful to avoid arrogance and never indulges in dense verbiage for the sake of appearing superlearned. Most important of all, he is careful to avoid becoming a propagandist and engaging in the promotion of an unproved hypothesis simply because he thought of it.

It might prove useful at this point to briefly note the major differences between the quacks and crackpots, i.e., the pseudoscientsts and the real articles. A few years ago, Fred Gruenberger, in an amusing article called "Measure For Crackpots" (1962), listed thirteen major differences between the crackpot (CP) and the scientist. First is *public verifiability*—the scientist encourages replication of his work, whereas the CP says he and his followers are the only ones who can do it. Next, the scientist makes *predictions* on the basis of his data and admits those predictions that didn't come true, whereas the CP lists all possible outcomes and notes after the fact that one of them was, indeed, correct! Third, the scientist seeks to devise *controlled experiments* if he can, whereas the crackpot seeks to avoid them or, if some are performed, invents marvelous excuses for why they did not support his theories. Fourth, the scientist uses "Occam's razor," i.e., he prefers the explanation requiring the fewest assumptions or the simpler explanation, whereas the CP embraces either an unstable hypothesis—e.g., God or the Devil did it—or explanations so complex and convoluted they are almost impossible to test. Fifth, the scientist's work tends to lead to more *fruitful* results, i.e., new ideas, new approaches, new results, whereas the CP's arguments lead to dead ends. Sixth, the scientist immediately submits his work to known and recognized *authorities* for both opinion and testing, whereas the CP will usually refuse to allow the authorities to test his claims. Seventh, the scientist seeks out *established channels* for the publication of his results, whereas the crackpot avoids these channels or establishes his own private publication sources. Eighth, the scientist tends, in general, toward *humility,* whereas the CP seldom—if ever—demonstrates such avoidance of the limelight. Ninth, in general the scientist gravitates toward *open mindedness,* whereas the CP is generally dogmatic and arbitrary. Tenth, the CP is frequently identified by what Gruenberger calls the "Fulton Non-Sequitur." Here the CP argues that since they laughed at Robert Fulton and his steamboat and now they are laughing at me, I, too, must be a genius like Fulton! Eleventh, the crackpot most often suffers from *paranoia.* He feels the world is against him and opposes his project because it *is* so important! Twelfth, the CP is always overimpressed with the value of his discovery—it's earthshaking and very valuable in dollars and cents, i.e., the *dollar complex,* whereas the scientist, if he ever considers its financial aspects, considers these last. Finally, the CP suffers from the *statistics compulsion* and not only uses them, but continuously explains them and often uses them inappropriately, whereas the scientist usually assumes his readers are informed and seldom ends his sentences with explanation points.

Quacks, in addition to the above sins, also promise quick and dramatic cures, display credentials unrecognized by responsible scientists or educators, claim they're being persecuted by organized medicine and that their work is being suppressed because it is controversial, use disclaimers couched in pseudomedical jargon, cite anecdotes and testimonials rather than laboratory studies in support of their claims, or use reports from the mass media rather than controlled studies published in reputable peer-reviewed journals to validate their arguments. Investigators should also be familiar with a number of excellent books dealing with various health scams and frauds. One of the best is Stephen Barrett's *Health Schemes, Scams, and Frauds* (Consumer Reports Books, 1991). Despite the long efforts of skeptics and medical authorities, quacks and faith healers still manage to extract millions of dollars yearly from credulous people who fall into their traps.

It also behooves every paranormal investigator to familiarize him- or herself with the skills and techniques of the professional magicians. As you are probably aware, many claims of supernatural powers and abilities, for example psychic surgery, mind reading, key bending, and predictions, are nothing more than "tricks" or basic effects well known to professional prestidigitators. There are, surprisingly enough, only a few basic "magic" effects. While it could be said that all of magic can be classified as one effect—that of change or alteration in a seemingly impossible fashion— it is not very useful or revealing. Most magicians would support a classification schedule similar to the one below:

1. Productions (from not being to being—appearances, creations, multiplications)
2. Disappearances (vanishings, obliterations—from being to not being)
3. Transpositions (from being here to being there—a change in location)
4. Transformation (from being in this way to being in that way—changes in appearance, character, or identity)
5. Defying the Laws of Natural Science:
   a. antigravity (levitation and change in weight)
   b. magical animation (movement imparted to the inanimate)
   c. penetration (putting one solid through another—matter through matter
   d. restoration (making the destroyed whole)
   e. attraction (mysterious adhesion)
   f. invulnerability (injury proof)
   g. sympathetic reaction (sympathetic response)
   h. rapid germination (miraculous growth and development)
6. Mental Phenomena:
   a. prediction (foretelling the future)
   b. divination (discovering hidden knowledge)
   c. mental control (mind over the inanimate)
   d. thought reading (mental perception, mind reading)
   e. thought transmission (mental perception, mind reading)
   f. extrasensory perception (unusual perception, other than mind)
   g. psychometry (obtaining complex mental images from inanimate objects)

h. physical anomalies (contradictions, abnormalities, freaks)
i. spectator failure (magician's challenges)
j. identification (specific discoveries)
k. hypnotism (controlling others' behavior via suggestion)
l. memorization (unusual memory feats)
m. lightning calculation (using mathematical tricks)

Within each level of class there are, of course, hundreds of specific tricks or effects. These tricks and effects are spelled out in detail in a large number of excellent books on magic. Some of the better ones of these are *The Amateur Magician's Handbook* (4th edition) by Henry Hay (New American Library, 1987); *Mark Wilson's Complete Course In Magic* (Courage Books, 1988); *Magic: Scientific Diversions & Stage Illusions* by A. A. Hopkins (Arno Press, 1977); Marvin Kaye's *The Handbook of Magic* (Dorset Press, 1973), as well as the same author's *Handbook of Mental Magic* (Stein & Day, 1975); and *Magic and Showmanship: A Handbook for Conjurers* by Henning Nelms (Dover, 1969). If these are difficult to find or not available, most any good library will have others of equal merit. Any work by Walter Gibson, Houdini, Dunninger, or Kreskin will also be valuable. Most strongly recommended are the works of James Randi. Particularly important are his *Flim-Flam!* (Prometheus Books, 1982), *The Magic of Uri Geller* (Ballantine, 1975), and *The Faith Healers* (Prometheus Books, 1987). Also highly recommended are the works of Milbourne Christopher, particularly his *The Illustrated History of Magic* (Crowell, 1973), *ESP, Seers & Psychics* (Crowell, 1970), and *Mediums, Mystics & The Occult* (Crowell, 1972). Extremely useful is the latest edition of the Abbott Magic Manufacturing Company's catalog. Order from Colon, Michigan 49040.

Every paranormal investigator must also be familiar with the schemes and scams of the so-called mediums and psychics. Two books that every serious investigator should be intimately familiar with are *The Psychic Mafia* by M. Lamar Keene (St. Martin's Press, 1976) and *Powers: Testing the Psychic and Supernatural* by Dan Korem (Intervarsity Press, 1988). Both of these volumes, along with Randi's work, provide an excellent overview of the trickery and con games that so-called "psychics" use to bilk a naive and credulous public. An earlier classic concerned with exposing mediums is Harry Houdini's *A Magician Among the Spirits* (Harper & Row, 1924). *Dunninger's Complete Encyclopedia of Magic* (Lyle Stuart, 1967) and Ruth Brandon's *The Spiritualists* (Alfred A. Knopf, 1983) also describe techniques used by mediums and spiritualists to hoodwink their followers.

Every serious and would-be investigator must also be familiar with or have read the "Classics" in the skeptical field. Beginning with MacKay's

Extraordinary Popular Delusions and the Madness of Crowds originally published by Richard Bentley in London in 1841 (Bonanza Books, 1980) and including Joseph Jastrow's *Error and Eccentricity in Human Belief* (Dover, 1935); Martin Gardner's *Fads & Fallacies in the Name of Science* (Dover, 1957); D. H. Rawcliffe's *Illusions and Delusions of the Supernatural and the Occult* (Dover, 1959); Bergen Evans' *The Spoor of Spooks* (Alfred A. Knopf, 1954); Andrew Neher's *The Psychology of Transcendence* (Prentice-Hall, 1980); Martin Gardner's *Science: Good, Bad, and Bogus* (Prometheus Books, 1981); Singer's *Science and the Paranormal* (Charles Scribners Sons, 1981); Kendrick Frazier's *Paranormal Borderlands of Science* (Prometheus Books, 1981) and his companion volume *Science Confronts the Paranormal* (Prometheus Books, 1986); Paul Kurtz's *A Skeptic's Handbook of Parapsychology* (Prometheus Books, 1985); James Alcock's *Parapsychology: Science or Magic* (Pergamon, 1981); Philip Klass's *UFOs Identified* (Random House, 1974); *UFOs Explained* (Vintage, Random House, 1976); *UFOs: The Public Deceived* (Prometheus Books, 1983); and *UFO Abductions: A Dangerous Game* (Prometheus Books, 1988); Robert Sheaffer's *The UFO Verdict* (Prometheus Books, 1981); Joe Nickell's *Inquest on the Shroud of Turin* (Prometheus Books, 1983) and *Secrets of the Supernatural* with John Fischer (Prometheus Books, 1988); Lawrence D. Kusche's *The Bermuda Triangle Mystery—Solved* (Harper & Row, 1975); Melvin Harris's *Investigating the Unexplained* (Prometheus Books, 1986); and Terence Hines's *Pseudoscience and the Paranormal* (Prometheus Books, 1988). The dedicated paranormal investigator should also look into the area of anomalistic psychology and be familiar with the contents of several of the textbooks in the area, particularly Zusne and Jones, *Anomalistic Psychology* (Lawrence Erlbaum Associates, 1982); Marks and Kamman's *The Psychology of the Psychic* (Prometheus Books, 1980); and Graham Reed's *The Psychology of Anomalous Experience,* rev. ed. (Prometheus Books, 1988).

The paranormal investigator has, of course, a lot in common with the legendary private investigator and it would behoove the former to learn as much as he or she can about the work of the latter. Edward R. Smith's *Practical Guide for Private Investigators* and James L. Drake's *Private Intelligence Secrets* (Alpha Publications, 1989) are two excellent introductions to PI work. Also of use in this regard are Fallis and Greenberg's *Be Your Own Detective* (M. Evans & Co., 1989); Palmiotto's *Critical Issues in Criminal Investigation* (Anderson Publishing Co., 1990); and a yearly subscription to *P.I. Magazine* (755 Bronx, Toledo, Ohio 43609, $10 per year) is also invaluable for the latest information as to tricks of the trade, techniques, equipment, and so forth. Specialized books may also come in handy in certain of your inquiries: Ed Ferraro's *You Can Find Anyone*

(Marathon Press, 1989); Lee Lapin's *How to Get Anything on Anybody* (Wolfe Publishing Co., 1983); and French and Van Houten's *Never Say Lie* (Loompanics, 1987). You should also be informed as to the best and proper ways to go about interviewing and questioning people. Some excellent sources in this connection are Burt Rapp's *Interrogation: A Complete Manual* (Loompanics, 1987); *Criminal Interrogation and Confessions,* 3rd edition, by Inbau, Reid, and Buckley (Williams & Wilkins, 1986); and *The Confession: Interrogation and Criminal Profiles for Police Officers* by Macdonald and Michaud (Apache Press, 1987).

Another ever-present possibility for the paranormal investigator is the hoaxster and the practical joker who delights in fooling everyone with his fake UFOs and UFO photos and his simple as well as intricate and convoluted "crop circles." Moreover, you can also expect to encounter out-and-out crooks and con men who will do anything to separate the dupe from his money. Essential reading in this area is Curtis MacDougall's *Hoaxes* (Dover, 1958); Richard Saunders's *The World's Greatest Hoaxes* (Playboy Press, 1980); Walter B. Gibson's *The Bunco Book* (Citadel Press, 1986); Robert A. Steiner's *Don't Get Taken* (Wide Awake Books, 1989); Maurice Beam's *It's a Racket* (Macfadden Books, 1962); David Maurer's *The Big Con* (New American Library, 1962); M. Allen Henderson's *Money for Nothing* and *Flim-Flam Man* (Eden Press, 1989); and Victor Santoro's *The Rip-Off Book* (Loompanics, 1984).

In summary, what kind of individual makes a good or "ideal" investigator? Fortunately, this question is one that is easy to answer: *Ideally* he or she should be a combination scientist, experimental psychologist, detective or private investigator, professional magician, scholar, knight in shining armor, and miracle worker. In other words, he or she should do his/her damnedest to emulate the authors! As an insightful humorist once remarked, "The true title of every book ever written is: HOW TO BE MORE LIKE ME, no matter what it says on the cover." In the present case nothing could be truer or more appropriate. Seriously, we can only write about what we know and have experienced. We hope our work and experiences will be of use and value to you in the pursuit of reason and sanity in a world that seems daily more determined to dwell in a universe of irrationalism and the supernatural. We started, a moment ago, to say that it is impossible to write about what one doesn't know, but then we remembered that philosophers, reporters, and psychics do this routinely. Let us look now at the world of the paranormal, its history and scope, and some of the people who live there.

Part 1

General Principles

1

The World of the Paranormal

Evidence of seemingly paranormal goings on come in from all over—
from many different fields, from many different belief systems, and from
all corners of the earth.

—Bernard Gettelson, *Intangible Evidence*

In looking at the paranormal as a field of human interest, it should be
helpful at the outset to consider the major types of phenomena that are
included in this field. The so-called *paranormal* includes extrasensory perception (ESP) or telepathy; clairvoyance or remote viewing; dowsing; psychometry; precognition and retrocognition; psychokinesis (which includes
telekinesis, teleportation, psychic healing, and psychic surgery); as well as
survival phenomena which include ghosts and apparitions, bilocation, out-
of-body-experiences (OOBEs), hauntings and mediumistic phenomena, near-
death experiences (NDEs), channels, and poltergeists. Recently the paranormal has expanded to embrace a number of phenomena related to the
above, such as unidentified flying objects (UFOs) and extraterrestrial alien
visitors (ETs), past-lives regressions and memories suggesting the possibility
of reincarnation, demon possession, levitation, miraculous visions, religious
miracles of one sort or another, amulets and crystal powers, hypnosis and
hypnotic powers, unnatural powers and forces, astrology, vampires, palmistry, pryamid power, Satanic forces and powers, witchcraft, glossolalia, and
xenoglossy. While these things make up the major forms of paranormal
phenomena, other things such as firewalking, spontaneous human combustion, and cryptozoology must also be included.

Telepathy or *ESP* is usually defined as having access to another per-

39

son's thoughts by means not involving the known senses or logical inference. Examples are: a man dreams of riding a merry-go-round while his wife is reading about it in a book. A man has a pain in his head at the exact instant his son is shot in the head in a war several continents away. *Clairvoyance,* literally "clear seeing," is defined as the gaining of information about an object, location, or event by means not involving the known senses or logical inference. A modern version of this is called "remote viewing." In this instance, a person moves to a geographical location and another "viewer" some distance away attempts, successfully, to locate and describe, i.e., to remote "view" the exact location of the sender. Clairvoyance, rather than being mind-to-mind communication, refers to an awareness of physical things or realities rather than mental events. Typically, the clairvoyant "sees" something at a distance or "hears" something, i.e., uses *clairaudience* ("clear hearing") or "smells," "tastes," or "touches" something, i.e., shows *clairsentience.* Swedenborg "saw" Stockholm burning even though at the time he was three hundred miles away.

Precognition is defined as the acquisition of information about an object, location, or event *in the future* by means not involving logical inference. An example would be dreaming about a plane crashing in the lot across the street, and two days later a plane does, indeed, crash in a lot across the street. While a look into the future is always more exciting than a look into the past, the phenomenon known as *retrocognition* is also often reproted. This is a direct, present, and fresh perception of a past event. Related to this is the almost universal experience of *déjà vu* (literally, "already seen"), the experience we have when we encounter something for the first time and yet feel strongly that we've encountered it before. Retrogression also often takes the form of what Jung calls *psychic localization,* wherein a specific place seems to store experiences that can be clairvoyantly perceived by a psychic or sensitive individual.

We also have *psychometry* or "object reading," defined as the extrasensory ability to determine information relating to an inanimate object merely by handling the object or concentrating on it or thinking about it. Some paranormal authorities consider this a particular form of clairvoyance.

As for *psychokinesis* (PK), this refers to movement or changes in physical matter brought about or caused by mental activity. A vase can be caused to fall off a table or a light bulb made to explode by will power alone. Besides the movement of objects, PK includes acoustical, electrical, and other forms of physical aberrations or supernatural events, e.g., spoon-bending, levitations, fire-walking, auras, psychic photographs, apports (i.e., producing physical objects out of thin air by transporting them from one place to another by mind power alone), out-of-body experiences, and so forth. A particular form of psychokinesis that supposedly shows up whenever poltergeists (literally from the German meaning "noisy and boisterous spirits") appear is known as RSPK or *recurrent spontaneous psychokinesis.* When the mental influence takes place at a distance it is called *telekinesis.* When objects are moved mentally from one place to another, the term *teleportation* is applied. Recently in Asia and South America a number of shamans allegedly performed "psychic surgery," i.e., surgical operations on willing patients using only the surgeon's fingers to remove "diseased" tissues and organs from the patient's body cavity. Careful study of this phenomenon has shown that no surgery actually occurs. As for the surgeon, by the clever manipulation of his hands and fingers, he makes it "appear" he has entered the patient's body. The blood and tissues shown to witnesses and the patient usually come from chickens or other small animals.

Bilocation, or one body being in two places at once, the *doppelgänger phenomena,* or seeing one's double, OOBEs, or the sensation or feeling of having one's consciousness leave or become independent of the body itself have been widely reported since the beginning of time, particularly by mystics, dreamers, psychics, and others—as well as by a few people who have come close to dying. The latter also report in their *near-death experiences* (NDEs) sensations of moving through a dark tunnel, encountering an extremely bright light, a panoramic view of their lives, and an intensely realistic *out-of-body experience* (OOBE). The experience of having a free-floating mind or consciousness without the physical presence of any bodily sensation is very common and can be brought about in a number of different ways. Deep relaxation coming from meditation, suggestion, or hypnotic procedures, or as a result of the ingestion of a number of drugs—particularly ketamine hydrochloride, an anesthetic—can also bring about the OOBE experience. Starvation, physical exhaustion, extreme stress, or periods of sustained emotion can also cause this subjective feeling that one has no bodily sensations. People with a superstitious or spiritual bent will, however, interpret the experience in supernatural terms, usually as evidence that there is such a thing as a "soul" that exists independent of the physical body.

This belief in the existence of an animator or *soul* is also the basis for the belief in *apparitions,* or *ghosts, spirits, revenants,* or *haunts* of the dead. The terms are used interchangeably with the exception that the original meaning of "revenant" was to describe any being that returned from the dead after a long absence. *Vampires,* for example, were believed to be revenants, having the power to revive themselves after having been dead for some while. They might wait years or even centuries before appearing for the first time. *Apparitions* also can be of the living as well as of the dead. There are, in fact, three kinds of apparitions: *crisis apparitions—*

where illness, danger, or death is involved; *haunting apparitions*—where a single figure is seen repeatedly in the same place; and *experimental apparitions*—where a living person projects an appearance of himself to another. Interestingly enough, there are many different types of ghosts, including animal ghosts and specific ghosts such as the *ankou* or graveyard-watcher ghost that guards cemeteries; *bogies* of the bogie-man fame; *banshees*—an Irish ghost that foretells an impending death; *shins*—Chinese evil ghosts; *spooks*—benevolent rather than harmful spirits; *trickster spirits* —that haunt the Everglades; the *undine* or *ondine*—beautiful female ghosts that haunt stretches of water in Europe; and *will-o'-the-wisps*—ghostly lights that are souls of the dead that wander across the landscape. Also notorious is the famous or infamous *incubus*—an evil spirit that comes at night to seduce young women and make them sell their souls to the Devil. A ghost-like creature, the incubus usually appears in the form of a handsome young man. The reverse of this demon-lover is the *succubus*—a demon in the form of a lovely young woman that seduces young men for the same evil purpose. Many legendary creatures like elves and trolls were believed to be the offspring of the incubi and succubi. G. N. M. Tyrell, in his 1953 book *Apparitions,* argues there are four types of ghosts: *experimental*—spirits of people who are still alive; *crisis ghosts* that appear to relatives at or just after the death of a loved one; *post-mortem ghosts* that appear long after death and look and seem so real they are shocking; and *true ghosts*—the most widely reported and seen by people who have no connection with them. True ghosts are not restricted by time, i.e., they can appear centuries after their deaths, but they are, however, usually restricted to a specific single locality. Ghosts, interestingly enough, are world-wide phenomena, reported throughout history, appearing in many different shapes and forms, and with a variety of purpose, e.g., revenge, to complete unfinished business, to deliver messages to the living—warnings, locations of lost or hidden valuables, etc. The most commonly reported ghosts are, of course, the ghosts of human beings appearing as mist-like entities, roughly human in shape, and appearing and disappearing suddenly and mysteriously. Ghost stories have been ever popular and are just as popular today as they were in nearly every century before. More than likely the crews of spaceships in the future will while away the long hours on flights between the stars telling tales of ghostly spacemen and space-women and haunted starships.

It might also be helpful here to distinguish between the *paranormal,* i.e., those things lying outside the range of normal human experience, and *parapsychology,* which is a branch of psychology (the study of experience and behavior) that studies unusual or anomalous human experiences like telepathy and encounters with spirits. For all such uncanny or ostensibly paranormal experiences the generic term *psi* is used. Parapsychology has been the object of scientific investigation for well over a hundred years but still has little in the way of hard material facts to support its claims and pretensions. Most serious students of parapsychology, i.e., those who approach the subject from a scientific perspective, resent the fact that their work is indiscriminately grouped with aspects of the occult and supernatural such as astrology, spiritualism, Scientology, Transcendental Meditation, crystal gazing, Tarot cards, and such. They also resent, in Mishlove's words:

> . . . personal attacks on imagined or irrelevant characteristics of individual investigators; group derogation of parapsychologists as gullible, incompetent, emotionally unstable true believers; unsubstantiated allegations of fraud; allegations of fraud based on rumor and innuendo; appeal to authoritarian opinion that does not confront the issues; religious belief in the supremacy of a particular and limited form of rationalism that can and must conquer all challenges; and apocalyptic rhetoric regarding the intellectual dark ages that will follow the rise of parapsychology.
>
> (Mishlove 1988, p. 17)

Most upsetting of all to the scientifically minded parapsychologists is the lack of familiarity with the experimental work and the hard data thus far accumulated on the part of the critics. Equally upsetting is the critic's confusion of the scientific study of psi phenomena with popular abuses. As Mishlove notes, "The problem is insidious, as this confusion is fostered not only by overzealous believers and overzealous skeptics of parapsychology—but also by the theoretical controversies within parapsychology itself. Such associations have touched the raw nerves of many parapsychologists, inspiring an urgent need to create as much distance as they can between the scientific and the personal approaches to psi" (p. 30). Vessey in 1969 summed up the position neatly: "There is no common ground between the psychical rsearcher and the occultist, for the simple reason that the former is attempting to pursue an exact science, whereas the latter is neither exact nor scientific." (Mishlove 1988, pp. 30–31) Unfortunately, too many parapsychologists who venture onto the wild sea of superstition in their small boats of scientific objectivity are overcome and drown. John Beloff, for example, once considered astrology as an archetypical pseudo-science and in 1978 acknowledged that after looking at the data, he is now convinced that such subjects as acupuncture, astrology, UFOs, and psychotronics should be partially included within the legitimate domain of parapsychology. Mishlove also believes that all of the paranormal claims should be considered as having something to offer their consumers in that, "for all their offensiveness, the cults may be partially satisfying a social need that parapsychology is partially stimulating" (p. 51). Therefore, Mishlove tries to find some good in even the worst and most primitive of the *psi* systems. Mishlove's main concern, however, is to encourage the *development of psi abilities,* or "supersensory reality," and he believes that a number of prescientific traditions and contemporary systems do exactly this. The prescientific traditions that do it are: Shamanism, Divination, Yoga, Buddhism, Sufism, Judaism, and Ceremonial Magic. The contemporary systems that do it are: Spiritualism, theosophy, anthroposophy, the Rosicrucian Order (AMORC), Hermetics, Scientology, Silva Mind Control, Philippine Spiritualist Training, Milan Ryzl Training, Transcendental Meditation, Alan Vaughan Training, The Monroe Institute of Applied Sciences, LeShan Psychic Healing Training, Soviet Psi Training, UFO-related psi development patterns, Jack Schwarz Training, Foundation for Mind Research, The Church of Divine Man, Annette Martin Training, Adventure Trails, A Course in Miracles, New Frontiers Institute, and Radionics. Mishlove admits that "pseudoscience and strangeness are relevant parameters of some contemporary development systems." A description of each of these "systems" is provided by Table 1-1. This table provides a broad overview of a number of paranormal world views and taken as a whole gives considerable insight into the workings of the *paranormal mind.* As one would suspect, there are hundreds of other similar developmental systems today competing with these.

The purpose of all of these psi development systems is to produce a *psychic,* that is, an individual who has in his possession a large number of different kinds of supernormal or paranormal abilities and skills such as the ability to read minds, see events that transpired in the past, predict the future, or by holding objects in his hands, to determine who owns or owned the object and events of importance associated with the object. Most psychics claiming these abilities and skills acquired them naturally, i.e., they were born with these wild talents. Modern psychics are particularly astute at contacting the dead, speaking with ghosts, and in *predicting* earthquakes and other disasters such as plane crashes, train wrecks, floods, and hurricanes. Most of their predictions are in error but this does not dissuade them. If just one of these predictions ever comes to pass they will be famous forever! Among the most famous and ballyhooed of the psychics are Peter Hurkos, Ingo Swann, Alex Tanous, Clarisa Bernhardt, Tony Cordero, Beatrice Rich, Eileen Garrett, Ruth Montgomery, Jeane Dixon, Dorothy Allison, Gerard Croiset, Beverly Jaegers, Greta Alexander, Noreen Renier, Frances Baskerville, Judy Belle, Dixie Yeterian, Nancy Czetli, Ginette and Louis Matacia, and, of course, Uri Geller. Many of these psychics use skills other than their alleged "psychic" ones in the process of helping find lost objects and working with the police in homicide and missing-person cases. The *cold-reading* technique (Hyman 1977), using

Table 1-1

Paranormal or Psi Development Systems
(After Mishlove)

Prescientific Tradition

BUDDHISM: Right living and thinking are urged; meditation and visualization are practiced; postures, breathing, physical exercises, and contemplation are practiced.

CEREMONIAL MAGIC: Magical potions, dreams, herbs, magical stones, images on gems, incantations, magical ceremonies, alchemy, astrology, charms and amulets, numerology, dream interpretation, conjuring, drugs, and potions are used.

DIVINATION: Future predicted from intestines of slaughtered animals, fire, smoke, movement of snakes, shape of plants, murmuring of brooks and streams, etc. I Ching, Runes, precious stones, throwing of bones, and dreams are studied to predict the future.

SHAMANISM: Master of spirits, rituals, myths, drugs and trance techniques. Trained via use of drugs, solitude, fasting, and other austerities that cause visions and hallucinations. Drumming, chanting, and dancing are also used. Spells, magical charms, and suggestion are used to heal.

SUFISM: Prayer, devotion, ascetic discipline, along with spiritual exercises are used. Chanting, singing, dancing, and rituals are employed.

YOGA: Good habits are practiced and bad habits are controlled. Specific postures and breathing exercises are used. Physical exercises and mind-control exercises also are practiced. Concentration and meditation are encouraged.

Modern Systems

A COURSE IN MIRACLES: This course is based upon spirit dictation supposedly given and coming from Jesus Christ himself through Helen Schucman, a psychotherapist. Reading the books and contemplating what has been read constitutes the training.

ADVENTURE TRAILS: Here ESP is developed via survival training and isolation techniques. By doing so one develops "frontal lobe experience." Also included as a basic tool is the "sexual orgasm," which is believed to induce a "whole brain orgasm" which is supposed to awaken one's psychic awareness.

ALAN VAUGHN TRAINING: Uses meditational practices and artistic pictures as targets for concentration and visualization of desired ends. Practice with such targets and feedback, plus meditation and relaxation, can be beneficial.

ANNETTE MARTIN TRAINING: This system specializes in psychic medical diagnosis. It uses relaxation and identification with the patient, i.e., jumping into the patient's body to discover the problem. It uses spirit guides and Edgar Cayce techniques—simple meditational practices and tests with feedback to attain the goals.

ANTHROPOSOPHY: Literally, "man-wisdom," founded by Rudolf Steiner. Involves mind training via concentration, exercises to control attitudes, feelings, and emotions. Open-mindedness is encouraged and the goal is to attain a "spiritual vision" and devotion to truth and knowledge. Quiet, lonely, and intense contemplation of higher moral things and nature and animals is encouraged. Bodily rhythms and homeopathic and herbal medicines are employed.

CHURCH OF DIVINE MAN: This Berkeley, California, organization was founded by the Reverend Lewis Bostwick to help people become more perfect. Religious and metaphysical concepts such as reincarnation, spirit guides, and auras are used. Chakras, psychometry, and telekinesis are emphasized, as well as concepts of spiritual healing.

FOUNDATION FOR MIND RESEARCH: Robert Masters and Jean Houston have developed an intensive program of hypnotic trance work and consciousness-expanding-sensory-visualization exercise, including yoga exercises, as well as the Feldenkrais and Alexander physical techniques to expand the mind.

HERMETICS: Refers to Hermes Trismegistus (thrice great Hermes) or the name given to the Egyptian God Toth who is identified with the Grecian god Hermes. There is airtight secrecy kept on the exercises compiled by Franz Bardon in his *Initiation Into Hermetics* (1926). The exercises draw on Tarot cards, mental electricity and magnetism, classical Hermetic philosophy, Christian kabbalist thought, and theosophical concepts. There are ten stages of practice and three sections of application: magic mental, magic psyche, and magic physical training. The last includes introspection, concentration, empty mind, breathing exercises, physical stimulation, baths, body control, thought projection, and automatic writing.

JACK SCHWARZ TRAINING: Schwarz is able to control his sense of pain, and he uses self-control and biofeedback procedures, as well as visualization techniques plus psychophysiological exercises to help people attain altered states of consciousness. While in the altered states, people make contact with their psi abilities.

LeSHAN PSYCHIC TRAINING: In a five-day program this training promotes psi-healing abilities through strengthening the ego, changing one's concepts of one's self, space, and time, and producing an altered state of consciousness which is associated with healing.

MILAN RYZAL TRAINING: Uses "hypnosis" to activate and cultivate ESP and then teaches one how to control this in a normal waking state. Nothing but pure suggestion is employed.

MONROE INSTITUTE OF APPLIED SCIENCE: Robert Monroe, in Afton, Virginia, teaches how to attain an out-of-body experience (OOBE) via alert relaxation techniques and audio binaural beat effects which stimulate the brain and induce deep relaxation. The entire effect is due to relaxation, expectation, and suggestion.

NEW FRONTIER INSTITUTE: This is a Bay Area (San Francisco) group that uses group hypnotic trance techniques as well as regression and visualization practices to achieve a merging with the "divine Radiance" which solves all problems.

PHILIPPINE SPIRITUALIST HEALING: Through the use of prayer, laying on of hands, and psychic surgery, i.e. the placebo effect, many people are healed. Also employed are trance mediumship and channels for helping spirits.

RADIONICS: This is a method of medical diagnosis and healing that uses complex instruments, or "black boxes," to determine ills. From the technical point of view the instruments are senseless, but the box does serve as a ritual object for the user to focus his mind on. Any and all resulting effects are due to suggestion and the placebo effect.

ROSICRUCIANISM: The Ancient Mystical Order of Rosae Cruces (AMORC) supposedly dates back to ancient Atlantis. Offers mastery of life via auras, premonitions, and telepathy. Rules for living include prayers, honesty, humility, concentration, Egyptian rituals, mantras, meditation, rituals, and ceremonies. Use is made of numerology, symbolism, secret alphabets, and daily exercises and rituals which are essential for mind control and psychic development.

SCIENTOLOGY: Founded in the 1950s by L. Ron Hubbard. It is a blend of science and mysticism and an outgrowth of an earlier movement called Dianetics. All human behavior is controlled by unconscious reactive patterns developed during times of stress—these trauma patterns are called *engrams*. Via *auditing,* the engrams people have can be made conscious and brought under the individual's mental control. This is done by talking freely, e.g., psychotherapy. By using an E-meter (a galvanometer), the auditor for the person's emotional responses triggers an engram, and he then zeroes in on these topics until the emotional upset is gone, e.g., systematic desensitization. Scientologists believe higher training levels lead to the development of psychic abilities.

SILVA MIND CONTROL: Promotes basic exercises in concentration, relaxation, and visualization over a forty-eight-hour period and argues this leads to ESP ability. The training is supposedly of one's brain waves, but it is, rather, intense suggestion which causes neuroses in some people.

SOVIET PSI TRAINING: Techniques used here include surrounding the sender with a weak magnetic field, stimulating certain acupuncture points with needles, giving mental suggestions, and Yogic breathing exercises to do the job.

SPIRITUALISM: Séances, mediums, automatic writing, spirit photographs, human auras, chakras (energy centers in the body), self-hypnosis and trances, i.e., suggestion, are employed. Prayer, concentration, meditation, speaking in tongues, and sitting in circles with other believers.

THEOSOPHY: Founded in 1875 by Helen Blavatsky. Ideas taken from ancient mythologies involving the astral body (soul), the etheric body, thought forms (ideas that materialize), drugs, self-hypnosis, reading past lives, and communing with nature spirits. Does not use the unconscious trance for psychic work.

TRANSCENDENTAL MEDITATION: Employs a mantra form of meditation to block thought and induce deep relaxation. Through thought concentration one can supposedly learn to levitate, read minds, attain enlightenment, and so forth.

UFO RELATED PSI-DEVELOPMENT PATTERNS: Supposedly psi abilities are sent by extraterrestrials in UFOs. One Ted Owens claims he is in contact with aliens who "gave" him PK and ESP abilities. Owens also claims rainmaking and lightning striking abilities. Self-hypnosis and the Rolfe memory system training also help.

There are many other systems which allegedly will develop psychic abilities in those who follow their dictates religiously. According to Mishlove: "The possible permutations and combinations of system components for psi developments is truly enormous and like hardy biological species, programs seem to develop in order to fill every possible social-evolutionary niche" (Mishlove 1988, p. 179).

---

highly general statements and feedback from the client, as well as careful observations to convince the client that the "psychic" knows all about him or her, is well known and used by most of the seers. If the paranormal investigator keeps a close tab on the predictive accuracy of the "psychics," something most interesting emerges. Most do no better than chance, i.e., no better than guessing, and seldom—if ever—are their predictions exact and precise. Even when they are correct, one has to stretch the limits to get them in the ball park. Jeane Dixon's prediction of Kennedy's assassination, for example, was merely that the man elected president in 1960 would die in office. Hardly anything to send up rockets about.

Astrology is the belief that the planets of the solar system have a direct influence on individuals and on the course of human affairs. Central to this belief is the concept of the *zodiac*—a circular band in the sky through which the planets are seen to move. It is divided into twelve equal sections known as signs of the zodiac. In astrology, a planet's influence varies according to which part of the zodiac it is occupying. Almost everyone in the United States and western Europe today knows his or her zodiacal sign, i.e., the sector of the zodiac through which the sun was passing when he or she was born. The concept of the zodiac was evolved during the Babylonian era as an ancient measuring device. It consists of twelve sectors, each measuring thirty degrees, and each sector is named after a fixed star constellation: Aries, Taurus, Gemini, Cancer, Leo, Virgo, Libra, Scorpio, Sagittarius, Capricorn, Aquarius, and Pisces. If, for example, a person says he was born under Taurus it means his birth occurred between 21 April and 22 May when the sun was between zero and twenty-nine degrees in the Taurus sector. According to serious believers, the popular astrology columns printed in the newspapers are childish nonsense, but the *scientific astrology,* i.e., analyzing your personality from your horoscope using exact times and precise geographical locations, is an exact science with high validity. Unfortunately, orthodox science and the science of astronomy do not support this view. Nevertheless, popular belief in the power of the stars to control human destiny continues unabated.

Similarly, belief in *numerology,* or that numbers themselves have magical properties, is based upon the Pythagorean notion of vibration ratios. Numerology is most often used for character analysis and prediction. For example, if you have the person's name and birthdate, that is all that is needed to build up an entire character portrait. By adding the numbers of the birth date one can also determine the individual's future and chance for success and happiness. The study of the hands, or *palmistry,* came about as a result of man's fascination with his hands—things he possessed that the animals were denied. These things of power that enabled him to shape tools and make impressions with must be magical indeed. When he began to see them also as mirrors of his fate and containing his future, the first steps in the art of palmistry, or *chiromancy,* had been made. By studying the lines, mounts, valleys, and other configurations of the palms, along with the shape, size, and texture of the hands themselves, one could predict the fortunes and fate of the individual. The belief that there is a relationship between these physical features and man's nature is deep-seated and has a long tradition. Palmistry is generally studied under three headings by the modern practitioner: first, medical or therapeutic chiromancy —diagnosing physical and mental illness; second, psychotherapeutic chiromancy—describing the consultant's character and praising the good qualities and warning of the weak ones; and, third, divinatory chiromancy —telling the past and predicting the future. Good palmists are careful in making predictions and never foretell misfortune or death without qualifying the reading and showing how the tragedy can be averted. Some people are so suggestible that they themselves may unconsciously bring about a predicted disaster.

The powerful and mysterious *Tarot cards* are also used to tell fortunes and predict the future. Consisting of a deck of seventy-eight cards divided into two groups, twenty-two highly symbolic picture cards—the Major Arcana—and fifty-six cards much like those of a regular deck— the Minor Arcana—the Tarot serves as a map of the human mind. Supposedly they touch virtually every aspect of our inner landscape and stir our unconscious as well as our unconscious associations. When used for divination purposes the fortune-teller shuffles them thoroughly, insuring that some cards are face up while others are face down, then after cutting them three times, the significator—the card representing the client, usually a king for a man and a queen for a woman—is placed face up on the table. The reader then lays out the cards over the significator in the form of a celtic cross, the Orsini Oracle method, or the Golden Dawn method. Depending upon the cards' pattern of distribution over and around the signficator, one can then divine the individual's fate. Also with the Tarot the divinator asks a question, shuffles the cards, and then deals in a set pattern, thus establishing the significance of the fact that you obtained that particular sequence of cards out of all possible sequences. This kind of thinking is what Jung has called *synchronicity*—a way of looking at events not as part of an endless chain of cause and effect, but as simultaneous expressions of a given moment. There is, according to Jung, a universal connective principle joining things and events together.

With the *I Ching,* or *The Book of Changes,* the Chinese made a science of synchronicity. Based upon a group of sixty-four six-line drawings, or hexagrams, with broken (no) and unbroken lines (yes) and each having a particular message, the user tosses coins or plays counting games with yarrow stalks to come up randomly with one of the hexagrams. When properly interpreted, this hexagram will offer an answer to the question you ask. You could use just about anything at the time you ask your question—passing cars or street noises—but since the hexagrams are easier to interpret, they are used. One must be of an extremely superstitious nature to place great credence in the chance workings of the universe and such esoteric concepts.

We must also remember that divination and prophecy can be carried out with almost anything: e.g., the pattern of distribution of *tea leaves* remaining in the bottom of one's tea cup; the self-projected images one sees when staring into the depths of a *crystal ball* or at a flickering candle flame or flames in a fireplace or most any shiny surface—a procedure known as *scrying;* or the use of a system of small, thumbsize stones marked with hieroglyphics called *runes,* whose symbols can tell your fate and fortune. And while we are in the area we must not forget *graphology,* or character reading through handwriting analysis, and *biorhythms*—those rhythmic cycles of life that affect all human beings and the physical, emotional, and intellectual cycles that each individual experiences. By knowing our own personal cycles we can become better tuned into life and happiness and all the other goodies.

Along with these pseudo-sciences and strange beliefs we must also include *cryptozoology,* or the study of animals that may or may not exist— monsters in a word. Included are *humanoids* like Bigfoot, the Abominable Snowman, the skunk man, wildmen, and Mo-Mo—a Missouri half-ape, half-man; *land monsters* such as the behemoth, the giant anaconda, the okapi, the woolly mammoth, and the Tasmanian Tiger; *monster birds and bats* such as the athol, the moa, the roc, the thunderbird, and the vampire bat; *phantoms* such as the black dog, the talking mongoose, the monster who left the devil's footprints, and phantom lions and kangaroos; *river and lake monsters* such as Chessie, the Loch Ness monster, the Ogo-pogo, Slimey Slim, the Giant Boa, and the White River Monster; *sea monsters* such as the Coelacanth, the Kraken, the Leviathan, giant octopi and squid, the Plesiosaur, and sea apes and serpents; and finally, *visitors from strange places* such as outer space aliens, little green men, Mothman, the Mad Gasser of Mattoon, and the Men In Black. In this category we also find many of the weird creatures from folklore such as *vampires, were-wolves, zombies, unicorns, dragons, fairies, elves, mermaids, giants,* and the *Griffin,* the *Hydra,* the *Basilisk, gnomes, ogres, leprechauns,* and other fearsome and legendary critters such as the *hoop snake,* the *hodag,* the *flitterbick,* and the *goofus.* A delightful review of all such strange and wonderful creatures can be found in Daniel Cohen's delightful *Encyclopedia of Monsters* (Dodd, Mead and Co., 1982).

Paranormalists are also fascinated with the subject matter of *hypnosis* and hypnotic sorts of phenomena like *past-lives regression* and *future-lives progression.* In the former, people are "hypnotized" and told to go back in time to years before their birth, whereupon they suddenly discover they have lived before—not just once before but many times before and in many cases as members of the opposite sex. In the latter, when people are put into a "hypnotic trance" and told to go into the future, they can move ahead hundreds of thousands of years and see themselves living future lives. The terms "hypnosis" and "hypnotic trance" are put in quotation marks because neither of these conditions exists. Through the use of *suggestion* on the part of the hypnotist and *imagination* and *compliance* on the part of the subject, people play these roles and act out their past and future lives with relative ease. For additional information on these role-playing games that most ordinary people and especially *fantasy-prone individuals* play with great skill, see the author's book *They Call It Hypnosis* (Prometheus Books, 1990). While in these so-called *trance states* many individuals are able to "speak-in-tongues," i.e., talk fluently in a strange, unknown language (*glossolalia*) or talk in foreign languages they never had an opportunity to learn normally (*responsible xenoglossy*). Interestingly enough, many other supernormal skills and abilities are supposed to accrue while people are in trance states, e.g., superstrength, superstamina, ability to levitate, ability to become invisible, clairvoyant and ESP abilities, etc.

As part of the paranormal picture we find reports of *spontaneous human combustion,* a condition in which human beings suddenly and mysteriously burst into flame and are consumed from within; and *crop circles,* a condition in which large circles, triangles, and humanoid-like shapes and diagrams appear overnight in ripe fields of wheat, oats, and barley—particularly in England, where they have been most often seen and reported.

Careful scientific investigations of both these phenomena have clearly shown that in the case of the former, it was neither *spontaneous* combustion nor *human* combustion. In every case that has been properly investigated it has been clearly shown that a flammable substance was involved and that it was externally caused. As for the crop circles, they are clearly the work of a group of human hoaxsters and, in fact, the BBC telecast a program last year in which a group of the hoaxsters demonstrated the technique and made a large and lovely crop circle for the television crew and national audience. Also of interest are a number of alleged paranormal skills such as *metal-bending*—of usually keys or spoons, *seed-sprouting*—causing seeds to germinate before one's eyes, *fire-walking*—walking across a bed of burning coals without harm, and *starting dead watches*—causing broken watches to start ticking again. All of these are nothing more than tricks or taking advantage of simple physical and mechanical principles. The keys and spoons are surreptitiously bent either in one's belt buckle or in a handy door crack; sprouting seeds are substituted for dormant seeds via sleight-of-hand; using the proper kind of coals and walking quickly and firmly across the ash layer in the fire pit does not produce burns on anyone; and most watches will—when shaken—start ticking again, but not for long. Again, all paranormal investigators must be ever on the lookout for legerdermain and tricksters.

The New Agers have been particularly prone to revive the most ancient of superstitions and attribute magical powers and properties to *rocks and crystals* in a modern version of sacred charms and amulets. Quartz crystals and precious and semi-precious stones are attributed magical powers and properties, and they can even be mentally "programmed" by the mind of the true believer pretty much as one programs his home computer. *Colors* are also attributed magical powers, and certain ones can make you sick or well and develop your personality and increase your spirituality. Finally, even the shape of certain objects have magical powers. *Pyramids*—large, medium, or small—have the ability to keep meat fresh, sharpen razor blades, and cure human ailments if one sits inside one.

Along with religious, drug, and altered states of awareness phenomena, these make up the body of the most common and frequently reported paranormal experiences. Before going any further, a brief history of the paranormal field might be helpful.

A Short History of Paranormal Phenomena

The history of paranormal (literally, beside, above, or beyond the normal) or occult (literally, "hidden," secret, or mysterious) events is buried in the remote past, but it most likely began with attempts on the part of primitive man to divine the future. The Old Testament refers to the existence of soothsayers and prophets and the prophetic powers of dreams as reported in dreams of Joseph and Jacob's dream of a ladder to heaven. The Greeks had specific temples with oracles that were able to tell the future. Plato discussed prophecy and direct knowing of the future via the soul. Aristotle spoke of the role of dreams in showing us the future. The Chinese *I Ching* was used to show how, by throwing yarrow stalks, the future could be known. The ancient Indian Vedas spoke of yogic practices that would lead to knowledge of both past and future lives and how the soul could be freed from the body via certain disciplinary measures.

During the early years of the Christian era psychic experiences and paranormal events were linked with the forces of evil and satanic influence, but by the time of the Renaissance psychic events were seen as part of religion and the religious mystical experience. In the Middle East astrology, numerology, and the kabbala were created and, along with other mystical experiences such as communing with spirits, leaving the body, and seeing the future, these became part and parcel of the Jewish and Islamic religious practices.

During the Middle Ages—and even in the Renaissance—prophets were common and revered. Among the most notable were Roger Bacon (1219–1294), Robert Nixon (1467–1485), Mother Shipton (1488–1561), Nostradamus (1503–1566), and William Lilly (1602–1681). Some of the most famous of all the seers include David Goodman Croly (1829–1889), Cheira (1886–1936), and Edgar Cayce (1877–1945). We even have such claimants today in the persons of Jeane Dixon, Ruth Montgomery, and a number of lesser psychics.

By the sixteenth and seventeenth centuries ghosts, apparitions, and psychic events were accepted as part of the everyday world of reality and were interwoven into the popular culture. Ghosts, witches, spells, portents, mystics, and spirits are liberally sprinkled throughout Shakespeare's plays. Defoe, Henry Moore, and others wrote about apparitions, poltergeists, and demon possession. Swedenborg, in the early eighteenth century, was widely read and his powers of clairvoyance were legendary. In a reputedly "well-documented" instance Swedenborg allegedly saw and reported a fire that was ravaging his home city of Stockholm while he was visiting Göteborg three hundred miles away. The philosopher Immanuel Kant was so impressed by this paranormal event that he wrote a book, *Dreams of a Ghost Seer,* in 1766 trying to explain it.

When the Age of Reason began in the seventeenth century, a reaction to the earlier superstitions brought materialism and a scientific outlook to the fore. This belief in rationalism gave momentum to the development of science and the anti-supernaturalism spirit lasted well into the eighteenth century. Unfortunately, the spirit did not extend to the uneducated masses and it came too late to prevent the horrible Salem witch trials of 1692 and the beliefs in satanic and demonic possession that plagued both Europe and the New World.

In the early part of the nineteenth century there was a world-wide resurgence of belief in occult and supernatural phenomena. Hoffman and Poe were creating ghostly tales of demons, ghouls, and evil spirits in the 1840s. What has been called the Age of Spiritualism began in Hydesville, New York in 1848 with Kate and Margaret Fox who claimed they were receiving communications from dead spirits in the form of ghostly knockings or "raps." Their later exposure—revealing the "raps" were nothing but the popping of their finger and toe joints and that all of their alleged communications were fraudulent—did little to stem the tide of eager believers. Horace Greeley, editor of *The New York Tribune,* was both a believer and a supporter of this nonsense and encouraged the craze of spiritualism that swept the nation and brought so-called "mediums" fame and fortune. Despite the fact that scientists and rationalists exposed the mediums time and again, the will to believe brought the eager and trusting public back to the séance time after time. Séances were even held in the White House under the auspices of Mary Todd Lincoln and it is rumored that Lincoln himself often looked to mediums and their dead spirits for guidance. Lincoln's papers include a letter allegedly written to him by the dead spirit of a close friend. The letter, sent to him by way of automatic writing through a well-known medium, is written in reverse and can only be read in a mirror.

Mediums such as the Italian Eusapia Paladino, the American Margery, the Englishman D. D. Home, Mrs. Piper, the Brothers Davenport and Andrew Jackson Davis—also Americans—became world famous, and the scientists who investigated them—Hereward Carrington, Sir Oliver Lodge, Charles Richet, Henry Sidgwick, Harry Price, and the famous American philosopher-psychologist William James—also shared the limelight. Difficult as it may be for us to believe, to the religious-minded and the mystically inclined spiritualistic theory was considered quite reasonable. For most of us, our knowledge of the physical world and the human body causes us, in Tabori's words, "to gag at clairvoyance and spirit communication. . . . The psychologist cannot conceive the human personality surviving *without* the physical brain" (Taplinger 1972, p. 93). As for the mediums, the more careful and intense the study and investigation of their alleged powers, the more certain it became that cheating and chicanery were behind every instance of the so-called supernatural. In the words of Anatole France, "I attended numerous spiritualist gatherings, formed acquaintances with famous mediums and watched them during their work. But I did not experience even once anything interesting, anything that would have deserved serious thought or anything that passed beyond the frontiers of the mind. . . . Remember, how unimportant and commonplace the alleged utterances of the most famous 'spirits' are! . . . I think all psychical researchers should devote themselves to the unmasking of the crooks and tricksters proliferating in this field. . . ."

"And if they find something that they consider genuine?" France was asked.

"Then they should be investigated themselves . . ." laughed the great writer.

Despite the popularity of the spiritualists and reports of miraculous events created by mediums such as D. D. Home and Leonora Piper, most of their so-called psychic miracles were gross exaggerations and, unfortunately, many of their claims were never carefully or intensively investigated. Sadly enough, many famous luminaries fell prey to their desire to believe in the possibility of life after death and the medium's wily shenanigans. The creator of Sherlock Holmes, Sir Arthur Conan Doyle, spent the last fifteen years of his life arguing the validity of psyhic phenomena. More deplorable still, Doyle was even taken in by two young girls who cut pictures of fairies from books and pasted them over other photographs and convinced Doyle that fairies were real! Although Doyle was originally a skeptic, when he attended a séance and received word from his wife's dead brother, he became an ardent believer. Doyle's gullibility eventually alienated his good friend Harry Houdini, who became one of the mediums' greatest enemies. Time after time Houdini unmasked case after case of mediumistic fraud, and in his lectures and articles he demonstrated how the mediums produced all of their apparitions, apports, voices, ectoplasm, and all other physical manifestations supposedly due to spirits.

It is important to note here that Doyle was by no means alone in his belief in the paranormal. Thackery, the novelist, supported D. D. Home and attended séances with the Fox sisters. Victor Hugo spent years communing with spirits of the dead and Mark Twain not only considered himself blessed with ESP and precognition—primarily via dreams—but also attributed his wife's cure from paralysis to the intervention of a psychic healer. Hawthorne not only believed in ghosts but wrote about them. Thomas A. Edison also claimed to have worked on a device to contact the dead, and the British scientist Sir William Crookes, among others, carried out serious scientific investigations of the "unexplained."

Because of such highly placed scientific interest, the Society for Psychical Research was founded in London in 1882. Three years later, due primarily to the work of William James and Simon Newcomb—aided by

Richard Hodgson and James Hyslop—the American Society for Psychical Research was created in Boston in 1885. James was convinced of the legitimacy of Mrs. Leonora Piper and the validity of her abilities. Her true abilities were, unfortunately, never adequately tested under controlled conditions. While most of the scientifically trained investigators were skeptical when dealing with spiritual communications, apports, ectoplasm, etc., they did readily accept the existence of telepathy, psychokinesis, etc., as the explanation for the medium's apparent powers. The investigator Edmund Gurney, for example, suggested that apparitions were hallucinations created by telepathic messages coming into the brain of the observor and that all the physical manifestations were due to psychokinesis. The early work of the British and American psychical research societies resulted in the publication of Edmund Gurney, F. W. H. Myer, and Frank Podmore's *Phantasms of the Living* in 1886 and Myer's *Human Personality and Its Survival of Bodily Death* posthumously in 1903. In 1889–90 the British society also carried out a survey of the English public, asking questions about psychic experiences, and approximately 10 percent of the population reported encountering apparitions.

In 1920 William McDougall, an Oxford psychologist who transferred to Harvard, took over as head of the American Society and, after moving to Duke University in 1927, persuaded a young biologist named Joseph B. Rhine and his wife Louisa to join him. These two men were responsible for establishing the first parapsychological laboratory at Duke and making the study of psychic phenomena respectable in the academic world. In fact, it was McDougall himself who created the term "parapsychology" to distinguish it from the fraudulent and pseudoscientific work of the very popular mediums. McDougall and the Rhines wished to bring the study of psychic phenomena into the laboratory and establish such work as a part of scientific psychology. McDougall and the Rhines also introduced the terms "extrasensory perception" and "psychokinesis." Though Rhine was at first a member of the Duke Psychology Department in 1935, he established the Parapsychology Laboratory as a separate entity and became its first head. The *Journal of Parapsychology* began publication in 1937. Because of the Rhines' success in making the study of psychic phenomena respectable, other universities in western Europe and the Soviet Union also established parapsychology departments.

Despite the parapsychologists' careful and intensive labors, little reliable or useful knowledge about paranormal behavior was discovered. Their work along with numerous scandals and revelations of mediumistic fraud was successful in shoving the mystique of the spiritualists into the background and causing a shift in public attitude. In 1957 the Parapsychological Association, made up of people with a professional interest in scientific research, was founded and, in 1969 due primarily to the efforts of Margaret Mead, the organization was admitted to the American Association for the Advancement of Science (AAAS), a marriage that was not at the time nor in the succeeding years a happy one.

Rhine's death in 1980 did have a somewhat dampening effect upon academic parapsychological research, but the work of Montague Ullman, Stanley Krippner, and Alan Vaughan on telepathic dreams (*Dream Telepathy: Experiments in Nocturnal ESP,* Macmillan, 1973), and the more recent work of Schmidt and Jahn on mental effects on microevents (1969, 1979, and 1982, 1987), the "psychic" exploits of Uri Geller, and the work of Targ and Puthoff on remote viewing managed to keep interest alive.

In its earlier stages most parapsychological research was of the "proof" variety, that is, attempts were made via controlled laboratory studies and statistical analysis to "prove" that "psi" exists. Fortunately or unfortunately, despite strenuous efforts for well over some fifty years, such proof is still lacking. Despite a decided increase in the sophistication of methodology and equipment, the long-sought-after repeatable experiment is still missing.

For a while during the 1960s and 1970s there was a concentration on the study of a number of so-called gifted individuals such as the Russian Nina Kulagina and the Americans Ted Serios and Ingo Swann. Early tests of these "superpsychics" in some laboratories by credulous investigators led to the championing of their abilities. When subjected to more careful tests by skeptical scientists, all of these so-called psychic abilities fell by the wayside. It soon became clear that in spite of the claims of the psychic "stars," none of them should be taken seriously. Nor have recent studies of dream telepathy, remote viewing, the Ganzfeld effect studies of Charles Honorton, or the automated machine scoring work of Schmidt and Jahn been any more persuasive. While Honorton and others have argued that the Ganzfeld studies *do* constitute the long-sought repeatable experiment, flaws in the methodology and the lack of replicability by neutral or hostile investigators have caused the main body of science and the majority of scientists to reject such claims.

No review of the field of parapsychology and the paranormal could be considered complete unless one discusses the Edgar Cayce phenomenon. Cayce, born in Hopkinsville, Kentucky in 1901, was a self-educated "psychic" physician who, while in daily self-induced trance states, was able to successfully diagnose and cure numerous human ailments. Using a "spirit guide" Cayce would describe the individual's ailment, presribe specific treatment, and "heal" the ailing individual in hundreds of cases where orthodox medicine was reputedly unsuccessful. In addition to "physical readings" Cayce also gave "life readings" that included information about the individual's "past lives" and their present spiritual status as well. Cayce also claimed prophetic abilities and gave many "readings" in which his spirit guides told him about history, science, religion, psychic phenomena, as well as the future. These readings total approximately fifteen thousand in all and are on file at the Cayce Foundation—The Association for Research and Enlightenment—located in Virginia Beach, Virginia. As a prophet Cayce leaves much to be desired. Many of his predictions have not come to pass and never will. Time, it seems, has a way of making fools of anyone brave enough to attempt to figure out her secrets.

With the birth of the so-called "New Age" in the late 1960s and early 1970s, there was a rebirth of interest in communicating with spirits. Rather than referring to the communicators as "mediums" however, now they are called "channels." Jane Roberts led this revival in the 1960s with several volumes of spiritual wisdom dictated to her by the discarnate spirit Seth. In 1965 the psychologist Helen C. Schucman began to hear an inner voice and to write down what this voice told her. The more she wrote, the more she heard until she had recorded some twelve hundred pages of what she labeled *A Course in Miracles* (1975). Later on she was convinced that the inner voice she heard was that of Christ. A few years later, as a result of the publicity given them by the actress-author Shirley MacLaine in her best-selling autobiographical books *Out On A Limb* (1983) and *Dancing In The Light* (1985), two other channels, J. Z. Knight and Kevin Ryerson, came into the limelight. Knight channels a thirty-five-thousand-year-old spiritual and political leader from fabled Lemuria (now India) named Ramtha. Knight is an attractive forty-year-old blonde who has parlayed the words of Ramtha into several volumes of psychological and spiritual counseling and lectures that have made her a fortune. Ryerson, an articulate and clever individual who channels a number of different entities, is in touch with the soul of the universe and channels a number of spiritual sources, particularly an Essene Hebrew named John and an Elizabethan named Tom. He, too, has become famous and wealthy. Jach Pursel and his entity, Lazaris, has also become famous. Lazaris is somewhat different in that he has never been either human or physical, but is a discarnate, free-floating spirit filled with the wisdom of the universe. Literally hundreds of other individuals calling themselves channels have jumped aboard this quite profitable bandwagon and have managed for some time now to amass fame and fortune. A detailed and fascinating report of this revival of turn-of-the-century spiritualism can be found in Jon Klimo's *Channeling: Investigations on Receiving Information From Paranormal Sources* (J. P. Tarcher, 1987).

Another source of amusement and entertainment for the credulous has been the growth and proliferation of the so-called *psychics*. Psychics, in case you didn't know, are those fortunate individuals who are endowed with special power and abilities that enable them to penetrate the boundaries of space and time and see the past and the future, contact the dead, locate missing persons and things, cure the sick by the laying on of hands, and generally do whatever it is that needs doing. Today they are everywhere. One Los Angeles psychic earns over $1,000 a day making economic predictions. Another specializes in locating archeological artifacts. A group calling themselves Professional Psychics United claims an 87 percent success rate helping the police with unsolved crimes. Even the FBI Academy for some time used a presentation on "How Psychics Can Be Useful" as part of their training program. It is also rumored that ABC-TV hired a psychic at a salary of over $50,000 a year to advise their programming staff. They have also been used by several branches of the Armed Forces to spy on the Soviets via out-of-the-body trips and to use psychic powers to locate missile silos, destroy weapons, caches, and so forth.

Despite the absence of positive evidence for the existence of psi, the lack of a repeatable experiment, the hundreds of cases of proven fraud, deceit, and human gullibility, the belief in the paranormal continues and the search for the irrefutable proof of the paranormal and the permanent paranormal object (PPO) wistfully wished for by John Beloff (1990) goes on. Loyd Auerbach, one of the more reputable investigators and one who unashamedly and unabashedly calls himself a parapsychologist, has in his book *ESP, Hauntings and Poltergeists* (Warner Books, 1986) mounted a strong defense for continuing the search for psi despite decades of negative results. Auerbach argues that:

> Psychic phenomena exist; that is, there are psychic interactions between people, and between people and the environment, that are unexplained by current mainstream science. . . . I and others think that to ignore any out-of-the-ordinary happenings (what can be called anomalies in the natural world) is to ignore the process of science. . . . People are having experiences which *appear* to be paranormal, psychic. . . . Parapsychologists are the ones who look into these experiences, hoping to add to the sum of human knowledge and to work out a new form of interaction with the environment and with other people. I will admit the possibility that what we are studying may be no more than "airy nothing," common effects and experiences that are misunderstood. But what if they are something more?

Auerbach goes on to stress the fact that the overwhelming majority of people who report such experiences are neither "crazy" nor "weird." He also notes that the experiences exist but what they are remains to be seen. They are mysteries in need of solving. Even if the paranormalists are wrong, Auerbach argues, we may well discover the solution to why people have such experiences. Auerbach sums up his argument with the statement:

Personally, I believe we *will* find something here. I have had a few psychic experiences myself, although, believe it or not, I've never seen a ghost. In addition, I am trained as a magician and mentalist—of course, I'm talking about stage magic and phony mind-reading—which has provided some insight into how people really perceive the world around them, and how they can misunderstand ordinary happenings. Yet, while I maintain a skeptical outlook, and in the true spirit of skepticism keep an open mind, looking at all sides of a situation before deciding what's going on, I still believe there are psychic happenings. Interestingly enough, so do quite a large number of professional magicians and mentalists . . . this book is meant to enlighten you as to what parapsychologists are really up to and what people do experience. It's meant to impress upon you the importance of keeping an open mind while at the same time questioning reports of psychic happenings, especially when reported by the mass media. (Auerbach 1986)

Conclusions

Several years ago the sociologist Sorokin (1957) argued there was a basic split in Western epistemology, two separate mentalities that he tagged the *Sensate* and the *Ideational.* In his words:

> At one extreme is a mentality for which reality is that which can be perceived by the organs of sense; it does not see anything beyond the sensate being of the milieu. . . . Those who possess this sort of mentality try to adapt themselves to those conditions which appear to the sense organs. . . . At the other extreme are persons who perceive and apprehend the same sensate phenomena in a very different way. For them they are mere appearance, a dream, or an illusion. True reality is not to be found here; it is something beyond . . . different from this material and sensate veil which conceals it. . . . whether (true reality) be styled God, Nirvana, Brahma, OM, Self, Tao, External Spirit, l'elan vital, Unnamed, The City of God, Ultimate Reality, *Ding für und an sich,* or what not, is of little importance. What is important is that . . . true reality is usually considered supersensate, immaterial, spiritual. (Sorokin 1957, pp. 25–26)

In our contemporary civilization the sensate subculture is of course dominant since science and materialism and the associated beliefs of individuals, progress, and utilitarianism are ascendant. The Ideational elements of our civilization play a secondary role even though large numbers of people concern themselves with occult and supernatural phenomena. The extent of such beliefs was noted earlier. It is also important to note that members of the Ideational subculture safeguard the integrity of their knowledge by reinforcing their beliefs with organizations—both large and small—that publish books, newsletters, propaganda tracts, and so forth, hold periodic meetings and rallies; and support whenever possible organized attacks on the unbelievers. Most members of these groups also have a large emotional investment in the organization and its aims and they strive to learn and grow spiritually and intellectually within the bounds of the belief system. Every new belief, no matter how bizarre, is taken as a sign of progress. Members of the Sensate subculture immediately assume the particular belief is delusional, proving it is not quite as easy as it might seem. The very idea of "reality testing" presumes a Sensate epistemology and those with an Ideational philosophy can always claim that an empirical test constitutes no proof at all. Although we like to think that our scientific observations are unbiased, they are instead selected and interpreted within the very framework they are supposed to test. People in the Ideational subculture abhor the Sensate beliefs and argue that only by turning off our rational conscious minds can we open up the subconscious, intuitive, alogical mind and make contact with the higher spiritual realities.

Many philosophers with an Ideational bent argue the wisdom of this position but fail to realize the subsequent dangers of becoming dependent upon irrational and alogical information coming from the subconscious. We cannot ever rid ourselves of the issue of *truth and falsity* with regard to belief. Delusions are universally defined as false beliefs. Societies, as well as smaller social groups, have and can easily become delusional, deranged, and supportive of false and dangerous beliefs. Delusional beliefs held by entire societies—beliefs in witches, Satan, devils, demons, ghosts, and the like—and particularly religious beliefs have plagued mankind since the beginning of time. If we look at the Sensate-Ideational split in the light of human welfare and the future well-being of the human race, there is little in the way of choice. Beyond question the Ideational mind-set has caused more human horror and misery in the name of religion and supernatural beliefs than any force in history. There is no ferocity or mania that comes close to matching that of the religious zealots and sanctimonious idealogues acting in the name of their god or gods. Rape, wholesale murder and slaughter, massive torture of children and the innocent and the aged, unspeakable acts of unimaginable horror have all been carried out in the name of delusionary religious beliefs. Endless wars have been and continue to be waged over which delusionary belief system is true and which is false, and both are justified by the Ideational mentality. A catalog of these horrors perpetrated by individuals with such mind-sets has been recently compiled by James Haught (1990). Delusions have been, are, and can be dangerous—very dangerous—especially when held by groups of people. They can also be very dangerous to the individuals who hold them and perhaps even more dangerous to others who unwillingly become victims of those holding bizarre and lethal convictions. To argue that one man's delusion is another man's truth is to argue that we utterly lack or eschew the power to discriminate and that there is no "right" or "wrong," and no way to discriminate between truth and fiction. Fortunately, such arguments are mostly academic and lack consensual validity. Most of us know right from wrong and can get through the day, month, year, and even decade without confusing the two. Most of us, while we may well harbor an illusion or two, engage in odd thoughts now and then, and on certain rare occasions even have a hallucination or two, for 99 percent of the time or more we are able to tell the difference between reality and dreams and fact and fiction. Most of us know that we must obey the physical laws of the universe or suffer the consequences. We are not like the Russian psychic who, after stopping horses, bicycles, and cars, held the deluded (and unfortunately fatal) belief that he could stop a train. Most of us have moral and humane standards and principles that we live by, and we do—for the most part—respect and honor the rights of others. We acknowledge and respect the power of science and scientific laws and we do not allow our religious beliefs—if we have any—to dominate and control our behavior and overrule our common sense. We are, for the most part, reality oriented and we know the difference between sane and insane thinking and rational and irrational behavior. Although we may not be as intellectually astute and as sophisticated as professional logicians and academic specialists, we are not fools either. Fortunately, education —primary, secondary, and higher—is not a total failure. Though we may carry and share many illusions of one sort or another, we still have only a few (and rare) delusions and hallucinations. We are, most of us that is, of the sensate mind-set and look askance at those who find their reality in some otherworldly dimension rather than this one that all of us—both Ideational and Sensate—must and do inhabit and share. Is this a Sensate bias? Yes, indeed, and thankfully so since it leads to survival and the enhancement of human welfare. While it can be claimed that the Ideational also emphasizes the "higher aspects" of human existence and leads man to higher levels of exaltation, the historical record tells us another and far different story.

Of utmost importance is the fact that in the Ideational world all beliefs are of equal validity. The only way that the truth or falsity of an Ideational belief or even its utility can be determined is by entering the Sensate world and using the tools and operations of science. This should be obvious. This fact and the difference between the two modes of thought

—between the two mentalities—are profound and of the utmost significance: it is the difference between science and superstition. Those with vested emotional interests in the Ideational view will probably never understand or comprehend the Sensate position, and vice versa. Let us pray that few in the Sensate camp will ever want to do more than merely understand the origin of supernaturalism and the roots of what Kurtz terms the "transcendental temptation." Once one has entered the camp of the paranormalists, one develops a disease of the mind from which few ever recover. Unfortunately, there is neither an antidote nor a cure. Neither is there a preventive vaccine. Like AIDS, the best we can do is to make sure that the young and innocent are never exposed to the Ideational virus. This, as most of you are aware, is much easier said than done—especially when nearly every media source is flooding the landscape with New Age legends and urban mythologies.

As a paranormal investigator you must also be cognizant of the fact that even though you may solve the msytery to your satisfaction and to the satisfaction of the Sensate and scientifically oriented community, this in no way guarantees that anyone in the Ideational community will ever give you an ear or acknowledge your existence, much less accept the validity of your findings. For most members of the Ideational community empirical work that challenges or fails to validate a deeply held belief will never be accepted. Instead, it usually serves to harden the resistance, stiffen the opposition, and strengthen the original belief. Don't be too disappointed if your diligent work, your brilliant logic, and your magnificent solution falls upon unhearing ears and unseeing eyes. To be forewarned is to be prepared. Do not expect acceptance and understanding from those with deep emotional investments and public commitments to Ideational claims. As many wise men have noted, the logical and emotional gulf between the opposing points of view may well be unbridgeable.

Psi Investigators

The most visible and vocal groups of individuals opposing the world of paranormalists and psychics is the *Committee for the Scientific Investigation of Claims of the Paranormal* (CSICOP) and its seventy-two state and international subgroups. As one would expect, these organizations have met with considerable outraged opposition from psi supporters. CSICOP's official journal is *The Skeptical Inquirer,* a quarterly, that aims to provide the public with the truth about all paranormal claims. Of this journal, which is edited and published by some of the most credentialed and reputable scientists in the world, Leslie Shepard in *The Encyclopedia of Occul-*

tism and Parapsychology states, "It is difficult to combine an attitude of impartial inquiry with a stance of scientific authority when there is an implicit initial assumption that all claims of the paranormal are erroneous or fraudulent." The problem with this statement and most of the other attacks upon and objections to CSICOP's exposure of case after case after case of erroneous and fraudulent claims is that it is so incredibly difficult to the point of being impossible to find any *valid or legitimate example* of a paranormal claim that is not either the result of human error or misperception or due to human deceit and deception. Bernard Gittelson in his pro-psi and highly credulous work *Intangible Evidence* (Simon & Shuster, 1987) derisively refers to members and supporters of CSICOP as "psi cops," self-appointed and arrogant "thought police." What Gittelson forgets is that it is a cop's duty to monitor social behavior and to see that society's laws are obeyed. Many policemen are feared and disliked and accused of being arrogant, especially by lawbreakers who have the most to lose. It is also easy to understand why Gittelson and his kind are terrified of the "psi cops" who are seeking to uphold and support the laws of nature. To be called a "psi cop" is, rather than a term of opprobrium, a compliment and an honor. In this regard it is important also to remember that the implicit initial assumption behind every paranormal claim is that the phenomena reported is something supernatural and beyond the powers of human science to explain.

Anti-psi forces are also accused of attacks on the personal integrity of serious parapsychologists and of being sarcastic, hostile, and authoritarian. Such accusations, as far as dealings with legitimate parapsychological science are concerned, are blatantly false as can be seen by the articles in and the tone of *The Elusive Quarry: A Scientific Appraisal of Psychical Research* by Ray Hyman, James Alcock's *Science and Supernature: A Critical Appraisal of Parapsychology,* and *A Skeptic's Handbook of Parapsychology* edited by Paul Kurtz. All of these scholarly tomes are published by Prometheus Books. There is, perhaps, some element of truth in the charges when serious and dedicated scientists are forced to confront total and abysmal scientific ignorance and superstitious nonsense. Being human they do, on occasion, lose their tempers and make sarcastic and hostile remarks, especially to creationists and Bible-thumpers who argue that man and the dinosaurs coexisted.

Another favorite argument of the "psi-cophants" is that there is a real and important distinction between what a mentalist or sleight-of-hand artist can do on a stage and with preparation, and what can be done spontaneously. While a clever magician can bend spoons surreptitiously and can appear to pick up "psychic" information from a gullible audience member with a stooge's help—this is not in any way scientific proof that legitimate psychics do it the same way nor does it rule out the possibility that the psychic does use supernatural skills. Furthermore, if one catches the medium or the psychic cheating on one occasion, it in no way proves that he cheats on *every* occasion that he reads another person's mind! To the true believer and *psi-cophant* there is no such thing as a convincing demonstration.

Psi-cops are also accused of being so afraid of psi that they rationalize it away even when it is staring them in the face. Rather than immediately leaping to a paranormal explanation for every strange or unusual event, the psi-cop first attempts to explain the phenomenon in natural terms. To the impatient psi-cophant this is a deliberate refusal on the part of the psi-cop to face the paranormal fact. Months ago a friend told me of going to a movie and, while waiting in the lobby before the movie started and perusing the billboards, he suddenly thought of a friend that he hadn't seen or heard from in years. Following the movie and as he was coming out of the theater, lo and behold, there was his friend in front of him. He, too, had just seen the movie. After renewing acquaintances it was clear that while looking at the billboards he had heard his friend's voice at the candy counter and this had triggered the association. What was apparently a paranormal event after study becomes clearly something quite simple and natural. Unfortunately, the simple and natural are, apparently, neither simple nor natural to the psi-cophant.

The Paranormal Literature

The sincere paranormal investigator should definitely familiarize him- or herself with the paranormal literature. While it is admittedly vast, you should at least become familiar with those sources that provide both a broad overview of the field and that are reasonably coherent and provide at least some supporting evidence for the belief. Among the more reasonable and readable sources written from the paranormal viewpoint are: Laile Bartlett's *Psi Trek* (McGraw-Hill, 1981); Bernard Gittelson's *Intangible Evidence* (Simon & Schuster, 1987); Louis Stewart's *Life Forces: A Contemporary Guide to the Cult and Occult* (Andrews and McMeel, 1980); Jeffrey Mishlove's *PSI Development Systems* (Ballantine Books, 1988); Jenny Randles's *Beyond Explanation* (Salem House, 1985); Loyd Auerbach's *ESP, Hauntings and Poltergeists* (Warner Books, 1986); Jon Klimo's *Channeling: Investigations on Receiving Information from Paranormal Sources* (Jeremy Tarcher, 1987); *Exploring the Paranormal: Perspectives on Belief and Experience* edited by Zollschan, Schumaker, and Walsh (Avery Pub. Group, 1989); and *The Handbook of Parapsychology* edited by Benjamin

B. Wolman (Van Nostrand Reinhold, 1977). In addition to these volumes there are a number of magazines and journals that provide timely and up-to-date reports of the latest fads and fallacies in the paranormal world. Particularly recommended are: *Fate,* monthly ($22.95 per year from P.O. Box 1940, 170 Future Way, Marion, OH 43304-1940), $1.95 per single copy; *Strange,* twice a year, $4.95 per issue ($17.95 for four issues from *Strange Magazine,* P.O. Box 2246, Rockville, MD 20847); *Critique,* three times a year, $5.00 per issue ($15 per year from *Critique,* c/o Bob Banner, P.O. Box 11368, Santa Rosa, CA 95406); *Gnosis,* quarterly, $4.00 per issue ($15 per year from *Gnosis,* P.O. Box 14217, San Francisco, CA 94114-09217); *Magical Blend,* quarterly, $3.95 per issue ($14 per year, *Magical Blend,* P.O. Box 11303, San Francisco, CA 94101-7303); *Body, Mind & Spirit,* bi-monthly, $2.95 per issue ($15 per year, *Body, Mind & Spirit,* P.O. Box 701, Providence, RI 02901); *New Age Journal,* bi-monthly, $2.95 per issues ($24 per year, P.O. Box 53275, Boulder, CO 80321-3275); *Infocult: The Journal of Strange Information,* quarterly, $2 per issue, ($9 per year, P.O. Box 3124, East Hampton, NY 11937); *Connecting Link* (channeling), bi-monthly, $3.95 per issue ($20 per year, 9392 Whitneyville, MI 49302);*Creation Spirituality,* bi-monthly, $4 per issue ($20 per year, 160 East Virginia Street, San Jose, CA 95112); *Meditation: Vision to Reality,* bi-monthly, $4 per issue ($22 per year, 17211 Orozco Street, Granada Hills, CA 91344); and *Fortean Times: The Journal of Strange Phenomena,* sporadic (intended to be quarterly), $6 per issue ($16 per four issues, back issues available, Fortean Times, 20 Paul Street, Frome, Somerset BA11 1DX, England). In addition to these books and journals Time-Life Books, Inc. has published a series of ten separate volumes in their *Mysteries of the Unknown* series which are worthy of reading. The ten volumes are: *Miracles, the UFO Phenomenon, Psychic Voyages, Hunting for Monsters, Spirit Summonings, Mystic Places, Future Visions, Psychic Powers, Mind Over Matter,* and *Phantom Encounters.* A second and related series called the *Time-Life Library of Curious and Unusual Facts* is also available. The ten volumes in this series are: *Coincidences, Vanishings, Feats & Wisdom of the Ancients, Mysteries of the Human Body, Forces of Nature, Amazing Animals, Inventive Genius, Lost Treasures, A World of Luck,* and *The Amazing Mind.* The volumes in both series sell for approximately $15 each plus shipping and handling and can be obtained from Time-Life Books, 1450 E. Parham Road, Richmond, VA 23280-9985.

Finally, Richard S. Broughton, Director of Research at The Institute for Parapsychology in Durham, North Carolina, has argued in his recent book *Parapsychology: The Controversial Science* that not only has parapsychology come of age but that it is now ready to be applied in the everyday world (1991). Broughton bases his arguments on the fact that the statistical technique *meta-analysis* shows the *ganzfeld* experiments are producing consistent positive effects. Unfortunately, not only are there a number of weaknesses with the meta-analytic technique itself, but Broughton's arguments that a theory-less largely anecdotal, unreliable, and extremely quixotic set of experiments carried out by biased believers constitutes a "science" are extremely hard to swallow. What Broughton's book shows, as James Alcock, Ray Hyman, and Martin Gardner have noted in the past, is that rather than being a "science," parapsychology today, as it has been in the past, is instead a "faith," i.e., a religion.

For the naive and budding investigator some of the claims presented and discussed in these books and journals might be the place to begin. Picking a single topic you find intriguing, you can gather the available information, consult the original sources and claimants, and then draw your own conclusions. This process is recommended because most of us who have jobs and professions do not have either the time or the finances to travel halfway across the continent in search of UFO abductees, haunted houses, or screaming skulls. We must make do with the local mysteries we hear about or stumble across. These may well be few and far between in most locales, so if you wish to pursue psi investigating as a full-time recreation you may have to begin with your local library or bookstore. And, in fact, this is a truly appropriate and excellent place to start.

2

Investigatory Tactics and Techniques

The Scientific Method

The rational basis upon which the work of today's skeptical investigator is predicated can be traced back to ancient times, to the first glimmerings of what we now call science. Although man's earliest efforts to comprehend his strange world were essentially magical—a mixture of spiritism and other occult thinking—more and more he became the possessor of empirical knowledge.

Empirical (from the Latin *empiricus,* "experienced") refers to that which is learned from one's own observation. Underlying the empirical attitude is a belief that there is a real, knowable world that operates according to fixed rules and that effects do not occur without causes.

As the practical knowledge gained from man's experience and observation was slowly accumulated, the shaman or magician-priest attempted to put it to use. Thus, as Colin A. Ronan explains in his *Science: Its History and Development among the World's Cultures* (1982), "by degrees the magician came to be the first in the lineage of experimental investigators, and the remote ancestor of the modern scientist" (p. 11).

With the expansion of empirical knowledge, recourse to purely supernatural beliefs diminished, and explanations for natural phenomena began to be admixtures of the rational and the magical. Such a set of observed "facts," beliefs, standards, and methods constituted a paradigm (or model) to explain some part of man's mysterious world. According to Ronan:

Our present scientific synthesis is another step along the road to a more comprehensive picture, but it is not the final one. Our current paradigms will one day give place to new and improved bodies of theory, just as those we now accept replaced the paradigms before them. For example, whereas it was once universally agreed by Western scientific philosophers that the stars and planets were fixed to crystal spheres centered on the Earth—a belief which was pregnant enough with puzzles in celestial motion to tax the most brilliant minds—this was replaced by a concept of motion in empty space, which again presented new problems to challenge the intellect. Now we have moved on to motion guided by universal gravitation in a relativistic space-time universe; this represents the present pinnacle of modern cosmological thought. It is greatly superior in many ways to the doctrine of the spheres, but it is not the last word. A new and more widely embracing paradigm will doubtless come to replace it. (Ronan 1982, p. 11)

The scientific paradigm functions something like a partially completed jigsaw puzzle. It readily indicates just where problem areas are and which ones deserve the most serious effort, while at the same time seeming to promise that the problems are capable of being solved. As science writers William Broad and Nicholas Wade (1982) state:

But the tranquility of normal science does not last. Sooner or later, scientists trying to extend the paradigm find that there are puzzles they cannot solve. Often such anomalies were there from the outset but could be ignored during the heady process of paradigm explication. In fact, during normal science, scientists try to suppress novelties. Yet against the background of the paradigm the anomalies stand out with increasing prominence. The time comes when they can be ignored no longer. Then the field enters into crisis, such as befell earth-centered astronomy before Copernicus, or the phlogiston theory of burning before the understanding of oxygen. (p. 132)

Here we see science in its self-correcting aspect. Those who criticize "orthodox" scientists (often with a view toward advancing their own pseudoscientific notions) claim that science is rigid and that scientists are close-minded defenders of their orthodoxies. That has sometimes been the case, as distinguished science writer Martin Gardner concedes in his classic text, *Fads and Fallacies in the Name of Science* (1957): "It would be foolish, of course, to deny that history contains many sad examples of novel scientific views which did not receive an unbiased hearing, and which later proved to be true." He adds:

Probably the most notorious instance of scientific stubbornness was the refusal of eighteenth-century astronomers to believe that stones actually fell from the sky. Reaction against medieval superstitions and old wives' tales were still so strong that whenever a meteor fell, astronomers insisted it had either been picked up somewhere and carried by the wind, or that the persons who claimed to see it fall were lying. Even the great French *Académie des Sciences* ridiculed this folk belief, in spite of a number of early studies of meteoric phenomena. Not until April 26, 1803, when several thousand small meteors fell on the town of L'Aigle, France, did the astronomers decide to take falling rocks seriously.

Still, Gardner observes:

One must be extremely cautious, however, before comparing the work of some contemporary eccentric with any of these earlier examples, so frequently cited in crank writings. In medicine, we must remember, it is only in the last fifty years or so that the art of healing has become anything resembling a rigorous scientific discipline. One can go back to periods in which medicine was in its infancy, hopelessly mixed with superstition, and find endless cases of scientists with unpopular views that later proved correct. The same holds true of other sciences. But the picture today is vastly different. The prevailing spirit among scientists, outside of totalitarian countries, is one of eagerness for fresh ideas. In the great search for a cancer cure now going on, not the slightest stone, however curious its shape, is being left unturned. If anything, scientific journals err on the side of permitting *questionable* theses to be published, so they may be discussed and checked in the hope of finding something of value. A few years ago a student at the Institute for Advanced Studies in Princeton was asked how his seminar had been that day. He was quoted in a news magazine as exclaiming, "Wonderful! Everything we knew about physics last week isn't true!" (pp. 9–10)

Indeed, an excellent example of a scientist's willingness to change his opinion occurred following the Apollo moon landing. Harold Urey—who had authored one textbook theory concerning the origin of the moon's surface—was able to examine the moon rocks recovered by the Apollo astronauts. Immediately, Dr. Urey realized that his theory was incompatible with the hard evidence before him. "I've been wrong!" he announced in true scientific spirit ("Twenty 'Scientific Attitudes,' " 1989).

As anthropologist Kenneth L. Feder notes, "Though individual scientists may be swayed by personal biases, wishful thinking, or peer pressure, data cannot be explained away for very long." Feder (1990) cites an extreme case, the notorious scientific hoax represented by the alleged discovery of man's fossil ancestor, Piltdown Man. Although most of the evolutionary scientists at the time did not wish to relinquish the brain-centered evolutionary paradigm, they did when increasing evidence indicated that brain expansion was not as old as upright posture. Feder says that with the mounting evidence "Piltdown became trivial, even before it was finally proved fraudulent."

In addition to its self-correcting aspect, science also has a self-policing system—at least to an extent. Its purpose is to guard against the type of fraud exemplified by the Piltdown hoax, as well as less blatant forms of dishonesty such as that known as "cooking." The term was coined in 1830 by Charles Babbage in his *Reflections on the Decline of Science in England*. As he wrote:

> Cooking is an art of various forms, the object of which is to give ordinary observations the appearance and character of those of the highest degree of accuracy. One of its numerous processes is to make multitudes of observations and out of these to select those only which agree, or very nearly agree. If a hundred observations are made, the cook must be very unlucky if he cannot pick out fifteen or twenty which will do for serving up. (Babbage 1830)

Those accused of cooking their results include the Abbé Gregor Mendel, the pioneer geneticist, although whether his fudging of data was conscious or unconscious is debatable (Broad and Wade 1982, pp. 29–33).

Science's self-policing system is comprised of three major aspects: peer review, refereeing, and replication. Peer review refers to the work of committees of experts who advise government agencies as to which scientists should be given funding for their research. This is a safety mechanism meant to insure that reputable, competent scientists are engaged and to guard against fraudulent research proposals (Broad and Wade 1982, pp. 61–62).

Similarly, the referee system is a peer-review process applied to scientific journals. The journals routinely send out the manuscripts of submitted articles to expert authorities who attempt to spot any deficiencies (e.g., in scientific methodology or argument). The experts may favor publication, or urge returning the manuscript for revision, or recommend against publication (Broad and Wade 1982, pp. 17, 62).

Finally, replication is a strong defense against bad or bogus science. Attempted replication means that other scientists will try to reproduce an experiment (or other research endeavor) to see if they obtain results—that is, to try to verify or refute the work. To permit replication, in submitting his work for publication a scientist is expected to describe his methodology or experimental procedure in sufficient detail—usually in a format having these (or analogous) major divisions: Introduction (including the immediate background of the problem and a review of the applicable scientific literature), Materials and Methods, Results and Discussion, and Conclusions. This permits referees to judge whether replication could be attempted and whether there are perceived methodological or other problems (Broad and Wade 1982, pp. 61–52; Houp and Pearsall 1988, pp. 443–57).

How the replication procedure can work is illustrated by an example concerning Dr. Charles T. Tart, a parapsychologist at the University of California at Davis. Tart reported successful scoring in ESP tests that, according to Martin Gardner (1981, p. 207) "far exceeded anything obtained before in the history of parapsychology." Subsequently, three mathematicians were asked to review Tart's raw data, while Gardner called attention to serious flaws in the experiment. As a consequence, Tart corrected some of the flaws and repeated the test himself but obtained negative results. Nevertheless, he stated: "Because the level of scoring in the first experiment was so high, it would be absurd to argue that the results of the second experiment mean that the results of the first experiment were a mere statistical fluke." Gardner replied:

> Tart's last statement leaves me so staggered that I can respond only with a parable. A parapsychologist finds a psychic who can levitate a table forty feet. He investigates this under poorly controlled conditions, but is so convinced the phenomenon is genuine that he writes a book about it. The book is published by a gullible university press. After skeptical magicians—those terrible spoilsports!—patiently explain how the levitation could have been accomplished by trickery, the parapsychologist agrees to test the psychic again, this time with adequate controls. The table does not rise at all. The parapsychologist then writes a formal report that concludes: "In view of how high the table rose during the first experiment, it would be absurd to contend that the failure of the second experiment in any way casts doubt on my previous observations." (pp. 211–212)

This prompted an angry rejoinder from Tart and a final reply from Gardner (pp. 212–214). The latter concluded:

> When reputable scientists correct flaws in an experiment that produced fantastic results, then fail to get those results when they repeat the test with flaws corrected, they withdraw their original claims. They do not defend them by arguing irrelevantly that the failed replication was successful in some other way, or by making intemperate attacks on whoever dares to criticize their competence.

As the previous case demonstrates, despite the various safeguards that supposedly help insure good scientific research, problems can occur, and they can arise at any stage of the process. However, being aware of their potential can at least mitigate against them, as will be discussed in the pages and chapters to follow.

Conducting Investigations

Attitude is an essential element in investigative work. All too often in the emotionally charged arena of debate over paranormal issues, polarization takes place with the result that on the one side are ranged "believers" and on the other "debunkers." The former seem (at least to the latter) entirely too credulous in their heralding of potentially wonderous phenomena; conversely, the latter appear (at least to the former) altogether too close-minded and prone to dismiss out of hand that which might upset their orthodox views.

The serious investigator should steer between either extreme, seeking neither to foster nor suppress mysteries but rather to solve them. Recognizing that objectivity is the surest path to truth, he will suspend judgment and adopt a skeptical attitude toward the data he encounters. Actually, since skepticism is "simply a doubting state of mind," what is needed is not so much skepticism as *discernment* (Korem 1988, p. 29) or critical thinking. Such thinking does not inhibit the truth; instead the demand for rigorous proof helps insure that it emerges from the cacophony of controversy. From this perspective comes a guiding principle of a distinguished international investigating body, The Committee for the Scientific Investigation of Claims of the Paranormal. Note that investigation is its middle name, that it "Does not reject claims on a priori grounds, antecedent to inquiry, but rather examines them objectively and carefully."

Critical thinking, then, "*is not merely negative thinking.* It also fosters the ability to be *creative and constructive*—to generate possible explanations for findings, think of implications, and apply new knowledge to a broad range of social and personal problems." Therefore, continue Wade and Tavris (1990), "Critical thinking cannot really be separated from creative thinking, for it's only when students question *what is* that they can begin to imagine *what can be*." Critical/creative thinking is essential to the problem-solving requisites of investigation, the mechanics of which we now turn to.

The typical investigation begins with a fact-finding phase. Generally speaking, people obtain information in two essential ways: (1) *empirically* —that is, through their own observation and experience, and (2) *indirectly*—from specific sources. As Feder (1990, p. 10) points out, people often assume that the first of these—direct experience—is preferable, but "This is unfortunately a false assumption because most people are poor observers."

Trained observers are, of course, another matter, and the observations of a specialist or an experienced field investigator can have great probative value. In marked contrast is the response of John Taylor, a mathematical physicist at London's King College, who was fooled by mischievous children who were allowed to perform their alleged paranormal effects—such as bending paper clips—*out of view*! (Gardner 1981, pp. 181–82) Such examples offer an obvious lesson for investigators. As Gardner challenges:

> You suspect someone of habitually cheating at cards. Whom would you hire as a secret observer to settle the matter? A physicist?
>
> A self-proclaimed psychic goes about performing miracles exactly like the feats of magicians who specialize in what the trade calls "mentalism." You suspect the psychic of cheating. Whom do you call upon as an expert witness? A physicist?
>
> One of the saddest, most persistent aspects of the history of alleged psychic phenomena is that there always has been a small, noisy group of scientists who, combining enormous egotism with even greater gullibility, actually imagine that *they* are competent to detect psychic fraud. (p. 293)

Direct observation is only one of the information sources available to the investigator. Published materials represent essential source material as well, as do interviews and other means. Access to a good reference library (especially if it includes interlibrary loan privileges) may enable one to obtain information on a particular subject (say "spirit photography"); background facts on a specific case (e.g., "The Amityville Horror"); biographical knowledge (as on an alleged "psychic detective"); scientific data (on meteors as potential explanations for UFOs, for instance); and the like. (See Bibliography: Part 2: Reference Sources for the Investigator.)

The personal interview is another important source, whether it is of someone who claims to have experienced some paranormal phenomenon, or an expert from whom one is seeking an opinion, or perhaps someone else with useful information to impart such as a fellow investigator willing to share data. (Interrogation techniques are discussed in chapter 3.)

By positing the bottom-line question in a case—say, "Is such-and-such a house really haunted?"—and defining any necessary terms (haunting, ghost, etc.), subsidiary questions will naturally follow: Where do these allegations originate? Are there sightings of the supposed ghost? If so, under what conditions do these occur? Are there ghostly noises? What potentially naturalistic sources might there be for such sounds? And so on. Making a list of such questions and considering possible sources for the answers to them—newspaper files, interviews of the caretakers, inspection of the premises and its environs, etc.—can represent a general plan for attacking a problem.

Sooner or later, one finds oneself beginning to formulate potential explanations or *hypotheses* in the case. As David A. Binder and Paul Bergman state in their legal text, *Fact Investigation: From Hypothesis to Proof*:

> Investigation is often all too readily thought of as merely a time to learn evidence. But remember that the evidence gathering phase of investigation is normally preceded by an analysis which ultimately dictates what evidence one pursues. This analysis concerns in part the potential legal theories and factual hypotheses that one may pursue during investigation. (Binder and Bergman 1984, p. 162)

Additionally, W. Beveridge, in his *The Art of Scientific Investigation*, describes the significance of hypothesis in investigation:

> Hypothesis is the most important mental technique of the investigator, and its main function is to suggest new experiments or new observations. Indeed, most experiments and many observations are carried out with the deliberate object of testing an hypothesis. Another function is to help one see the significance of an object or event that otherwise would mean nothing. For instance, a mind prepared by the hypothesis of evolution would make many more significant observations on a field excursion than one not so prepared. Hypotheses should be used as tools to uncover new facts rather than as ends in themselves. (Beveridge 1950, p. 63)

In the investigative process, the hypothesis may function in somewhat the following manner. The study of a particular problem triggers (or at least yields) one or more potentially applicable hypotheses. At the same time, or subsequently, the investigator considers the problem in light of each hypothesis. Deficiencies in each are noted and prompt additional factual investigation. In both the testing of hypotheses and the search for additional evidence, the investigator draws upon his intellectual resources (his experience, creativity, common sense) as well as upon various tools available to him (a certain compendium perhaps, or even some scientific analysis) in his search.

The goal of the investigator—who abandons or modifies hypotheses as necessary—is the development of proof, in favor of one hypothesis, that is sufficient to solve the original problem. (Rules of evidence will be discussed at length in chapter 3.)

A cautionary note regarding hypotheses involves bias (touched on earlier), and Beveridge urges the "Intellectual discipline of subordinating ideas to facts." As he explains, "A danger constantly to be guarded against is that as soon as one formulates an hypothesis, parental affection tends to influence observations, interpretation and judgment; 'wishful thinking' is likely to start unconsciously." He quotes Claude Bernard, who stated: "Men who have excessive faith in their theories or ideas are not only ill-prepared for making discoveries; they also make poor observations." Warning that "Unless observations and experiments are carried out with safeguards ensuring objectivity, the results may unconsciously be biased." Beveridge cites instances in which that occurred in science, including the experimental work of Mendel mentioned earlier. Beveridge adds:

> The best protection against these tendencies is to cultivate an intellectual habit of subordinating one's opinions and wishes to objective evidence and a reverence for things as they really are, and to keep constantly in mind that the hypothesis is only a supposition. (pp. 67–68)

The "wishful thinking" Beveridge warns against can even lead to a hypothesis being imposed on the data. A case in point is a 1982 article that attempts to identify Sir Arthur Conan Doyle, the creator of Sherlock Holmes, as the perpetrator of the Piltdown Skull hoax. Ignoring the considerable *prima facie* evidence pointing to Charles Dawson—who not once but twice "discovered" sets of the doctored bones and was otherwise linked to the hoax—the writers seem to have arrived at Conan Doyle by drawing his name out of a hat. Having once done so, however, they manage to marshal numerous insinuations and innuendoes as supposed evidence for their notion: Conan Doyle lived near the gravel pit where the bones were discovered (and hence could have planted them); he had a special knowledge of skulls; and so forth (Winslow and Meyer 1983). In sum, the article seems a classic example of starting with the answer and working backward to the facts. Much more successful was the approach of the earlier Piltdown investigators who allowed the evidence (including Dawson's suspicious discoveries and his fabrication of other ancient finds) to indicate a plausible solution to the mystery (Weiner 1955, Jones 1990).

One way to escape the effects of prior bias is to employ the tools of logical reasoning known as *deduction* and *induction* (Myers 1989, p. 297). In deductive reasoning, one argues from the general to the specific. That is, we begin with a body of facts or a general premise which we then employ to reach particular conclusions. For example, in research into the authenticity of the "shroud" of Turin—the alleged burial cloth of Christ—the laws of geometry precluded the image on the cloth having been imprinted by simple contact, since the figure lacked the wraparound distortions that would have necessarily resulted (Nickell 1988, p. 79).

In inductive reasoning one generalizes from particular instances—that is, employs observations to reach a hypothesis. According to Myers (1989, p. 297), "Many thinking tasks involve both types of reasoning. The skills involved in playing chess include a well-practiced ability to reason deductively (from the rules of the game) and inductively (generalizing from past experiences)."

Apart from such general guidelines for the formulation of hypotheses and the avoidance of bias, it is difficult to specify investigatory procedures. Cautioning that "Investigation is a process of reasoning before it is a series of discrete tasks," Binder and Bergman observe that, "By and large, once one has identified potential evidence, one then chooses the investigatory vehicles . . . that will most likely enable one to ferret it out." They add: "It would be wonderful if some system, such as 'Depose one, interview two,' could be devised. However, such mechanical advice is better left to instructional books on how to dance or how to knit. Litigated disputes are too varied to permit any such step-by-step approach" (pp. 35–36). The same may be said of allegedly paranormal matters requiring investigation. Since approaches to such matters must necessarily be tailored to specific circumstances, they are apt to be almost as varied as the mysteries themselves. Even cases falling within the same general investigative area, and even having similar goals, may require such different approaches as ultimately to have little in common from an investigative standpoint.

Investigatory Strategies

Having pointed to some of the factors that make it difficult to prescribe easy formulas for assigning investigatory procedures, we can nevertheless describe a few of the general strategies that have been proven effective in investigating cases of allegedly paranormal phenomena. These approaches at least represent some basic options for consideration and should also help stimulate thinking toward the creation of new ones.

1. *Check details of an account of paranormal events.* Such an approach proved exceedingly effective in the case of "the Amityville Horror" house in Amityville, New York. This most famous of American "haunted" houses —where Ronald DeFeo murdered his parents and siblings in 1974—was purchased the following year by George and Kathy Lutz. Allegedly, they and their two sons experienced an astonishing variety of phenomena: strange music, green slime oozing from the ceiling, damage to windows and a heavy front door, demonic hoof tracks in the snow, and more.

Soon after the appearance of a popular book, *The Amityville Horror* by Jay Anson, investigators went to Amityville to check out details of the events the Lutzes had related to Anson. As it happens, the earliest newspaper account of the alleged events, although quoting George Lutz, failed to mention any damage to the house. Despite claims that a priest who had blessed the house had experienced sinister phenomena and that police were called to the house to investigate, the latter denied they had ever been to the scene, and the priest stated he had never entered the house. Moreover, when investigators checked weather reports they found that on the day the hoof tracks had reportedly been seen, there had actually been no snow on the ground.

Thus, it was revealed that the reported events were untrue; it turns out they were merely part of a deliberately concocted hoax. DeFeo's lawyer, who had been planning to write a book, eventually confessed that he and the Lutzes had "created this horror story over many bottles of wine." Money had been the motive (Anson 1978, Lester 1979, Moran and Jordan 1978, Morris 1977-78).

2. *Attempt to recreate the "impossible."* Frequently encountered cases that call for creative thinking and experimentation are those in which something that is apparently of human manufacture is instead held to have a non-human origin, i.e., is attributed to miraculous powers, extraterrestrial beings, or the like. Consider, for instance, the enigmatic lines and other markings—including giant drawings of animals, birds, and other creatures—that are drawn on the Nazca plain in Peru and which have been attributed to "ancient astronauts."

Although the drawings date from the time of the ancient Nazca Indians, resemble those found on Nazca pottery, and are associated with other facets of the Nazca culture (Nickell 1983), Erich von Däniken suggests another origin. He believes that the great size of the drawings—so large they can only be viewed from the air—argues against their having been made by the primitive Indians, unless with the help of extraterrestrials (von Däniken 1970).

To test the hypothesis that the figures *could* have been made by the Nazcas, presumably for some religious or ceremonial purpose, a reconstruction was attempted using a means von Däniken conceded might have been used: "working from a model and using a system of coordinates," to lay out a figure (p. 17)—in this case the giant "condor" measuring 440 feet long. The reconstruction required only a crew of six, some sticks and knotted cord, and it was accomplished in just two days (Nickell 1983). According to *Scientific American* ("Big Picture," 1983), it was "remarkable in its exactness" to the Nazca original.

Other applications of this investigatory approach include conducting experiments in quarrying, carving, transporting, and erecting the large stone statues on Easter Island—again in response to von Däniken (Heyerdahl

1958); producing a "negative" image like the supposedly supernatural one on the Shroud of Turin (Nickell 1988); creating a "spirit" picture (Nickell with Fischer 1988, pp. 58-59); and duplicating "mind-over-matter" effects (to be discussed presently). Of course such reconstructive work does not, of itself, prove the original was produced in the same manner, but it can have significant value in the context of other evidence.

3. *Devise an experiment to test a claim of paranormal ability.* An example of this approach was an investigation of the psychokinetic ("mind-over-matter") skills of James Hydrick, a twenty-one-year-old ex-convict and martial arts instructor of Salt Lake City, Utah. Touted by an Associated Press wire story, the now-defunct TV program "That's Incredible," and other media sources, Hydrick's apparent powers seemed to gain scientific support when a former assistant professor of electrical engineering made tests which he believed indicated the genuineness of the phenomena. Hydrick's reputed feats included moving a delicately balanced pencil by pointing at it and turning the pages of a telephone book from several feet away by merely staring.

However, when Hydrick appeared on another television show, "What's My Line?" (February 24, 1981), magician James Randi was there with a challenge. This was a standing $10,000 offer to anyone able to demonstrate genuine paranormal powers, and he placed a check for that amount in the custody of a panel of judges chosen to adjudicate the challenge. Having studied videotapes of Hydrick's performances, Randi thought he knew how the effects were produced and he easily duplicated them. But Randi was not using psychokinesis; instead, albeit imperceptibly, he was *blowing*.

To rule out Hydrick's using the same trick, Randi set up a simple test. He scattered feather-light Styrofoam pieces onto the table, surrounding the phone book, and challenged the would-be psychic to again turn the pages—this time without disturbing the Styrofoam pieces. If Hydrick were merely blowing to spin the pencil and flip the phone book pages, as Randi's hypothesis held, that mechanism would be revealed for all to see. Hydrick hesitated, expended the next hour and a half pretending to psychokinetically affect the pages (only a few minutes of which were actually aired), and gave up, contending his powers were weakened. Randi reclaimed his $10,000 check. Eventually, as related in Dan Korem's *Powers: Testing the Psychic & Supernatural* (1988, pp. 86-163), Hydrick confessed, boasting how he had "tricked the whole world" (p. 149).

4. *Research precedents.* That is, seek out previously investigated cases that may have features similar to those of the one under study. It is possible that similar cases may have similar solutions, although, of course, that must not be assumed. James Randi made use of this approach in the

"Columbus poltergeist case," specifically citing what has been learned from previous investigations.

In March 1984 the home of John and Joan Resch in Columbus, Ohio, was reportedly attacked by a poltergeist (or "noisy ghost"). Furniture was overturned, picture frames were smashed, glass objects were broken, and a telephone handset was thrown from its cradle. Stated Randi (1985): "Since the record of past cases indicates that when these destructive phenomena take place very frequently an unhappy adolescent is in the vicinity and they cease when the youngster is recognized and satisfied, explanations other than supernatural ones immediately suggest themselves."

Among the past cases Randi may have been referring to were some related in magician Milbourne Christopher's *ESP, Seers & Psychics* (1970). One occurred in 1951 in a Louisville, Kentucky, home. Bottle caps, boxes, and other objects were flung about, but eventually an eleven-year-old girl confessed that she was guilty of the disturbances. While her mother was away in the hospital, the girl had simply wanted some attention (149).

Another case transpired in 1964. In an office in Oakland, California, a water cooler was overturned and a hanging light bulb reportedly "unscrewed itself" from its socket, flew through the air, and smashed. Soon police interrogated a boy who worked for the company and he confessed, although he later retracted his confession, which he claimed had been coerced (p. 142).

Yet another series of disturbances plagued the C. A. Wilkinson family of Tulsa. Mr. Wilkinson suspected "wild electricity" of being the causative agent, but as Christopher states:

> Even objects that were not operated by electricity took on sudden motion. Chairs and tables seemed to vibrate. Pots leaped into the air. One night the commotion was so great that Wilkinson, his wife, and his twelve-year-old adopted daughter bedded down outside in the family automobile.
>
> As usual the disruptions drew curiosity seekers, reporters, and investigators. A trap was laid for a possible human culprit. A light coating of powder was dusted over potential flying objects. The *Tulsa Tribune* duly noted that after the disturbance that followed telltale marks were found on the girl's hands. She confessed that she was the cause of hitherto mysterious turmoil. (p. 146)

As it happened, in the Columbus case fourteen-year-old Tina Resch was an adopted child described as "hyperactive and emotionally disturbed" (Randi 1985). Tina was suspected of the shenanigans, which typically occurred when witnesses were looking away from the girl. However, photographs and television newstapes caught her red-handed—toppling a lamp, for example—and a TV technician saw her secretly move a table with her foot. As to the teenager's motive, Randi (1985) says, "She was admittedly under stress and had good reason to want to attract media exposure: she wanted to trace her true parents, against the wishes of the Resches. And her 'best friend' . . . had a fight with her and broke off their friendship two days before the phenomena began."

5. *Consider an innovative analysis.* Quite often there is an opportunity to utilize some specific discipline or even unique field of study in the investigation of some particular claim. Take, for example, the synchronistic (or "meaningfully coincidental") case of the "two Will Wests"—the criminal lookalikes whose astonishing resemblance was termed "one of the strangest coincidences in all history" (Blassingame 1975, p. 12). The 1903 case helped prompt the use of fingerprint identification in America.

Reasons to doubt that the pair's resemblance was coincidental, and instead to hypothesize that they might be identical twins, were numerous: the men were described as looking "as alike as twin brothers" (Thorwald 1964, p. 95); they had similar names, Will West and William West (if they were twin siblings they might have been named—in the sound-alike way often common to twins—Willy and Billy); and there were other indicators of possible twinship.

What was needed was scientific or documentary evidence bearing on their possible relationship. Today, such a case would be easily solved by recourse to genetic factors in blood samples, but this was not possible since the Wests are deceased. However, a geneticist and a fingerprint analyst —both with expertise in twins' fingerprints—were able to study the Wests' fingerprint patterns. While these were not identical, they were extremely similar with the same types being found on the fingers of both men. For instance, both had distinctive double-loop whorl patterns on their right thumbs. The experts concluded the evidence for the pair's twinship was highly probable.

Other evidence that the Wests were monozygotic (identical) twins came from their ear patterns. These were more similar than would have been expected even for dizygotic (fraternal) twins, according to the world's foremost expert on ear identification, Alfred Iannarelli.

Finally, documentary evidence corroborated the scientific studies. For example, correspondence logs from Leavenworth Penitentiary showed that while incarcerated there the Wests wrote to the same brother, the same five sisters, and the same uncle. Also a fellow prisoner's deposition turned up in the files. One George Bean stated that he personally knew the pair and knew them to be "twin brothers" (Nickell with Fischer 1988, pp. 75–88).

Another example of an innovative analysis being used in paranormal research was the application of linguistics to a case of alleged "channeling." Distinguished linguist Sara Thomason, who has conducted considerable research into claims of past-life regression (1987), was asked by the Kentucky Association of Science Educators and Skeptics (KASES) to examine a tape recording of a channeler through whom, allegedly, spoke a long-dead Scotsman. Dr. Thomason's excellent professional analysis revealed that the supposed Scotch dialect was bogus, that it was in fact merely an amateurish imitation (Thomason 1989).

Although in some cases an expert will be commissioned to conduct the analysis and reach a determination, it falls to the investigator to recognize the potential application of the analysis in the first place; therefore, to whatever extent he or she may be a specialist, the investigator must attempt to have a generalist's knowledge of as many options that may be available as possible. Also, it is the investigator who will assimilate the proffered expert opinion with other evidence in the case.

Of course, numerous other strategies, or permutations thereof, could be listed; however, our intention was not to compile an exhaustive list but rather to suggest some possibilities and to prompt the serious inquirer to think in terms of investigatory strategies. Although investigations often progress "organically" rather than by formula (that is, one discovery may prompt a new avenue of pursuit that was not anticipated in one's original strategy), still, having a plan of attack for a problem can pay dividends.

Tools of the Trade

In addition to a trained mind, the serious investigator often needs some specific tools or equipment. Here we suggest some of those that have proved useful, together with some tips on their selection and use.

For fieldwork a small notebook and pen are essential, and experience will show that a watch, magnifier, measuring tape, and combination knife are occasionally useful as well, as are, perhaps to a lesser extent, a flashlight (or penlight) and a small lensatic compass (for direction finding as in UFO fieldwork, surveying and sketching a site where some event was reported, etc.). Such items may easily be kept in the pocket or purse for convenience.

A good camera is a must. One should eschew the "pocket" models intended for amateur use. Instead, as Adrian Holloway advises in his *The Handbook of Photographic Equipment:*

> If you want a better quality, more adaptable camera which is still portable
> and quick to use, a 35mm direct vision camera may suit you. The choice

of film in the format is wide, and enlargements are more satisfactory. The trend in 35mm direct vision models is toward automation, higher quality, interchangeability of lenses, and compactness. Automatic exposure rangefinder focusing, and the facility for electronic flash are now common; autowinders, built-in flash, and autofocus are growing more popular. (Holloway 1981, p. 8)

For crucial, nonrepeatable photo opportunities, an instant-picture camera can serve as a useful backup system. It permits correcting for mistakes and helps ensure that one will not come away empty-handed, a victim of any of the misfortunes that can befall the photographic process. While most instant-picture film does not yield a negative that will permit additional copies to be made, a print can be professionally copied and a negative provided (Holloway 1981, pp. 54, 134).

As to film, color naturally provides more visual "information," which is why it is standard, for example, for crime-scene photographs. However, black-and-white film can be used for copy work (discussed presently) and is preferable when a photo is being made solely as an illustration (say for an article or book) that will be reproduced in black and white. (However, black-and-white prints *can* be made from color negatives.) When photographing in low light, choose a color film that is "fast" (has a high ASA/DIN number) or a black-and-white film that is "slow." With the latter, fast films (400 ASA and higher) will minimize a "grainy" appearance in enlargements (Holloway 1981, pp. 126, 142).

One should practice with the camera—guided by the manufacturer's instructions and a good beginner's manual—before relying on it for serious work. Then, one should emulate professional photographers who take lots of pictures; film is cheap, they observe. Relying on only one or two shots is to ignore "Murphy's Law"—the cynical, if all-too-often-correct dictum that if something can go wrong it will: A subject may blink, for example, rendering his eyes closed in the photo; and there are many other potential problems that lie in wait. Extra negatives are good insurance.

Professionals also recommend "bracketing"—i.e., providing a range of exposures as insurance against inaccurate readings from the camera's built-in light meter. (Erroneous readings can result from backlit subjects, "contrasty" scenes, or other causes.) In bracketing, in addition to taking shots at the optimum aperture setting indicated by the light meter, the photographer makes one or more additional shots that are deliberately overexposed (by adjusting the aperture accordingly, say, one major f-stop) plus one or more that are underexposed (Holloway 1981, pp. 27, 203). Bracketing thus increases the likelihood of obtaining a picture—or permitting a detail thereof to be enlarged—with the desired exposure.

The experienced investigator will give thought to *why* he or she is taking a picture and let that *raison d'être* govern how the shots are composed. Because *context* can be crucial, significant features should be photographed not only in isolation, but should also be shown in their relationship to other features. (For example, a crime-scene photographer does not just take a shot of a corpse and then a close-up shot of a nearby pistol; rather the body and gun are also photographed together so as to best illustrate their proximity.)

Also, so that the intended audience for the photograph can grasp the relative size of what is being represented, some indication of *scale* should be given. Therefore, to demonstrate the great size of the Nazca "condor" reconstruction mentioned earlier, the project investigator was photographed standing inside one of the giant bird's feet, and that picture was published (in *Arthur C. Clarke's Chronicles of the Strange and Mysterious*) beside an aerial photo of the entire bird (Fairley and Welfare 1987, pp. 45-47). As another example, in order to properly document a "spirit" picture, a metric scale was included in the photograph (Nickell with Fischer 1988, p. 53).

Photographic copying represents a common use of the camera in investigative work—whether it is copying a picture, document, or similar item. While special copying units are available, simple copying stands (or copying tables) are more economical, and they can even be improvised. One need only obtain a tripod for stabilizing the camera, a drawing board on which to mount the picture to be copied, and two photoflood lamps in reflectors. Use a close-up lens if available. Set up the tripod so that the camera is aimed at right angles to the copy. Then,

> Set photofloods on either side of camera, at about a 45° angle to the center of copy, and each at the same distance from it. Look at copy from camera's point of view. Copy must be fully and evenly lighted. Shift lights until reflections are gone. If shooting copy under glass, use Polaroid filter to cut glare.
>
> In copying line drawings and prints, develop your film for maximum contrast. Use a slow pan film and give it full development. Photographs or black-and-white pictures are best copied with fine-grain panchromatic film. Underdevelop slightly to keep contrast down. Use fine-grain pan film for color pictures, and correct for redness of photofloods with yellow-green filter on camera. (Zim, Burnett, and Brummitt 1964, p. 146)

Another investigative tool is the tape recorder, used primarily to record interviews. According to Fletcher:

> Because you are recording within the limited range of the human voice, you do not need any very expensive equipment. You don't want the cheapest

recorder you can find, but on the other hand you don't want anything close to the top-of-the-line model. A middle-price-range cassette tape recorder will do just fine. Try to get one with built-in "internal noise control," which is a special circuitry that diminishes clicks and whirrs on your tape made by the moving parts of the recorder itself. Check to be sure the tape recorder has a microphone, either built-in or as a separate unit.

Use 90-minute cassettes, and, when buying tape, buy a fairly top-quality brand. (Not so much for super high fidelity, but so the tapes won't break or tangle up.) Always take at least two blank tapes with you. . . .

He adds:

When you are conducting the interview, be sure to keep an eye on the tape as it approaches the end of a side. Some audio recorders don't have a signal to tell you when the tape has run out, and you can miss recording important information if you don't realize that the tape has run out and needs to be turned over.

Keep a pen handy during the interview, and as one tape is used up, immediately write on its label the date, place, person's name, the interview title, and maybe a few themes discussed on the tape. If you are right in the middle of an important thought when the tape ends, just pop a new tape in and go on; but always remember to write the date, place, and name of the narrator on the tape label before you leave at the end of the session. It's easy to mix up tapes and get them out of sequence. (Fletcher 1986, p. 4)

Pocket recorders, about the size of a pack of cigarettes, are useful for vocal note-taking; also those whose professions require one to be prepared to record an interview at a moment's notice—journalists for example—use them extensively. (Interrogation techniques are given in chapter 3.)

Videotape camera-recorders or "camcorders" allow one to make a visual record of activity—say a test of a dowser's ability—at the same time an audio recording is being made. Modern models have hook-up cables for playback on a TV screen or for copying to a VCR. A tripod is essential if the camera is to be kept stationary, as during an interview, but the camcorder is also designed to be hand-held. Since this equipment is rather expensive, one may wish to rent it when needed (see the Yellow Pages for "Videotape Recorders—Rentals"), and the video store personnel can give a crash course in its use (Fletcher 1986, pp. 4-5; Quinn 1986, pp. 16-17, 99-100).

A VCR unit attached to a television set is exceedingly useful for recording TV documentaries and news items concerning paranormal topics. It also permits viewing of instructional videotapes (we recommend purchasing one on magic tricks, for example), as well as educational tapes and one's own camcorder cassettes.

Other equipment that has been put to good use in investigating paranormal claims includes a radio receiver, used to interpret secret messages broadcast to an alleged faith-healer by his backstage confederate (Steiner 1986); a two-way mirror, to permit the detection and secret videotaping of cheating during psychokinetic metal-bending tests (Gardner 1981, p. 182); and an argon laser, whose light revealed solvent rings around "spirit" pictures that were actually transfers from newspapers (Nickell with Fischer 1988, pp. 55–57).

Given the vagaries of investigative work, many other tools, devices, and gadgets may find occasional use as, for example, in examining and documenting the mysterious "crop circle" phenomenon in rural England (characterized by flattened circles, typically having a diameter in the 5 to 25-meter range, that have appeared by the scores in cereal crops over a number of years). Researchers utilized an airplane for reconnaissance plus cameras with zoom lenses. On the ground they experimented with "poles of various lengths with mounting brackets for cameras on top," but at least one researcher preferred to take pictures from a stepladder. To prevent getting only a partial view in photographs, they equipped their cameras with wide-angle lenses, and, for taking closeup shots of marks on plant stems, they used macro lenses. They also employed a video camera and made use of many miscellaneous items:

> The accessory bag holds many useful items including collapsible tripod, boxes of film, lenses, first aid kit, compass, maps, marker rods, 20-metre tape, clip board with writing pad, vacuum flask, and sandwiches. When we set off to visit a new site, we are prepared for most eventualities. (Delgado and Andrews 1989, p. 149)

A look at a portion of their approach indicates how some of the items are used:

> When we reach a new site, first we photograph general views outside the circle, then walk carefully across the floor to examine the centre and take pictures of it. We place a compass on the ground in the central area. One person holds the measuring tape about 0.5 metres above the compass, while another takes the other end and walks magnetically north to the wall. The measurement is noted on a prepared plan of a circle with the eight main compass points marked on it. The eight measurements are

recorded, usually counter-clockwise because it is easier to hold the tape in your right hand against the circle wall if you are right handed. (p. 150)

In short, these researchers have done some praiseworthy photographic documentation and information gathering, although their follow-up work—including recourse to dowsing and their haste in dismissing the hoax hypothesis (especially since some circles have definitely been produced by hoaxers)—leaves something to be desired (Delgado and Andrews 1989, pp. 155, 177-78).

In addition to the use of dowsing rods and pendulums, there is much other questionable—even outright pseudoscientific—use of equipment in paranormal research. One example is that of employing certain photo-enhancement techniques to "discover" tiny figures inhabiting the eyes of the "miraculous" Image of Guadalupe in Mexico. Critics suggested a "pious imagination" instead may have been operative (Tierney 1983; Smith 1983, pp. 79-83, 111-112). Among other examples is that of attaching lie detectors to plants to monitor their alleged emotions in response to human thoughts. It was later discovered that the same reactions could be obtained from pieces of Styrofoam (Tompkins and Bird 1973, pp. 40-42; Gardner 1981, p. 161).

The lesson in all of this is that one should choose the right tools and techniques for the task at hand. Above all, a discerning mind, the willingness to persevere, and a desire for the truth are among the investigator's greatest assets.

3

Getting at the Truth

The Art and Science of Interrogation

Because people are a major source of information for the investigator in his attempts to ferret out truth and solve mysteries, the techniques of interviewing and interrogating are essential ones. There are several steps that should be followed in conducting an interview.

The fact finder's first step is determining who to interview. Usually, sources will fall into one of three categories: (1) eyewitnesses to, or participants in, events; (2) scientists or others whose expert opinions are being sought; and (3) fellow investigators or others with relevant knowledge to impart.

Some of those in the first category—perhaps including someone who feels she was victimized by a fortunetelling scam, or a person who believes he has a ghost for a roommate—may present themselves to you, seeking your help. Others—possibly including those with an alleged paranormal ability—may become known to you through the news media or other source, such as a friend or student. Still others will need to be searched for.

Witness or informant location can present a challenge to the investigator's resourcefulness, but there are many options available. Paying a visit to the scene of some alleged paranormal event—a Bigfoot sighting for instance—and making inquiries in the vicinity (a "neighborhood canvass," detectives call it) is a standard approach. So is asking those who may turn up if they can suggest others who may be interviewed. Journalists as well as private detectives know the technique of using a city directory (in which names are arranged by street location) to identify persons living near some address that is of interest. Telephoning the public library, chamber of commerce, or other source may also turn up something. (For example, one of us needed information about a "mysterious disappearance" alleged to have occurred in Rhayader, a village in Wales. Whom to write to? A letter addressed simply to the "mayor" brought a response from that officeholder; he in turn interviewed townsfolk and made inquiries of the police, and as a result concluded the disappearance tale was a hoax [Nickell with Fischer 1988, p. 64]). Other approaches will no doubt come to mind.

Persons in the second category—those who can give an expert opinion —may be identified from a variety of sources. Some (like document examiners) advertise in the Yellow Pages. Others (such as scientists) may be identified through various professional directories found in the library's reference room. A phone call to the appropriate department of a university may put the investigator in touch with someone who can provide the necessary assistance or who may be able to recommend someone who can. An excellent source is the list of "Scientific and Technical Consultants" that appears in each issue of the *Skeptical Inquirer.* Thumbing through back issues of *SI* would be another very good approach, since over the years experts from various fields have published in its pages. (Some criteria for choosing experts are given below under "Rules of Evidence.") Knowledgeable people are often glad to share what they know, but be aware that the professional persons may expect to charge for their consultations.

Other potential interviewees—those of the third category—may provide valuable information. The names of persons who have already been associated with a case, such as fellow investigators, journalists, or the like, may turn up in the initial, fact-finding phase of an investigation. Again, looking through the pages of *SI* could be helpful, as could searching for other articles or books on your topic in such standard sources as *Reader's Guide to Periodical Literature* and *Books in Print* (see Appendix I). Here is another phase of investigative work wherein the ability to think creatively is an important asset.

After scheduling the interview, one must prepare for it. Journalist D. L. Mabery advises:

> Probably the single most important step you can take to prepare for a successful interview is to do research on your topic. If you are interviewing someone who is an expert on that topic, you should know as much as you can about the topic so that the person will not have to spend too much time explaining it to you.
>
> Experienced reporters know that their job at the interview is to col-

lect the greatest amount of information in the smallest amount of time. Frequently some of the information a reporter might wish to obtain in the interview can be found before the interview even takes place. A reporter doesn't want to waste any time getting answers he or she could learn through research. (Mabery 1985, pp. 20–21)

Again, *Reader's Guide* and other research sources listed in part 2 of the bibliography can prove helpful in providing background information. Following this research, the investigator should reflect on the information the informant may be able to provide and then draw up a list of questions. These should be planned so that one leads logically into the next; otherwise confusion may be sown and the interview will not be as effective as it could be. Special thought should be given to questions that might be unsettling, since the informant could become uncooperative at that point and even terminate the interview. Placing such questions at the end of the session would insure that the less sensitive material would at least be covered (Mabery 1985, pp. 25–26).

In conducting the interview, begin in a way intended to break the ice and put the subject at ease. Be a good listener, letting the interviewee do most of the talking; you are there to obtain information, not impart it. Open-ended questions (those not answered by yes, no, or other limited response) will allow the person to answer more fully and in his own way (O'Leary 1976, p. 26). More focused questions can be used in following up, and they can be scribbled during the session as they come to mind.

Ask one question at a time, keep questions simple, and try to relate to the subject on his own level, adapting your speech accordingly. Do not let rambling discourses prevent you from obtaining the desired information; keep the subject on track, and make use of a technique called "shunting," i.e., asking a question which is related to the digression but which will return the conversation to the original point. Finally, avoid "leading" questions—questions that suggest or imply an answer (O'Hara 1973, pp. 94–96, 113)—except when querying an expert witness.

Interviewing a suspect (say someone who might have perpetrated a UFO hoax) or a hostile witness is known in police parlance as *interrogation* (O'Hara 1973, p. 109). While the paranormal investigator lacks legal authority, he or she can take some tips from police investigators. Despite what one may see on TV crime shows, the successful police professional is usually one who cultivates an interest in people and their problems and who thus inspires confidence. While one may "act as though he were angry or sympathetic as the circumstances suggest," one should never be coercive, never lose control, and never lose sight of the objective. In addition, the investigator should avoid smoking, "doodling" and other distractions, and convey an attitude of wishing to set things right (pp. 112–113).

You will need a record of any interview. Good reporters learn to take quick notes, being able to "jot down key words and phrases and later reconstruct a man's conversation in every important detail" (Woodward with Graham 1967, p. 45).

If an informant may be inhibited by note-taking, the interviewer can follow the approach of many professional private investigators, paralegals, and journalists. As one of the latter relates:

> I have often found that it is better to leave my notebook in my pocket during an interview. Then, when the subject has told me everything I think I am going to get, I can go back over some of the things he has said and jot down the correct spelling of a name or the precise figures he may have mentioned. After leaving him, I sit down alone and transcribe what he has told me. (Woodward with Graham 1967, p. 47)

Whether or not the notes are taken from the outset, *always* retire to a quiet place immediately after the interview and write out a complete narration from what was said. If you are out of town, for example, do not wait until you return home to transcribe your notes; instead go to a restaurant and accomplish the task over a cup of coffee. Be sure to *date* the record.

A tape recorder can be even more inhibiting than note-taking and it should be avoided if it does seem to intimidate the subject. Otherwise, it is recommended for its several advantages: it insures accuracy and preserves intonations; it permits eye contact to be maintained; and it protects the investigator against the subject later charging that he or she has been misquoted (Mabery 1985, pp. 29–30; Woodward with Graham 1967, pp. 46–47).

Interviewing at a distance can be accomplished either by telephone or by mail. The latter has the advantage of providing its own documentation (although phone conversations can be recorded—see your electronics store staff). This can often be handled in the form of a query in letter format. However, if you choose this method and have more than one or two questions, number them so as to minimize the chances of any being overlooked. Your respondent can then number his answers accordingly, at a convenience to him. For queries sent to agencies, companies, etc., where you do not know the name of an individual to address, you may use such titles as "Curator," "Reference Librarian," "Director," or the like. (But in the greeting of your letter avoid such unnatural forms as "Dear Librarian" as well as sexist salutations like "Dear Sir" or "Gentlemen." One option is the form "To the Director" followed by a colon.) It is preferable, however, to address queries to real individuals whenever possible.

Your reference librarian or business-desk librarian can probably help you identify someone to write to (or to telephone), along with his or her correct title. Various directories of museums, organizations, and so on are available for this purpose (again see Bibliography: Part 2).

An even more extensive interview by mail can be conducted by sending a cover letter and a separate list of questions, with the exchange being repeated one or more times for follow-up questions. Enclose a self-addressed stamped envelope (S.A.S.E.) for your correspondent's convenience, except when writing to a person in another country. In that instance, send a return-addressed but stampless envelope along with an "international postal reply coupon"; you can purchase one at your post office and your correspondent can redeem it at his. Finally, always send a thank-you note to anyone who has answered a query. If you make many queries and find writing thank-yous burdensome, consider having some thank-you cards printed with a brief message (e.g., "Sincere thanks for your recent help with my research") and your name. You can pen an additional note on these if desired.

In contrast to a written record of an oral interview is the written statement. In this case, information is taken down by the investigator and signed by the informant; an affidavit is such a statement sworn before a competent authority, generally a notary public. All such written statements should contain several parts. The *heading* should include the name of the person making the statement, the name of the interviewer, and the date and location—for example: "Statement [or Affidavit] of Jane Smith made to Richard Jones, January 10, 1990, 10:00 A.M., at 36 Locust Street, Evanston, Illinois." The second paragraph—the *identification*—identifies the person and should contain sufficient information to permit the witness to be relocated in the future. The *body* sets forth the information supplied by the interviewee, and should avoid a language foreign to him or her; indeed, odd phraseology or slang expressions should even be incorporated into the statement so as to make it more credible. (If it were shown that the deponent or affiant—that is, the one making the statement or affidavit —did not understand certain words that were used, the statement's value would be compromised.) The body may be in narrative or question-and-answer form. The statement's *close* should read something like this: "I have read the foregoing three-page statement, finding it true and correct, and have signed each page." The deponent should make any corrections in his or her own handwriting and then affix his signature, immediately below the text on each page, followed by that of the investigator as witness. If an affidavit, the document must be signed *in the presence* of the notarizing official. A sworn statement may be some protection (not a guarantee of course) against deliberately false information.

Eyewitness Behavior and Misbehavior

A competent eyewitness—that is, one who has personally observed an event—is in a position to provide valuable information. However, as Levin and Cramer point out in their *Problems and Materials on Trial Advocacy* (1968, p. 269):

> Eyewitness testimony is, at best, evidence of what the witness believes to have occurred. It may or may not tell what actually happened. The familiar problems of perception, of gauging time, speed, height and weight, of accurate identification of persons accused of crime all contribute to making honest testimony something less than completely credible.

In law, for a witness to be held competent to testify, he or she must be able to observe adequately and to receive proper impressions, to remember, to recount or narrate, and to have a moral compunction to tell the truth. Thus, a witness may be impeached by demonstrating prejudice or bias, an incapacity to testify due to an inability to observe or recollect, a poor reputation for veracity (often presumed from the commission of certain crimes or acts of misconduct), and the making of previous statements that are inconsistent with the current testimony (Hill, Rossen, and Sogg 1978, pp. 84–85, 105).

Among the more notorious examples of the limitations of eyewitness behavior are faulty identifications. For example, in 1896 and then a second time in 1904, a London man named Adolph Beck was misidentified as the swindler William Thomas and sent to prison. The men's strong general resemblance, coupled with their walrus mustaches, led to the error of justice. Fortunately, Thomas's subsequent arrest and correct identification kept Beck from having to serve out the second term (Blassingame 1975, pp. 14–16).

But eyewitnesses are similarly unreliable in giving testimony as to events. Memory (as we shall discuss in the next part of this chapter) is fallible, and often what is reported is quite different from what actually happened. For example, a psychology professor showed her students a film of an automobile accident, then asked them to fill out a questionnaire. One group was asked, "About how fast were the cars going when they smashed into each other?" In the other group's questionnaire, "smashed into" was replaced by "hit." The result was that more than twice the students in the first group reported they had seen broken glass when in fact there was none in the film (Loftus and Palmer 1974, pp. 585–89). Terrence Hines concludes from this (1988, p. 172), "Thus, a leading question given *after the fact* can alter a memory, not only for the actual subject of the question—speed, in the present case—but also for related material."

Not just average people but supposedly "reliable witnesses" can misperceive, as Klass (1981) has reported. In one case, for example, an astronomer failed to recognize that he was seeing the rocket-engine plume from a distantly launched missile, and he found that he had written into his report "several inaccuracies and inconsistencies" (p. 312). In another case, there were multiple witnesses who—viewing the event independently—had a UFO experience: one person saw a formation of three small craft; a group of three witnessed a large saucer with glowing windows; still others saw a cigar-shaped UFO complete with illuminated windows and rocket exhaust. Actually, what everyone must have seen was a Soviet booster rocket that fell back toward Earth at the time of the UFO sightings and broke up as it reentered the atmosphere (p. 314; see also Klass 1976, pp. 10–15).

As a result, Klass states as the very first of his ten "UFOlogical Principles" that

> Basically honest and intelligent persons who are suddenly exposed to a brief, unexpected event, especially one that involves an unfamiliar object, may be grossly inaccurate in trying to describe precisely what they have seen. (Klass 1976, p. 16)

Even so, his "UFOlogical Principle #2" holds:

> Despite the intrinsic limitations of human perception when exposed to brief, unexpected and unusual events, some details recalled by the observer may be reasonably accurate. The problem facing the UFO investigator is to try to distinguish between those details that are accurate and those that are grossly inaccurate. This may be impossible until the true identity of the UFO can be determined, so that in some cases this poses an insoluble problem. (p. 26)

Similarly, researchers into eyewitness behavior do not assert that the testimony of eyewitnesses is generally unreliable; rather, they "research variables that help estimate or control eyewitness accuracy" (Wells and Loftus 1984, p. 7).

We have already seen that postevent information can color eyewitness testimony; among other factors that can affect eyewitness accuracy is the age of the witness. Young persons are generally more apt to be influenced by suggestion and imagination, whereas elderly witnesses tend to be comparatively less credible in certain other respects. (For example, incompetent, elderly subjects were twice as likely as young adults to misidentify a bystander as the assailant when he was perceived to be "criminal-looking" [Yarney 1984]).

Still other factors that can have a detrimental effect on eyewitness reporting are the individual's expectations; problems in perception (of faces, for example, and of time); viewing conditions and duration; recall, and the conveyance to others of the recollected information; salience of event features (i.e., details thought to be peripheral are more likely to be misremembered than those that were salient or central to the event); stress; and others (Wells and Loftus 1984, *passim*).

Nevertheless, despite the numerous factors that plague eyewitness reporting, the observations of a competent witness who cannot be impeached and whose testimony may be corroborated in important respects can still be a useful resource for the investigator of paranormal claims.

The Fallibility of Memory

As indicated in the previous discussion, one's recall—the ability to remember information—can be a perishable commodity. Events may be misremembered or quite simply forgotten.

Memory has three distinct stages: sensory register, a momentarily held record of sensory data; short-term memory, an active memory which—unless consciously attended to—will decay in about twenty seconds; and long-term memory, the largest component of one's memory system, which stores information that is only minutes old as well as that which has been held for decades. Indeed, when people talk about memory, they are usually referring to long-term memory—the more permanent component of the system, comparable to a library in both its storage capacity and its retrievability (Loftus 1980, pp. 14–15).

Unfortunately, the stored memory is not a precise record of a person's experiences. According to Elizabeth Loftus, in her book *Memory: Surprising New Insights into How We Remember and Why We Forget* (1980),

> Memory is imperfect. This is because we often do not see things accurately in the first place. But even if we take in a reasonably accurate picture of some experience, it does not necessarily stay perfectly intact in memory. Another force is at work. The memory traces can actually undergo distortion. With the passage of time, with proper motivation, with the introduction of special kinds of interfering facts, the memory traces seem sometimes to change or become transformed. These distortions can be quite frightening, for they can cause us to have memories of things that never happened. Even in the most intelligent among us is memory thus malleable. (p. 37)

Such are memory distortions, then, that quite often "people are generating not memories of true events but fanciful guesses, fantasies, or plain confabulations" (p. 45). An example is a nineteenth-century case that was originally supposed to provide proof of the appearance of an apparition. It is discussed in C. E. M. Hansel's *ESP: A Scientific Evaluation* (1966, pp. 186–89), and is worth studying briefly.

The events were recalled, some years after they had transpired, by Sir Edmund Hornby, a Shanghai jurist. One night he was awakened by a newspaperman who had arrived belatedly to get the customary written judgment for the next day's edition. Hornby told him to get the writing from his butler, but instead he sat on the bed, looking "deadly pale," and refusing to leave until he was given the information. He did say apologetically, "This is the last time I shall ever see you anywhere." Finally, the judge relented, giving a verbal summary which the man took down in shorthand in his pocket notebook. After expressing his gratitude, he left. In the meantime Lady Hornby awoke and her husband explained to her what had happened.

The following day at court the judge was surprised to learn that the newsman had died during the night. Hornby asked for particulars. Supposedly the man had gone up to his room to work on his papers. Queried later by his wife, he answered, "I have only the Judge's judgment to get ready, and then I have finished." Still later—after the time Judge Hornby had talked with the man in his home—his wife again went to see about him and discovered him dead. Although the man's wife and servants were certain he could not have left the house without their knowledge, on the floor was the notebook, containing a summary of Hornby's judgment!

After this tale was reported by psychical researchers, a correspondent pointed to discrepancies betweeen the judge's account and certain facts in the matter. (Recall investigative strategy number 1 in the previous chapter.) For example, the man did not die at the time reported (about 1:00 A.M.) but much later—between 8:00 and 9:00 in the morning after a restful night. Moreover, the judge could not have told his wife about the event at the time since he was then between marriages. Finally, although the story depends on a certain judgment that was to be delivered the following day, no such judgment was recorded.

Confronted with this evidence of his faulty recall, a bewildered Judge Hornby commented:

My vision must have followed the death (some three months) instead of synchronizing with it. . . . If I had not believed, as I still believe, that every word of [the story] was accurate, and that my memory was to be relied on, I should not have ever told it as a personal experience. (Hansel 1966, pp. 188–89)

The case had been presented as one having considerable credibility due to its trustworthy source, "But," concludes Hansel (1966, p. 189), "the story illustrates that an eminent judge is no less liable to errors of memory and recall than anyone else."

Numerous factors can cause memory loss, including the following: clinical depression, fluid imbalance, adverse effects of medication, malnutrition, low blood sugar, anemia, lung disease, small stroke, poor blood circulation, and severe hypothyroidism—all of which are treatable (Mark 1990), as well as such permanent causes as Alzheimer's disease.

Not surprisingly, attempts to retrieve one's theoretically trained "original" memory, as by hypnosis (or similarly through the use of truth serum), are fraught with difficulty. Not only are there no convincing studies to support the contention that recall during hypnosis is more accurate than ordinary waking recall, but "What is worse," adds Loftus (1980, p. 58), "people under hypnosis have been known to 'recall' events from their past confidently and to fabricate future scenarios with the same confidence." The *American Bar Association Journal* expressed similar views:

> People can flat-out lie under hypnosis, and the examiner is no better equipped to detect the hynotic lie than any other kind. Even more serious, a willing hypnotic subject is more pliable than he normally would be, more anxious to please his questioner. Knowing even a few details of an event, often supplied in early contacts with police, may provide the subject with enough basis to create a highly detailed "memory" of what transpired, whether he was there or not. (*ABA* 1978)

Such well-intentioned—if questionable—attempts to enhance memory are modest compared to certain extreme applications of hypnosis. Among these are what is termed "past-life regression"—the hypnotic coaching of individuals to "remember" their previous incarnations. The best known case of hypnotic regression was that of Bridey Murphy in the early 1950s. An amateur hypnotist named Morey Bernstein hypnotized a neighbor, a Wisconsin housewife named Virginia Tighe. Soon, speaking in an Irish brogue, Mrs. Tighe described her previous existence as an Irish lass named Bridey Murphy. Eventually, however, reporters learned that when Virginia lived in Chicago as a child, a woman named *Bridey Murphy* Corkell had once lived across the street. It was also learned that Virginia had participated in school performances, in which she had practiced speaking in an Irish brogue. These and other revelations showed that—consciously or unconsciously—Virginia Tighe was merely acting out a role as Bridey, not giving evidence of reincarnation (Baker 1990, pp. 225–29; Gardner 1957, pp. 315–20).

Another abuse of regressive hypnosis has been in the supposed authentication of UFO abductions. The most famous case of this sort is that of Betty and Barney Hill, who were subjected to hypnotic regression following their sighting of a UFO. Actually, their "memories" of being taken aboard a flying saucer were soon recognized as having been based on Betty's dreams, the details of which she had repeatedly described to her husband (Baker 1990, pp. 237–39).

Such pseudomemories and other limitations on accurate recall must give the investigator pause whenever alleged remembrances are the basis for extraordinary claims.

Charisma and the Power of Suggestion

Everyone is susceptible to subtle forms of suggestion, but some people are prone to being influenced easily. A charismatic individual may be able to overcome their critical thinking, to dispose them to abandon rationality, and show blind faith in that individual's capacities (Bailey 1988, p. 91).

By *charisma* is meant "a certain quality of an individual personality by virtue of which he is considered extraordinary and treated as endowed with supernatural, superhuman, or at least superficially exceptional powers or qualities" (Weber 1978, p. 241). The intentional enhancement of charisma, i.e., a strategy to manipulate others, is known as "numenification" (Bailey 1988, pp. 91–94).

Another example stems from man's attempts to foretell the future and thus dispel uncertainties about his fate. According to Charles Mackay in his mid-nineteenth-century classic, *Memoirs of Extraordinary Popular Delusions and the Madness of Crowds* (1841, p. 281), "Upon no subject has it been so easy to deceive the world as on this." Decrying "the sciences, so called, of astrology, augury, necromancy, geomancy, palmistry, and divination of every kind" (p. 282), he observes that they flourish wherever "death and ill-fortune" haunt people's thoughts.

In addition to emotional anguish (including fear, grief, and guilt), physical suffering (such as pain, exhaustion, and hunger) can cause one to become vulnerable to manipulation by charlatans. For instance, unrelenting pain may drive one into the clutches of the medical quack, or the death of a family member may permit one to be lured to the séance table.

Such victims are often described as *gullible*, a pejorative term which suggests they should have known better. Their psychological needs, however, have weakened their critical defenses, and permitted their perceptions of events and their recollections of them to become distorted. Thus, the very people who could give evidence against charlatans are often the ones supporting them with testimonials. Among the pathetic examples of this are endorsements made by the victims of a "psychic dentist" in Palatka, Florida. He is the Reverend Willard Fuller, a faith-healing "dentist" who—if his clients could be believed—fills teeth miraculously. He also claims he can straighten crooked teeth, turn silver crowns into gold, and perform other dental wonders—all through the power of Jesus. Alas, however, as Hines (1988, p. 247) concludes, "In spite of the usual testimonials, Fuller is nothing more than a practitioner of sleight of hand."

X-rays showed that underneath some of the miraculous new "fillings" the old cavities still ate away. Some skeptics even went so far as to suggest that a pellet of filling material had just been secretly smeared over the cavity during Fuller's preliminary examination. In other cases, those who were convinced they had new fillings learned otherwise from their dentists; they had been duped by faulty memory and simple suggestion from a charismatic "healer." None of the more outstanding of his alleged miracles is scientifically documented, yet Fuller—who himself has several missing teeth—has attracted a considerable following. His appeal may be greatest among dental phobics, of which there are an estimated thirty million in the United States (Spraggett 1970; Randi 1987, pp. 207–12).

Numerous additional examples could be given. For instance, the charismatic "giggling guru," the Maharishi Mahesh Yogi, sold thousands of admiring disciples on the notion that they could learn to levitate, to float in the air by mental power alone. Actually, they merely bounced up and down on mattresses, but they were encouraged to *believe* they were, momentarily, levitating (Randi 1977, 1979). Just such a relationship—of too-credulous followers succumbing to the fantasies and deceptions of manipulative, charismatic individuals—characterizes much of that realm known as the paranormal and is a major obstacle to the truth.

Not only charismatic individuals, but other forms of perceived authority may exert influence on people—the news media for instance. Take the case of the ubiquitous panda. On December 10, 1978, a zoo in Rotterdam reported that a small panda had escaped. As the newspapers hit the stands, the Netherlands experienced a wave of panda sightings—over one hundred—that extended over the next few days. But a single panda could not have traveled so far in so little time, and, as it happened, only a few hours after it was discovered missing the panda was found. Rather, its body was, for it had wandered only about five hundred yards before being struck by a train.

What had the numerous eyewitnesses actually seen? Influenced by suggestion and thus "programmed" to see a panda, many people probably superimposed a mental image of one onto a glimpse of something else—another animal perhaps.

In any case, such a "flap" or flurry of reports—like those that occur with UFO sightings, hauntings, and the like—represents what psychologists term "contagion." Analogous to a contagious disease, psychological contagion is transferable; that is, some idea or custom or emotion can be spread from person to person until many become affected. Contagion is often called "mass hysteria" (Van Kampen 1979; Harre and Lamb 1983, p. 119).

Rules of Evidence

It is by marshaling of *evidence* that the investigator seeks to accomplish his task. The term (from the Latin *evidentia*) refers to that which makes something evident, or manifest; more specifically, it denotes the facts that are presented so that people can reach a decison in a matter. Therefore, *proof* is an effect or a consequence of evidence.

In all areas of controversy—legal, scientific, scholarly—it is a rule that the burden of proof is on the advocate of the idea. That is, whoever asserts a fact has the responsibility of proving it, and not anyone who would deny or doubt it. Although as a practical matter both asserters of fact and challengers of the assertion usually present affirmative as well as rebuttal evidence (Binder and Bergman 1984, p. 13), in the final analysis one must not lose sight of who has the onus of proof.

Yet, with disconcerting persistence in controveries over paranormal claims, proponents attempt to shift or at least cast off the burden of proof. Quite often they assert, "you can't prove it isn't so"—where "it" is the authenticity of a supposedly miraculous relic or the reality of extraterrestrial visitations, or some other emotionally held belief. The difficulty of proving a negative can be profound. For example, suppose you attempt to disprove the assertion that a flying saucer has just landed on the roof. You go outside and point triumphantly to the vacant roof, whereupon your opponent states: "It flew away."

In such cases, when one hears the assertion that something is true because it cannot be proved untrue, the proper response is to point out the fallacy involved. This is the fallacy of argument *ad ignorantiam*—that is, literally, an appeal "to ignorance." The mirror-image argument, skeptics should take note—that something is untrue because it cannot be proved —is likewise an argument *ad ignorantiam*. (However, in this instance, because the onus is on the asserter of fact, his or her position cannot be held to be commensurate with that of the skeptic. Indeed, as Martin Gardner observes [1957, p. 81], "If a man persists in advancing views that are contradicted by all available evidence, and which offer no reasonable grounds for serious consideration, he will rightfully be dubbed a crank by his colleagues.")

Ray Kytle (1987, pp. 124–25) gives several examples of the *ad ignorantiam* fallacy including these arguments: "If evolution is true, why has it stopped?"; "If you think psychokinesis isn't possible, then how do you account for Uri Geller's ability to bend keys just by looking at them?"; "If there were such a thing as the human soul, then certainly doctors, who have dissected every part of the human body, would have discovered it"; and "I know the stars influence the way people are. Can you prove they don't?"

Among the other fallacies that plague paranormal research are those of inductive reasoning known as *faulty causation*. There are three basic types: *oversimplification,* i.e., the presumption of a single cause for a phenomenon whereas there actually may be multiple causes; *post hoc ergo propter hoc* ("after this, therefore because of this"), the assumption that since one event follows another it was caused by it; and the *hasty conclusion,* which results from insufficient evidence. It is possible to guard against such fallacies. To begin with, remember that "Correlation is not causation." Kytle illustrates the value of this dictum:

> For example, it was discovered some years ago that a higher percentage of people died of respiratory diseases in Arizona than in any other state: a fact. This finding produced a great deal of consternation. Living in Arizona *caused* lung disease—or so many people inferred. Actually, however, what had happened was this: Many people with *existing* respiratory disorders such as asthma, hay fever, bronchitis, and emphysema had moved to Arizona seeking relief from their illnesses and had remained there until they died. Correlation, yes; causation, no. The truth of the matter lay in an *alternative explanation.* (p. 86)

As can be seen, it is always premature to accept that a cause-and-effect relationship is proven until alternative possibilities are considered and then decisively eliminated. In other words, before positing a supernatural explanation for some phenomenon (e.g., before attributing strange noises in an old house to a "ghost"), one must clearly rule out all naturalistic—including human—causes (for example, expanding pipes, hoax claims, etc.).

Another fallacy is the *ad hominem* ("to the man") one, sometimes called the genetic fallacy, which replaces substantive discussion with a personal attack, the implication being that so contemptible a person could not have ideas with merit (Kytle 1987, pp. 117–18, 179). Of course mere name-calling should be eschewed; however, sometimes a person's traits are relevant to a discussion, as when there is a question of competence (e.g., one may lack the scientific training and experience to perform some analysis) or in certain other instances. (For example, evidence that Charles Dawson perpetrated other hoaxes is relevant to the question of his guilt in the Piltdown skull affair—although it does not *of itself* constitute proof.)

The opposite side of the *ad hominem* coin is the fallacy of *appeal to authority*—the supposition that someone who has achieved a good reputation must have correct views. Of course he or she may, which is why we cite expert opinion; however, to be relevant and credible such opinion should meet certain criteria: the expert should be generally recognized as such by his peers; his opinion should be within his area of expertise; it should reflect the consensus of others in the field; and the expert should not have a strong personal interest (pecuniary or otherwise) in the position being advocated (Kytle 1987, pp. 120–21).

Some other common fallacies are the following: diversion (raising an irrelevant issue in order to divert the argument—also known as the "red herring" fallacy); emotive language (using emotionally charged wording to preempt reason and objectivity); overgeneralization (moving from a tentative assertion to a categorical one); false analogy (implying that two situations which have *some* things in common are alike in other respects also); and others (to which Kytle [1987] is an excellent introduction). Remember that all arguments consist of a *claim* that is supported by *reasoning* which in turn is based on *evidence;* the latter must be *true* and the reasoning *sound* for the claim to be valid (Kytle 1987, p. 50).

Turning to the level of proof required to effectively solve some mystery in paranormal research, one should keep in mind the old journalistic maxim, "Extraordinary claims require extraordinary proof." No precise standards have been codified, but the requisite level of proof can be characterized by analogy to the two standards found in civil law—namely, a "preponderance of the evidence" and "clear and convincing evidence" (Hill, Rossen, and Sogg, 1978, p. 49). (The highest legal standard, which is required in criminal cases and is known as "proof beyond a reasonable doubt," would seem impractical for paranormal research, although such a standard might well be achieved.)

The first, or lower, standard should be represented in paranormal research by establishing the preferred hypothesis—that is, from among the hypotheses that can be advanced, arriving at the one which best accounts for the evidence.

When there are competing hypotheses capable of accounting for the facts, the preferred hypothesis may be determined by invoking what is known as "Occam's razor." Named for fourteenth-century philosopher William of

Ockham, the principle is expressed as *non sunt multiplicanda entia prae-ter necessitatem*—i.e., things must not be multiplied beyond necessity. Also referred to as "the maxim of parsimony," it thus affirms that the simplest tenable explanation—i.e., the hypothesis with the fewest assumptions—is most likely to be correct and is to be preferred (Beveridge 1950, pp. 115–16; Shneour 1986, pp. 310–11).

The second, higher level of proof—the "clear and convincing" standard—would apply to a hypothesis that had been rigorously tested or would otherwise be upgraded from hypothesis to *theory* (as a very well supported hypothesis is termed). Yet as Martin Gardner cautions (1957, p. 7), "there are no known methods for giving precise 'probability values' to hypotheses."

In general, admissibility of evidence is governed by logical relevance. One legal maxim holds that the "best evidence must be given of which the nature of the case permits." Therefore, *direct* evidence (that which immediately establishes some fact) is preferred over *circumstantial* evidence (that which establishes collateral facts from which the main fact may be inferred). Of course, multiple pieces of evidence, even circumstantial evidence, may be mutually *corroborative*—that is, one piece supportive of another—and such an array of evidence can be quite probative. An example would be eyewitness testimony that a suspect fired a fatal shot, plus his fingerprints on the murder weapon, together with gunpowder residue on his hand ("Evidence" 1960).

Nevertheless, quite often those who are emotionally committed to a point of view and are consequently unable to accept even an impressive array of corroborative evidence will attempt to attack it piecemeal. Consider the evidence pertaining to the Shroud of Turin. The reported confession of a medieval artist that he "cunningly painted" the image is supported by the lack of any record for the shroud prior to that time; also the suspiciously still-red "blood" and presence of paint pigments on the image are fully consistent with artistry, as are numerous other factors including stylistic similarities to Gothic art. Nevertheless, those who advocate the cloth's authenticity offer one explanation for the absence of historical record (the shroud may have been hidden away), another for the confession (the bishop who reported it could have been mistaken), yet another for the pigments (perhaps they were splashed on by some artist who copied the image), and so on.

But note that each explanation is independent of the other, giving the effect of separate rationalizations, whereas the preponderance of *prima facie* ("at first view") evidence (i.e., evidence sufficient to establish a fact, unless rebutted) clearly points to a single hypothesis: the "shroud" is the handiwork of a medieval artisan. Shroud proponents lack any viable hypothesis for the image formation ("miracle" scarcely qualifies even if expressed quasi-scientifically as "flash photolysis," an imagined radiant energy from Christ's resurrection); therefore the artistic hypothesis is obviously the preferred one in light of Occam's razor.

In summary, following certain basic rules of acquisition and admissibility, and avoiding fallacies in argument, the investigator collects such relevant facts and marshals such evidence of sufficient weight so as to constitute the probable solution to the mystery at hand.

The Fallibility of Truth-Seeking Devices

Lie detectors do not detect lies; rather, they measure physiological changes which are held to indicate deception. The standard machine, known as a *polygraph* because of the multiple tracings it makes, has three features: (1) a blood pressure cuff, placed on the upper arm of the person being tested and used to measure variations in blood pressure and pulse; (2) a tube fastened around the subject's chest which indicates changes in breathing; and (3) a device for measuring the skin's electrical conductivity. Some instruments have an additional unit, one for measuring movements and pressures. These devices activate pens which trace graphs of the various changes (Inbau, Moenssens, and Vitullo 1972, pp. 156–57).

Unfortunately, while polygraphs do detect nervousness, Hines correctly observes (1988, p. 304) that "not everyone is nervous when telling a lie and not everyone is calm when telling the truth." Factors other than nervousness that may affect the responses are physical handicaps, moral attitudes toward veracity, location of the test, personality of the examiner, and the subject's state of mind ("House Measure" 1985). Still other factors that may affect results include pain, drunkenness, fatigue, and illness, especially certain respiratory ailments and mental illness, as well as the influence of a sedative, low intelligence, nervous or excitable temperament, and emotional stress (O'Hara 1973, p. 124).

One technique in which the polygraph may help produce valuable results is known as the "peak of tension" test. As Inbau, Moenssens, and Vitullo explain in their *Scientific Police Investigation*:

> When a person who is to undergo a polygraph examination has not been informed of all the important details of the offense under investigation, the examiner can conduct as part of his examination what is known as a "peak of tension" test. It consists of the asking of a series of questions in which only one refers to some detail of the offense, such as the amount of money stolen or the kind of object taken or the implement used to commit the offense—something that would be unknown to the subject

unless he himself committed the crime or unless he had been told about it by someone else. For instance, if a suspected thief has not been told about the exact amount of money involved, he may be asked a series of questions which refer to various amounts, one of which will be the actual amount stolen. The theory behind the peak of tension test is that if the person tested is the one who took the money, for instance, he will be apprehensive about the question referring to that amount, whereas an innocent person would not have such a particularized concern.

Before conducting a peak of tension test, the examiner prepares a list of about seven questions, among which, near the middle, is the question pertaining to the actual detail. The list is then read off to the subject, and he is informed that during the test questions will be asked in that precise order. A truth-telling subject, aware of the accuracy of any one question, will not ordinarily be concerned about one more than any of the others. On the other hand, a lying subject will have that question in mind as the test is being conducted and, in anticipation of it, he is apt to experience a buildup of tension that will climax at the crucial question—in other words, that will reach a "peak of tension." (Inbau, Moenssens, and Vitullo 1972, p. 164)

If such a test produces information that can then be corroborated, then it has served a valuable purpose.

A cheap type of "lie detector" is a galvanometer (one of the previously mentioned instrument that comprise the polygraph—which measures the skin's conductivity or "galvanic skin response"). Sensitive but subject to glitches, the galvanometer is even less trustworthy than a polygraph, which has additional instruments to provide a check on the skin response.

Another type of "truth evaluator" is especially useless. Known as a Psychological Stress Evaluator (PSE), it supposedly indicates untruthfulness by analyzing stress in a subject's voice. However, according to tests of its accuracy, the PSE was, at best, less reliable than the polygraph; it has often been shown to yield no more accuracy than tossing a coin (Klass 1980).

So-called "truth serum" (e.g., sodium pentothal) represents yet another, even more dubious, means of obtaining honest responses. Predicated on the assumption that the drug relaxes the subject to the extent he or she no longer expends the effort to lie, the approach is undermined by the fact that the subject may no longer feel constrained to tell the truth—indeed, in his or her drugged state may not know what the truth is. As with hypnosis, the subject who is administered truth serum may babble the wildest imaginings.

Given the limitations placed on such techniques—especially restrictions on use of the polygraph for employment screening, many businesses have regrettably turned to graphology. Also known as "handwriting analysis," it supposedly reveals one's character traits. Dubious at best, this approach becomes especially ominous—and a basic violation of peoples' civil liberties—when it is used to screen out job applicants whose handwriting is alleged to reveal "dishonesty." (See Beyerstein and Beyerstein 1992 for a discussion.)

Tips from Magicians and Professional Investigators

Stage magicians—who make their living as professional deceivers—know that it is possible to mislead anyone, given the right circumstances. It may be said that the person who believes he cannot be fooled has just fooled himself. According to magician/investigator James Randi:

> Many "men of science" stupidly assume that because they have been trained in the physical sciences or the medical arts, they are capable of flawless judgment in the investigation of alleged psychics. Nothing could be further from the truth. In fact, the more scientifically trained a person's mind, the more he or she is apt to be duped by an enterprising performer. (Randi 1982, p. 7)

The magician's fundamental means of deception is called *misdirection* —drawing observers' attention away from the real action. The old saw, "The hand is quicker than the eye," is only a magician's ploy (and sometimes a joke followed by the clarification, "That's why there are so many black eyes!"). In fact, the hand is *cleverer* than the eye, and this cleverness involves misdirection. For example, while the conjurer is showing one hand empty, and thus luring the audience's attention there, his or her other hand may be deftly making what in magicians' parlance is termed a "steal," i.e., secretly gaining possession of an object (Hay 1949, pp. 362–63, 439).

Or the magician may take advantage of an observer's inclination to shift his or her attention. Bright, quick-witted people are used to thinking ahead; therefore (to cite a hackneyed example), if the conjurer looks up, then drops the hand that is holding a ball as if to toss it in the air, his audience will tend to shift their attention and look upward in anticipation. They will not see (what a child might see, if strategically placed) the magician smoothly drop the ball into a secret pocket in his coattail. (Although his hand now comes up empty, some observers may later insist— due to the mind's retention of the image of the ball—that they "saw" it tossed from his hand and "witnessed" its evaporation into thin air.)

Magicians—or phony paranormalists using their tricks—employ other principles of deception: utilizing confederates (that is, persons planted in the audience who assist them), special gimmicks and apparatus, and outright lying. Because they lie so readily in the service of entertainment, stage magicians will often be notably truthful in their other endeavors. However, the same may not be said of the bogus "psychic" who pretends to work wonders by special power; he is likely to be a deceiver both on stage and off.

Uncovering trickery and deception involves the awareness that comes from knowledge and experience. More and more skeptical investigators are widely studying conjuring—finding it an entertaining hobby in addition to a rewarding means of gaining insights into human perception, plus an excellent form of training for exposing fake psychics' legerdemain.

A word of caution is in order here: learn humility and remember that a little learning is indeed a dangerous thing—that there is often more than one means of accomplishing some trick or effect. Therefore don't jump to the conclusion that some phenomenon is not produced by trickery, just because you have determined it was not accomplished by a trick familiar to you. (Recall the fallacy of argument *ad ignorantiam* explained earlier.) Remember, too, the value of videotaping (as disccussed in the previous chapter) in permitting the investigator to study an otherwise fleeting series of actions.

Detecting verbal deception—lying—has no easy prescription, but experienced investigators look for inconsistencies and improbabilities in the subject's statements and/or obvious evasiveness that may be indicative of deception. The investigator's best insurance in this regard is prior research and follow-up investigation which may tend to contradict or corroborate an interviewee's statements. Attempting to correlate one witness's statements with those of others is useful not only in detecting deception but in uncovering unintentional errors of fact as well (O'Hara 1973, pp. 94, 121). As we have seen, these may be due to perceptual errors, faulty memory, bias, suggestion, and other factors.

If children must be questioned, consider that (according to O'Hara 1973):

> The child may indulge his fancy in an imaginary journey to strange places and relate a series of unreal events. The distinction between truth and unreality may be lost on the child without any intentional desire to deceive. A child under six may invent a story in reply to a question. An older child, from six to ten may tend to distort the story. (O'Hara 1973, p. 97)

O'Hara adds:

The chief advantage of the older child as a witness, however, is the ability to observe, remember, and express himself and the absence of motives and prejudice. (p. 97)

For any type of suspected deception, consider setting a trap. That is, rather than taking a confrontational position that may warn the trickster away from attempting his deception—thereby producing only ambiguous results—actually provide good opportunity for any deception to take place, while having devised some means of exposing it. For example; one can be lax in the controls used in testing, say, someone suspected of using sleight of hand, while secretly observing and filming the activity. Or, one could take a tack like that skeptics have employed to expose bogus spiritualists. While at first going along with the protocol of the dark-room séance, investigators have then grabbed ghostly forms which invariably proved to be fake; on other occasions they turned up the lights and found the "ghosts" were the medium's confederates (Mulholland 1938, pp. 133–38).

Yet again, investigators have given dishonest spirit photographers the opportunity of substituting for a blank photograph plate one that had been preexposed; thus a "ghost" would appear along with the sitter's photo when the plate was developed. But, unknown to one photographer, the investigator had used x-rays to secretly mark the unopened plate that he had brought to the session. Therefore, when the plate with the ghostly image lacked the secret mark, the investigator knew that the plates had been switched (Mulholland 1938, p. 152). Houdini used a different method: when the photographer was not looking, he turned the plate around; it was developed with the "ghost" upside down in relation to the portrait of the magician (Gibson and Young 1953, p. 123).

Police investigators recommend a similar ensnarement approach when confronting a suspect they believe may be lying. According to O'Hara (1973):

The witness who is obviously lying can often be brought into the investigator's camp by careful maneuvering. He should be permitted to lie until he is well enmeshed in falsehoods and inconsistencies. The investigator can then halt the interview and dramatically announce that he recognizes the witness's statements as falsehoods. He can sustain his point by one or two examples. . . . (p. 100)

If the resulting confrontation does not produce results, the investigator can fall back on some of the other strategies and techniques we have discussed in the last two chapters. After all, it is rare that an entire case depends solely on the veracity of one informant.

Part 2

Specific Applications

4

Investigating Ghosts, Haunted Places and Things, Poltergeists, and Other Nonentities

As for ghosts there is scarcely any other matter upon which our thoughts and feelings have changed so little since early times.

—Sigmund Freud

When I'm asked if I believe in ghosts, in "dead guys" floating around, I usually say that I'm not sure, that we must wait and see. What I mean by this is that I'm simply unconvinced, one way or the other, that the spirits of the dead can come around and communicate or be seen by us living folks. . . . On the other hand, I absolutely believe that people *experience* encounters with apparitions.

—Loyd Auerbach, *ESP, Hauntings & Polergeists*

Even though ghosts or apparitions may exist only in the minds of their percipients, the fact of that existence is a social and historical reality: the phenomena represent man's inner universe just as his art and poetry do.

—R. C. Finucane, *Appearances of the Dead*

Ghosts: An Overview

According to the dictionary, an *apparition* is a supernatural appearance or a *ghost,* a *spirit,* or a *specter.* Most authorities do not bother to make sharp distinctions between the terms and some simply refer to the subject as "dead guys." Even so, some authorities like G. N. M. Tyrrell divide apparitions into four main classes: (1) *experimental cases* in which the agent deliberately tries to make his apparition visible to a particular person; (2) *crisis apparitions* in which the agent is seen, heard, or felt when he is undergoing an emotional crisis during illness, danger, or death; (3) *post-mortem apparitions* in which the apparition is seen, heard, or felt long after the death of the agent; and (4) *haunting apparitions* where a single ghost is seen repeatedly in the same place. Crisis apparitions can involve both the living and the dead. No matter what their former shape, ghosts are world-wide phenomena and have appeared in many different forms and shapes throughout history. The most common form is, of course, the ghost of a human being, but ghosts of nearly every living creature have also been reported.

We have every reason to believe that the belief in ghosts grows out of and in response to some basic and universal human need. The need, of course, is for some assurance of survival after death. Throughout history, and even in prehistory, ghosts were an integral part of religious belief. Since religion has always carried the promise of immortality, this means that the spirits of the dead had to be taken into consideration since, quite obviously, the body does not survive. In any small group or tribe the ghosts of one's forebears would naturally be the most prevalent. In most cultures one's ancestors were also seen as protectors and they had the power to intervene between supernatural evil and the living. If the goodwill of our ancestors' ghosts were not guided and maintained, then nothing stood between them and disaster: disease, crop failure, accidents, and death would result. Thus, whenever these things did occur, it was obvious to supersti-tious primitive man that the ghosts were angry. To calm them propitation was necessary. This appeasement took many forms: sacrifice, magic spells, burial ceremonies, dismemberment of corpses, gifts of money and food to the dead, or by taking steps to keep the dead away, e.g., burning fires before one's door, or by keeping the dead in their graves, e.g., by placing heavy stones (tombstones) atop their graves. Sometimes steps were taken to prevent the dead from doing harm. Since ghosts have a poor sense of direction, many corpses were buried head down or in the center of crossroads. When they returned they would most surely lose their way and be unable to haunt the living. We must not forget that *animism*— the belief that every man has two things belonging to him, a life and a phantom in close connection with the body—was the earliest and most primitive religious concept. Both the life enabling it to think, feel, and act, and the phantom or second self or image are seen as separable from the body, the life as going away and leaving the body insensible or dead and the phantom or soul as appearing to people at a distance from it.

As part of the primitive religious concepts, every society created a place where the soul or phantom or spirit could go, e.g., the Happy Hunting Grounds, the Elysian Fields, Valhalla, Paradise, or Heaven. Suppose, for some reason or another, the poor phantom wants to go there but cannot; what is it to do? This led to the idea of wandering ghosts and to the reasons for their appearance. Many ghosts are the spirits of murder victims wandering the earth in search of revenge. Others have returned to life to see that wrongs are righted and that justice is done. Many others came back because of improper burial, while many others return to take care of unfinished business—something important was left undone. Others simply cannot believe they are dead and are lost. They simply don't know where to go or what to do, or how to get to where they are supposed to be. No wonder so many ghosts moan, groan, howl, and shriek.

Although most ghosts are human in form, they can be in the form of other things: ships, such as that of The Flying Dutchman, for example; spectral animals such as dogs, cats, and horses; ghost trains are also frequenty reported—the train bearing Abraham Lincoln's coffin is occasionally seen in New York State. Revenants (one who comes back from the dead) can also show up as skeletons, decaying corpses, a skull, a face, clouds of mist, or eerie, moving lights. While the forms that ghosts take and their habits are incredibly varied, their reasons for returning, according to the folklore, tend to be fairly limited. The ones that are the most feared, however, are those who return out of sheer malevolence like vampires, who come back to drink blood and create others like themselves, or the ghosts of executed witches who come back to wreak havoc on the living. Others return to reenact their death scene, to punish the guilty, to obtain redress for wrongs, or to dog those who wronged them until they confess or atone for their sins. Many will pester the living until the living carry out the unfinished business of the dead.

Some ghosts are good-spirited and benevolent and return to warn the living of impending disasters. In World War II a number of soldiers were saved by the ghost of Joan of Arc, and numerous "ghostly hitchhikers" appear to warn motorists of unsuspected dangers lying ahead. Other ghosts return to comfort the living and to prove that there is, indeed, "life on the other side." Some appear to announce the coming death of people who are still living. Josephine's ghost is alleged to have appeared to Napoleon some days before he died.

Despite the goodliness of many specters, there is still an almost universal fear of them and their appearances. We have every good reason, of course, to associate this fear with the universal fear of death and dying. While belief in survival has existed since the beginning of time, few individuals seem to be eager to die. Most prefer to cling to life on this earth and it is of no little interest that many ghosts have the same preference, i.e., they don't want to go either, and they reveal their reluctance by haunting or hanging around the place where they met their fate.

For people who believe in or are haunted by ghosts, the major question is: How do you get rid of them? If you lack the ghostbusting equipment —portable nuclear-powered particle accelerators—that Dan Aykroyd and Bill Murray used in *Ghostbusters,* you might do what primitives do. Along with propitiatory ceremonies involving food, dance, prayer, sacrifice, and the casting of spells, the primitives also often use disguise. They dress up in ritual funeral costumes, e.g., veils and black cloth, and cover themselves with ashes so the dead will not know who they are. Then, if appeasement fails to work, the natives will don horrible demonic masks, beat tom-toms and drums, shake gourds and rattles, brandish spears and swords, and shout imprecations and scream—all to frighten the dead away. Huge bonfires and totems are also helpful. One can also cooperate with them and help them fulfill their goals and aims—once you are able to determine what they are. If none of these procedures work, then the best way to be rid of ghosts is to confront them, i.e., assure them you are not afraid of them and that they have no power to harm or hurt you. An ancient Irish legend says that if you run from a ghost he will haunt you forever, but if you turn and face him he will never bother you again. Truer words were never spoken.

On rare occasions one will encounter ghosts who are very stubborn and who are not so easily dismissed. They keep coming back time after time. These are the *haunts*—ghosts that seem condemned to eternal restlessness. Some, though they are not condemned to stay, freely choose to do so. In most of the cases we find they are either evildoers or their victims. Most haunts are victims. Many of course haunt old buildings—houses, castles, towers. Some, however, are known to haunt jetliners and cruise ships, as well as barns, caves, mines, cabin cruisers, and houseboats. In fact, ghosts have been found in every nook and cranny occupied by a human being. Many ghosts are quit famous, depending on their fame while they were alive. The ghost of Anne Boleyn is seen stalking the Tower of London, sometimes with her head under her arm and other times with it on her shoulders. Elvis Presley's ghost is even more famous. Elvis is not only seen everywhere all over the nation, but he is even the subject matter of an entire book devoted to his post-mortem appearances written by perhaps the world's foremost advocate of near-death experiences, Dr. Raymond Moody. Moody's book is titled *Elvis After Life: Unusual Psychic Experiences Surrounding the Death of a Superstar* (Peachtree Pubs, 1987; Bantam, 1989). One of the episodes in the book concerns a truck driver on his way to Memphis who is flagged down by a hitchhiker in the middle of the night. As dawn approached and it grew lighter, the driver suddenly realized his passenger was Elvis. When they neared Graceland, Elvis's home, the singer asked to be left off and promptly disappeared! This is a modern variation of the ancient Vanishing Traveller story—a world-wide legend told and retold in every country and language on earth. Abraham Lincoln is often seen haunting the White House.

Haunts of suicides are also plentiful. Many times the haunts reenact the event or the crimes that caused their deaths. Some ghosts are also very difficult to identify and many haunts appear to be stupid, acting like sleepwalkers or robots—walking aimlessly or repeating the same routine walks or acts. A few appear to be aware of what they are doing, most do not. Monks in grey cowls walking down corridors and grey ladies on staircases going up and down endlessly are universally reported in churches and monasteries and in old homes. Such reports are timeless and universal and differ only in the superficial aspects such as costumes and settings.

Perhaps the most fascinating fact of ghostlore is that in all of the many reports of ghostly encounters and in all of those cases where living persons and apparitions came face to face, *there is no record of a ghost or spirit ever harming a human being.* This fact alone clearly indicates that all ghosts and apparitions are, in some way or another, illusory. Interestingly enough, this is one thing that even those who most strongly support their existence will agree to. If anyone has ever been hurt or died as a result of an encounter with an apparition it has been because of fear. True, a number of natives have been literally frightened to death and it is possible that the fear itself could have caused a number of deaths. Fear, of course, can also be the cause of many misperceptions since we know that strong emotion can also affect our perceptual accuracy, the accuracy of our judgments, and our ability to observe and report accurately. According to Hans Holzer, one of the world's best known ghost hunters, "Ghosts have never harmed anyone except through fear found within the witness, of his own doing and because of his own ignorance as to what ghosts represent" (Holzer 1971, p. 14). Therefore, it is perfectly safe to be a ghostbuster. If any harm comes to you, you can be sure it will come from the hand of the living, not from the dead.

Ghost Theory

According to Loyd Auerbach, one of the most reasonable and sophisticated of the parapsychologists, when most people use the term "ghost" they are referring to anything truly unusual—an image, sound, smell, feeling, emotional state, or movement of objects—and they usually mean some sort of force left over after a death, but the force can just as well be that of someone who is still alive, what Tyrrell calls "apparitions of the living." Therefore, keep in mind that the apparition you see could be someone "on a sightseeing trip or trying to alleviate a bit of bordom." Feeling the presence of someone or of something intelligent is also often reported and connected with a ghost.

To explain how a mind without a body can contact the living Auerbach brings in the concepts of ESP and psychokinesis. Since a ghost doesn't have a voice box to speak with, the only way it can get a message through to a living person (or another ghost) is through the use of telepathy from the mind of the ghost to the mind of the living person. Another hypothesis is that the ghost can create a bodily form and even a larynx out of that spirit substance known as ectoplasm. It is well known that apparitions appear much more easily than they speak. Moreover, most ghosts do not look like white-sheeted figures or the green goblins shown in *Ghostbusters.* Instead, they look like people and seem to be pretty solid, although some may be a little faded or fuzzy around the edges.

Ghosts are also notoriously difficult to photograph. As Auerbach notes, "The truth is . . . there are no good photos of 'ghosts' and most are suspected of being produced through fraud or intentional error. The main contradiction here is that when an apparition has appeared before more than one person at a time, *not everyone sees it.* This makes no sense if there were in fact a physical materialization that is really seen, i.e., that is capable of reflecting light" (pp. 44–45). Another possibility is that humans do have an astral body composed of invisible energy or matter that only those with psychic abilities can see. If you are not psychic then you can't see it. Neither can the camera. As for hauntings, unless you are psychically sensitive you will be unable to receive the recorded information and the replay of past events. Auerbach suggests another possibility: a ghost is simply a part of the human mind that can coexist in the physical world outside the physical body—either split off during life, or surviving at the death of the body—and as an energy field floats around in its pure disembodied state and uses psi abilities to receive information and interact with people and objects. If this is true, why is it that ghosts are rarely —if ever—seen in the nude? Not only do they always appear fully clothed, but they often carry all sorts of other objects—tools, weapons, lamps, torches, etc. Where do these come from? Why, they are projected by the mind of the apparition, of course. A telepathic message is sent so that the observer sees exactly what the ghost wants him or her to see. Therefore, anything is possible. If telepathy is used, sights, sounds, smells, tastes, and anything else can be impressed upon our minds and translated into sensations and perceptions, giving rise to experiences we interpret as "real."

Holzer agrees. According to Hans, in physical terms ghosts are electromagnetic fields originally encased in an outer layer called the physical body. When death occurs this outer layer is dissolved leaving the inner self—also referred to as the *soul* or the *psyche*—free to drift out into the nonphysical world where it can move forward or backward in time and space, motivated by thought and all of its intact earthly memories. Not so in the case of ghosts. Here the electromagnetic field is unable to move into the wider reaches of the nonphysical world but instead is held captive within the narrow confines of its former emotional entanglements. Ghosts, therefore, are the surviving emotional memories of one who has died traumatically and usually tragically but is unaware of his death. Unwilling to leave the physical world, these personalities remain in the very place their tragedy or emotional attachment occurred prior to their death. According to Holzer, "true" ghosts do not travel, follow people home, or appear at more than one place. While some "free spirits" or "discarnate entities" that can travel and have appeared to several people in various locations may exist, they are few in number and not like the average ghost. True ghosts simply do not understand their predicament and are rooted to one spot by their emotional ties. They are doomed to relive over and over again the events that led to their unhappy deaths. While most parapsychologists do little to help these trapped souls, Holzer always tries to help by recruiting a trance medium and allowing the ghost personality to use the medium's body to express himself. Once the ghost personality is known and tells his grievance, Holzer does a quick analysis and eases the ghost into his proper dimension. Holzer also argues that since the human personality is electrical in nature, its impulses can be recorded and measured. Instruments along the line of Geiger counters can be used to detect the presence of ghosts. Additionally, ghosts can also be photographed provided one uses *psychic photography.* Psychic photography requires not only the presence of a camera and film, but most importantly the presence in the immediate vicinity of a person with the gift of *photographic mediumship,* i.e., a person having in his or her body some substance that makes the process of psychic photography possible. Certain glands, it seems, secrete this substance only when the medium is in "operating condition." According to Hans, "I myself have on occasion been able to get psychic photographs when there was someone with that special talent in my vicinity. The light-sensitive surface of film or paper seems to become coated with invisible but very sensitive psychic matter which in turn is capable of recording through imprints from beyond the world of matter" (p. 15). Clever Hans does caution the unwary about the ever-present possiblity of fraud including faulty equipment, light leaks, double exposures, faulty development or printing, reflections, refractions, and even delusions of the viewer. If, however, you take all these possibilities into consideration and eliminate them, then if there is nothing left, it must be paranormal! Belief springs eternal in the breast of the credulous! For, according to Holzer, "Try as man might, ghosts can't be explained away, nor will they disappear . . . ghosts are indeed nothing more or nothing less than a human being trapped by special circumstances in this world while already being of the next. Or to put it another way, human beings whose spirit is unable to leave the earthly surroundings because of unfinished business or emotional entanglements" (p. 16). In other words, ghosts are more to be pitied than censured.

Also representing the sympathetic or humanistic view are the thoughts of Raymond Moody. Moody also sees "ghosts" as evidence of psychic experiences. In most cases the study of ghosts turns out to be a quarrel on the part of skeptics and believers over whether or not these experiences are "real." Moody sees all such arguments as fruitless and a waste of time. What is important here, he maintains, is the sympathetic exploration of the emotional context of these experiences. Instead of trying to "prove" or "disprove" the "reality" of these experiences, we should look at them in terms of their human meaning. Most are anecdotal, derived from fallible human memory, and the result of highly emotional arousal. This does not mean the experiences were *unreal,* however—it only means their reality or lack of it can never be established. There is still a lot we can do with such experiences, especially if they are the result of grief and bereavement. We can take their emotional nature into account and counsel the living. Moody, nevertheless, clearly lets us know that his sympathies lie with those who believe that what they saw was indeed the spirit of the deceased.

With regard to theories about ghosts, Peach (1991) has recently provided an excellent overview in her study of apparitions, *Things That Go Bump in the Night.* She sees apparitions as primarily mental hallucinations, etheric images created by a mental act, psychological disturbances, the spirits of the departed, or, as the occultists would have it, astral or etheric bodies. Although her attempts to come to a satisfactory conclusion are somewhat limited, she does provide a very interesting discussion of the various points of view. While she fully agrees that 90 percent or more of all reports of apparitions are due to natural causes, she still holds out the hope and belief that maybe something does survive after all.

In summary, it seems that ghosts and apparitions are in some way or another illusory, i.e., hallucinatory. Ghosts are, most simply, subjective hallucinations, i.e., the perception of sights, sounds, and other sensory experiences of things that are not actually real or present. They are imaginary objects—things seen, heard, and felt—that, mostly, do not exist for others. Yet, to those experiencing these hallucinations, the ghosts are very real. Of course! Hallucinations are defined as *false* perceptions—perceptions which appear to be very, very "real," but aren't. If you are *psychic,* however, ghosts will come as a matter of course. In fact, Holzer states categorically, "Anyone who sees or hears a ghostly phenomenon is by that very fact psychic. You do not have to be a professional medium to see a ghost, but you do have to be possessed of more than average ESP abilities to tune in on the defined 'vibrations' or electromagnetic field that the human personality represents after it leaves the physical body. There are of course millions of such people in the world today, most of them not even aware of their particular talent" (p. 17). So there, all you would-be investigators, you may well be one of these lucky millions who has the ability to see ghosts but doesn't know it. Unfortunately for poor Loyd Auerbach, despite his many years of parapsychological investigating, he reports that he has not yet seen a ghost!

A final point: if the idea that inanimate objects can also return from the dead strikes you as ridiculous or strains what little credulity you have left, fear not; the fact that spectral clothing, weapons, armor, and such— even entire ships, planes, and trains—are reported lends even further weight to the idea that all of these apparitions are merely hallucinations of one kind or another.

Haunted Places

If you feel inclined not to go along with the idea of free-floating electromagnetic fields as the solution to the problem of ghosts, you will probably feel even less inclined to support the old but still viable notion of *psychometry.* This is a psychic power possessed by certain individuals which enables them to divine the history of, or events connected with, a material object with which they come in close contact.

Dr. J. Rhodes Buchanan was the discoverer of this phenomenon and gave it its name. The Civil War General Bishop Polk told Buchanan that he was so sensitive to atmospheric, electric, and other physical conditions that if he touched brass in the dark, he immediately knew it by its influence and the offensive metallic taste in his mouth. Following up on this idea, Buchanan began to experiment and found that medical students could receive distinct impressions from medicines held in their hands—even when the substances were disguised. Buchanan soon became convinced that some emanation is thrown off by all substances which certain sensitives are able to feel and interpret. Buchanan boldly declared, "The past is entombed in the present! The world is its own enduring monument; and that which is true of its physical is likewise true of its mental career. The discoveries of Psychometry will enable us to explore the history of man, as those of geology enable us to explore the history of the earth. There are mental fossils for psychologists as well as mineral fossils for geologists. . . . Aye, the mental telescope is now discovered which may pierce the depths of the past and bring us in full view of the grand and tragic passages of ancient history." In the past trance mediums would ask for objects belonging to the dead in order to make contact, and many claimed that they were merely the instruments and that the spirits actually did the reading. Others, however, repudiated spirit intervention and claimed that the ability to see the past in objects once owned by the dead was a personal gift, a sensitivity to the influence of which objects are possessed. According to those so gifted, very slight contact is sufficient to impart such personal influence. Often only the name of the dead person will suffice. In one instance, pieces of blank paper from the bottom pages of the letters of eminent persons, just below their signatures, was sufficient for successful readings and identifications of the persons who wrote the letters! The visions sometimes come in quick flashes of images to the psychometrist and are so fast and frequent an effort of will is required to slow them down. As for the visions themselves, they may be small or large enough to encompass the entire area and there is no definite order in their emergence. The pictures are often kaleidoscopic and while there is an oscillation in periods, images of more important events seem to be stronger and clearer and return more often. According to the psychometrists, the exercise of this faculty requires a relaxed, receptive mind. When the clue is handed over, some psychometrists feel they are back on the location of the event immediately, while others have to make the trip in time and space. As a rule, however, a "clue" containing an "influence" is indispensable for a successful reading. Buchanan believed that with some of the more gifted psychics the "clue" could be supplanted by nothing more than the name of the deceased written on a piece of paper.

Most fascinating of all, however, is the fact that psychometry has been called in to solve the mystery of hauntings. As the theory goes, whenever a human being undergoes a highly emotional or traumatic experience, this "mind stuff" somehow or other interpenetrates all surrounding material environmental objects and a record of these events is made. In somewhat the same manner that you would photograph and tape-record the event, the surrounding material objects imprint the event. At a later date, when the properly attuned psychic visits this site, he or she is able to watch the original event in its entirety. This is what is meant by a "haunting." If you are sufficiently sensitive and you enter a hotel room where a gruesome murder took place some years ago, sooner or later you will be able to see the original murder take place again before your very eyes. Even credulous persons like Sir Arthur Conan Doyle were troubled by the rank illogic of this nonsense. In his book *The Edge of the Unknown* Doyle mused,

> That the victim of some century old villany should still in her ancient garments frequent in person the scene of her former martyrdom, is indeed, hard to believe. It is more credible, little as we understand the details, that some thought-form is shed and remains visible at the spot where great mental agony has been endured. But why such a thought form should only come at certain hours, I am compelled to answer that I do not know. (p. 121)

Certainly, as the theory goes, the psychometric impression should always be there and thus should always be perceived. But this is not the way the ghost works, it seems—sometimes you see it and sometimes you don't. This is the case even with the most psychically gifted. Even the most gifted are not always percipient and they often are embarrassingly in error, especially when magicians like Houdini trick the psychics by giving them artifacts of living females and telling them they are objects of dead males.

Nevertheless, as far as hauntings go and a theory as to why hauntings occur at all, there has been nothing in the way of progress theoretically since Buchanan's work of a century ago. Some psi-cophants might take exception to this, however, and counter that Gertrude Schmeidler's and Michaeleen Maher's statistical approach, Tart's electronic instrument approach, and Randles's speculations about normal reality and synchronistic reality modes are true modern indicators of progress. We beg to differ. Schmeidler's and Maher's use of psychics to roam through allegedly haunted houses to pick spots they believe to be haunted and to see if these picks agree with the places where family members reported having seen the spooks is hardly a new theoretical approach (Cochran 1988). The same may be said about having both skeptics and psychics pick "cold spots," i.e., ghost spots, or having psychics attempt to describe the personality of the ghost and compare it with the actual knowledge of the dead person. Tart's suggestion that the use of much more sensitive electronic detector devices (heat sensors, infrared imaging devices, strain gauges, biosensors, and magnetic and radiation sensors such as Geiger counters), which are hooked up to a computer so that changes can be charted and correlated from moment to moment and any existing pattern immediately will become apparent, hardly represents anything new. Here again, the supposition is that the ghost is some sort of energy form that is a part of the electromagnetic spectrum and is thus detectable. As Susan Blackmore says, "Much of the research is based on pseudophysical theories. The problem with this field is that we keep coming up with mad ideas that lead nowhere" (Cochran 1988).

Jenny Randles's explanation for hauntings is in terms of human beings partaking of two types of "realities"—the *normal reality mode* and the *synchronistic reality mode*. The normal reality mode is the everyday world of science, logic, and material reality, whereas the synchronistic mode is the world of the subjective, mystic, psychic, intuitive, and synchronistic (in the Jungian sense). When we experience or are in the synchronistic mode we see ghosts in haunted houses or talk with them because our energy fields ("life fields" in her nomenclature) interact and harmonize. Emotions can cause "ripples" in these life fields and these "ripples" give rise to psychic experiences, ghosts, and such. In her words,

> Information from the past can be absorbed and experienced in several ways: detecting feelings, especially tragic or evil ones (we call that a "presence" or more graphically a "ghoul") and picking this up in more concrete terms (as with telepathy), when we perform psychometry or, in more extreme cases, mediumship. When we do the same thing with information about the "future," this can again just be as feeling (a presentiment or sense of impending doom) or in more concrete images as a prediction. (p. 163)

If you were expecting something more concrete or satisfactory or something more rational or persuasive in the way of explanation, you will not find it in the works of any of the aforementioned psi-cophants. As far as the psi-cophants are concerned, haunted houses exist, ghosts exist and are real, psychic energy fields exist, and psychometry is the explanation for why places are haunted.

Let us now look at the problem of haunted houses and places from the psi-cop point of view. From this point of view *there are no such things as haunted houses; there are only haunted people.* Any and all houses alleged to be haunted have not been fully or properly studied by qualified and capable investigators. When such investigations are made, in nearly every instance a natural, purely physical, psychological explanation is found for the so-called ghostly presence.

Exposures of haunts and haunted houses is as old and as common as the ghosts themselves. In McKay's *Extraordinary Popular Delusions and the Madness of Crowds,* published originally in 1841 but still in print, a chapter is devoted to haunted houses and the procedures used by earlier skeptics to eradicate such superstitions. A house in Aix-la-Chapelle, supposedly haunted and filled with specters in white robes and mysterious knockings, was found to be not haunted at all. The sounds were due to a broken door and window, which caused the knockings. As for the white-robed spooks—there were none. A Scottish haunting was found to be due to a trapped rat that could only lift the door of his trap but could not escape. This resulted in a series of ghostly bangs. Until someone mustered enough courage to investigate, the banging was attributed to ghosts. Some monks of the order of Saint Bruno who wished to acquire an ancient palace proceeded to haunt it themselves until the king was told they would rid the place of the demons if he would allow them to live there. The king agreed and the hauntings ceased. McKay also provides a number of additional stories of chicanery and deception in which numerous other individuals were able to persuade their fellows that valuable pieces of real estate were haunted in order to lower the value. It is ironic indeed that McKay closes his chapter with the following words, "It is to be hoped that the day is not far distant when lawgivers will teach people by some more direct means, and prevent the recurrence of delusions like these, and many worse, which might be cited, by securing to every child born within their dominions an education in accordance with the advancing states of civilization. If ghosts and witches are not yet altogether exploded, it is the fault, not so much of the ignorant people, as of the law and government that have neglected to enlighten them" (p. 618).

One hundred and fifty years after McKay's statement we find in bookstores all around the country a new book titled *The Black Hope Horror* by Ben and Jean Williams (William Morrow & Co., 1991). The Williamses recount the haunting of their home and a neighbor's home because their houses were built atop the graves of black slaves in the Black Hope cemetery in a suburb of Houston, Texas. Despite the fact that the entire subdivision is also built over the graves, no one else in the subdivision reported any hauntings except the Williamses and their next-door neighbor, a Mr. Haney—the individual responsible for starting the rumor that their houses were haunted. As for the rest of the people in the subdivision, there are no ghosts, only Haney's and the Williamses' overactive imaginations.

Our own investigations over the past twenty-five years clearly support the work of McKay and other ghostbusters. As of this date and after investigating a total of forty or more individual claims, we have yet to find anything that defies a natural explanation for the reported phenomena. On several occasions we set out to investigate supposedly haunted property only to discover the premises had never been haunted in the first place. A typical example of this is the Hannah House, a stately red brick mansion in Indianapolis that was reported in *Haunted Heartland* by Beth Scott and Michael Norman (Warner Books, 1986) as being haunted by the ghost of a mysterious man in a frock coat who wanders the hallways. Other bizarre phenomena supposedly included the overpowering odor of decaying flesh, many instances of crashing glassware, pictures that fell off the walls for no apparent reason, and mysterious and numbing cold spots at various place in the mansion. Moreover, a local psychic reported that she saw the ghost of a pregnant woman in one of the haunted bedrooms and that this woman had given birth to a stillborn child. A Mr. and Mrs. O'Brien, who operated an antique business in the house for a ten-year period, reputedly saw many apparitions. Sott and Norman also report that the Indianapolis Jaycees, who used the house for their annual Halloween project for youngsters, experienced some strange noises and swinging chandeliers, and a local psychic who was brought in was able to sense cold spots.

When a local skeptical investigator, Dr. Robert Craig, systematically began to investigate these claims, he was unable to confirm any of them. Interviews with the local Jaycees revealed that none of the supposed happenings had actually occurred and they were only rumors supposedly started by some local psychics who hoped to drum up business. Hoping to find something to investigate, Craig was left instead with only some improbable tales and empty rumors. Craig's experience is in no way rare. Both of us have individually encountered similar claims that, upon investigation, turned out to be baseless. In other words, many houses and places reputed to be haunted aren't and never were in the first place. In many cases you will find that, like the famous Borley Rectory in England, the rumors of the place being haunted were deliberately started in order to draw tourists or visitors, to decrease the value of the property if someone is out to get revenge, or, in the case of a store or place of business, to draw more customers. Nowadays the lure of—the mere possibility of—encountering a real live spook is almost irresistible.

Most rumors of haunted houses that we have investigated over the past twenty-five years have been due to the misinterpretation of normal and natural sights and sounds, or the inability to identify, locate, or explain the unusual happening. One of our first cases involved the notorious Bell Witch—a character famous throughout the entire southwestern part of the nation—and a cave she supposedly was haunting in Christian County, Kentucky, near Hopkinsville. People passing the cave mouth would, on occasion, hear moans and groans from inside. To determine the cause a local magician and a skeptical friend spent several nights in the cave until one evening they heard the moans and groans. Upon investigating, they discovered a crack in the cave roof. When the wind blew from a certain direction across this crack, natural pipe organ sounds were generated.

A Jeffersonville, Indiana, house was supposedly haunted by the crying of an infant. Attempts to find the crying child were fruitless and the residents only experienced the sounds periodically. Careful investigation determined that a hole in the foundation of the house permitted stray neighborhood cats to crawl under the floor and build a nest in which to drop litters of kittens. The mewing of the kittens before the mother took them away was interpreted as the sound of an infant's wailing.

In a small frame house in Lexington, Kentucky, a series of natural events also convinced a family that the house was haunted. Of two upstairs bedrooms identical in every way, one room was normally warm and the other was abnormally cold. The teenage daughter complained that she felt strange in the cold room. Every morning around six o'clock the house was rocked by several loud banging noises that no one could explain. On several evenings when the mother was sewing in her bedroom, she would see a flash of something white cross her door leading into the hall. These events plus other strange noises convinced the family their house was haunted. The loud bangs were the worst since none of the neighbors reported hearing any such sounds. When we were called upon to investigate in the month of February the heat was on in the house. When we went into the furnace room we discovered that the banging noises were due to the expansion and contraction of the duct pipes as they cooled in the early morning. The cold bedroom was the result of cold air pouring in from a broken window whose break was hidden from view by a wooden valance. The white flash was due to the reflection of light from a full length mirror on the back of the bathroom door directly across the hall. When lights were on in the bath or the headlights from a passing car shown in the bathroom window, they were reflected off the mirror in the door, and when the door moved it was as if someone had flashed a searchlight across the bedroom door. Despite our explanations for the disturbances, the family moved and refused to return.

Most other reputed hauntings were of a similar nature. Many involved animals such as squirrels, rats, birds, mice, and owls haunting attics, inner walls, and so forth. One particularly amusing incident involved a squirrel dropping his acorn shells from a height of about twenty feet onto a tin patio roof in the middle of the night. Another involved a rat whose left hind foot was inextricably caught in a large spring rat trap that he dragged across the attic floor nightly after the family had retired. When they investigated, he hid in the corner. We were able to catch him by making him think everyone had left. When he skittered again, I caught him in my flashlight beam and trapped him in a fishing net. The hooting of nesting hoot owls, which only come around seasonally, can also be quite provocative. Another unusual case involved a family in the coal mining area of western Kentucky who were religious fundamentalists. Periodically they would smell sulfur dioxide (SO_2) which they interpreted as the smell of brimstone, which the Bible says indicates the presence of the Devil. On at least two separate occasions the perceptual expectancies of some of the family members led them to report seeing "a flash of red," which, of course, was old Satan himself. When we first investigated, no smell was encountered nor could we discover where the smell came from or how it could have entered the house. We requested that someone call us the next time the smell was encountered. When we returned a few weeks later, we found the house filled with SO_2 but could not discover its source until we went outside and inspected the foundation of the house. When the area sustained a dry spell, the earth pulled away from the house foundation and large fissures were opened in the soil, allowing the natural gases in the area to well up from the coal deposits below and enter the house through the ventilators. Following a normal amount of rain, the soil filled up and closed the fissures, thus shutting off the gases. Could it be SATAN? No, nothing but gas.

Many other cases of haunting we found were the result of hobos and tramps moving into deserted farmhouses for shelter and warmth, foundations settling, underground streams eroding the ground and causing strange noises, excessive humidity from structural leakage, CB transmissions being picked up unintentionally, microwaves causing vibrations of pipes and wires, high and low frequency sound waves beyond the hearing range, the passing of heavy buses and trucks, and a number of other electrical and magnetic anomalies that gave rise to unusual experiences which the percipient concluded were haunts.

Two recent and unusual hauntings here in Kentucky involved first, a haunted houseboat and second, an eldery couple whose furniture—rather than their house—was haunted. In the case of the houseboat moored at a marina, an elderly couple lived in the houseboat until the husband became ill and was forced to move to a hospital and his wife to their old home in a nearby small town. Shortly after the move the husband died and the wife put the houseboat up for sale. The following summer the twenty-five-year-old caretaker of the marina reported one evening that he saw lights on in the houseboat. Upon investigating, he found the boat locked as usual from the outside, but in spite of this the interior of the boat showed signs of recent occupancy. After straightening up the premises, turning out the lights, and locking all the windows and the only door, the caretaker went back to the marina office. A few minutes later the lights came on again, and again the caretaker investigated, finding nothing and no explanation for the lights. The next evening the same thing happened again, but this time the caretaker, his girlfriend, and one of the local residents all visited the illuminated houseboat. While there the caretaker swore that someone unseen flushed the toilet, opened a sliding glass door, and sat in a rocking chair while the three were on the premises. Moreover, the caretaker disconnected the only source of electrcity going to the houseboat, but in spite of this lights continued to go on. Finally in desperation, the caretaker wrote a note to the ghost asking what he wanted. He also left paper and pencil for the ghost's use in responding. The following morning not only had the ghost replied, saying he only wanted to be left alone, but the ghost also wrote a friendly note to the Kentucky State Police river patrolman stationed at the lake. This proved to be the ghost's fatal mistake. The patrolman compared the handwriting of the ghost with the handwriting of the deceased and also with the handwriting of the caretaker. The handwriting of the ghost and the caretaker were identical. Upon being confronted, the caretaker admitted the haunted houseboat was a hoax. He thought that publicity would sell the houseboat and increase business at the marina.

The case of the haunted furniture was distinctive because of its clear illustration of another unusual, but by no means uncommon, psychological phenomena known as *folie à deux,* a French phrase meaning "folly of two" (Sachs 1988). An elderly couple in a small Kentucky town went to an auction of belongings from an old building that had formerly served as a home for the aged. The couple purchased a complete bedroom set of oak furniture in the summer of 1978. From the time they moved the furniture into their house trailer home, they were tormented by demons that banged on closet doors, created gusts of cold air in the middle of their rooms, awakened the couple while they slept, called out their names in the middle of the night, and switched the lights off and on for no apparent reason. The wife was the first one to see and hear the ghostly demon and the husband remained unconvinced until he was awakened one evening by a voice calling out his name. From this moment on he, too, was a believer and began to have similar experiences. The husband's younger sister, who lives nearby and is a frequent visitor, has never encountered the ghost nor have the couple's next door neigbhors ever seen or heard anything unusual. Interviews with all concerned revealed a typical pattern: the younger, dominant personality—highly imaginative and convinced of the existence of ghosts—persuades the less imaginative member of the duo that specters exist. Soon both are seeing and hearing what their imaginations have created. Ergo: *folie à deux.* Odds are that the ghostly voice calling the husband's name in the middle of the night was that of the wife. We tend to see and hear those things we believe in.

While it is not commonly known, locating the source of and the distance of sounds from the ears of the listener is unusually difficult. On numerous occasions the listener will confuse the location of a sound and swear it is close by when it is, actually, hundreds of yards away. Similarly, the reverse is also true and sounds miles away are detected as near at hand. It is also uncommonly difficult to pinpoint the size or distance of a light source in total darkness. Because of the saccadic movement of the human eye in total darkness, stationary points of light are perceived as moving back and forth. In poor light and under conditions of reduced visibility, it is also difficult to accurately gauge the size and shape of even familiar objects much less the size and shape of unfamiliar objects. All of these facts must be taken into account when we listen to the eyewitness accounts of people who report encounters with ghosts, haunts, demons, and monsters of one sort or another.

Haunted People

As noted earlier, there are no such things as haunted houses, only haunted people. People are easily haunted especially at night after retiring. One of the most common experiences occurs in the middle of the night when the sleeping person suddenly awakes and finds to his astonishment a ghostly figure standing by his or her bed. On many occasions this figure may be a vision of someone near and dear who has just died, or it may well be a vision of a monster or a demon or an alien spaceman. The person experiencing the vision is also startled to discover he is paralyzed, unable to move, and often experiences a floating sensation of moving across the room, out the door, through the walls, etc. Accompanying this experience is a feeling of calm and detachment as if the experience is happening to someone else. After the vision disappears or the experience is over, the percipient usually calmly goes back to sleep as if nothing has happened. If such an experience occurs when a person is falling asleep, it is called a *hypnogogic hallucination*. If such an experience occurs after the person has already been asleep and after they are wakened, it is called a *hypno-pompic hallucination*. These experiences are also known as *waking dreams* or, in times past, as *night terrors* (Liddon 1967). There are always a number of characteristic clues that indicate a hypnogogic or hypnopompic hallu-cination. First, it always occurs before or after falling asleep. Second, one is paralyzed or has difficulty in moving or, contrarily, one may float out of one's body and have an out-of-body experience. Third, the hallucination is usually bizarre; i.e., one sees ghosts, aliens, monsters and such. Fourth, after the hallucination is over, the hallucinator typically goes back to sleep. And fifth, the hallucinator is unalterably convinced of the "reality" of the entire experience. Whitley Streiber's *Communion* (pp. 172–175) is a classic textbook description of a hypnopompic hallucination, complete with the awakening from a sound sleep, the strong sense of the reality of being awake, the paralysis (due to the fact that the body's neural ciruits keep our muscles relaxed and help preserve our sleep), and the encounter with strange beings. Following the encounter, instead of jumping out of bed and going in search of the strangers he saw, Strieber typically goes back to sleep. Strieber even reported his electronic burglar alarm was still working—proof again that the intruders were mental rather than physical. Strieber is, of course, convinced of the reality of these experiences. This, too, is expected. If he was not convinced of their reality, then the experience would not be hypnopompic or hallucinatory. In nearly every collection of reputedly "true ghost stories" one can expect to encounter typical hypnopompic and hypnogogic hallucinatory experiences again and again. In fact, of all the various tales and reports of ghosts you will encounter, this source will be the one most frequently used to explain away the ghostly experiences of human beings.

A definitely atypical and unusual case, however, was that of a haunted couple bothered by the ghost of the wife's uncle. The spirit was the ghost of the wife's father's dead younger brother. The uncle had been very fond of his niece when she was a child, frequently visiting, bouncing her on his knee, and bringing her toys. He died at the age of thirty-five when his niece was eleven, and put in his first ghostly appearance when she reached puberty. His first five visitations were made when she was in bed alone. Then he began to appear on occasions of her romantic liaisons with eligible young men. One time the uncle showed up at a petting session in the local lover's lane. Another time he appeared in front of her boyfriend's car on the way home from a movie. According to the woman, the uncle was clearly and unmistakably jealous of any and all attentions she received from other men. Although her uncle's visitations had tapered off for a while, they became increasingly frequent when she started going steady with her husband-to-be. Moreover, the ghostly appearances intensified following their engagement, culminating in regular and almost nightly hauntings after the honeymoon.

Following their marriage, the ghostly uncle would synchronize his visits with the couple's lovemaking activities. During this time the husband had never seen the apparition but had relied on his wife's reports. Approximately a week before the husband showed up in my office for counseling, he was making love to his wife, when she suddenly exclaimed, "Oh, no! He's here again!" Quickly turning his head, the husband caught a glimpse of a man wearing a green sweater (the uncle's favorite haunting garment). Further attempts on the husband's part to see the ghost more clearly were futile. The couple was understandably distraught, and in the husband's words, "We're so nervous now we can't perform. He's ruining our love life!"

At this point in his narration, the husband suddenly stopped and said, "I feel him here right now. I can always sense his presence even though I can't see him. He's in the room with us right now!"

This gave me a golden opportunity to ply my trade and implement my ghost-busting technique. I leaped to my feet, glared viciously at the far wall, and snarled through gritted teeth, "You goddamned, stinking, dead son-of-a-bitch! Get the hell out of my office and don't ever come back! If I ever catch you in here again or if I ever hear of you bothering this man or his wife again, I'll come after you with all the power of Christ behind me and I'll dig up your corpse and drown you in holy water so deep that your soul will rot in hell for a thousand eternities! You have no power here! The power of life and love is infinitely stronger! You can't hurt these people and it will do you no good to bother them any further! From now on they're going to ignore you. You have had it, you ghostly bastard! So get lost and stay lost!"

The husband gaped at me in pure astonishment, his mouth hanging open.

"Do you still feel his presence?" I asked.

"Oh no. He's gone," the husband replied.

"That's right," I followed. "And if he knows what's good for him he'll stay gone. The way to handle Uncle G. from now on," I stressed, "is to threaten him. The only way he has power over you is for you to fear him. As long as you and your wife continue to be afraid of him, he will continue to haunt you. He has the power to plague you only as long as you are afraid of him. Once you show him that you're not afraid of him, all his power is gone. You and your wife were afraid of him, weren't you?"

"Yes," the husband replied. "We were. The wife more so than I because she's the one that kept seeing him all the time."

"Well, if he ever shows up again and if either of you ever see him again, I want you both to stare him straight in the eye and give him hell. Say, 'I'm not afraid of you. You are dead, dead, dead, and the dead have no power over the living. So you might as well get the hell out of here and stop bothering us.' Has your wife ever looked him in the eye?" I asked.

"No," the husband said. "We've been told that if you look a ghost in the eye, it'll steal your soul."

"Baloney," I rejoined. "That's simply nonsense, an old wives' tale. In fact, the opposite is true. What ghosts and spirits are most afraid of is your lack of fear. There's an old Irish legend that says, 'If a ghost is chasing you, it will continue to pursue you as long as you run.' If you stop and face it, it will go away. All ghosts feed on fear, and if you show them you're not afraid, they dry up and blow away."

"Didn't you feel his presence a few minutes ago?" the husband asked.

"No, I did not, and I couldn't see him either. Your ghost is not out there in the environment somewhere. Uncle G. is inside your head and inside your wife's head. That doesn't mean he's not real. As far as you two are concerned he is real. You're not crazy or anything like that. It's just that he's not haunting me; he's haunting you two. And since I don't know him, never heard of him, don't give a damn about him, and, God knows, certainly don't fear him, he has no power over me in any shape, form, or fashion. But I have power over him and any and all ghosts, because I know and understand them and how they operate. So, from now on, don't let him threaten you. You threaten him instead! Okay?"

"All right. He sure went away as soon as you hollered at him," the husband agreed.

"Certainly he did. Of course," I replied. "And I doubt very seriously that he'll ever show up again. If he does, you now know what to do. Stare him right in the eye and tell him to get the hell out of your life. If he doesn't disappear instantly, call me, and I'll finish him off completely, totally, and once and for all! Now since it is your wife that has the most trouble with him, it is particularly important that she do exacty as I have said. Make sure that the next time he shows up she gets very, very angry and screams and throws things at him, and that she looks him straight in the eye and tells him he has no power over her and that it will do him no good to ever bother her again. If you are there with her and you sense his presence—even though you don't see him—you also threaten him. Okay?"

With this the husband rose, thanked me, assured me that both he and his wife would follow my prescription, and left.

Eighteen months have elapsed and, so far, Uncle G. has stayed away. We confidently predict he will never be seen again by either the husband or his wife. The Freudian implications of the wife's sexual problems with the uncle aside, quite clearly guilt and childhood trauma are involved in the apparition's appearances. Nevertheless, superstitious fear is the source of the problem and it is most likely responsible for the persistent manifestations. Both husband and wife felt a sense of helplessness and needed to be given a source of power and, in their eyes, an effective means of dealing with the periodic irritations. Once they are able to cope, their major problem disappears. This is not to argue that all of the wife's deeper conflicts and sexual hang-ups have been resolved. It is doubtful they have, but at least she now has a tool—an effective way to fight, a weapon for dealing with her externalized fears.

We have discussed this particular case in some detail because in the event that you, in your investigations, chance upon such a ghostly psychological hang-up, this is one specific way to deal with irrational fear, i.e., giving the client a means of fighting not only the ghost, but his own fear, which is, of course, *the* problem.

Another quite unusual case of haunting concerned a young housewife who began to see the ghost of a golden-haired three-year-old girl playing in her backyard. While the housewife would be cooking or washing dishes, upon looking out the kitchen window she would see the little girl playing in the yard. On opening the back door the little girl would disappear. The housewife would often hear the footsteps and laughter of the little girl running through the upstairs hall. Upon climbing the steps, however, no one was ever there. Neither the woman's husband or any of the neighbors ever saw or heard the ghostly child. After investigating the case and talking with the housewife, she reported that she was barren and that both she and her husband desperately wanted children. After counseling and recommending that they adopt a child, not only did the little girl ghost disa pear, but the couple soon had a child of their own, as well as an adopted daughter. In this instance, the wife's longing and hunger created the very thing her heart most desired.

Examples of such "psychological ghosts" or apparitions due to grief and wish-fulfillment are not only very common, but are also well documented. Nandor Fodor, the prominent psychoanalyst and psychic researcher, has written several books detailing numerous cases in which he exorcised both ghosts and poltergeists, using psychotherapy. In most of Fodor's cases the ghosts are pure inventions of the hauntee's subconscious, but they are, nevertheless, vastly entertaining and we strongly recommend Fodor's books, particularly *The Haunted Mind* (New American Library, 1968); *The Unaccountable* (Award Books, 1968); *Haunted People* (E. P. Dutton, 1951); *Between Two Worlds* (Parker, 1964); and *On the Trail of the Poltergeist* (Citadel Press, 1958).

In many instances the ghosts and/or the hauntings are due to medical problems or physical disorders. In one case in upper New York State, a woman suffering from the neurological disorder known as "restless legs," an involuntary trembling of the lower limbs, was certain the condition was due to demons who seized her lower limbs every time she lay down. In a fascinating story called "The Woman Who Couldn't Watch TV," the neurologist Harold Klawans, in his book *Toscanini's Fumble and Other Tales of Clinical Neurology* (Contemporary Books, 1988), tells of one of his patients with Parkinson's disorder that he put on L-dopa and Artane. The drugs did wonders for her until one day when she told Klawans she was having trouble watching TV. Because Artane also blocks acetylcholine in the brain and also affects visual convergence and visual accommodation, Klawans assumed that all he had to do was lower her Artane dosage. In talking with her about her TV viewing habits she said she wasn't able to sit in her favorite chair and watch TV. When Klawans asked in what way her eyes bothered her, she told him her eyes had nothing to do with it. "It's because of my Uncle William," she replied. "He sits in my chair right in front of the set." "Well, why don't you tell him to move?" "I can't," she replied. "He's dead. He died in 1961." It was, of course, a hallucination and even she knew he wasn't really there. She also knew that the recurrent vision of her dead uncle was due to the drugs which she did not want to give up since they had done her so much good. Later, she also developed nightmares and frightening dreams, again as a direct result of the drugs. In your investigations of haunted clients, make sure that you ask about any and all drugs and medications that have been ingested prior to the sightings of apparitions, as well as any neurological disorders or pathologies such as epilepsy, for example, that might be responsible for the ghostly appearances. In most instances you will not find any such disorders and deficits simply because most sightings of ghosts are seen by people who are quite normal, but who have developed perceptual expectancies and attitudinal sets that make misperceptions and imaginal errors both common and frequent.

Polters and Other Such Geists

By far the most fascinating and sensational of all the apparitions are those of the hell-raising and noise-making variety known as *poltergeists,* from the German words for "noisy ghost" or "racketing spirit." The theory behind this phenomenon is that a ghost or spirit is at work in the house and that in order to make contact with objects, the destructive demon must work through a living person—a medium. Since many of this destructive type of haunting have centered on young boys and girls (although not all), the children are assumed—particularly adolescents who are in a highly vulnerable or sensitive state—to be responsible for the physical manifestations. The forces that upset furniture, smash dishes, destroy crockery and glassware, tilt tables and chairs, rip phones from the walls, pull down draperies and pictures, and persist in all sorts of devilment are, supposedly, due to recurrent spontaneous psychokinesis (RSPK), a psychic unconsciously operating through the adolescent. The misapplication of sexual energies is seen as the cause and the root of the problem. Skeptics and magicians who have spent time and have explored this sort of ghostly outbreak intensively are not as convinced as the psi-cophants that sex has anything to do with it.

Arthur C. Clarke has investigated a number of poltergeist cases and in a number of them he has managed to catch, on camera, human beings surreptitiously tossing objects when no one was supposed to be looking, pulling up rugs and doilies to dump glassware, and jerking light and phone wires to bring down lamps and telephones. In other words, you can rest assured that there is a living human rather than a ghostly hand busily at work in poltergeist phenomena. Perhaps the most famous case in recent history was that of Tina Resch of Columbus, Ohio. Tina was first investigated by parapsychologist William Roll, an authority on RSPK and poltergeist phenomena and author of *The Poltergeist* (Nelson Doubleday, 1972). Roll's preliminary investigations convinced him that Tina was for real and the phenomena were, indeed, genuine. The Resch poltergeist was so elusive that no one ever actually saw a single object even start to move of its own accord. James Randi, the magician and CSICOP fellow, also investigated the case and, unbeknownst to Tina, had a TV camera watching her every move. He thus revealed that Tina had cheated by pulling and throwing the objects when she was not observed. Tina's explanation was that she "only cheated sometimes." Roll, convinced of Tina's abilities, took her to his laboratory in Georgia and while there became even more certain of her RSPK skills. Records of the lab work are, by no means, convincing. In every case of RSPK demonstrations, many opportunities for Tina to cheat were provided and the controls were unacceptably loose. Moreover, as Randi noted, "Roll is myopic and wears thick glasses; he is a poor observer" (Randi 1984–85).

Our own encounter with a suspected case of poltergeistic activity came about in Lexington a few years ago. A middle-aged woman, her husband, and their twenty-three-year-old son, as well as the woman's mother, lived in a modest but comfortable three bedroom brick home with a full basement and garage. Several months before strange things began to happen, the son purchased a Corvette whose original owner had been killed in an accident with the car. The son and one of his friends began to restore the car by working on it at night in the basement of the house. The mother passed by the car one evening and swore she saw her son sitting in the driver's seat. When she came upstairs immediately afterward, she found her son sitting in the living room. One night when she went downstairs after turning on the basement light, the light was suddenly turned off even though no one was there. On another occasion the son and his friend removed the head gasket and set it on a shelf on the wall over the car. A few minutes later the head gasket was thrown violently onto the hood of the car, even though no one was near it. Shortly after these occurrences, the woman and her mother went upstairs when they heard the pool balls on the pool table clacking together just as if someone were playing on the rec room pool table downstairs. When the woman went down to see if her son or husband had come home unexpectedly, no one was there nor was anyone playing pool. A few days later, when the woman was vacuuming the hall, the phone in her kitchen rang. She shut off the vacuum and went to the phone in the kitchen. While she was on the phone, the vacuum cleaner suddenly started up even though no one was present. Two days later her next-door neighbor came over for a visit and, while using the small bathroom between the bedroom and the kitchen, dried her hands and opened the door to the kitchen. Suddenly and without warning, someone violently slammed the door leading to the bedroom behind her back. Less than a week later, the woman, her husband, and the next-door neighbor and her husband were all sitting at the kitchen table drinking coffee. After the woman had gotten up from the table, gone to the stove for the pot, and had filled up all the cups and returned to the table—suddenly, without any warning, the telephone flew off the telephone table next to the wall and landed under the kitchen table where they all were sitting. Finally, a few days later while the woman was preparing dinner, the front doorbell rang. Since she was in the process of melting some butter, the woman took the pan holding the melted butter and moved it from the front burner to one of the pans of water sitting over a flame on the back burner. When she returned from answering the front door, approximately a three-minute conversation, she found the pan of congealed butter sitting in the middle of the kitchen floor. None of the butter had been spilled.

This was, as far as the woman was concerned, the last straw. She went to the phone and called the University of Kentucky psychology department and asked for someone who knew something about poltergeists. We received the phone call and agreed to look into the woman's problem. After talking with her and her family and examining the artifacts and the environment in question, it was very easy to establish the fact that no poltergeist existed nor had one ever existed. Since both the woman and her family were well educated and very intelligent, they quickly dismissed the idea of a noisy and malevolent ghost once the cause of the problems was discovered. First, the windows of the Corvette were tinted and dark. As she passed by the windows of the car and glanced at it, she saw her own reflection in the tinted windows. Since the son had been working inside the car for the past week, she assumed it was him and not her reflection. The reason for the lights being extinguished was the result of a faulty downstairs switch. The head gasket was covered with oil and the shelf over the car was slanted downward. When the oily gasket was carelessly laid on the slanted shelf, it took only a few seconds before it slid off the shelf onto the car's hood. The pool rack containing the pool balls was affixed to the wall next to the table and suspended from the top with a single screw. Whenever heavy trucks rumbled past on a major interstate a few hundred yards away, this ball rack shook and the pool balls rolled back and forth in the rack, clicking together.

As for the vacuum cleaner, after examining it and turning the switch to the place where it was barely off and then giving it a kick with my foot, the vacuum cleaner suddenly popped back on. I asked her whether anything had been in the hall while she was on the phone. She said she did remember that she saw the family beagle in the middle of her bed in the bedroom. The only way he could have gotten into the bedroom was through the hall. She admitted that she had just "flipped" the switch off on her way to the kitchen. Clearly, just like my kicking had restarted it, the dog bumping into it had also done the job. Repeating the neighbor's experience in the bathroom, I shut the door to the kitchen and left the door to the bedroom open. After washing my hands and drying them, I grabbed the kitchen door and pulled it open very quickly. As I did so the air pressure in the small room slammed the bedroom door shut behind me. As for the flying telephone, I noticed that two cords ran from the phone and the answering machine across the floor next to the kitchen table to a wall outlet a few feet away. Both cords were lying loose on the floor. Repeating the woman's actions in moving her chair back to the stove and returning, I sat her chair legs inside the loose phone cords on the floor. Then, scooting the chair up to the table, I dragged the phone and the answering machine from atop the telephone table under the kitchen table. I had, beforehand, put a pillow on the floor to catch the phone. Clearly the woman had dragged the phone from the table when she returned and sat down. Repeating her sequence with the pan of butter, we all saw the boiling water on the rear burner shake the butter pan off, saw the butter pan skitter across the front burner off the stove to the floor and land upright with none of the now cold butter spilling. Heat and vibration had done the trick.

The concatenation of all of these odd and unusual events, plus the fact that the superstitious seed about the "haunted car" had already been planted, was fully enough to do the trick. The sequence of events one after the other was certainly odd enough and strange enough to make the woman believe something weird was going on even though her common sense told her it couldn't be. Even though the woman accepted the explanation and agreed that this was the most likely explanation for the events, she still felt very nervous about the house. Fortunately for both her and the family, nothing else of a *geisty* nature has happened since.

The most fascinating aspect of this case is just how clearly it demonstrates the power of expectation and how our attitudes and mental sets can influence our perceptions and beliefs. In cases like this one the perceptual errors were of little or no consequence. On certain occasions they can even be a source of amusement, as with the teenagers at a high school "pot" party who got stoned on tea leaves they were led to believe were the real thing. On other occasions these mental sets and misperceptions have led to tragic consequences. A few years ago the crew of the U.S.S. *Vincennes* shot down an Iranian Airbus, killing two hundred and ninety innocent people. This was an even clearer example of the perceptual expectancy principle at work. Fearing an attack, both the commander and the crew believed they were in jeopardy and fired in self-defense. Military psychologists have long been aware that soldiers, sailors, and airmen in their first battle suffer considerable stress before and during, and may confuse their expectancies with reality (Basowitz et al. 1955, Grinker and Spiegel 1945). Not only do such tragedies make it doubly important that we carefully check our facts before jumping to conclusions, but also that we recognize and pay more attention to the limitations and deficiencies of normal human perception. As for *geists*—polter or otherwise—before blaming them for every domestic anomaly we cannot explain, we would do well to apply Harrington's principle of "least astonishment." In his book *Dance of the Continents* (1983) Harrington states:

> Understanding is a sport of participation and therefore something of a game. . . . The game has only one rule: draw the least astonishing conclusion that can be supported by the known set of facts. . . . Every least astonishing conclusion is a winner, judged to be the most probable choice of all the available competitors. (pp. 36–37)

How to Bust Ghosts, Haunted Houses, and Other Such Nonentities

Whenever you are called upon to investigate the claim of a ghost or apparition, a "haunted" house, or a suspected poltergeist, you must keep in mind that as an investigator there is nothing to be afraid of. As we reported earlier, in the entire history of ghostly investigations, there is no case on record or any evidence of any ghost or apparition ever harming a human being. Ghosts, apparitions, and such can never harm you. This however, is *not,* repeat, *not* true of the living. They *can* harm you—especially if they are mentally deficient or disturbed, i.e., psychotic or delusional. You must also keep in mind that in most of our cases you will find that perfectly normal and natural events are misconstrued or misinterpreted and seen as evidence of the supernatural. In most cases of ghosts and haunted houses you are facing a *psychological problem:* a problem of misperception, perceptual expectancy, delusion, or hallucination. A principle worth remembering in this regard is: *There are no haunted houses, only haunted people!* Although many people *believe* that they have encounters with the dead, these encounters are purely subjective and are products of the observer's own minds or else they are victims of deliberate hoaxes and intentional deceptions. Neither is there any case on record worthy of serious scientific consideration that offers anything in the way of proof that the dead have ever returned or have been able to make physical contact with the living. Despite the thousands of séances and hundreds of mediums both here and abroad during the Age of Spiritualism, we have nothing that emerged from all of this silliness that is worthy of any current thinker's time and attention. The "dead" simply do not fit anywhere in our current concepts of known physical laws, and the current level of psicophantic thinking about the issue is and has never been grounded in anything more substantial than fanciful speculation. Therefore, when someone calls or reports contact with "spirits" or the deceased, you should do two things: (1) try to determine the normal, natural, or physical cause or causes for the experience, and once this has been accomplished (2) try to determine the mental or psychological cause of the experience. In doing these things you should look for the answers to two questions: (1) Why did this experience happen to this person at this particular time? (2) What motive did the percipient have that seeing or experiencing an apparition would resolve or satisfy?

In the second half of Peach's book (1991) dealing with the practical side of ghostly investigations, she provides an excellent set of approaches to carrying out a thorough and systematic study as well as a truly exhaustive set of questions for use with witnesses and claimants. All would-be investigators will profit from following her guidelines.

On first contact, the third question that needs an immediate answer is: Is this case investigatable? Or can this case be investigated? Once you answer either "yes" or "no," then you should follow it up with the question, Can *I* or should *I* be the one to take it on? If your contact says to you that last week his sister saw a face floating in the moonlit clouds that looked just like her dead boyfriend and that the face talked to her —such a rare, historical, once-in-a-lifetime, reported, second-hand event— even though it may be theoretically possible to investigate, it is neither practical nor feasible to do so. You would be better off simply recommending psychotherapy for the young lady and looking elsewhere. In other words, it is simply not worth your time and trouble. Only if the financial reward is sufficiently large enough to make the effort worthwhile should you consider it.

You must also remember that it is very difficult for any investigator to get out of bed every night and hurry over to meet a ghost who is waiting patiently for you to show up. Most of the time you will be the one who will have to wait patiently for people who have encountered the spirit to come to you. Of course if you are really eager to get underway, you could always advertise in the newspapers or put an ad in the yellow pages. This, however, is not necessary nor should it be of any concern. Once you have established a reputation as a ghost hunter or ghostbuster, people will flock to your door. One case will lead to another and another, and so on as the word spreads. Ghosts are—especially since the release of the two *Ghostbuster* films and the romantic movie *Ghost*—very, very popular. In our own cases most of our investigations come about as the result of people contacting the university and/or CSICOP, asking for someone interested in or familiar with the paranormal or occult phenomena. Once your reputation as "someone who is interested" is established, then every year, shortly before and after Halloween, you will be sought after by TV, radio, and newspaper representatives anxious for a story relevant to the season and by hundreds of curious or bedeviled citizens in need of advice or counsel. While you can expect to receive inquiries almost any time during the year, the number of seriously interested parties tends to peak around the last week of October and the first few weeks of November.

Upon first contact, which is usually by phone, try to determine whether or not it is something you are really interested in and whether or not it *can* be investigated. Many individuals do not want to discuss experiences over the phone that may make others think they are "crazy." They want face-to-face contact so they can "prove" to you that they aren't "nuts." Many times, however, it is quite clear from what is said that they are "nuts" and there's little you can do. For example, last year I received a phone call from a distraught young lady insisting that I help her stop a group of Satanists in her home town who were killing babies by stealing their souls. With the souls gone the babies lived for several years before having to be buried. Even after burial the Satanists stand over the graves and talk to their victims. According to my caller, it is impossible to tell who's living and who's dead, i.e., without a soul. My caller said she had been to the police, but they wouldn't listen to her and must be in cahoots with the Satanists. That's why she was calling me! I assured her there was little I could do unless she could obtain some evidence— tapes, photos, testimonials, etc. She alleged this was impossible because they would see her gathering the information and would kill her! I insisted there was nothing I could do until she had proof. That was the last time I heard from her. I was stymied because she even refused to give me her name, address, or phone number.

Contactees such as this one are rare. Most fall into a number of types or categories. The largest group is people who have misinterpreted normal, natural sights and sounds and have jumped to a paranormal conclusion prematurely. Reports of odd noises, strange lights, weird odors, etc., all clearly suggest a physical basis or cause and one that should yield easily to a careful and patient probe. The second largest group consists of individuals who are terribly frightened by some unusual or unexpected encounter or series of encounters occurring to them most frequently in the middle of the night while they are in bed. Usually they are aroused from a sound sleep, find themselves unable to move, and in the presence of a ghost or someone recently dead, a monster, an extraterrestrial, or a rapist. They may also have an out-of-body experience or find themselves floating on the ceiling while they can see their body in bed below. These "waking dreams" or hypnopompic or hypnogogic hallucinations were discussed earlier. Any such report that involves waking up in the middle of the night and encountering a ghost or demon is immediately suspect.

A third group commonly met consists of individuals who are actively hallucinating due to the ingestion of some consciousness altering substance, i.e., alcohol, narcotics, pot, cocaine, tranquilizers, and so forth. Since we live in a pill-popping, drug-using society, the number of people who hallucinate and misperceive daily due specifically to poisoning of the Central Nervous System (CNS) number in the thousands, if not millions. Make sure during your initial contact—if you discover that drugs are involved —that you also do your best to find out *what specific drugs* are involved and *how much* your contact has ingested.

Fear, is of course, the most common reaction shown when an apparition is met and your contactee will want your help in bringing an end to the terror. Your job is first to reduce this fear through reassurance, knowledge, and moral support. *Never, under any circumstances belittle or make fun of the contactee or in any way insult his or her intelligence. Arrogance has no place in this business!* Politeness, patience, kindness, a listening and helpful and sincere posture of interest and concern is paramount—even in the face of those reporters who are obviously under the influence of alcohol or drugs or who are patently mentally disturbed. The role of a counselor-friend is especially important when dealing with the latter.

Principles of De-Haunting

Most of the time the people who seek your help want the haunting to cease. They are frightened by these things and want them to end. The poorly kept secret of dealing with spooks—particularly evil or scary ones— is to fight fear with fear. This principle is well known to all witch doctors, medicine men, and shamans from Timor to Tibet. The horrible masks, horns, dragons, firecrackers, loud screams and screeches are all designed to frighten the evil spirits away. For de-haunting houses our twenty-first-century equivalents are high-fi equipment and electronics. On several occasions, as soon as we were informed of the whereabouts of said wraith, we assembled several loudspeakers and stroboscopes and went to work. Our procedure is somewhat analogous to fumigating, except our purgatives are light and sound rather than toxic gases.

For one pair of elderly apparitions who kept showing up after dark at a small farmhouse outside of Louisville and who wore turn-of-the-century garments, we were able to apply the full power of our tools without disturbing the neighbors.

On the appointed evening, the haunted vacated the premises and spent the night with friends. Using two 1,000 watt Pioneer portable speakers and a Realistic STA-860 high power amplifier with a tape deck and a variety of tapes featuring some hard-rock bands, e.g., *Raid, Billy Idol,* and *Devo,* supported by a portable 7¾-inch Xenon super-strobe light capable of illuminating a 60-by-90-foot area, we were in the house shortly after dark. The strobe light, when set to flicker at ten to twelve flashes per second, is particularly disconcerting to all spirits—both living and dead. After equipping ourselves with earplugs and sunglasses, the tapes were played at maximum volume while the strobe was systematically flashed in every room and hallway—including closets, basement, and attic—of the entire house for a two-hour period. Paradoxically, instead of raising the dead, thunderous hard-rock sound actually drives them away. It is also most effective in repelling senior citizens.

To ensure maximum results, all of the haunted family members must be present for the first few minutes of the de-haunting procedure. They are required to feel the full effects of both light and sound in order to appreciate what the unfortunate ghosts are having to endure. Once the hauntees are safely away from the premises, it is permissible for the ghostbuster to terminate the light and sound after a few minutes, provided of course that there is no chance of the hauntees returning unexpectedly and prematurely. They must leave with the firm conviction that the flashing cacophony will continue till dawn.

These procedures were sufficient to stop the ghostly visits and, after some needed repairs were made to the cornices and soffits of the house, the moaning and groaning from the northwesterly winds also ceased.

The de-ghosting of apartments and condominiums is, expectedly, a little more tricky. Here you will have to consider both neighbors and the local police, especially if you use tapes featuring machine-gun and artillery fire, thunderstorms, steam whistles, and sirens. These can be most effective for the more persistent *geists*—polter, quiet, or what have you. These realistic sounds are highly recommended for crowded or densely populated areas, because the use of hard-rock tapes will often attract hordes of teenagers who will mistake your efforts for a party. No spirit in his right ectoplasm is able to withstand this realistic sort of auditory onslaught for long. In fact, very few of either the living or the dead, haunter or hauntee, can tolerate it for more than a few minutes. For this reason and to avoid angry confrontations with neighbors and police, a reduction in volume is advisable.

For caves, cemeteries, and older rural domiciles—places minus the benefits of rural electrification services—portable generators may be required to power your electronic torches, bones, and gourds. While many ghostbusters have also used masks and other sorts of Halloween grotesqueries, we have never found such supplementary aids to be necessary. Yet if some particularly stubborn spooks who are both nearsighted and hard-of-hearing show up, then you may have to not only wear the masks but also sprinkle holy water around. The latter is nothing more than tap water drawn from the nearest faucet. If the client is suspicious, draw it from a church and have it blessed by a priest. If a priest isn't handy, bless it yourself but don't let your client know. In any case it should be dispensed from a cross-marked container. The point and purpose of all this is to convince the hauntee that the spirits have been dispersed. Although this is not the typical type of exorcism most folks would expect, it can, nevertheless, be very effective with nearly everyone afflicted by spooks.

In all of your de-haunting efforts you should always have an assistant. At least two people are required to load, unload, set up, and arrange the noise and light show. Also, the more slamming and banging the better, and experience has shown that two busters are noisier than one. Just in case you might encounter a flesh-and-blood spook, it is always nice to have an ally and an extra pair of fists. A helper is also handy in the event you are required to bring into play any kinds of instrumentation. Dale Kaczmarek, president of the Ghost Research Society, and others, too, recommend that many different kinds of sophisticated equpment may be required to ferret out some of the more subtle natural causes of spooky phenomena—especially electric or magnetic anomalies—including microwave and ultrasonic detecters, magnetometers, spectrum analyzers, video cameras, strain gauges, cameras normal light and infrared recording devices, diode tape-recorders, etc. (1987) as a normal part of a ghostbuster's equipment. In such cases you *must* have an assistant. Moreover, in case of multiple witnesses, a second interviewer can also save time as well as collect corroborating or contradictory evidence from a second interview. For most cases, however, little more than paper and pen or a pocket tape-recorder will be required. Whenever any equipment is used, the more unobtrusive it is the better. It must never be used in such a way that it will interfere with or upset the psychological conditions that caused the haunting in the first place.

Again, it should be emphasized that most of the people who will be seeking your assistance will not be as interested in solving a mystery or in determining the cause of the disturbance as you are—they are most interested in having it stop and go away. Nor will most of them be very interested in your philosophy of how the universe works nor have any great desire to be converted to materialism. Rather than attempting to convert them, your best bet is to solve their problem, i.e., find the ghost and get rid of it ASAP. The more efficient you are in doing this, the better they will like it. *After* you have found it and *after* you have exorcised it, *then* you can put in a good word for naturalism, science, and CSICOP. It is not a good idea to do it ahead of time simply because most of the hauntees want results, not philosophy. Deliver the desired results and you will have considerably less difficulty in selling your philosophy. Dissipate the emotion and fear and people become much more reasonable.

Tricks of the Trade

Shortly after the British Society for Psychical Research was founded in 1882, reports of supernatural events poured in from all corners of the Empire. In investigating new reports the Society put forth ten basic questions every reporter was required to answer about any apparition:

1. Could it have been an ordinary person, a shadow, a hanging coat, etc., or someone playing tricks?
2. If you heard ghostly sounds, could they have been normal—a cracking branch, birds, ordinary footsteps, your own breathing, wind in the chimney, or a hoax?
3. Has the place a reputation for haunting? If so, did you know, and were you expecting a ghost?
4. Why are you sure you weren't dreaming?
5. Did you recognize the apparition; if so, how?
6. Did anyone else see it before or afterwards, without either knowing about the other's experience?
7. If anyone else was with you, did he see it? If he did, could the words you spoke have given him a clue to what you had seen?
8. If it was the apparition of a living person, were there any unusual features (e.g., clothes, behavior) which you later found to be correct?
9. Did you or anyone else who saw it make a written record? If it foretold something—e.g., a death—did you write it down BEFORE the prophecy was fulfilled?
10. Have you had any other apparently psychic experiences? If so, how many and what kind? (Haining 1988, p. 119)

From the above questions it is apparent that members of the Society were fairly sophisticated psychologically even back in the nineteenth century and they clearly recognized the dangers of social influence, perceptual expectancy, social contamination, and so forth. Since this time the professional ghostbusters and parapsychologists have learned a great deal about people who report apparitions and have become a bit more sophisticated in approaching them over the years. Auerbach, for example, suggests that upon hearing of a reported haunting or paranormal incident, there are five things to do:

1. Determine as best you can if there is a "normal" explanation keeping in mind the initial interview may not be sufficient to enable you to make this decision.
2. Determine what motivated the call or contact. Do they want information, counseling, help in busting the ghost, or are they merely reporting something they thought might interest you?
3. Determine whether there is a need for an on-site investigation or interview or whether or not it is worth your time and effort in taking it further; how current is the event, how frequent, how many witnesses?
4. Can the experience/event be verified by other witnesses and is it worth investigating?
5. Should you go to the site or should they come to you? Is the experience or event site-centered or not? If not, they can come to you. If site-centered, then you should go to them because of psychological dynamics and setting-person interaction.

If you cannot visit the person or site immediately, by all means have them keep a journal or record of the time and place and circumstances of the event or experience. If there are multiple witnesses, have them take notes and make observations independently of each other. They need also to report their physical, emotional, and mental states during the time of the event or experience. Notes should be taken down immediately—as soon after the event as possible. If it recurs, then a notebook or journal should be kept. If you are able to interview the experient, ask about noises, voices, movement of objects, emotional state, smells, feelings before, during, and after the event. If there were more than one witness, interview each witness separately. Reliability can also be checked by having the same witness tell his story several times. Beware of giving the experient suggestions and putting words in his or her mouth. Memories can also be jogged with a recreation of the event, and it is important to remember that you should look at what is *not* reported, as well as what was. It is also important to look for eyewitness contamination. Frequently hearing reports from one witness will cause the second witness to unconsciously add details to his account he would not have mentioned had he not heard the other's story first. Watch your own biases and don't put words in the witnesses' mouths by jumping to a natural explanation prematurely or by assuming it was definitely this or that. Look for cases of perceptual expectancy and misdirection, imagination and suggestibility, as well as intentional and unintentional prevarication. As noted earlier, video monitoring can be very revealing, especially in claims of poltergeist activity. Remember also the belief system and the motivation of the experient are always your most important and significant clues. People with a strong religious background and fundamentalistic beliefs in Satan and demons can offer a considerable challenge. Though most such people are unaware of it, the Catholic Church itself is adamantly opposed to spiritism and has been for many years. In fact, on April 24, 1917, the Vatican condemned all attempts to communicate with the dead, except through prayer, and it banned recourse by the faithful to séances if they felt they needed help. In 1957 Pius XII had a conference on spiritist experiences organized and the conclusion was: "Spiritism is the mistaken explanation for natural phenomena. Communication with the spirits of the dead is impossible." In the words of Brazilian bishop Bonaventura Kloppenburg, "I have taken part in séances for 40 years and today, I am more convinced than ever that no spirit ever came to visit or ever will" (Valente 1991). In general, the Church's position is that people who seek exceptional signs from the beyond are abandoning their Christian faith. If they do this then, "Faith is no longer verified by life, by real living, and so people look for something to cling to." It is important that all paranormal investigators understand that many modern theologians are as opposed to fundamentalistic beliefs in ghosts, demons, and little red devils running around the landscape as they are. Unfortunately, these enlightened theologians are as embattled with the forces of unreason as we are and, when all things are considered, may have an even more difficult fight on their hands than we do.

Being a paranormal investigator is a great deal like being a private detective or investigator (PI). Both are primarily concerned with solving mysteries. Despite what you may believe or may have been told, all real PIs (as opposed to the TV and movie variety) are very, very careful about breaking the law. Even the police are very sensitive to the fact that both the U.S. Constitution and the law limit them in their investigations. If *they* are limited, think how much more limited *you* are. You are neither a professional nor a policeman/policewoman nor are you licensed in any way. As an amateur, you should not sell your services for money. If you accept money for your services, then you are a professional whether you think so or not. To our knowledge, no state issues licenses to either ghost-busters or paranormal investigators. Nevertheless, when you start selling your services, you may be inviting some problems with local ordinances, the Internal Revenue Service, etc.

You should be particularly careful about trespassing. You cannot go onto private property unless you have, in legal terms, license and privi-lege. The latter, of course, is the owner's permission. Believe it or not, you cannot legally stand on a person's lawn and look in his window. Un-less you have the owner's permission, you're guilty of the crime of tres-passing. Even though an old deserted house may appear to be deserted and abandoned, it is wise to make the proper inquiries and get the owner's permission before you barge in and start your ghostly fumigations; other-wise you might wind up in jail. Similarly, no matter how above board and honest your intentions, you must never—under any circumstances—damage or destroy any property of any kind. In your zeal to get at a specter hiding in the woodwork, you might be tempted to use a crowbar to pry up a panel to get at the source of the noise behind it. Don't you dare, unless you have the owner's explicit permission to do so! No matter how old, worthless, or decrepit the premises may appear—don't aggravate the damage. If you do, you could wind up in court or jail and paying out lots of dollars from your own pocket.

You must also be very careful about invading other people's privacy. No matter how intriguing the mystery, how right you may feel you are and how wrong the private citizens you are dealing with may be, you must respect their right to privacy, otherwise you may be sued for harassment. As a general rule, if a person says he doesn't want to talk to you, *leave*. If you are told to stop following them, *stop*. You have a right to your privacy and so do they.

These facts of civilized living, however, should never become insurmountable obstacles. If you are an adept investigator, you will learn to overcome them by winning the permission and gaining the cooperation and confidence of your opposition. Once gained you then should have no trouble with your ally. To make a friend, you need to sharpen your interpersonal skills and the gentle art of verbal seduction as well. To get consistently reliable and valid information you need to be a good inter-viewer. With good interpersonal skills, although a good interview is never guaranteed, it certainly makes it more probable. Good interpersonal skills begin with at least a rudimentary understanding of human nature and particularly with good manners. By good manners we mean being consid-erate and thoughtful of other people, understanding their feelings, and treating them fairly and squarely. Being considerate of their feelings and emotions and putting them at ease is a fundamental requirement of a good interview. For a skeptic dealing with people who believe in psychics, ghosts, UFOs, and the like, it is particularly important that he or she not antagonize the believer at the outset and create a hostile witness before any questions are asked. Sugar, as the saying goes, catches many more flies than vinegar. If you are asked directly, "Don't you believe in (ghosts, UFOs, demon possession, etc.), be noncommittal, smile, and say, "Well, I'm not sure." After getting the story you came after and knowing where you stand, then you can probe the belief system of and the experiences of the believer, help with the dilemma, and play counselor if counseling is indicated.

It is never a good idea to make up your mind about a witness ahead of time. You should be flexible enough to shift or change your initial stance as the interview progresses. Good manners, kindness, and consideration are essential in making initial contact and putting the witness at ease. Being a good listener and keeping the communication channels open are paramount. The more disturbed the witness and the more bizarre the witness's behavior, the more important it is to treat him or her kindly and gently, to draw them out, and to get the full range of their delusion, as well as their complete cooperation. Almost everyone wants not only to be believed, but also to be understood, respected, and appreciated. Never destroy anyone's dignity! Doing so will make a lifelong enemy as well as a fiercely uncooperative witness.

The better you understand the person you are to interview, the easier it will be to understand what they tell you in their report. If possible, you should review all of the facts surrounding the case ahead of time and also try to determine the attitude—friendly or hostile, believer or skeptic— of the witness in advance. Since people react differently in different environments, if possible try to pick a place where they will feel at ease and be willing to talk. A pen and notebook is essential and a small pocket tape recorder is recommended. There are a number on the market that are so small they can be hidden in your pocket, and a complete taped record of any conversation can be obtained surreptitiously in the event the witness does not want to go on record or for you to take notes. Even if he has no objections, a taped record is much better than hastily scrawled, illegible, or even inaccurate notes. Unless you've mastered shorthand, the recorder can easily store every detail a notekeeper might miss or overlook. Finally, the writing down of notes also prevents you from watching the facial expressions and reactions of the witness as he tells what happened. These are important aspects you should observe and that you might miss if your eyes are on the notebook instead of the witness's face.

During the interview smile, establish rapport, put the witness at ease, and keep him or her talking. Prepare ahead of time a list of questions and follow-up questions you want to ask so that you will be assured of getting all the important information needed. A good strategy here is to assume you have to write up the entire event and explain it to someone else. This will help you decide exactly what information you need and the questions you need to ask so that your story will be complete and make sense to your reader. This approach will almost insure that you will know ahead of time exactly what it is you *need* to know. Don't fail to ask "closed" as well as "open-ended" questions. Closed questions are simple and specific for getting basic facts and can be answered "yes" or "no" for the most part. They do not provide much detail. Open-ended or general questions allow the individual to tell it in his own words and supply all the details, e.g., "Exacty what did you see?" or "What did you think it was?" You should also keep control of the interview. That is, do not allow your witness to ramble on with irrelevancies for hours on end. Keep him or her on track and on the subject of concern. Neither should you allow yourself to get sidetracked.

If possible, it is also desirable to conduct the interview in private. Even with multiple witnesses it is advisable to interview them one at a time and separately. This will allow you to check on the accuracy and agreement —or lack of it—between the witnesses. On occasions it is also desirable to have your witness tell his story several times to see to what extent his or her accounts agree. Or two different interviewers can carry out separate interviews and then cross-check the stories for reliability.

Additional points worthy of consideration for the investigator concern using language familiar to your witness, using silence to make the witness uncomfortable and to draw him or her out, knowing when to be blunt or confrontational, knowing when and where to appear stupid, when and where to lie, in knowing how to control your own ego—don't allow yourself to feel superior to your witness—arrogance always shows even when you think it dosen't. Also, during the course of the interview keep your opinions to yourself. Remember it is an interview—not a debate. Keep your focus on the question being answered. Don't make up a second question while the first one is being answered. If you do, you may miss the answer.

If the witness's memory is faulty, help him or her by picking a specific reference point and working backward or forward from this. It is well known that emotionally traumatic events are more difficult to recall than those less emotionally disturbing. Memory also plays tricks on people and they make up information to fill in the gaps. This is known as *confabulation* and it is particularly common when the witness is hypnotized or is under pressure to come up with an answer. If the event happened months or even years before and was highly traumatic, getting the witness to relax and see it as if it were happening to someone else on a TV or movie screen can be helpful and can also increase the accuracy of recall. The technique of walking a witness, step-by-step forward or backward in time is also an excellent way to jog a person's memory. It is particularly helpful for locating lost objects. For example, a student lost an expensive ring given to her on her birthday and had no idea what happened to it. In helping her find it we made her go back to the last time she was certain that she had it in her possession. When she went back and recounted every event of every day from this time forward, she remembered that on the night of the first day she went into the dormitory bathroom before bedtime, took off the ring to wash her hands and face, dried her hands, picked up her soap and toothbrush, and went back to her room—*leaving the ring on the shelf.* Since over fifty coeds used the facility, it was obvious where it went.

Finally, although you have nothing to fear from either spirits or "dead guys and gals," this is certainly not the case when we come to the living. In making your rounds you very well may encounter kooks, cranks, creeps, and fanatics who will be quick to hit you, shoot you, knock you down, and so forth if you threaten either their deep-seated beliefs or their fragile self-esteem. Take care. Beware of both fundamentalists and fanatics. Such weirdos do not hesitate to handle rattlesnakes, moccasins, and copperheads, or drink strychnine or cyanide-laced Kool Aid, so they certainly will think little of sending you to either hell or the happy-hunting grounds if you give them cause. When dealing with such people, discretion is definitely the better part of valor. Before challenging or confronting anyone, make sure you know who they are, where they come from, and what their stake is in the issue at hand. Believe it or not, some of our fellow citizens believe, literally, everything they read and see in *Weekly World News,* the *Globe,* or the *National Inquirer.* Feeling them out should always precede confrontation. Never forget that you will not always be walking in the company of those who think and believe as you do. Be careful, but at the same time, don't forget to have fun.

5

Investigating Amazing Powers

Much of today's controversy over paranormal issues centers around people who claim to have extraordinary abilities—those beyond the range of normal experience and nature. Such powers include prophecy, clairvoyance and eyeless sight, mind reading, levitation, firewalking, psychokinetic ability, and others. In this chapter we provide background discussions of each, together with a review of relevant investigations; finally, we provide guidelines for testing of paranormal powers.

Prophets and Astrologers

As we have already seen (chapter 3), attempts to mitigate against the uncertainties of life by attempting to divine human destiny are age-old. "Perhaps the oldest divinatory art," says Owen Rachleff in his *The Occult Conceit* (1971, p. 2), is astrology, which is founded on the superstitious beliefs of ancient stargazers.

Although its roots can be traced to Babylonia, modern astrology is predicated on the writings of Ptolemy (i.e., Claudius Ptolemaeus, a second-century Greek scholar who lived in Egypt). In his *Amalgest* he compiled prior astronomical lore and offered his belief that the earth was the center of the universe, around which all the stars and planets orbited; his *Tetrabiblos* repeated the conviction of the Babylonian priests that the planets, which were believed to be gods, controlled people's destinies.

According to astrology, at the same time a newly born infant draws its first breath (the gestation period is not considered), it also absorbs the influence of the planets as they are then positioned. Thus, a person's physical characteristics, personality, health, profession, and fate are largely pre-determined by his or her natal debut.

If this sounds simplistic and far-fetched, wait: by analogy, even abstractions can be "born" and so receive the impress of heavenly influence. Thus, it is that the American astrological soothsayer, the late Evangeline Adams, once wrote, in her glib and facile manner:

> The Sun was in Cancer when the United States was born, but Gemini, the third sign of the Zodiac, was "rising," as we astrologers say, at the moment of birth, and is, therefore, most influential in determining our destiny. Gemini is itself a very nervous, restless, versatile, and highly mental sign. The fact that the United States was born so strongly under its influence would be enough, according to astrology, to account for much which is significant in American character and history. But that is not all. The ruling planet of the sign Gemini is Mercury, "The Messenger of the Gods," which governs the mind, the imagination, and the nerves. This combination of celestial influence explains why we are the world's greatest travelers, greatest advertisers, greatest salesmen—and why, incidentally, we are so subject to the American disease of "nerves." (1942, xix)

The zodiac—which is the basis for drafting a horoscope, or astrological chart "of anybody or anything" (as Adams said, p. xvii)—is an imaginary belt along the apparent path of the sun and is divided into twelve equal parts, each one named for a constellation. Thus, although the planets are at varying distances from the earth, astrologers treat their supposed influences as uniform. Moreover, according to Milbourne Christopher,

> Forecasts are based today not on the actual movements of the planets in our twentieth-century sky but as they appeared in the heavens at the time of Ptolemy. The position of the earth in relation to the planets has changed considerably since then. Aries has moved into the area Ptolemy ascribed to Taurus, and the other divisions of the ancient zodiac have changed accordingly. Few modern astrologers are interested in the current movements of heavenly bodies. . . . (1970, p. 102)

In addition, as philosopher Paul Kurtz and astronomer Andrew Fraknoi point out in their "Scientific Tests of Astrology Do Not Support Its Claims" (1985),

> . . . we now know that a person's personality and physical characteristics are determined by his or her genetic endowment inherited from both parents and by later environmental influences. Several decades of planetary

exploration have confirmed that there is no appreciable physical influences on the earth from planetary bodies. Indeed, the obstetrician hovering over the infant during delivery exerts a much greater gravitational pull than the nearest planet. (Kurtz and Fraknoi 1985, p. 210)

As Kurtz and Fraknoi observe, "exhaustive tests" of astrological claims have failed to substantiate them. For example, since astrologers claim that persons born under certain signs are more apt to become politicians or scientists than those of other signs, the birth dates of those two groups could be expected to be clustered in those signs. But when physicist John D. McGervey of Case Western Reserve University checked the birth dates of scientists (16,634 listings in *American Men of Science*) and of politicians (6,475 in *Who's Who in American Politics*), he found that the dates were distributed just as randomly for those signs as they were for the general public (McGervey 1977).

Again, astrologers maintain that persons born under certain signs are more—or less—compatible with each other. But this is not supported by the evidence. Psychology professor Bernard Silverman of Michigan State obtained the 1967-68 Michigan records of marriages (2,978 couples) and divorces (478 couples), but found no astrological correlation. Those who were born under supposedly "compatible" signs married and divorced with equal frequency as those whose birth signs were supposed to be "incompatible" (Kurtz and Fraknoi 1985).

Nevertheless, today some 1,200 North American newspapers carry astrology columns and a majority of young readers, at least (55 percent of those in the thirteen-to-eighteen-year-old range, according to a 1984 Gallup poll), believe that astrology works (Kurtz and Fraknoi 1985). How it seems to do so becomes clear from a single experiment performed by psychologist C. R. Snyder and his colleagues at the University of Kansas. They drew up a generalized personality description which they showed to three groups of people: those in the first being correctly told it was a universal sketch, those in the second that it was a horoscope for their astrological sign, and those in the third that it was their *personal* reading. Asked to rate how well they were described by the profile on a scale of 1 to 5, the groups responded with average ratings of, respectively, 3.2, 3.76, and 4.38. Conclude Kurtz and Fraknoi (1975), "Apparently those who want to believe will do so!"

Astrological charlatans have long been able to capitalize on people's fears and to employ their hokum to gain power and influence. A classic example is Nostradamus—Michele de Notre-Dame (1503–1566), the French seer whose prophetic utterances occasionally contain specific astrological references. Eventually, although some viewed him as a heretic or warlock,

Nostradamus became wealthy and honored, especially at the French court. There, Henry II's queen, Catherine de Medici, was a patron of astrologers and sorcerers (Cohen 1985, pp. 143–50).

In recent times it has become fashionable to try to demonstrate that Nostradamus correctly prophesied modern events. However, Nostradamus's prophecies were written in quatrains whose vague and symbolic poetry could be subjected to different interpretations at different times. (Nostradamus admitted that the verses were written so "they could not possibly be understood until they were interpreted after the event and by it.") For example, consider this verse:

> Vn Empereur naistra pres d'Italie,
> Qui à l'Empire sera vendu bien cher,
> Diront auecques quels gens il se ralie
> Qui'on trouuera moins prince que boucher.

That is, according to one translator (Le Vert 1979):

> An Emperor shall be born near Italy
> Who shall be sold to the Empire at high price.
> They shall say, from the people he associates with,
> That he is less a prince than a butcher.

The second line is open to various interpretations, and the rest merely alludes to a ruthless ruler born "near Italy." Thus the quatrain could refer to Ferdinand II (the Holy Roman Emperor who ruled from 1619–1637) or to Napoleon, or—today's popular view—to Adolf Hitler. Still other interpretations are possible, and similar chameleonesque properties have been demonstrated for other quatrains, which have often been improved by biased translators (Randi 1982b; Hines 1988, pp. 39–42). Owen Rachleff (1971, p. 138) characterizes Nostradamus's prophecies as "exquisite examples of ambiguity, aided by a keen sense of history."

In this century astrologer Evangeline Smith Adams (1868–1932) became known as "America's female Nostradamus"; more recently, Jeane Dixon (b. 1918) appears to have inherited the mantle. She claims she discovered her gift for prophecy when a gypsy saw portents in the lines of her palm and made her a present of a crystal ball. Milbourne Christopher comments:

> She has since explained that if she knows the astrological sign under which someone was born she can find the future in a special segment of her crystal. Some signs are tuned in better at the center of the sphere, others

are read to the left, right, above, or below. Julius Zancig, an earlier user of the crystal ball, once said that a doorknob could be used just as effectively. The object merely serves as a focal point for concentration. If one has a lively imagination the scenes conjured up can be quite entertaining. Prolonged staring, however, produces headaches. If you really believe you can see the future in the transparent sphere, some psychiatrists warn, this may be a sign of trouble on your personal horizon. (1970, p. 79)

Mrs. Dixon's fame rests largely on the claim that she predicted the assassination of President John F. Kennedy. The May 13, 1956, issue of *Parade* magazine did report: "As to the 1960 election, Mrs. Dixon thinks it will be dominated by labor and won by a Democrat. But he will be assassinated or die in office, though not necessarily in his first term." However, Christopher states:

As we know now, the election was not "dominated by labor." She did not name the Democrat she said would win; no date was given for the president-to-be's end; and his announced demise was qualified with Delphic ingenuity "assassinated or die in office, though not necessarily in his first term." Thus if the president served a single term, it would be within four years; if he was re-elected, there was an eight-year span. (p. 80)

Christopher continues:

Such a surmise was not illogical for anyone who has studied recent American history. William McKinley was assassinated a year after the turn of the century. Warren Gamaliel Harding and Franklin Delano Roosevelt died in office, and during Harry S. Truman's tenure an attempt was made on his life. Moreover, the normal burdens of the Presidency are such that it is commonly regarded as a man-killing office. Woodrow Wilson and Dwight Eisenhower were critically ill during their terms. Unfortunately for the nation, the odds against Mrs. Dixon's prophecy's being fulfilled were not too great—7 to 3, based on twentieth-century experience.

In January 1960 Mrs. Dixon changed her mind. Kennedy, then a contender for the Democratic nomination, would not be elected in November, she said in Ruth Montgomery's syndicated column. In June she stated that "the symbol of the presidency is directly over the head of Vice President Nixon" but "unless the Republican Party really gets out and puts forth every effort it will topple." Fire enough shots, riflemen agree, and eventually you'll hit the bull's-eye. (pp. 80–81)

Mrs. Dixon has fared less well with other predictions: Eisenhower did not "appoint five-star General Douglas MacArthur to an exceedingly important post." Neither did "Russia move into Iran in the fall of 1953," nor did CIO President Walter Reuther "make known to his Union followers that he intends to run for President of the United States" (either in 1960 or 1964 as alternately predicted). Red China did not "plunge the world into war" over Quemoy and Matsu nor—as she foresaw—use germ warfare against the United States. She was wrong in 1965 when she prophesied that "Russia will be the first nation to put a man on the moon," and wrong again the following year: on May 7, 1966, holding her crystal ball dramatically and peering over the footlights of an auditorium at the University of Southern California, Mrs. Dixon confidently announced that the Vietnam War "will be over in ninety days." Instead, it lasted nine more years. Again, she saw a "great future" for Senator Edward Kennedy but not the tragedy of Chappaquiddick, in which Mary Jo Kopechne drowned in his automobile. The list of Mrs. Dixon's wildly erroneous predictions and of her notable failure to "see" major events could continue *ad infinitum* (Christopher 1970, pp. 81–83).

Still more recently has come the revelation that astrology held sway over important matters in the Reagan White House. Nancy Reagan came under the influence of a San Francisco astrologer, Joan Quigley, who drew up horoscopes that were used to regulate the president's schedule. At one point his calendar was color-coded for "good," "bad," and "iffy" days. Apparently motivated by fear and superstition, Mrs. Reagan "seemed to have absolute faith in the clairvoyant powers" of the astrologer, said Donald Regan (1988). He wrote that she "had predicted that 'something' bad was going to happen to the president shortly before he was wounded in an assassination attempt in 1981." Commented Daniel S. Greenberg, editor of *Science and Government Report* (1988): "A contagious good cheer is the hallmark of this presidency, even when the most dismal matters are concerned. But this time, it isn't funny. It's plain scary." In response to the affair, the Committee for the Scientific Investigation of Claims of the Paranormal challenged Joan Quigley to a test of her claim that she is "a serious scientific astrologer." Quigley, however, failed to respond (CSICOP 1988).

Clairvoyants

In addition to astrology, fortunetellers often utilize such other divinatory methods as palmistry, reading tarot cards, and the like—which are presumed *somehow* (occultists are typically vague on this point) to yield clues about people's character and destiny.

Others—such as crystal gazers—rely not on elaborate systems but on clairvoyance or "clear seeing"—the alleged psychic ability to perceive things beyond the knowledge of one's senses. Parapsychologists regard it as a subtype of ESP, distinguishing it from another subtype, telepathy, in which the information is supposedly received by thought transference (a topic we will take up later in this chapter).

The alleged prophecies of Nostradamus might be attributed to clairvoyance, since he invoked astrology only occasionally and wrote that his visions came while he gazed into a bowl of water (Cavendish 1974, p. 157). However, as we have seen, no such theory is required to account for the supposed accuracy of his prognostications. The same may be said of the much-ballyhooed talents of a twentieth-century clairvoyant, the so-called "sleeping prophet," Edgar Cayce (1877–1945).

Cayce (pronounced "Casey") was supposedly able to diagnose illnesses at a distance. By entering a "trance" state, he gave medical readings to thousands of people who wrote for his help. His disciples point to some 14,000 case histories (housed in the library of the Association for Research and Enlightenment—a Cayce promotional institution founded by the required prophet's son) wherein they find many supposedly accurate diagnoses of, and testimonials from, people who believe themselves cured.

Yes, as Martin Gardner observes:

> Most of Cayce's early trances were given with the aid of an osteopath who asked him questions while he was asleep, and helped later in explaining the reading to the patient. There is abundant evidence that Cayce's early association with osteopaths and homeopaths had a major influence on the character of his readings. Over and over again he would find spinal lesions of one sort or another as the cause of an ailment and prescribe spinal manipulations for its cure. (1957, p. 217)

In addition to osteopathy, Cayce's prescribed remedies derived from homeopathy and naturopathy, with some folk medicine and sheer inspiration thrown in.

> There were special diets, tonics, herbs, electrical treatments, and such medicines as "oil of smoke" (for a leg sore), "peach-tree poultice" (for a baby with convulsions), "bedbug juice" (for dropsy), "castor oil packs" (for a priest with an epilepsy-like condition), almonds (to prevent cancer), peanut oil massage (to forestall arthritis), ash from the wood of a bamboo tree (for tuberculosis and other diseases), and fumes of apple brandy from a charred keg (for his tuberculous wife to inhale). (Gardner 1957, p. 218)

An obviously fantasy-prone individual (as a child he had imaginary playmates), Cayce never attended school beyond the ninth grade but worked in a bookstore and was an avid, if eclectic, reader. He read the Bible annually, but soon became a thoroughgoing occultist. He was arrested and charged with fortunetelling fraud in New York, but was acquitted on the basis of "ecclesiastical" freedom.

Thus Cayce progressed—if that is the right word—from ascribing homeopathic and osteopathic causes to ailments into linking them with the person's "Karma." He began to describe his subjects' previous incarnations and to "see" their "auras" from which he diagnosed character and health (Gardner 1957, pp. 218–219; Phillips 1978, 7: 13–16).

But did Cayce have clairvoyant diagnostic powers? James Randi finds in Cayce's readings "the myriad half-truths, the evasive and garbled language, and the multiple 'outs' that Cayce used." Randi explains:

> Cayce was fond of expressions like "I feel that . . ." and "perhaps"—qualifying words used to avoid positive declarations. It is a common tool in the psychic trade. Many of the letters he received—in fact, most—contained specific details about the illnesses for which readings were required, and there was nothing to stop Cayce from knowing the contents of the letters and presenting that information as if it were a divine revelation. To one who has been through dozens of similar diagnoses, as I have, the methods are obvious. It is merely a specialized version of the "generalization" technique of fortune-tellers. (Randi 1982a, p. 189)

Although Cayce was never subjected to proper testing, ESP pioneer Dr. Joseph B. Rhine of Duke University—who should have been sympathetic to Cayce's claims—was unimpressed. A reading which Cayce gave for Rhine's daughter was notably inaccurate (Gardner 1957, p. 219). Frequently, Cayce was even wider of the mark, as when he provided diagnoses of subjects *who had died* since the letters requesting the readings were sent. Instead of perceiving their profoundly altered state, Cayce blithely rambled on in his typical fashion, in one instance prescribing an incredible nostrum made from sarsaparilla root, Indian turnip, wild ginseng, and other ingredients. As Randi (1979, p. 53) says of Cayce's lapses in these instances, "Surely, dead is a very serious symptom, and should be detectable."

In addition to his remote diagnoses, Cayce also tried his hand at clairvoyant prognostications. For example, he predicted that the mythical sunken continent of Atlantis would rise again about 1968; it didn't. But before his death in 1945 Cayce told numerous clients that in their previous lives they had been Atlantean citizens (Phillips 1978, 9:66).

Not only dedicated practitioners of clairvoyance like Nostradamus and Cayce are able to "see" beyond space and time—according to proponents of ESP—but also ordinary people can. Witness the disaster of the Titanic. What has since been described as "the most astounding instance of prophecy" is found in an 1898 novel, *The Wreck of the Titan,* written by an obscure author named Morgan Robertson. Fourteen years after this disaster novel had slipped into obscurity, the events it described came shockingly true: The *Titanic*—the largest ship in the world—sank on its maiden voyage across the Atlantic.

Not only did the *Titan* and *Titanic* have similar names, but they were of similar size (70,000 and 60,000 tons, respectively) with too few lifeboats; both sank in April in the North Atlantic after striking an iceberg; and both resulted in a great loss of life (most of the *Titan's* 2,300 passengers and 1,503 of the *Titanic's* 2,206).

Prophecy? Clairvoyance on the part of Morgan Robertson? Apparently not: First of all, despite apocryphal claims to the contrary, Robertson never claimed to be prescient. Moreover, there were glaring differences between the two ships—Robertson's fictional one having an auxiliary sail that the *Titanic* lacked. Finally, there is every indication that Robertson had researched his topic and merely made extrapolations from available facts. Ships traveling the North Atlantic route faced no danger so great as that posed by icebergs, and the danger was at its peak in April. As to the similar names, both mean gigantic and either was thus an obvious choice; it is even possible that the novel influenced the naming of the real ship (Behe 1990; Cohen 1985, pp. 277–80).

Even so, after the sinking of the *Titanic* many survivors and others came forward to claim they had had forebodings or premonitions of the disaster. But as Daniel Cohen points out:

> Every major tragedy stimulates such accounts, and the sinking of the *Titanic,* being a tragedy of unprecedented proportions and publicity, called forth an unprecedented number of predictions reported after the fact. Dramatic as many of them are, they are not of much use as evidence of any real forewarning of disaster. A hundred or a thousand times in an average person's life he or she may have a dream or some other vague premonition of disaster. When disaster really does strike, we tend to think it was foretold, forgetting all the times the dreams and hunches were wrong. Add to this very human response another one, a selective memory that tends to add or subtract details in order to make them conform to what actually happened, and we have the psychological conditions that create an outpouring of "I knew it was going to happen," every time some unexpected and dramatic tragedy takes place. And the sinking of the great ocean liner was surely laden with both drama and tragedy. (Cohen 1985, p. 280)

Occasionally, there is quite a different relationship between dramatic events and an apparent premonition or clairvoyant vision. Such was the case in 1981 when Los Angeles "psychic" Tamara Rand allegedly predicted the shooting of President Reagan—foretelling that the attempted assassin would have the initials "J. H." and a surname similar to "Humley" (his name was John Hinkely), that Reagan would be shot in the chest during a "hail of bullets," and that the event would take place in the last week of March or the first week of April (it actually occurred on March 30). The predictions were reputedly given on a talk show taped January 6 in Las Vegas.

Associated Press reporter Paul Simon thought Rand's story was too good to be true and upon investigating, discovered that it was: the video-tape was a fake, filmed the day *after* the attempted assassination, as her co-conspirator, KTNV talk show host Dick Maurice, later confessed. Rand deliberately made her "predictions" less specific than possible to deflect suspicion (Frazier and Randi 1981; Hines 1988, pp. 43–44).

Another type of clairvoyant trickery was practiced by a faith healer who appeared to have Cayce-like powers. The Reverend Peter Popoff appeared to receive information about people and their illnesses by some mystical means. Actually, the "hearing aid" that Popoff wore was a tiny radio receiver, enabling him to obtain the information from his backstage broadcaster, Mrs. Popoff; she gleaned the information from cards that the religious faithful had filled out, or that had been obtained by other means, such as informal interviews conducted before the healing service. James Randi—who had communications specialist Alec Jason intercept and record these broadcasts—played them on Johnny Carson's "Tonight Show," syn-chronized with a videotape of Popoff's performance. The results were hilariously effective (Randi 1987, pp. 141–50; Steiner 1986).

But what about laboratory experiments that supposedly demonstrate the scientific validity of clairvoyance? Dr. Rhine argued that tests with spe-cial ESP cards (known as Zener cards, after a Rhine colleague, K. E. Zener) proved that clairvoyance as well as telepathy existed. The cards bore five distinctively different symbols—a square, circle, star, cross, and wavy lines —there being five of each in the twenty-five-card decks. Supposedly cer-tain talented subjects were able to guess which symbols would turn up at a rate much greater than that attributable to mere chance. But as Martin Gardner summarizes the problems:

> In testing individuals, when a score falls to chance or below, Rhine has a great many "outs" which make use of that score to support ESP rather than count against it. Thus the subject may be scoring not on the correct card (known as the "target") but on the card ahead. This phenomenon

is called "forward displacement." Or he may be scoring on the card behind ("backward displacement"). Such displacement of ESP may even
be two or three cards ahead or behind! Clearly if he can choose between
all these possible variations, there is a strong likelihood one of them will
show scores above average. If no displacement is found, however, a chance
score may be attributed to some disturbance of the subject's mental state.
He may be worried about his studies, or bored, or distracted by visitors,
displeased with the experimenter, ill, tired, skeptical of work, low in I.Q.,
neurotic, or in a state of emotional crisis. Even the experimenter, if he
is in any of these regrettable states, may inhibit the subject by unconscious telepathy. All these factors are specifically cited by Rhine as con-
tributory to low scoring. (Gardner 1957, pp. 303-4)

Gardner adds:

Of course when scores are high, no one is likely to look for "subtle
influences." But if scores drop low, the search begins. Naturally they will
not be hard to find. Usually if low scores continue, the tests are discon-
tinued. If the scores are extremely low, they are regarded as a negative
form of ESP. This is called "avoidance of the target." (p. 304)

Decades since Gardner wrote that critique, the status of ESP research
has changed little, although proponents adopted a new name: Psi research.
Time and again, astonishing new claims have been made for the reality
of some form of ESP, including clairvoyance, but just as often skeptical
investigators have found serious methodological flaws and/or are unable
to replicate the experiments (Hines 1988, pp. 77-108).

Eyeless Sight and Seeing the Unseen

An interesting form of alleged ESP—sometimes attributed to clairvoyance,
sometimes to telepathy—is what is known in magicians' parlance as "second sight." This is the ability of some persons to see while blindfolded,
or, alternately, to describe things that are hidden from view.

For example, in his *Discoverie of Witchcraft* published in 1584, Regi-
nald Scott described how a conjurer could receive secret information from
a confederate. "By this means," he wrote, "If you have any invention [i.e.,
inventiveness] you may seem to do a hundred miracles, and to discover
the secrets of a man's thoughts or words spoken afar off" (p. 191).

Some two and a half centuries later, in 1831, the same feats were being performed by an eight-year-old Scottish boy, Louis Gordon M'Kean,
who was billed as the "Double-sighted Phaenomenon." The kilted lad stood

blindfolded and facing away from the audience, yet readily described such objects as watches, coins, and snuff boxes. He, too, could repeat the words of others—even though they were whispered at a hundred yards away (Christopher 1970, p. 110).

A similarly gifted "extraordinary individual" was an Englishwoman who performed as "The Mysterious Lady." Her advertisement (reproduced in Christopher) asserted:

> By the exertion of a faculty hitherto unknown, this lady is enabled to perform apparent impossibilities. She will describe minute objects which are placed in such a situation as to render it wholly out of her power to see any portion of them. Repeat sentences which have been uttered in her absence, and perform many other paradoxical feats of mind. Justice cannot be done in description; suffice to say, it is the first exhibition of its kind ever seen in America, and independent of its novelty, is at once interesting, surprising and instructive. . . . (Christopher 1962, p. 63)

She toured New England in the 1840s and apparently served as a model for a remarkably similar character, "The Veiled Lady," in Nathaniel Hawthorne's novel, *The Blithedale Romance* (Nickell 1987, pp. 54–81).

The secret to second sight is a code used between the blindfolded adept and the person who goes among the spectators to obtain the objects to be identified. All that is required is for the pair to agree on a series of questions, the particular phraseology of each denoting a category of information. For example, "What is this?" could indicate timepieces, and "Can you divine what I am holding?" could indicate money. When the pretended clairvoyant answers correctly, his partner responds with another agreed-upon cue: for instance "Correct!" could indicate a gold pocket watch, "Right!" a common wrist watch, and "Good!" an unusual timepiece of some sort. By such memorized questions and responses, magicians have amazed their audiences for centuries (Dexter 1958, pp. 187–204; Mulholland 1944, pp. 105–24).

The standard methodology aside, what about a similar second-sight demonstration in which not a word was uttered? The great French conjurer, Robert-Houdin, worked this improved version in 1848, merely ringing a bell to signal when an object was being held up for identification by his son Emile. It, too, is a trick—a "silent code" form of second sight, somewhat analogous to a semaphore system: a turn of the head, a tug of the ear, and so on. (For a discussion, see Dexter 1958, pp. 196–98).

Of course such a semaphore system presumes the blindfolded person can somehow peek, although there are other ways of signaling which are not dependent on sight. Perhaps the simplest method is one that was used by the great magician Robert Heller.

Heller's lady assistant lounged voluptuously on a sofa, with her head resting sideways on the armrest. The pose wasn't for effect; having her ear to the sofa enabled her to hear the subtle buzzing tones that conveyed messages telegraphed by backstage assistants (Dexter 1958, pp. 195–96). Heller's approach foreshadowed—perhaps directly or indirectly inspired—that of Peter Popoff, discussed earlier.

A seemingly impossible extension of second sight is found in the dramatic demonstration known as "the blindfold drive"—i.e., a securely blindfolded person's being able to steer a vehicle effectively, even in traffic.

The nineteenth-century "thought reader," Washington Irving Bishop (1856–1879), performed this feat in the latter 1800s. Tying on a blindfold, Bishop mounted a carriage, took the reins, and set off at a gallop through Manhattan traffic, astonishing reporters who pursued him in other conveyances. He did once—in Minneapolis in 1888—crash into a tree (he was unnerved at learning his wife had won her suit for divorce), but he regained the reins and completed the demonstration.

The magician "Newmann the Great" (C. A. George Newmann of Minneapolis) duplicated Bishop's blindfold carriage drive (Christopher 1970, p. 76 and illus. fol. p. 191), and the feat has continued with the advent of the automobile. In its modern form, the wonderworker may have wads of cotton taped over his eyes, followed by a bandana blindfold and then a double thickness opaque cloth bag placed over his head and tied at the neck. Still the performer can work his apparent miracle of "clear seeing." But how?

Observers of one such demonstration, asked to guess how the trick was accomplished, came up with imaginative possibilities, including secret signaling methods and fiber-optic tubes placed up the magician's nose (Brown 1988)! A magician queried as to the method is apt to respond, conspiratorily: "Can you keep a secret?" "So can I!" We think it wise to follow a similar course; however, one of us did conclude a newspaper exposé of one blindfold-drive performer—a stage hypnotist who insisted no trick was involved—in this way: "Magicians are not permitted to reveal their secrets in news articles, but the serious reader may find the solution, with illustrations, in the magical textbook *Cyclopedia of Magic* by Henry Hay [1949, pp. 27–29]. Sh-h-h" (Nickell 1976).

Another blindfold feat is the purported ability of certain persons to "see" with their skin. Called "dermo-optical perception," it is known by such other names as paroptic vision, skin vision, and eyeless sight. Typically, despite bandaged eyes, the sensitive can read printed matter by means of the fingertips or can divine colors when objects are held to the cheek. Actually it takes some "cheek" to accomplish the feat, as we shall see.

In the 1840s the alleged phenomenon was associated with mesmerism, and in the following century—publicized by the book *Vision Extra-*

Retinienne by Jules Romains (1919)—it was attributed to a "delta-state" (something akin to hypnosis). Still further interest was sparked in the 1960s by experimental work in the USSR and the United States (Cavendish 1974, p. 192).

In 1962, for example, a Soviet newspaper reported that a twenty-two-year-old epileptic patient, Rosa Kuleshova, could read with her middle finger. She could even read print that was placed under glass or cellophane, and she was able to describe magazine pictures. Soon, other Russian women discovered that they, too, had this remarkable ability. For instance, Ninel Kulagina, a Leningrad housewife, could read while blindfolded and even perform other wonders, including causing small objects to move by concentration alone. Accounts of the women's remarkable abilities appeared in Soviet scientific publications and in the June 12, 1964, issue of *Life* magazine.

For *Life,* the kind of vision this really seemed to represent was *déjà-vu*. Once before—in its April 19, 1937, issue—*Life* had featured the phenomenon of dermo-optical perception, that time as exhibited by thirteen-year-old Pat Marquis, "the boy with the X-ray eyes." Upon being tested by J. B. Rhine, however, the boy was caught peeking down his nose (Gardner 1981, p. 67; Christopher 1975, p. 99).

Indeed, "nose peeking"—often betrayed by what is described as "the 'sniff' posture"—has time after time been revealed as the secret behind "eyeless sight." When the Russian marvels were subjected to stricter controls—whereby their ability to benefit from peeking was effectively eliminated—the remarkable phenomenon was curtailed. Peeking was unequivocally indicated by the tests of Mrs. Kulagina; she was subjected to "alternate experiments" in which peeking was either permitted or restricted, and her successes and failures corresponded accordingly. The scientist testing her concluded: "Thus the careful checking fully exposed the sensational 'miracle.' There were no miracles whatever. There was ordinary hoax" (Gardner 1981, pp. 63–73).

As we have seen, it is practically impossible to prevent peeking by employing a blindfold, and attempts to use screens with armholes have likewise permitted peeking. Gardner, however, has a solution:

> A blindfold, in any form, is totally useless, but one can build a lightweight aluminum box that fits over the subject's head and rests on padded shoulders. It can have holes at the top and back for breathing, but the solid metal must cover the face and sides, and go completely under the chin to fit snugly around the front of the neck. Such a box eliminates at one stroke the need for a blindfold, the cumbersome screen with arm holes, various bib devices that go under the chin, and other clumsy pieces of apparatus designed by psychologists unfamiliar with the methods of

mentalism. No test made without such a box over the head is worth taking seriously. It is the only way known to me by which all visual clues can be ruled out. There remain, of course, other methods of cheating, but they are more complicated and not likely to be known outside the circles of professional mentalism. (Gardner 1981, p. 67)

Some tricksters employ other means of convincing observers they cannot see. For example, Joaquin Maria Argamasilla, "The Spaniard with X-ray Eyes" who was investigated by Houdini in 1924, could tell the time of watches whose cases were snapped shut and read a calling card or other small bit of writing placed in a padlocked box. Although Argamasilla wore a simple blindfold, and Houdini knew he was peeking, that fact alone was insufficient to explain the tricks. Close observation, however—involving Houdini's maneuvering into a position so that he could peer over the shoulder of the wonderworker—enabled him to learn the tricks. In receiving a watch, Argamasilla would pause for a moment and then lower his hand with a sweep; this was sufficient for his thumb to slightly open the case and glimpse the hands, this fact being covered by the flexed fingers and the misdirecting motion. As to the other feat, the lid of the padlocked box permitted a corner to be raised with a thumb so as to admit a peek at the contents. As a test, Houdini made two boxes, neither of which would permit the slightest opening, but, as Houdini wrote, "Argamasilla failed by refusal to take a test in both instances" (Gibson and Young 1953, pp. 248–57).

There are also many ways to learn the contents of a sealed envelope —which any good book on conjuring will show (see, for example, Hay 1949). One spiritualist, who gave "psychic" readings at her Cosmic Church of Life in Santa Clara, California, used the direct approach—as investigator Robert Sheaffer discovered. She instructed her patrons to place three questions—to be answered by the spirits—in a sealed envelope. Subsequently she would repeat the question, apparently without having opened the envelope, and dispense the spirits' advice. Sheaffer visited the woman in the company of magician Victor Wong, and discovered her *modus operandi*.

She worked from a tiny, cloth-draped alcove from which only her head and shoulders were visible. Using appropriate misdirection, she would remove the envelope from view, slit it open, and pull out the paper it contained. She would then read it surreptitiously and tell the sitters what the spirits' answers were. After answering the questions, she would tear up the envelope and discard it. Afterward, Sheaffer went to the dumpster at the rear of the building and retrieved some of the discarded envelopes. Piecing them together, he discovered that each had been slit open with a blade.

To discover whether the medium had any genuine powers, Sheaffer tested her in a time-honored way: he asked for advice from his brother John, and wondered whether he should sell his boat so he could pay his debts; although Sheaffer had neither brother nor boat, the "spirits" answered in the affirmative (Frazier 1983)!

Dowsers and Mental Archaeologists

Another type of reputed power that may be associated with clairvoyance is dowsing—a form of divination by which one attempts to use a divinatory rod, pendulum, or the like to locate such hidden materials as water, gold, lost objects, and so forth. The practice can be traced to sixteenth-century Bohemian mining camps where forked hazel twigs were used to locate ore—the twig twisting in the dowser's hands when he walked over a rich vein (Vogt and Hyman 1979, pp. 14–15).

Experiments with dowsers indicate that unconscious muscular activity is responsible for causing the pendulum to swing or rotate and the divining rod to twitch. For example, in one experiment, when a sheet of glass covered a bowl containing the test substance (mercury), the dowser's pendulum (an iron ring on a cord) stayed motionless, but when the glass was removed, the pendulum swung, supposedly due to "magnetism." Christopher says of the dowser:

> Then he was blindfolded, and an assistant periodically covered the mercury with the glass barrier. It had no effect. Unless he knew the glass was there, it did not stop the apparent pull of the mercury on the iron. This proved conclusively that muscular action, not magnetism, made the pendulum swing. (Christopher 1970, pp. 137–38)

In an experiment with another dowser a physiologist attached a measuring instrument to the rod and then wired one of the dowser's wrist muscles to the apparatus. By this means it was demonstrated that the muscle's contraction preceded the movement of the rod by about half a second (Bird 1979, p. 5).

But how do we explain dowsers' successes? According to critics, dowsers tend to be seasonal outdoorsmen having considerable experience with the type of material being sought—water, gold, oil, etc.; that is, they typically specialize in the type of dowsing they do. Take water diviners for example; as Milbourne Christopher observed (1970, p. 139), the best such dowsers "are people who are familiar with the soil on which they walk, or who have through experience a knowledge of how the earth appears over areas beneath which there is water." (For instance, the type and amount of vegetation could be an indicator.)

In fact, however, dowsers do not fare well in properly controlled tests. In 1949, for example, the American Society for Psychical Research (ASPR) pitted twenty-seven dowsers against a geologist and a water engineer. As revealed by shafts that were subsequently sunk at the specified points, the scientists were relatively successful at locating water and estimating its depth, whereas the dowsers failed completely. The ASPR's report concluded: "not one of our diviners could for a moment be mistaken for an 'expert.' . . . We saw nothing to challenge the prevailing view that we are dealing with unconscious muscular activity. . . ." (Dale et al. 1951).

Again, in 1964, a professor of physics at the American International College in Springfield, Massachusetts, offered a reward to anyone who could locate water under controlled conditions. Professor James A. Coleman arranged ten garden hoses, spaced a few feet apart and covered with canvas; one of the hoses was hooked up to a water source. The challenge was to locate the correct hose seven times out of ten attempts. Three diviners tried. Two admitted defeat after failing four times in a row; the third did locate the correct hoses twice, but then failed four times (Christopher 1970, pp. 140–41).

Fifteen years later James Randi tested several Italian diviners whose task was to trace the course of a water pipe. Actually, there were three hidden pipes that irregularly traversed a small plot, but only one had water flowing through it. The dowsers were completely unable to divine the path of that pipe (Randi 1982a, pp. 307–24).

Tests of dowsers' abilities to locate gold have also yielded negative results. In one, an Australian diviner failed to locate which of several empty boxes contained an ingot—even though he had seen which box it was placed in. In showing that the empty boxes produced no reaction to the rod, he apparently became confused and mistook the target box for the empty one next to it (Smith 1982). In another series of tests, dowsers could not distinguish boxes containing gold nuggets from those containing "fool's gold" or other metals or even from empty boxes (Nickell 1988, pp. 94–101).

Tests have also been made of dowsers' ability to locate archaeological objects, but again, controlled conditions appear to preclude success. Of course dowsers, as well as psychics who claim to locate archaeological sites, could make use of commonsense factors—e.g., the proximity of navigable waterways—just as archaeologists do. Archaeologist Kenneth Feder states that he often has students peruse Geological Survey maps and suggest the locales of potential sites. As he says:

It is quite common for students to come up with precise locations where, indeed, sites have already been discovered. Therefore, even if a psychic could come up with an accurate prediction for the location of an unknown site, we would have to consider the simple explanation that, consciously or not, the psychic was merely relying on commonsense clues rather than ESP to make the prediction. The lack of control of these variables renders such tests impossible to assess. (Feder 1990, p. 161)

One controlled test was conducted by Martin Aitken (1959). Aitken, a pioneer in the use of proton magnetometry in archaeology, tested British dowser P. A. Raine. The target was a buried kiln that Aitken had initially located by high magnetometric readings, then archaeologically verified. However, Raine could not divine the location, and Aitken concluded that archaeological dowsing did not work. Concludes Feder:

> Though practitoners of dowsing hold quite strongly to their beliefs, they seem to be unable to produce under scientifically controlled conditions. Until they do, dowsing cannot reasonably become a part of the archaeologist's repertoire. (p. 168)

May I Read Your Mind—and Aura?

Telepathy, a subtype of ESP, is the reputed phenomenon of communication between the minds of two people—a sender or *agent,* and a receiver or *percipient*—without the use of the sense organs. Also known as thought transference and mind-reading, it differs from clairvoyance in that the putative source for the perceived information is the mind of another.

Anecdotal cases of supposed telepathy are common—notably the type that might be called the telepathic apparition, thought of by some as a form of communication between someone's spirit and another person (Cavendish 1974, p. 28). Owen Rachleff provides a personal example, but then relates its not-so-mystical denouement:

> Seated at a restaurant window one day having a late lunch, I believed I saw my grandmother walking across the street, although she lived many miles away. I said to a lady companion: "I believe that was my grandmother across the street, but what in the world is she doing way up here?"
>
> Several hours later news came of my grandmother's fatal heart attack and, soon after, of her death. The restaurant incident at once came back to mind and was, in those days, regarded as a mysterious form of telepathy or premonition. For weeks the idea persisted that grandmother had somehow communicated her crisis miles across space to me. The occultic

aspects of this typical incident evaporated rapidly when I again met my luncheon companion of that strange afternoon and asked: "Do you remember how I believed I saw my grandmother and how I had wondered about her presence in this part of town?"

"No," the woman replied. "You never said anything like that." (Rachleff 1971, pp. 161-62)

Rachleff continues:

> There is no reason to doubt the probity or sobriety of the young woman in question. This case, like so many others, is merely one of post-dated wish fulfillment. After a crisis—usually involving death—the bereaved is understandably burdened with loneliness and remorse and consciously wishes he might once again, even for a brief moment, see or communicate with the deceased. Subconsciously he begins to convince himself that in fact he had seen or spoken to, for one last time, the beloved party in some form of very private and mysterious communication. It is a self-preserving mental trick, a tender delusion like the alleged passing of one's whole life before one's eyes in the act of drowning. (p. 162)

Stage-performing thought readers or "mentalists" (magicians performing mind-reading and other ESP tricks) convince many people of the reality of telepathy. This is despite the disclaimers they often give. For example, "The Amazing Kreskin"—today's premier mentalist—always flashed a statement on the TV screen at the end of his popular television show; it advised that the preceding was for entertainment only and was not intended to foster belief in supernatural phenomena. But this went over the heads of many who believed the talented performer could indeed read minds. After all, he did seem to know the people's thoughts!

Mentalists may perform any of various pseudo-telepathy effects such as "The Book Test" (divining a word that has been chosen at random from a dictionary or other book), "Naming Any Number of Chosen Cards," "The Cryptic Die" (revealing the uppermost number of a die that has been sealed in a box), and so on (Hay 1949, pp. 29-32, 105, 184). Such tricks can be quite convincing to one who is not privy to the mentalists' clever secrets. These include a means of momentarily rendering envelopes transparent; special writing pads and clipboards that "remember" what has been written on them; and secret writing devices that enable the mentalist, who has *apparently* written or sketched something previously, to actually produce it quickly and indetectably *after* the target writing or drawing has been shown (Hay 1949, pp. 21, 463; *Abbott's* 1987, p. 342).

An interesting trick of some mentalists involves finding a hidden object —such as a ring, or, in Kreskin's case, his paycheck!—by apparently telepathic means. The performer takes the wrist of a member of the audience as an assist, and therein lies the secret. Called "muscle reading" or "contact thought reading," it is the acquired art of detecting the subject's unconscious signals to proceed in one direction or another. The methodology is explained in various texts (e.g., Hay 1949, pp. 323–26; Christopher 1970, p. 77), which also describe a more difficult, noncontact form.

Mentalists—and their charlatan counterparts, fortunetellers—often give their subject such a detailed character reading, complete with specific, factual information, that they seem truly to possess remarkable powers of telepathy and clairvoyance. How else could they know so much from simply glancing at one's palm?

Actually, the sitter's hands may reveal valuable clues to get the seer started—a smooth band of skin, perhaps on the ring finger (denoting one's former married state), or possibly guitar-player's calluses on the fingertips. Then maybe there's a draftsman's pencil or tire gauge in the shirt pocket, or a DAR pin worn on the blouse. In any event, certain observations can be made about the sitter's age, address, accessories, etc., and these provide a basis for making some preliminary inferences.

Then the seer employs a technique known as "cold reading." Ray Hyman (1977) explains how the seer, or reader proceeds:

> On the basis of his initial assessment he makes some tentative hypotheses. He tests these out by beginning his assessment in general terms, touching upon general categories of problems and watching the reaction of the client. If he is on the wrong track the client's reactions—eye movements, pupillary dilation, other bodily mannerisms—will warn him. When he is on the right track other reactions will tell him so. By watching the client's reactions as he tests out different hypotheses during his spiel, the good reader quickly hits upon what is bothering the customer and begins to adjust the reading to the situation. By this time, the client has usually been persuaded that the reader, by some uncanny means, has gained insights into the client's innermost thoughts. His guard is now down. Often he opens up and actually tells the reader, who is also a good listener, the details of his situation. The reader, after a suitable interval, will usually feed back the information that the client has given him in such a way that the client will be further amazed at how much the reader "knows" about him. Invariably the client leaves the reader without realizing that everything he has been told is simply what he himself has unwittingly revealed to the reader. (Hyman 1977, p. 22)

The less-skilled pretender to telepathic/clairvoyant powers, who has not yet mastered the art of cold reading, can fall back on a stock spiel such as this one:

Some of your aspirations tend to be pretty unrealistic. At times you are extroverted, affable, sociable, while at other times you are introverted, wary and reserved. You have found it unwise to be too frank in revealing yourself to others. You pride yourself on being an independent thinker and do not accept others' opinions without satisfactory proof. You prefer a certain amount of change and variety, and become dissatisfied when hemmed in by restrictions and limitations. At times you have serious doubts as to whether you have made the right decision or done the right thing. Disciplined and controlled on the outside, you tend to be worrisome and insecure on the inside.

Your sexual adjustment has presented some problems for you. While you have some personality weakness, you are generally able to compensate for them. You have a great deal of unused capacity which you have not turned to your advantage. You have a tendency to be critical of yourself. You have a strong need for other people to like you and for them to admire you. (As quoted in Hansel 1977, p. 23)

Many people find such a profile accurately describes them and provides proof of the reader's exrasensory powers.

Anecdotal evidence and pseudo-telepathists aside, modern scientific tests of telepathy and other forms of ESP took place in the 1930s under the direction of J. B. Rhine at Duke University. Rhine's scientific training was as a botanist, but he and his wife became interested in psychic phenomena after hearing a lecture on spiritualism by Sir Arthur Conan Doyle.

Rhine's first publication on the subject concerned a supposedly telepathic horse named Lady Wonder. Unfortunately, this was something of an inauspicious beginning for the father of ESP (he coined the term "extrasensory perception" in 1934). Rhine believed Lady actually had psychic powers and he set up a tent near her barn so he could scientifically examine her apparent abilities.

Lady was then only the latest in a long line of supposedly psychic animals, including a seventeenth-century "Learned Goose" exhibited in London that could read "any Person's thought." Lady was trained to operate a sort of enlarged "typewriter," consisting of an arrangement of levers that activated alphabet cards. Lady would sway her head over the levers, then nudge one at a time with her nose to spell out the answers to questions posed by earnest inquirers.

To assess Lady's talents, magician Milbourne Christopher visited her and her trainer, Mrs. Claudia Fonda, in 1956. As a test, Christopher gave his name to Mrs. Fonda as John Banks (after the man who exhibited an earlier, seventeenth-century "talking horse" named Morocco). When Christopher subsequently inquired of Lady, "What is my name?", the mare obligingly nudged the levers to spell out B-A-N-K-S.

Another test involved writing down numbers which Lady then divined. Given a narrow pad and a long pencil, Christopher suspected Mrs. Fonda might attempt a trick of professional mentalism called "pencil reading"—observing the movements of the pencel's tip to learn what was written. Christopher pretended to write a bold "9," but, while going through the motions, touched his pencil to the paper only on the downstroke to produce a "1." Lady, of course, indicated the number was 9.

In short, as Christopher observed, Mrs. Fonda gave a "slight movement" of her training rod whenever Lady's head was over the correct letter. That was enough to cue the swaying mare to stop and nudge that lever. Lady was merely a well-trained animal, not a telepathic one.

Rhine's tests of human subjects, using Zener cards, produced several impressively high scorers, but magicians pointed out that lax conditions in the testing would have made cheating easy. In fact, in tests involving a Methodist divinity student, Hubert E. Pearce, Jr., the scores were significantly high until a stage magician came to observe. The student's scores dropped to pure chance, then—after the magician left—resumed their high rate.

Again, when George Zirkle and his fiancée, Sara Ownbey, obtained phenomenal scores, mentalist Ted Annemann suggested trickery could be responsible. Although the two were in different rooms and used a telegraph key to signal when Sara was ready to concentrate, Annemann showed how a silent counting code could easily have been employed to achieve the startling results (Annemann 1938). On other occasions Sara simply *told* Rhine she had achieved phenomenal results; the credulous researcher pronounced her his best subject "if we take her unwitnessed records, as I am fully prepared to do" (Christopher 1970, pp. 23–24).

Other problems with the Zener card tests were discussed earlier in relation to clairvoyance. Further problems with those tests and with other experiments in thought transference are given in Hansel's *ESP: A Scientific Evaluation* (1966), an essential text on the subject.

However, in the 1970s a supposedly new psychic phenomenon—which was called "remote viewing" but which is really telepathy repackaged—was reported. It was promoted primarily by two physicists at the Stanford Research Institute (now SRI International), Russell Targ and Harold Puthoff. They made astonishing claims: the remote-viewing effect was seemingly obtainable by anyone, and the experimental results were reliable and could be repeated. "In fact," commented David F. Marks (1982), a noted authority on alleged psychic phenomena, "remote viewing was every parapsychologist's dream come true."

In the procedure, someone travels to some distant location while another person waits with the test subject. At any chosen time the subject attempts to describe the location; his description is tape recorded, and he may even try to make a sketch of the site. Later, researchers have judges attempt to match the subject's description with the target locations.

Unfortunately, review of the remote-viewing transcripts in the Targ-Puthoff experiments "revealed an enormous array of extraneous information and cues"—i.e., "bits and pieces of information about the experiments that enable the judge to place the transcripts in their correct sequence: dates, times, references to previously visited targets, statements made by the experimenter monitoring the subject (including leading questions), and other information of this type." In two of the series Marks discovered that "there are enough cues to place the transcripts in almost perfect sequence."

Attempts to replicate the Targ-Puthoff experiments, with the experimental flaws eliminated, were unsuccessful, and Marks concluded that "remote viewing is a cognitive illusion, an artifact of human error and wishful thinking."

Equally controversial are the so-called *Ganzfeld* or "blank field" studies in which the sender is thinking about some object rather than a location. The "blank field"—perhaps an opaque screen across the subject's field of vision, or a covering over the eyes—is used to reduce extraneous sensory input and to facilitate telepathy. Hyman (1985), however, reviewed forty-two such studies and found flaws in the experimental methods. He concluded: "I believe that the Ganzfeld psi data base, despite initial impressions, is inadequate either to support the contention of a repeatable study or to demonstrate the reality of psi."

In brief, no one, to our knowledge, has ever been able to demonstrate, under properly controlled conditions, the reality of mental telepathy —not in all the years the alleged phenomenon has been studied.

However, just as some alleged psychics claim to have telepathic powers, others claim the ability to see auras—fields of light that supposedly surround people (and possibly other living things) as a manifestation of their psychic energy force. The colors of the auras are supposedly related to an individual's personality and changing moods.

Such claims have not been taken seriously by the scientific community, in large part because of the subject's association with theosophy and other esoteric and occult teachings. When Dr. W. J. Kilner published his *The Human Atmosphere* in 1911, *The British Medical Journal* stated (in its January 6, 1912 issue), "Dr. Kilner has failed to convince us that his aura is more real than Macbeth's visionary dagger." Kilner had not only claimed to see the aura and used it to make diagnoses of patients' conditions, but he also uncritically accepted the validity of (nonexistent) "N-rays" and clairvoyant powers (Kilner 1911).

In the 1970s interest in the aura was boosted by the popularity of a technique known as Kirlian photography—in which a high-voltage, high-frequency electrical discharge is applied across a grounded object. This yields an air-glow or "aura" that can be recorded directly onto photographic paper, film, or plates. Supposedly, the aura of living things contain information about their "life-force," those of people indicating their psychic state.

Actually the same "energy" emanates from nonliving things as well—paper clips, coins, shears—and, in fact, the Kirlian aura is really only "a visual or photographic image of a corona discharge in a gas, in most cases the ambient air." Experiments yield "no evidence as yet" that any property of the aura pattern "is related to the physiological, psychological, or psychic condition of the sample" (Watkins and Bickel, 1986).

Disappointingly, tests of alleged psychics' abilities to see auras have met with failure. One involved placing either one or two persons in a completely dark room and asking the psychic to state how many auras she saw; only chance results were obtained (Leftin 1990).

James Randi conducted another test on his two-hour television special, "Exploring Psychic Powers—Live." Anyone who could detect auras or otherwise demonstrate psychic ability would win $100,000. Barbara Martin was the challenger in the aura-reading category. She had selected ten people she maintained had clearly visible auras, and—unseen by her—each was asked to stand behind a screen. Martin agreed that the auras would extend above the screens and that she would therefore be able to tell which screens had people standing behind them. Alas, she got only four out of ten correct guesses—less than the five that chance allowed (Steiner 1989).

Psychokinetic Marvels

Yet another alleged form of ESP is called psychokinesis or "mind over matter." It is the supposed ability to influence physical objects by mental power alone. Examples include moving a compass needle, bending metal, "repairing" watches, projecting "thought pictures" onto photographic film, and influencing the fall of dice.

One of the Russian practitioners of "eyeless sight" whom we discussed earlier, Ninel Kulagina, was also adept at moving small objects by psychokinetic (PK) power, or so she claimed. Actually, like James Hydrick—whose PK feats of spinning a pencil and flipping phone book pages were mentioned in chapter 2—Ninel employed trickery. In fact, USSR scientists caught her using concealed magnets and invisible thread to move small objects like matches and a salt cellar, and to levitate a ping-pong ball (Gardner 1981, pp. 244, 290).

A film circulated in the U.S. showed her causing objects to move even though they were covered with a transparent cube. This impressed laymen but not professional conjurers who recognized it as a standard trick. Thus, when the film was shown at a magicians' meeting, it produced not awe, but laughter (Christopher 1975, pp. 85–86).

A special type of alleged psychokinesis is the production of "thought pictures." The premier exponent of "thoughtography" was Ted Serios, who claimed he could project mental images onto unexposed photographic film. To accomplish this, he looked through a paper tube that he pressed against the camera's lens. A Polaroid camera being used, the resulting thought-photos were developed in moments, thus precluding film-switching and darkroom trickery.

Magazine and photo experts were skeptical, however, and after study-ing videotapes of Serios's work they suspected he was slipping a tiny "pro-jector" in and out of the paper tube. Soon they had improvised such a projecting gimmick, a hollow cylinder with a lens at one end and a photo-transparency at the other, and were duplicating the alleged PK-photogra-phic effects. Serios was unwilling to appear before a team of sleight-of-hand practitioners but finally responded to a public challenge made by *Popular Photography*. His appearance before the experts—in which he was unable to produce his amazing thoughtographs—was effectively his Wa-terloo (Eisendrath and Reynolds 1967).

Laboratory tests of psychokinesis have not fared well either, for a va-riety of reasons, including the fact that the truly dramatic PK demonstra-tors have invariably been exposed as fakes. So prevalent was the problem of trickery at psi laboratories and the unwillingness of parapsychologists to guard against it that in 1979 James Randi launched his "Project Alpha Experiment" that was to last four years. He had two young magicians, Steve Shaw and Michael Edwards, pose as psychics and visit the McDon-nell Laboratory for Psychical Research at Washington University in St. Louis. Their apparent PK feats convinced the credulous parapsychologists that the pair had genuine paranormal abilities.

For example, the "psychics" were allowed to take home sealed plastic boxes containing various objects that they were instructed to psychokineti-cally alter. One box contained a fuse that Randi was able to blow without tampering with the wax seal. He simply inserted pins and connected them to his car battery!

The conspirators even deliberately left traces of their tampering, and they leaked warnings that their PK marvels were accomplished by trick-ery. But the gullible parapsychologists stubbornly resisted being infected with skepticism until the trio of tricksters called a press conference and revealed all. Parapsychologist Walter Uphoff continued to believe Shaw and Edwards had psychic abilities even after the disclosure (Randi 1983)!

Dr. J. B. Rhine began experiments relating to psychokinesis in 1934, testing whether subjects could mentally influence the fall of dice. Despite the numerous tests that have since been conducted, and rash claims that PK had been demonstrated, critics find insufficient evidence to warrant any such claims (Hansel 1966, pp. 1653–63; Hines 1988, pp. 99–100). Indeed, the results were actually so poor at Rhine's Institute for Parapsychology that the director, Walter J. Levy, Jr., faked an experiment to demonstrate the apparent PK powers of rats. He later resigned in disgrace (Gardner 1981, pp. 76, 126).

Walking on Air and Across the Fire

Among the many feats associated with Hindu fakirs, two of the most dramatic are floating in mid-air and walking barefoot over blazing coals. Such feats seem to defy natural laws and convince many people that magical powers do exist.

In the late 1820s self-levitation was reported in Madras, India. An old Brahmin mystic was able to sit cross-legged some four feet above the ground, while his hand grasped an upright cane that fitted into a bench. After his death in 1830, a fakir by the name of Sheshal, known as "the Brahmin of the Air," performed the same feat. And in 1866, Louis Jacolliot, Chief Justice of Chandenagur, witnessed the great fakir Covindisamy perform the so-called cane levitation (Gibson 1967, p. 81).

Actually, the feat is not truly a *levitation*. In stage magicians' parlance that term is reserved for effects in which the person appears to float freely in air. For example, in "The Floating Lady" illusion, a hoop is passed over the lady's body to prove that, ostensibly, there are no hidden wires or supports. (For the secret, see Gibson 1967, pp. 114–16, or Hay 1949, pp. 291–92.) Quasi-levitations like the fakirs performed—in which there is some visible connection between the person's body and the ground, floor, or stage beneath—are properly called *suspensions*.

By the time of Covindisamy's performances, European magicians had perfected the much more convincing levitation effect, but over the years exaggerated tales of the fakirs' powers of "levitation" persisted. Then in the late 1930s, the trick that had originated in Madras more than a century before was brought to London where it was finally photographed. The pictures, says Gibson (1967, p. 82), "indicated what had been suspected all along."

In actuality, the bamboo cane was a metal rod which was securely attached to the bench. It connected with a curved rod that extended under the fakir's loose sleeve and continued down his back. There it terminated in a seat, hidden beneath his floating garments, that comfortably supported the "levitating" fakir—or in this case, faker. Says Gibson:

> Yet despite the obvious trickery involved, many people still believe that Hindu yogis possess the power of levitation. Stories are told of adepts who cross ravines by striding boldly through the air. Others are said to sit in Himalayan caves and gradually float upward through the aid of breathing exercises that render their bodies weightless. (Gibson 1967, p. 83)

It is this legendary tradition, obviously, that lies behind the Maharishi Mahesh Yogi's claim (mentioned in chapter 3) that he could teach his credulous disciples to levitate. His Transcendental Meditation's Ministry of Information even issued a photograph depicting a TM student sitting in the lotus position and apparently levitating several inches in the air. However, her scarf was blown upward, revealing that the photo did not depict her in tranquil levitation, but rather caught her in the act of *bouncing*. Skeptics quickly duplicated the obviously fake photograph. (See Randi 1983, p. 103, for the two photos.)

Spiritualist mediums have likewise claimed the ability to levitate. In 1869, Daniel Dunglas Home (1833–1886) reportedly floated out one upstairs window and in another at Ashley House, Westminster. However, investigation has since cast doubt on the credibility of those witnessing Home's feat (Mulholland 1938, pp. 100–102), and there are plausible theories as to how Home—a known trickster—could have accomplished the apparent levitation (Stein 1989). Other such mediumistic levitations range from suspected to proven fakes (Mulholland 1938, pp. 50–51; Christopher 1970, pp. 176, 185–86; Stein 1989).

Firewalking, on the other hand, is not a trick—although, as the saying goes, there is a trick to it. An ancient Asian art, it is still witnessed frequently in Sri Lanka, India, Japan, the Philippines, and elsewhere, including the Fiji Islands. It is typically associated with a religious ritual, part of an elaborate ceremony that begins with the preparation of the fire itself and that culminates in the chief firewalker leading a procession of initiates across the hot coals.

Beginning about 1984, firewalking became something of a cultish activity in the West. Thousands of people flocked to firewalking classes taught by Tolly Burkan. Explains investigator Michael R. Dennett, who took the class and actually participated in a firewalk:

> Increasing numbers of firewalking students are giving testimony that the experience can add a new perspective to life. A San Francisco area physician says the course helped him to conquer his fear of flying. A tennis

pro said his game has improved since walking on fire. Some claim that firewalking class has improved their sex lives or helped them kick cocaine habits. Perhaps the most bizarre are claims that the feat sparks an ability to heal oneself. Failing eyesight can be restored and malignant tumors sent into remission. In short, firewalking is the most direct route to both mental and physical health. (Dennett 1985, p. 36)

Firewalkers attribute their ability to withstand burning to various exotic physiological effects or vague mystical powers, including "mind over matter" (Leikind and McCarthy 1985).

On the other hand, skeptics have proposed more mundane explanations. They have suggested that because firewalkers typically go barefoot, their feet become toughened and are thus more resistant to burning. Another notion was that the soles of the feet were coated with some special preparation that protected against burning. But these explanations are now largely discounted.

In fact, various tests conducted by British investigators, beginning in the 1930s, yielded valuable information about the phenomenon. For instance, an Oriental firewalker was able to walk about twelve feet (a few quick steps) across a bed of coals that had reached a temperature of 1,130 degrees Fahrenheit; however, when the trench was extended to twenty feet and the heat increased to 1,405 degrees, his feet received burns.

Investigator Bernard J. Leikind, a research physicist who, like Dennett, has himself performed a firewalk, explains that several physical factors are involved in the phenomenon. First of all, different materials at the same temperature have different thermal capacities and conductive abilities, and wood (unlike metal, say) is a poor conductor of heat. Among other factors involved in firewalking is the total time of contact. Says Leiking (in an article co-authored with fellow firewalker William J. McCarthy):

> Thus, so long as we do not spend too much time on the embers our feet will probably not get hot enough to burn. In fact, because the capacity of the embers is low and that of our feet relatively high, the embers cool off when we step on them. How do I know this? Well, the color and intensity of the light from the embers tells us their temperature; yellow embers are hotter than orange, orange hotter than red and so on. When I watched people walking across the bed of coals I could clearly see darkened footprints where the coals had cooled because of contact with the feet. In a couple of seconds the combustion reactions restored the embers' temperature and glow. (Leikind and McCarthy 1985, p. 30)

Of course, due to variables in the firewalk experience—the number of steps taken, whether one walks where the embers are deep or shallow, and so on—some people may become burned while others do not. Nevertheless, firewalking requires no mystical theory to explain it—as the courageous investigative work of Michael Dennett, Bernard Leikind, and William McCarthy clearly demonstrates.

Testing Claims of Paranormal Ability

The investigator must be prepared to subject individuals who claim to have paranormal powers to appropriate testing. Quite often the alleged wonder-worker will refuse to perform under strict conditions that would rule out trickery, and such refusal will—to all but the gullible—place the claimant in the proper light.

If the psychic or similar claimant agrees to submit to examination, the investigator should proceed in a very careful, thoughtful manner. James Randi—the world's foremost challenger of persons with alleged paranormal powers—has a statement that he circulates in connection with his longstanding $10,000 offer to anyone who can demonstrate such powers under satisfactory conditions (Randi 1982a, pp. 253–54). We have relied heavily on his statement for the following suggestions:

1. Have the claimant make preliminary (noncontrolled) demonstrations of his or her ability so that hypotheses can be formed and, in turn, tested.
2. If at all possible, film or videotape these demonstrations so they can be carefully studied.
3. Assemble a committee of observers to watch the demonstrations and/or study the videotapes. Select the observers for their relevant expertise (for example, physicists appropriately studied firewalkers, and magicians and photographic experts examined Ted Serios, the "thoughtographer").
4. Draw up ground rules for the test in the form of a written agreement.
5. As part of the agreement, have the claimant state just what paranormal abilities or powers will be demonstrated and clearly specify what will constitute a successful or unsuccessful demonstration. Especially, the claimant must clearly agree to what will constitute proof that he or she does *not* possess the alleged powers, to preclude after-the-fact rationalizations for failure.
6. Emphasize in the agreement that only what has been specified therein can be considered as part of the test.
7. Have the claimant acknowledge in the agreement that all the conditions for the demonstration or test are satisfactory.

8. Also have the claimant certify that he or she has not employed any trickery or deception in the past and will not do so during the demonstration.
9. Incorporate legal protections into the agreement: Have the claimant agree to allow all data (including videotapes, etc.) to be used subsequently in whatever way(s) the investigator(s) may choose and to surrender all rights to legal action (as for personal injury, emotional damage, financial loss, etc.) against the investigator(s).
10. Incorporate into the agreement such other protocols as seem wise, and have the document reviewed by the observers and other knowledgeable persons.
11. Have the claimant sign the agreement before a notary public.

When Randi notes in his statement (1982a, p. 253) that "specific rules will be formulated for each individual claimant," he acknowledges the great variety of paranormal claims that may be encountered and the way they may be demonstrated. To take just one example, consider the case of winsome young Suzie Cottrell, who performed alleged psychic feats using a deck of playing cards. Among other demonstrations, she could apparently predict, in writing, what card someone would select from a deck that was spread out, face down, on the table. She had performed this feat on "The Tonight Show," and her father had subsequently contacted CSICOP to request that she be tested. As Randi explains the protocol:

> After some negotiations, the date of March 16, 1978, was agreed upon, and Paul Kurtz, Chairman of the CSICOP, gave Martin Gardner and me responsibility for designing and controlling the procedure. We prepared a testing area by installing a videotape camera and outlining with white tape the exact area to be covered by the camera. This was to be the limited test area in which all action had to take place. Should Suzie's hands or any of the cards wander out of the test area, the experiment was to stop immediately and return to "ground zero," all materials being confiscated and held for examination. We had a good number of decks of cards, all labeled and fresh. And, most important of all, we were going into the fray with a definitive statement that had been read and understood and agreed to by Suzie Cottrell and her group. (p. 256)

Letting Cottrell perform her feat once without controls and without the video recorder running (although with another one recording every action!), the magicians learned her trick: In handling the deck, she glimpsed the top card, then employed a standard magician's "force" to ensure that it was the one selected. However, when the serious testing began, Randi insisted on cutting the cards just before they were spread, and as a result

Cottrell failed to score. (She also failed several other tests arranged by the committee.)

Although different protocols would be warranted for different situations, the Cottrell case provides an instructive example. Other approaches will be evident from the investigations that are summarized throughout this chapter. As always, experience, good judgment, innovative thinking, and a desire for the truth are assets that will stand the investigator in good stead in investigating those who claim to have paranormal powers.

6

Investigating Things in the Sky
and Alleged Abductions

If you assumed that UFOs, flying saucers, and the like are a modern invention you are badly mistaken. Since the beginning of time men have reported seeing strange things in the sky. UFOs definitely did not begin on the 24th of June 1947 when thirty-two-year-old businessman Kenneth Arnold, piloting his private plane, saw what he described as a chain of nine "saucer-like" objects flying from north to south near Mt. Rainier in Washington State. Throughout the ages records have clearly shown that strange objects in the skies have intrigued and frightened man since prehistoric times.

The ancient Sanskrit epics—*The Ramayana* and the *Mahahbarata*—describe *Vimanas* or aerial chariots and provide descriptions of air-battles that sound like modern nuclear weapons or laser beams: "flowing flashes which sped from a circled bow." Even in the Christian religion the Old Testament contains a number of ambiguous but highly evocative descriptions of aerial phenomena such as "the pillar of fire" in Exodus, the spectacular visions of Ezekiel, and the "flying scroll" in Zechariah. If we are confused today by strange things in the sky, what do you think the ancients were with their primitive science and their superstitions? Even something as simple as rain was a miraculous occurrence to them. They believed there were great bodies of water in the sky held back by a crystal globe with many windows. A rainstorm was, obviously, a leaky window. The great flood was, of course, due to someone "opening the windows of heaven." Rainbows were also miracles—God's promise to man of beneficence. Moses' burning bush or St. Elmo's fire was also miraculous. Stories like that of the crossing of the Red Sea we see now as more than likely due to what meterological optics calls an *inferior mirage.* A person in the desert on a hot day will see the sky spread out below him, giving the appearance of a large lake. Walk forward and the blue waters recede, appearing to open up a path of dry land across the receding craters. People coming from behind will seem to be swallowed up and drowned as the water closes over them. Bicycle Lake at Barstow, California is an excellent example of a true biblical "miracle." Jesus, allegedly walking on water, can be similarly explained. We also have good reason to believe that Jacob's Ladder (the biblical one—not the movie) was a corona—a remarkable astronomical formation that occasionally occurs in association with the *aurora borealis.* Electrons and atoms from the sun, when focused by the earth's magnetic field, give the appearance of an enormus ladder or barrel stretching up in the sky toward the magnetic zenith.

As for Ezekiel's fiery wheel, it is an excellent description of a mock sun display, i.e., the well-known solar halo complete with mock suns or sun-dogs, or the well-developed *parhelion.* This spectacular display is caused by the sun's reflection off a collection of ice crystals in the upper atmosphere. The claim that the wheel is actually a spaceship (Blumrich 1974) is a lot less credible than the natural event explanation. The argument that the Earth has been visited from the dawn of history by extraterrestrials is even supported by the biblical statement in Genesis 6: 2 and 4:

> That the sons of God saw the daughters of men and that they were fair and they took them wives of all whom they chose. . . . There were giants in the earth in those days; and also after that when the sons of God came in unto the daughters of men and they bare children to them, the same became mighty men which were of old, men of renown.

Such ideas have, of course, continued unto our own time with arguments by Eric von Däniken, Leslie Desmond, and Lepoer Trench that the earth is, indeed, populated by beings from the heavens.

Since Roman times writers have talked about the *prodigia,* a bow-shaped object often seen in a clear sky over the Temple of Saturn in Rome in 173 B.C.E. In the fifteenth century Pierre Della Francesca (1402–1492) of Arezzo, Italy, painted a number of religious frescoes that included lenticular clouds that look remarkably like flying saucers. During the sixteenth and seventeenth centuries there was great religious and political upheaval in Europe. Aerial phenomena were commonly reported and were always seen as divine warnings. In the years 1561 and 1566 in Basel and Nuremberg, woodcuts were carved containing flying globes and crosses, closely resembling modern reports of UFO sightings.

In a book published in London by William Fulke in 1640, there are long descriptions of strange things seen in the skies: flying dragons or "firedrakes" and reports of the devil. Fulke plays down and debunks all of these things. Particularly interesting is Fulke's discussion of sun dogs or mock suns referred to earlier. Fulke also described in detail the fire drakes or "flying clouds of smoke in which the devil flew." Fulke reported that many people swore they saw the devil flying up and down over the Thames, a remarkable UFO report made before 1600. Lions, ships, and armies were also reported as having been seen in the skies, and since many of the reports occurred in the daytime over water, this suggests some of them may have been due to atmospheric conditions and a type of mirage known as a *Fata Morgana*—a type of mirage in which astigmatic vertical magnification of distant objects occurs. Since this type of mirage was frequently seen across the Straits of Messina in Italy and gets its name from Morgan Le Fay—the fairy sister of King Arthur—and an enchantress whose visions of cities and harbors lured sailors to their doom—a physical source for the reports is available. It is important to note that double images of low altitude stars and planets have been the source of many UFO reports in our own time.

In 1885 in the French journal *L'Astronomie* there appeared what has been called the first photograph of a UFO, taken on August 12, 1883, at the Zacatecas Observatory in Mexico by one José Bonilla. He was observing sunspots at the time when he saw over three hundred strange dark objects crossing the solar disc, of which, with the aid of wet photographic plates at 1/100th of a second, he was able to take several pictures, Subsequently, it has been determined that what Bonilla saw were flocks of high flying geese. However, it wasn't until 1878 that there appeared what was, perhaps, the first mention of the term "saucer" in connection with an aerial object. This year it seems that one farmer, John Martin of Dallas, Texas, describing something he saw in the sky to a local reporter from the *Denison Texas Daily News,* told the reporter that the large orange object he saw while he was out hunting looked to be "about the size and shape of a large saucer" when it was directly overhead.

Sightings of things in the sky reached their peak a few years later. From November 1896 until the middle of 1897 thousands of people throughout the United States reported that they had seen the lights of an airship in the sky. In 1884 it was reported that four cowboys witnessed the crash of a cylindrical object in Nebraska. They allegedly found pieces of machinery and cog wheels that were glowing with heat. On April 17, 1897 an airship was seen to pass over the small Texas town of Aurora. It was traveling slowly and losing altitude, eventually crashing into a windmill. When Aurora's citizens inspected the crash site, they found the craft was composed of an unknown metal resembling silver and aluminum. A paper was also found containing hieroglyphics, and the pilot, according to Army signal officers, was identified as a Martian! Supposedly, the body was buried in the Aurora cemetery. Within the next few years, similar stories cropped up all across the country. Weird and fantastic stories also surrounded the sightings. One such case supposedly involved 135,000 witnesses at St. Paul, Minnesota, on April 13, 1897. At 9:04 A.M. a cigar-shaped object with huge wings landed on the courthouse square. After a few minutes the crowd of onlookers saw a hidden door open in the silver-coated craft and three beings stepped out. Although these creatures shared some human physical characteristics, there was no separation between the nose and mouth and they had large gills on both sides of their heads with huge fins sticking out of their backs. Their eyes looked like boiled eggs, their hands were claws, and they had suckers on their feet that prevented them from slipping. Such stories were, of course, never corroborated and the mysterious force that made people see airships then is the same one that makes us see UFOs today. Looking into the claims of the airships, however, quickly uncovered the fact that the fantastic stories were nothing more than journalistic hoaxes designed to attract publicity and increase newspaper sales.

The United States was not alone in its airship sightings. All across England and Europe similar sightings took place shortly before World War I. After the war, in the 1920s, 1930s, and 1940s came the age of the "dime novel" and the science-fiction pulp magazines, which offered the public science fiction, sexual titillation, and occasionally some tips on mechanical and electrical matters.

Influenced by the work of Jules Verne (1829–1905), H. G. Wells (1866–1946), and Edgar Rice Burroughs (1875–1950), in 1929 Hugo Gernsback created a pulp magazine called *Amazing Stories,* but by 1938 its huge circulation had dwindled to some twenty-five thousand copies and it was bought up by the Ziff-Davis Publishing Company of Chicago. Ziff appointed Ray Palmer, only twenty-eight years old at the time, as editor. Palmer, a science-fiction fan since childhood, had a vivid imagination and was not averse to creating controversy by writing under several pseudonyms—even in his own magazine. In the early 1940s *Amazing Stories* received a long letter—supposedly genuine—from a Richard Shaver on demonic troglodytes called Deros, upon whose heads a host of human misfortunes could be laid. By 1946 the "Shaver Mystery" had boosted sales of the magazine to 250,000 copies and Palmer had found his career and his market. Palmer then took off with lots of bug-eyed monster (BEM) stories and, when readers wrote in with their personal sightings of BEMs and DEROS, Palmer had drawings made and published them in the magazine. It was not unusual for odd, circular-shaped spaceships to decorate the covers.

Possibly no one in the world was more surprised than Ray Palmer by Kenneth Arnold's 1947 story, which triggered the modern error and gave the phenomenon the popular name of "flying saucers." Amazingly, *Palmer's fiction had now become reality!* Palmer was so impressed with all that was going on that he put out his own magazine in 1948 called *Fate* and named Curtis Fuller as its first editor. It has carried UFO stories ever since. The first issue of *Fate,* in fact, ran Arnold's sighting of the previous year and ran on its cover an exaggerated picture of one of the saucers. In 1952 the story was published in book form as *The Coming of the Saucers* and was jointly written by Arnold and Palmer. Of course, no mention was made of the possibility that what Arnold saw was nothing more than mirages due to a temperature inversion. Arnold reported that the air at his flying height of 9,500 feet was clear and still—characteristic of such an inversion. Air Force files also pointed out inconsistencies in Arnold's estimates of the probable sizes and distances of the objects, indicating that they were probably much closer to him and slower moving than he proposed. One must never let a few little facts, however so accurate, get in the way of a really good story.

The Arnold and Palmer book was not as popular as Major Donald Keyhoe's *Flying Saucers Are Real,* which was published in 1950 and, along with numerous other popular publications, set off a rave of sightings all across the nation. In the October 1947 issue of *Amazing,* Palmer wrote in an editorial:

> . . . a part of the now world famous Shaver Mystery has now been proved! On 25 June (and subsequent confirmation included earlier dates) mysterious supersonic vessels, either spaceships or ships from caves, were sighted in this country! A summation of facts proves that these ships were not, nor can be, attributed to any civilization now on the face of the Earth. (p. 2)

It is important to note that the arrival of the saucers did not surprise everyone. Readers of *Amazing* had already heard about them earlier when Palmer wrote about the European series of Ghost Rockets and phantom aircraft sightings in the 1930s and early 1940s. In the late fall of 1933 Scandinavians began to see strange lights in the sky, and in 1934 these sights and sounds became strange aircraft and rockets that were chased by the Swedish, Finnish, and Norwegian air forces. During the winter of 1933–34 a total of 487 cases were reported. Later investigation showed that misinterpretation of stars, planets, and other earthly lights provided the explanation for the bulk of the reports—especially during what was called the "psychosis periods"—in 1933–34 and 1936–37, when there was an abnormally high number of reports. Most were identified as lawful civilian or military aircraft and misinterpretations of natural things, but most disturbing were reports of strange cigar-shaped and rocket-like objects haunting the skies of Sweden from 1939—the first sighting—through 1946, when they reached a peak. In 1946 the Swedish Defense Staff received over two hundred reports of cigar-shaped objects—some with wings—many of which were seen in broad daylight. In fact, it seems that someone had developed "cruise missiles" long before their time. One cannot but recollect that the sightings came during the period when the German rocket scientists were developing their V1s and V2s and were trying their best to destroy England from their missile bases on the coast of the North Sea.

Following the Arnold publicity, there was an even more sensational case in January 1948 in which it appeared that the UFOs were definitely hostile. Air Force Captain Thomas Mantell was killed while climbing to intercept a high-flying UFO reported by ground control at Godman Field, Fort Knox, Kentucky. The careful Air Force investigation that followed concluded that Mantell was pursuing a Navy Skyhook balloon released that morning in the area. These balloons fly at altitudes of 60,000 feet or more, well above the operating height of Mantell's plane, which was without oxygen equipment. Despite the Air Force's conclusion that Mantell blacked out from oxygen deprivation during his climb and that the out-of-control plane spiraled to the ground, UFOlogists spread the word that weapon beams from the giant UFO "shot Mantell down" when he got too close. Interestingly enough, this case did bring the CIA into the UFO field because they were developing the Skyhook for photoreconnaissance of the Soviet Union and were worried not only that their secret would get out, but that some UFO cases might be sightings of Soviet balloons sent to spy on us. All such cases and the science-fiction setting, plus the U.S. developing space program had nearly every pair of eyes in the nation staring up at the heavens and set the stage for the gigantic UFO wave of the 1950s.

In the 1950s both UFO sightings and the publicity attending them escalated dramatically. In 1950 Frank Scully published a sensational book called *Behind the Flying Saucers* in which he alleged that a flying saucer had crashed on a remote desert plateau to the east of Aztec, New Mexico. The saucer, Scully claimed, was ninety-nine feet in diameter and contained the bodies of sixteen dead aliens. Scully hadn't seen it himself but was relying on stories he was told. Two years later the story was discounted as a hoax. A similar story was also reported concerning a crashed saucer seventy-five miles northwest of Roswell, New Mexico. The crash supposedly took place in July of 1947 and set off a chain of events and arguments that continues to this day. That something crashed is indisputable—but the argument is over exactly what it was. Skeptics and the Air Force say it was a balloon and offer balsa wood, foil, threads, paper, and so forth as material proof. Believers argue that there is a conspiracy afoot and that the Air Force is hiding evidence that the true residue is unearthly.

Under mounting public pressure to explain the apparent invasion of our domestic airspace, the U.S. Air Force started a series of investigations in 1948 with Project Sign. This was followed in 1949 by Project Grudge, and in 1952 they started the famous Project Blue Book, which was ended in 1969. To keep themselves honest, the Air Force also contracted with the Rand Corporation for an independent study of UFOs. The major reason for Blue Book was that in 1952 there were a total of 1,501 official sightings and reports. Headed by Captain Edward J. Ruppelt, top people of the Air Defense Command were briefed and their help was enlisted to use the nation's air defense system to detect the UFO invaders.

One series of sightings in particular captured Ruppelt's attention. Known as the Lubbock Texas lights, over a two-week period in August and September of 1951 people in the town saw strange lights in the skies. On August 25 a man and his wife saw a huge wing-shaped UFO with blue lights over Albuquerque. About twenty minutes later a group of three college professors in Lubbock saw a formation of lights sweep over the city at high speed so fast they could not be seen clearly. An hour later they came back. Local radar picked up a target at 13,000 feet moving at a speed that was nine hundred miles per hour faster than any jet in service. Five days later the lights returned and this time a college student, Carl Hart Jr., managed to capture the lights on 35 mm film, but the images were not exactly like what the professors had seen. When Donald Menzel, a Harvard astrophysicist and trained scientist, examined the pictures, he quickly pointed out that if the lights were moving as fast as claimed, they could not have been captured by Hart's camera. Moreover, Menzel duplicated the pictures in his laboratory and showed they were most likely natural in origin. Later analysis and work led the Air Force to conclude the lights were reflections off of flights of plovers.

In early 1952 *Life* magazine decided to do a definitive article on UFOs, and sought and received Ruppelt's cooperation. Unfortunately, when the *Life* story was published in April 1952, it really caused an uproar and dismayed Ruppelt. *Life* concluded that the UFOs were artificial devices created somewhere by intelligent beings and they cited Walter Reidel, the German rocket scientist, who affirmed that they were, indeed, extraterrestrial. The Air Force remained noncommittal. Unfortunately, following the *Life* story the monthly level of UFO sightings went from the normal ten to twenty per month to a total of ninety-nine reports in April alone and a total of one hundred and forty-nine in June. They came from every part of the nation and the number kept rising. In July there were five hundred and thirty-six—three times the June figure. On July 28 alone there were fifty formal reports. The wave began to subside thankfully in August with only three hundred and twenty-six sightings. The reports tailed off to approximately fifty per month for the rest of the year, when people finally went indoors.

Captain Ruppelt and Blue Book were, of course, overwhelmed. During the 1952 wave Ruppelt counted no fewer than sixteen thousand newspaper items about UFOs in one six-month period. As soon as things would start to calm down, some sensational new report would show up in the headlines and the reports of sightings would pour in once more. There can be no doubt whatsoever that reports of strange sights in the sky, when communicated in a sensational fashion by the media, causes every reader, listener, and watcher the next time they are out of doors to look up at the sky and, because of the power of suggestion, to begin to see things and to report them. One-time events in the sky are hard to confirm. It is much easier to learn from repeatable experiments in the lab than from sporadic views of celestial phenomena—which is one reason why less occult lore accumulates around a science like mechanical engineering than around astronomy. The first step in generating an eye-witness report is perception—the observor's intake of sensory stimuli. The problem is that this perception must be converted in the observor's brain into a conception—a step which involves subjective factors such as the association the person may make between the objects and concepts current in the culture. For example, witnesses almost invariably conceive meteors in terms of aircraft distances. They will report, "It landed just behind the barn," when, in fact, the meteor was hundreds of miles away. In reporting—the third step—the conceptions are transmitted to others. Through most of history this process was by word of mouth with second-hand reports and hearsay blending into the long-lived oral traditions that usually incorporated a lot of extraneous material, such as myths. Even today it is difficult to communicate conceptions accurately via words alone.

There is a classic UFO anecdote about a man early one winter morning reporting a large orange object on the ground sporting flashing red lights, with rows of lighted windows along the sides, and a number of small creatures inside. When the Sheriff screeched down the road to check it out, he found a school bus! In the context of UFO reports, simple, accurate words can lead many people to the wrong conception.

The quality of the reporting cannot be overemphasized because it does affect the beliefs of millions of people. Many people believe that if it appears in the newspaper or a book, it has to be true. Carl Sagan tells the story of a woman he saw reading a pseudo-astronomy bestseller filled with many factual errors and misquotes from Sagan himself. Sagan asked the woman if she knew the book was mostly nonsense and filled with mistakes. "It couldn't be," she said, "because they wouldn't let him publish it if it were not true." Not so. Books are published because they will sell and there is no other reason. Not only are the nonfiction shelves of most book stores filled with fantasies, but most of the UFO literature is pseudoscience. As for any and all of the UFO photographs, they are either (1) fakes or (2) photographs of natural phenomena. They are, indeed, easy to fake and most any professional photographer can tell you at least five or six ways to do it so that it will fool most any expert. For several years *Science Digest* magazine ran an annual contest for the best UFO fake pictures of the year. Some of the winners were held by many of the UFOlogists to be authentic.

A sociological fad-like element is shown by veritable waves of UFO reports following close on the heels of any well-publicized space event, such as the first Sputnik, the first photos from Mars, the first human in orbit, and the moon launch. Hoaxes also tend to show up in a similar fashion as they did within weeks after the first saucer report in 1947. Figure 6-1 shows examples of the sudden increases in the numbers of UFO reports correlated with the Sputnik launch and with the Mariner 4 close-up photos of Mars. Clearly the "waves" of sightings have social and psychological rather than physical causes.

As a primary result of all of the excitement about UFOs in the fifties and the forming of a number of private research groups to independently study the UFO phenomena, such as the Aerial Phenomena Research Organization (APRO), founded in Sturgeon Bay, Wisconsin, by Coral and Jim Lorenzen, and the National Investigations Committee For Aerial Phenomena (NICAP), headed by Donald Keyhoe during the 1960s, the UFO myth and the *extraterrestrial hypothesis,* i.e., the idea that the UFOs were extraterrestrial spaceships piloted by intelligent aliens, continued to grow and flourish. Because of the fact that so many people felt the government— particularly the CIA and the Air Force—was ignoring and debunking what they perceived to be a definite threat to our security and well-being, the Air Force decided to end the matter once and for all by bringing in the big guns of science to study the problem in depth. Therefore, in 1966 the Air Force commissioned the University of Colorado to conduct a study of the problem. The study was carried out under the direction of Dr. Edward U. Condon. Over a two-year period hundreds of cases were investigated and every conceivable aspect of the problem was looked at by a wide range of experts in all of the pertinent fields of science having a bearing on the problem, i.e., experts in radar, plasma physics, mirages, photographic

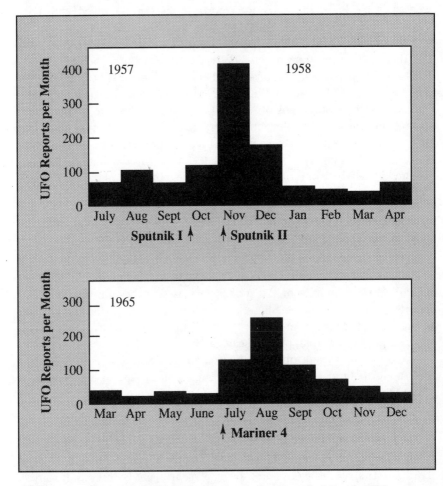

Figure 6–1 Examples of sudden increase in the number of UFO reports correlated with social factors such as the first satellite launches (top) and the first close-up photos of Mars (bottom). This correlation suggests that "waves" of sightings, discussed in many popular books, have social rather than physical causes. (From William K. Hartman, *Astronomy: The Cosmic Journey,* Belmont, Calif.: Wadsworth Publishing Co., 1978.)

analysis, and problems of perception. The report concludes that there is no evidence to justify a belief that extraterrestrial visitors have penetrated our skies and not enough evidence to warrant any further scientific investigation. This, as Condon himself anticipated, did not gladden the hearts of the UFOlogists, who argued vehemently that the study was biased and faulty from the outset. In an attempt to offset the storm of protest and the charge that the Condon report was a "whitewash," the Air Force had the National Academy of Science appoint a special panel to examine the report in detail, and to judge the adequacy of the methodology and procedures used in reaching their conclusions. The chair of this panel was was Dr. Gerald M. Clemence of Yale University and the former scientific director of the Naval Observatory. The rest of the panel consisted of leading specialists in fields relevant to the UFO problem: astronomy, atmospheric physics, meteorology, and psychology, The Academy's conclusion was unanimous and the Condon report was given straight "As," so to speak, in every aspect. In the words of the panel:

> We are unanimous in the opinion that this has been a very creditable effort to apply objectively the relevant techniques of science to the solution of the UFO problem. The report recognizes that there remain UFO sightings that are not easily explained. The report does suggest, however, so many reasonable and possible directions in which an explanation may eventually be found, that there seems to be no reason to attribute them to an extraterrestrial source without evidence that is much more convincing. The report also shows how difficult it is to apply scientific methods to the occasional transient sightings with any chance of success. While further study of particular aspects of the topic (e.g., atmospheric phenomena) may be useful, a study of UFOs in general is not a promising way to expand scientific understanding of the phenomena. On the basis of present knowledge the least likely explanation of UFOs is the hypothesis of extraterrestrial visitations by intelligent beings. (Condon 1969, viii)

As expected, neither did the panel's conclusions set well with the true UFO believers and at the time the reports were released they did everything in their power to discredit them, and they have done so ever since. The best way to appreciate what the report does to the myth of the UFOs is to read it in its entirety. It was published under the title *Final Report of the Scientific Study of Unidentified Flying Objects,* Edward U. Condon, Scientific Director, Daniel S. Gillmor, Editor, with an introduction by Walter Sullivan (Bantam Books, 1969).

Project Blue Book also was closed in 1969 and it, too, reached the same conclusion: that the so-called saucers presented no threat to national security, that the reports were most probably misinterpretations or fabrications, and that there was no evidence that saucers were extraterrestrial vehicles. Unfortunately, soon after Blue Book's reports were declassified, Brad Steiger, a UFOlogical psi-cophant, seized upon the reports and issued his own edited version in 1976 under the title *Project Blue Book* (Ballantine Books, 1976), in which he does all in his power to twist the conclusions to now support the ETP hypothesis! What is most revealing about the official documents—despite the claims made by Keyhoe and others during the 1950s and 1960s—is the fact that the Air Force knew no more than anyone else. As for the claims of "cover up," the Robertson Panel report, published in 1953, was also declassified and this CIA document also supports the fact that the Air Force had nothing to hide. Another interesting aspect of the Robertson report was the recommendation that the federal government launch a program to strip the UFOs of their mystery and to inform and educate the public in this regard.

Needless to say, this was not done. Instead, we saw a rapid increase in the popularity of science-fiction books, TV shows, and films exploiting the ET hypothesis. One individual having the most impact upon and influence in keeping the ET hypothesis alive was Dr. J. Allen Hynek, one of the nation's foremost astronomers who was one of the Air Force's consultants on Project Blue Book for nearly twenty years. Hynek at first started out as a debunker of UFOs, taking great pleasure in cracking what seemed to be puzzling cases. He was also an arch enemy of all those flying saucer groups and enthusiasts who during the 1950s so dearly wanted the UFOs to be interplanetary. His transformation was gradual, however, and by the late 1960s it was complete. According to Hynek, although the Condon report gave the *coup de grace* to the UFO era, "The UFOs, however, apparently did not read the Condon Report." Not only did the reports of sightings continue, but in the fall of 1973 a major wave of reports occurred and they continued throughout the 1970s and even into the 1980s. In 1972 Hynek published his first book, *The UFO Experience: A Scientific Inquiry.* In addition to listing and discussing a number of UFO case reports, he continued to defy normal explanation and set forth his famous classification system for UFO encounters of the First, Second, and Third kinds. The First is an encounter in which the observor reports a close-at-hand experience without tangible physical effects. The Second is an encounter in which measurable physical effects on the land and on animate and inanimate objects is reported. The Third is an encounter in which animated entities—often called humanoids, occupants, or UFOnauts—are reported. Hynek also had a fourth category, the "contactee" category, which also included individuals who claimed to have been abducted or who were invited aboard the spaceship and taken for a trip. Shortly after moving to Northwestern University, Hynek established the Center for UFO Studies and became its first Scientific Director. In 1977 Hynek published another book, *The Hynek UFO Report* (Dell, 1977), and in this volume confesses there is:

> . . . little doubt that an "intelligence" of some sort is operating. But what kind and there from?
>
> We must be extremely careful not to be too self-centered about this question. It is only too natural for us to think that all intelligence must necessarily be like our own—that visitors, if these they be, must think and act as we do. Indeed there are people in other nations whose actions we sometimes find difficult to understand; why, then, presume that the intelligence that appears to manifest itself in one way or another through the UFO phenomenon must be akin to ours? Or why assume that it necessarily operates under the conditions we are accustomed to? And, whence this intelligence? Does it really hail from afar, or is it perhaps much closer to us than popularly supposed? Is it meta-terrestrial rather than extraterrestrial? Or, going even further afield, is it in some way, as the psychologist Jung held, a strange manifestation of the human psyche? (pp. 8–9)

Clearly, Hynek has decided in favor of a mystery and some sort of alien intelligence at work. This possibility inspired Steven Spielberg, who borrowed the title of his spectacular film *Close Encounters of the Third Kind* from Hynek's book. After seeing the film, Hynek stated, "Spielberg has succeeded in capturing on film the essence of the UFO enigma, the mounting evidence that intelligence other than our own not only exists, but, in a manner peculiarly its own, is making itself known to the human race" (p. 9). Those who have seen the Spielberg film (and millions have) do not have to be told that the aliens in this film came from outer space. Hynek goes on to state that we study UFO *reports,* not UFOs, and that these reports are made by human beings who are often mistaken about what they observe. He proceeds, however, to argue that while the witnesses he interviewed *could* have been lying, *could* have been insane, or *could* have been hallucinating, he doesn't think so because their standing in the community, their lack of motive for perpetrating a hoax, their own puzzlement about the events, and their reluctance to speak of their experience all lend a subjective reality to their reports. Hynek is, however, an astronomer, not a psychologist, and the fact that there are other possible explanations for these reports—other psychological explanations he was unaware of—were never discussed. These reports are indeed human reports and thus subject to error, and are one and all highly suspect. Speculation with regard to alien visitors reached an all-time high in the 1970s. In 1974 a wave of reports appeared on radio and TV shows across the USA that the Air Force was harboring a captured UFO and its alien crew at Wright-Patterson

Air Force base in Dayton, Ohio. The broadcasts stated that President Gerald Ford would shortly make an announcement of this fact—sometime within the next two weeks. This announcement has, of course, yet to be made. The UFOlogists, as would be expected, insisted there was a conspiracy afoot and the entire Federal apparatus was engaged in a gigantic cover-up. Why? Well, because the public would panic, of course. Just like they did during the famous Orson Welles broadcast of the *War of the Worlds* drama. To suggest otherwise to the UFOlogists is to bring down their wrathful disdain.

We have every reason to believe that all such UFO flaps would never become "flaps" in the first place if they were not aided and abetted by the media. A dramatic illustration of this was shown in the late 1960s. In a high school sociology class in Westgate, Iowa, the students carried out an experiment involving a fake UFO incident to see what effects it would have on the public. On the night of the supposed "sighting," three students ig-nited gasoline in a pasture, burning a circular area about ten feet in diameter —the purported landing site of the UFO. They also added four smaller circles for the landing gear. No one except the nearest neighbor to the pas-ture knew of the plot. The following morning the students activated the plot by reporting the "sighting" to fellow students and the local radio station. Before 9:00 A.M. one of the students had been interviewed by a reporter from the radio station. By 10:00 A.M. a UFO expert had arrived at the school and public reaction escalated rapidly. Within a few hours the burned patch gained statewide and, finally, nationwide attention. The newspaper argued that the photos of the burned patch *proved* something *really did land!* Moreover, the media embellished the story, adding "a ball of reddish-orange flame" and "an oblong object reddish-orange at one end and red on the other." The mere fact of media coverage convinced many people that the UFO incident was true. The students also discovered that repeti-tion alone tends to make things believable. One high school girl in the class who wasn't in on the hoax didn't believe it at first, but after hearing report after report she finally insisted it was true. What the students learned was that: *one phone call and a burned patch of grass could trigger a national incident.* Of course, this is only possible when a populace has already been primed and their expectancies are high. From this little experiment it seems crystal clear that one can use the media for one's own purposes. After having learned a good lesson about the irresponsibility of the media and human suggestibility, the students then went to the newspaper and confessed that it was a hoax. Incredibly, many observers in nearby surrounding towns stated that they, too, had seen the UFO in the sky on the night in question. The students' final written report concluded:

1. Emotions increase suggestibility. (psychologically true)
2. Emotions tend to ruin one's perspective. (also psychologically true)
3. Interactions with other people fan emotions. (also psychologically true)
4. The media give reality to unreality. (True)
5. People tend to blame what they distrust, and believe what they fear. (psychologically true)
6. The media are not always reliable. (True)
7. The public can be rather easily manipulated. (True)
8. People seek excitement. (True)
9. Excitement grows with the number of people who are involved. (True)
10. People are not very well prepared for surprises. (True)

The media in general and TV in particular have been in relation to the UFO question enormously irresponsible. For every hundred reports lending support to the ET hypothesis, we are fortunate, indeed, if there is even *one* report discounting the UFO sighting and stating that it was actually a natural phenomenon, e.g., a meteorite, a bolide, or a manmade object such as a satellite, a weather balloon, a high altitude rocket test, etc. You see, UFOs from outer space are news; but UFOs that are merely searchlights are not.

Following the success of the prime-time series on UFOs and Spielberg's *Close Encounters* film, a number of lesser films kept the public interest and belief in alien visitations alive and kicking all through the 1970s and into the 1990s. Particularly effective in doing so was the second Spielberg film *ET* with its delightful and charming alien visitor, and three other films with not-so-charming aliens, starring Sigourney Weaver: *Alien, Aliens,* and *Alien³*. In the 1980s many movie makers and science-fictioneers went so far as to propose that we would soon see a vast influx of aliens so very much like ourselves that they would quickly be assimilated. This possibility cropped up in the movie and TV series titled *Alien Nation*. One could assume that any myth that year after year was unable to find one concrete bit of factual evidence to support it would quickly die from lack of sustenance. As Ian Ridpath noted, "Most scientists would draw their own conclusions from such an abject lack of results, but they do not have the indefatigable optimism of committed UFOlogists for whom the Perfect Case, like the Second Coming, is an article of faith." Just because not once in the last forty-four years has any alien spaceship landed on the White House lawn (or any other lawn for that matter) and its crew request to see our leader, should any true believer despair. They have something even better to sustain them: case after case of human-alien contact and alien abductions. These have managed to keep the faith alive; for as Ridpath and many others have noted, religion and UFOs have much in common and, for the masses, the basic appeal of UFOlogy is that it is a belief system rather than an area of scientific research and investigation.

To be adequately informed about the UFO phenomenon there are a number of books that must be read. Chronologically, by author, they are: Donald H. Menzel's *Flying Saucers* (Harvard University Press, 1953), and Menzel and Lyle G. Boyd's *The World of Flying Saucers* (Doubleday, 1963); and Menzel and Ernest H. Taves, *The UFO Enigma* (Doubleday, 1977); Philip J. Klass's *UFOs Explained* (Random House, 1974), *UFOs: The Public Deceived* (Prometheus Books, 1980), and *UFO Abductions: A Dangerous Game* (Prometheus Books, 1988); Robert Sheaffer's *The UFO Verdict: Examining the Evidence* (Prometheus Books, 1981); Allan Hendry's *The UFO Handbook* (Doubleday, 1979); Douglas Curran's *In Advance of the Landing: Folk Concepts of Outer Space* (Abbeville Press, 1985), and *Phenomenon: Forty Years of Flying Saucers,* edited by John Spencer and Hilary Evans (Avon Books, 1989). Investigators should also be familiar with some of the major UFO research organizations still active. Particularly important are: The J. Allen Hynek Center for UFO Studies (CUFOS), 1955 John's Drive, Glenview, Illinois 60025; The Mutual UFO Network (MUFON), 1034 Oldtowne Road, Seguin, Texas 78155; The Institute for UFO Contactee Studies, 1425 Steele Street, Laramie, Wyoming 82070; The New York Center for UFO Research (NYCUFOR), 134 West Houston St., Suite 1, New York, New York 10012; The British UFO Research Association (BUFORA), 16 Southway, Burgess Hill, Sussex, RH15 9ST, England; and the International Committee for UFO Research (ICUR), which can be reached at the BUFORA address.

There are also a number of magazines, journals, and newsletters concerned with the UFO phenomena worthy of serious consideration, The most noteworthy are the *IUR: The International UFO Reporter,* published bi-monthly at $25 per year (2457 West Peterson Avenue, Chicago, Illinois 60659) by CUFOS. The Hynek Center also publishes the *Journal of UFO Studies,* which is published annually at $15 per issue. The *MUFON UFO Journal* is published monthly and is included in the annual MUFON membership dues of $25 a year. Other publications include: *Caveat Emptor,* published quarterly by Cross-Country Communications, P.O. Box 4533, Metuchen, New Jersey 08840-4533 at $15 per year; *UFO Magazine,* 1800 S. Robertson Blvd., Los Angeles, California 90035, published bi-monthly at $15 per year; *Quest: The Journal of UFO Investigation,* 106 Lady Ann Road, Soothill, Batley, England, published bi-monthly at $25 per year; *Skeptics UFO Newsletter (SUN)* published by Philip J. Klass, 404 "N" Street SW, Washington, D.C. 20024 on a bi-monthly basis at $15 per year;

and *Saucer Smear,* published by James W. Moseley, P.O. Box 1709, Key West, Florida 33041 nearly every month. Although Moseley does not charge for his newsletter, contributions are recommended if one wishes to recieve copies regularly.

Alien Contactees and Abductions

Like the UFOs, tales of contact with extraterrestrials and claims of visits to the planets and stars and other worlds are, in no way, a modern invention. The Swedish mystic Swedenborg (1688–1772) claimed to have visited the various planets and described the conditions there. People on Mars were the best since they were God-fearing. There were two types of Venusians: the gentle souls and the cruel ones, and both are of gigantic stature. The Moon people, however, are quite small—like children—but they have voices like thunder. Another planetary traveller was one Fraulein Romer who, in 1813, went to the moon. Another early traveller, Victorien Sardou, went to Jupiter. In 1894 the famous Helene Smith, nee Catherine Elaine Muller, joined a spiritualist group in 1891, practiced typtology (table tipping), adopted Victor Hugo as her spirit guide before adopting another guide named Leopold, and proceeded to go into trances. While in her trances, she visited the planet Mars in 1894, described the flora and fauna, saw cars, houses, and other civilized artifacts, and even brought back the Martian language. The famous psychologist Flournoy, who described Helene's trips in his book *From India to the Planet Mars* (University Books, 1963), noted that her Martian language was syntactically like French. Then in 1895, one Mrs. Smead, nee Mrs. Willis M. Cleaveland, visited both Mars and Jupiter. According to Mrs. Smead, Jupiter was very nice because it was "babies heaven." We have every reason to believe that the astronomical work carried out by Schiaparelli and Percival Lowell, who were studying the planet Mars at the time, served as the source of inspiration for the ladies. Mars was a very popular planet for the mediums of the time. Then in 1916, one Eva Harrison introduced planetary visitors from Orion to her audiences, but to those listening to their speech it was apparent they came from places considerably closer.

As for abductions, these, too, are as old as the hills. The theme of the fair maiden abducted by a flying dragon to be rescued by the brave knight is the stuff of legends. Being the kidnapped victim of the little folk is also part of the fairy tale lore of nearly every nation. Riding on the witch's broom or being carted off by fairies is also common coin in the folk tales of many different peoples. Little wonder that we would encounter similar tales in our own time.

The ink on the UFO story was hardly dry before an uneducated, erstwhile evangelist named George Adamski (1891–1965) published a book, coauthored with the English writer Desmond Leslie, titled *Flying Saucers Have Landed* (British Book Center, 1952). According to Adamski, he got into the saucer business because he wasn't making as much money in the religious trade. Adamski toured the country peddling his book and lecturing about his trips to Venus, Mars, and Saturn. We were fortunate in attending one of his lectures in Louisville, Kentucky, during which he talked about walking across the surface of Venus. During the question period, we asked him if his feet had healed. "What do you mean?" he asked. "Well, since the surface temperature of Venus is somewhere close to 480 degrees Fahrenheit, your feet must have been badly burned." "Don't be ridiculous," he countered. "I'm not, you are!" was our conversation-ending response. Adamski wrote a second book, *Inside the Space Ships* (Abelard-Schuman 1955), with further tales of his trips to Jupiter, Saturn, and points elsewhere.

The year 1954 also saw the publication of Truman Bethrun's *Aboard a Flying Saucer* and Daniel Fry's *White Sands Incident*. According to the former, he was aroused one night while laying asphalt in the California desert by a three hundred-foot diameter UFO with small, olive-skinned men and a beautiful female captain. It seems they came from Clarion— a planet perpetually hidden behind our moon. While working at White Sands Proving Ground in New Mexico, Fry saw a UFO land. When he went over to it, he met an ET named A-Lan who invited Fry aboard and flew him to New York City and back in less than a half hour. A-Lan asked Fry to write a book warning people about nuclear war. Then, in 1955, Orfeo Angelucci published *Secret of the Saucers,* another fantastic gem in which Orfeo met some "space brothers" and took rides with them around the solar system. On one of these rides, Orfeo met Jesus himself who told Orfeo the incognito ETs were here to help us and start the New Age. On another trip to a distant planet, Orfeo met a beauty named Lyra, who told him he had been a spaceman named Neptune in another life. Howard Menger, a native of Brooklyn, saw his first saucer when he was only eight years old in 1932. Ten years later he began to see them routinely when he was in the army. Then he began to encounter a number of space brothers and sisters who talked with him and told him about other worlds. For a while Menger served as a "go-fer" for the ETs and in return they told him how to build a "free energy motor," which he built and showed off whenever he could find anyone who would listen. The motor, of course, was useless and did nothing except lie there. His various tales are recounted in his 1959 book *From Outer Space to You,* a book you should hardly wait to miss. This collective nonsense succeeded only in persuading most intelligent observors that the entire silly business of UFOs was ridiculous.

Public opinion would probably have stayed that way had it not been for the coming of the abduction cases in the 1960s. In the 1960s more and more people reported not only seeing UFOs, but being taken aboard the spacecraft against their will. Though the details differed, many of the incidents seemed to follow a standard pattern: People are driving along a lonely road; they see a light in the sky; their car stalls; they get out of their car and then they are surprised to find an hour or two has passed of which they have no recollection; in the days that follow they experience nightmares and flashbacks, or extreme anxiety; eventually they begin to recall—on their own or through hypnosis—that during the missing time they were abducted, i.e., taken aboard a spaceship by aliens.

One of the cases following this classical pattern, and perhaps the most famous UFO abduction case in history, was the story of Betty and Barney Hill, which broke in September 1966 and told of a UFO abduction five years earlier. The story first appeared in the October issue of *Look* magazine and was a two-part story by John G. Fuller. Fuller's book *The Interrupted Journey* (Dial Press, 1966), with an introduction by the Hills' hypnotist, Dr. Benjamin Simon, was published soon after. This case was one of the first to gain worldwide publicity and was one of the first to use hypnotic regression. To summarize the case, the Hills had been on a holiday in Canada and started back home in their car to New Hampshire. Nearing the town of Lancaster, Betty noticed a light in the sky and called Barney's attention to it. They stopped the car to look at it through their binoculars. The light proved to be a large spaceship that dropped down to tree level. Barney got out and started toward it, while Betty stayed by the car. Barney then thought he saw people in the vehicle looking at him, so he panicked and ran back to the car and the Hills drove off down the road. When they got home they realized they were about two hours later than they should have been. When Betty told her sister the next day, the sister suggested they might have been "irradiated" by the UFO. Betty then went to the library and checked out Donald Keyhoe's *The Flying Saucer Conspiracy* and read it. Several days later, Betty had a nightmare in which she dreamed she and Barney had been abducted, taken aboard the saucer, and examined. After Betty wrote to a national UFO organization, some interviewers came by to hear her story. When Barney went in to see an M.D. for his ulcers and hypertension, the physician recommended that Barney see a psychiatrist, Dr. Simon, who practiced regressive hypnosis. Betty went with Barney because she, in the meantime, had had several abduction dreams. Under regressive hypnosis, Simon found the Hills had seen something in the sky and had become frightened, but since they disagreed on the details of the alleged abduction, it was not a shared experience. Other discrepancies led Simon to conclude that the abduction tale was only a fantasy. This fact was not emphasized in Fuller's account nor did Fuller mention that more than two years had elapsed between the time of the UFO encounter and the sessions with Dr. Simon. Simon also noted that Betty's account of her nightmares and the account of the abduction were identical. Simon stated that in his opinion Betty's memories of the alleged abduction were based solely upon her dreams. The truth seems to be that her dreams were based on the material supplied by the investigators and the books she read. Some of the inconsistencies in Betty's account were very amusing. For example, Betty reported the aliens didn't understand our concept of time. Yet, as she was leaving the UFO one of the aliens supposedly turned to her and said, "Hey, wait a minute."

The Hill case is important because it contained all of the main components of future abduction claims: missing time, spatial dislocations, physical isolation from the rest of the world during the event, physical exams inside the UFO, and the interest of the aliens in the human reproductive system. All of these show up time and again in cases of alleged abduction revealed through hypnotic regression.

Following the Hill case, reports of UFO abductions began to proliferate. In October 1973, Charles Hickson and Calvin Parker of Pascagoula, Mississippi, reported they had been abducted and taken aboard a flying saucer for a superficial physical examination. According to them, their abductors were short, grey men with wrinkled skin, and rather than walking, they "floated." UFO experts, after interviewing Hickson and Parker, concluded that they were telling the truth. Claims were even made that Hickson successfully passed a lie detector test supporting his abduction story. A more rigorous investigation by Philip J. Klass (1989) discovered that the case was a hoax, that the lie detector test was flawed, and the abduction a "put up job" to make money.

Following the 1975 NBC television prime time movie "The UFO Incident," telling the story of Betty and Barney Hill, numerous other claims of abductions were made, including the notorious Travis Walton case. In this case, a group of woodcutters in one of the Arizona national forests was cutting wood when all of a sudden a hovering UFO "tapped" young Walton, one of the workers, and he disappeared. Five days later, Walton reappeared and told of being taken aboard a spaceship and given a physical exam. This case was unique in that there were multiple witnesses and a report to the authorities that was made while the abductee was still missing. There were, however, some discordant elements. First, the abduction occurred only two weeks after the NBC telecast. Second, Walton's older brother Duane assured everyone Travis wasn't even missing. And third, all of the Waltons were UFO buffs, and Travis had told his mother well before the incident that if he were ever abducted, she shouldn't worry. Subsequent investigation by Klass again uncovered a monetary motive behind this hoax (Klass 1989).

In the spring of 1979, one of the most incredible UFO abduction stories of all time appeared in a book titled *The Andreasson Affair: The Documented Investigation of a Woman's Abduction Aboard a UFO,* authored by Raymond Fowler, an experienced UFOlogist. According to Mrs. Andreasson, a Massachusetts mother of seven, in January 1967, only a few months after the Hill abduction gained international attention, she too was abducted. However, it was not until 1974—seven years later—that she decided to go public and attempt to collect the $100,000 prize offered by the tabloid *National Enquirer* for convincing evidence of extraterrestrial visitors. Despite the story she told under regressive hypnosis administered during fourteen separate sessions by one Harold Edelstein, she never collected the prize money. Even Fowler himself had some doubt about some of the bizarre details of Mrs. Andreasson's story. Since none of the details about the strange beings without heads and her visit to another world could possibly be verified, it seems clear that it is another excellent example of the imaginative skill of someone who is fantasy-prone.

The abduction phenomena reached its peak perhaps during the middle and later 1980s, when a number of claims were reported from all over the planet of numerous UFO contacts and abductions by aliens. In the wake of these claims came another phenomenon: the hypnotic-regression guru, an untrained, nonprofessional, amateur hypnotist specializing in contacting alleged abductees and eliciting strange and spectacular tales of abduction, examination, molestation, impregnation, and surgical implantation.

Typical of such gurus is Budd Hopkins, an artist by profession, who abandoned his trade for the more lucrative work of UFO-abduction propagandist. In his first book on UFO abductions, *Missing Time* (1981), Hopkins describes the adventures of some thirty-seven people from all walks of life who underwent a "missing time" experience and then later, under Hopkins's hypnotic ministrations, reported a classic UFO abduction fantasy quite similar to that of Betty and Barney Hill. Hopkins focuses on nineteen individuals, all of whom had body scars, missing time, and memories of alien faces. He stresses that all of the nineteen are normal, and even raises the possibility that their reports of alien abductions might be delusional. All such doubts as to the validity of such abductions were, however, quickly erased when Hopkins followed up his first book with a second one called *Intruders: The Incredible Visitations at Copley Woods* (1987), in which he discovered the motive behind the abductions! It is, incredibly, that the aliens are carrying out an extraterrestrial genetic experiment in which earthlings are unknowing and unwilling participants!

Nearly all of Hopkins's evidence is gathered from alleged victims who have sought him out in the hope that he can explain or explain away their "missing time" or "UFO contact" experience. With these initial expectations and Hopkins's "hypnotic style," it would be remarkable indeed if anything other than an abduction experience emerged.

The ABC program "20/20" on May 21, 1987, devoted a segment to UFO abductions. Hopkins was interviewed along with a number of other believers. The show also interviewed one skeptic, Dr. Martin Reiser, a psychologist and hypnosis consultant for the Los Angeles Police Department. After viewing videotapes of Hopkins interviewing a subject under hypnosis, Reiser concluded that Hopkins was telling the subjects ahead of time that abductions happen, that they are very common, and that there is no question that the alien abductors do exist. Hopkins's response was, "Well, these cases are so outrageous and the person feels so uncomfortable talking about them that, unless you assure that person by your manner that you believe them, you will not get the story." Reiser responded, "I think much of what was felt and perceived by these two subjects could be explained in rational, reasonable ways that don't have to involve UFOs or UFO experiences."

In the late '80s, Hopkins was out-gurued by Whitley Strieber, the occult novelist whose book *Communion: A True Story* (1987) was on the *New York Times* bestseller list for nearly a year and made his publisher, Beech Tree Books/Morrow, a fortune and made Strieber an international celebrity. The book is highly autobiographical and gives an account of Strieber's early life when he had a number of experiences that he was able, at a much later time, to relate to contacts with extraterrestrials. Some of this biographical material was recovered under hypnosis and is therefore highly suspect. Nevertheless, Strieber describes a number of "missing time" episodes, conversations with voices coming through his stereo system, and out-of-the-body experiences.

Things came to a head one night in October 1985 when Strieber was in his isolated cabin in upstate New York with his wife and son and another couple. After everyone was asleep, Strieber awakened and saw a blue light on the cathedral ceiling of the living room. He thought the house was afire. Though afraid and almost in a state of panic, he went back to sleep! He was awakened again by a sharp, loud noise like a firecracker. His wife and son and the guests also heard it and awakened, and the house was surrounded by a glowing light. Strieber went downstairs then and the light disappeared. He comforted his son and his guests and all went back to sleep. Later, under hypnosis, Strieber remembered being visited during the night by a little man with a hood but no head.

Three months later, on the day after Christmas, Strieber and his wife and son were again in the cabin. After shutting up the cabin, setting the alarm system, and checking the place thoroughly, he fell asleep. He was suddenly awakened by a whooshing noise from downstairs. He checked the alarm system, but there was no indication that there had been any intrusion. He saw the bedroom door open, and a small figure about three-and-a-half feet tall was staring at him. Then he was paralyzed and was floated out of the house, into the woods, and then into an alien space-craft. He was shown a needle and thought it was put into his brain. Then he felt he was being raped anally. Later, under hypnosis, he recalled more details of the experience. Later still, he had another "missing time" experience and several visits from little "dwarf-like" beings.

Strieber then started seeing a psychiatrist, Dr. Donald Klein, who uses regressive hypnosis, and after a number of hypnotic sessions concluded, "I have examined Whitley Strieber and found that he is not suffering from a psychosis. He appears to me to have adapted very well to life at a high level of uncertainty. He is not hallucinating in a manner characteristic of psychosis." Dr. Klein also wrote that many of Strieber's symptoms were consistent with temporal lobe abnormality, thus raising the question of possible organic brain disease. Subsequent EEG tests, however, revealed no abnormalities. Strieber also took a lie detector test and this test indicated that he honestly thought he perceived the things reported in the book. Exactly what happened to Strieber and why he thought he was abducted will be discussed in the following section.

About the same time that Strieber and Hopkins were vying for "King of the Abductionists" title, a reporter named Gary Kinder was extolling the experiences of a Swiss cabinet-maker named Billy Meier in a book titled *Light Years: An Investigation Into the Extraterrestrial Experiences of Edward Meier.* Meier was famous for his beautiful color photographs of spacecraft called "Beam Ships" that were supposedly from planets of the stars in the Pleiades. The space aliens were tall, stately, and fair of hair and skin, and one four-hundred-year-old lovely fell in love with Billy. Not only did Meier take trips with the aliens, he even journeyed back in time and talked wih Jesus Christ. Investigations, however, proved all of the lovely photos were those of models found in his workshop, and Meier's wife finally blew the whistle on her scheming old man.

To counter all of this nonsense, the early 1980s produced a number of books and magazine articles that would have ended the issue once and for all were the UFOlogical community not so religiously zealous in its commitments and belief. Two truly brilliant works dealing with the UFO issue were Robert Sheaffer's calmly reasoned work *The UFO Verdict* (Prometheus Books, 1981) and Douglas Curran's *In Advance of the Landing:*

Folk Concepts of Outer Space (Abbeville Press, 1985). William R. Corliss also published *Handbook of Unusual Natural Phenomena* in 1983 (Arlington House), which clearly indicated that many so-called UFOs were rarely seen natural phenomena. In 1981 Philip J. Klass published a devastating attack on the abductee claims in his article "Hypnosis and UFO Abductions" in the Spring 1981 issue of The *Skeptical Inquirer.* This article was the precursor of his book, published a few years later, *UFO Abductions: A Dangerous Game* (Prometheus Books, 1989), which should have brought an end to the abduction-by-aliens silliness, but unfortunately has not. Since Klass is a gentleman who never hesitates to "put his money where his mouth is," Klass has publicly offered to pay any abduction victim $10,000 provided that the victim reports the alleged abduction to the FBI and the FBI investigation confirms that the kidnapping really occurred. As of this date no one has attempted to collect the money. The reason for this is quite simple: anyone who knowingly reports a spurious kidnapping to the FBI is vulnerable to a $10,000 fine and up to five years in prison.

Another article, "The Aliens Among Us: Hypnotic Regression Revisited" by your senior author R. Baker (*Skeptical Inquirer,* vol. 12, Winter 1987–88), explained the experiences and behaviors portrayed in the alien-abduction books in a naturalistic and satisfying way by our understanding of anomalistic psychology.

Curiously enough, in addition to Budd Hopkins and his cohorts David Jacobs, a history professor and author of *The UFO Controversy in America* (Signet, 1976), and Thomas Bullard, a professor of folklore, a number of psychiatrists and psychologists not only took the alien abduction claims seriously, but some of them insisted that they, too, were abductees. Drs. Leo Sprinkle and Edith Fiore insisted that they were victims, and Dr. Fiore wrote a book containing interviews with a number of these victims titled *Encounters* (Doubleday, 1989). Dr. Fiore, a clinical psychologist with twenty years of experience, also believes in reincarnation and demon possession, i.e., that the spirits of the dead can take over the minds and bodies of the living. Two other psychiatrists who take the alien abduction claims quite seriously are Dr. Rima Laibow and Dr. David Gotlib, a Canadian. Dr. Laibow has coined a term for the abductees to dignify their claims and refers to them as victims of an "experienced anomalous trauma" (EAT). Dr. Gotlib, equally sympathetic to their claims, publishes a newsletter known as *The Bulletin of Anomalous Experiences,* which appears seven to eight times a year. Subscriptions are $20 a year and can be ordered by writing Dr. David Gotlib, 1365 Yonge Street, Suite 200, Toronto, Ontario M4T 2P7. Mention should also be made of the fact that both Strieber and Hopkins publish newsletters devoted to the experiences of alien contactees and abductees. Strieber's publication, known as

The Communion Letter, is published quarterly and subscriptions are $20 a year from The Communion Letter, P.O. Box 10234, San Antonio, Texas 78210-0235. The Hopkins newsletter, known as *IF—The Bulletin of the Intruders Foundation,* is published sporadically, and one can receive copies by becoming a member of the Intruder Foundation and sending $25 to Intruders Foundation, P.O. Box 30233, New York, New York 10011.

Understanding and Investigating UFOs

In what is without question the best book available on how to go about investigating, evaluating, and reporting UFO sightings—Allan Hendry's *The UFO Handbook*—Hendry argues convincingly in his Introduction that no formal training is required to study *Unidentified* as well as *Identified* flying object reports. In some ways formal academic training can be a hindrance in that one tends to see the entire UFO panopoly from the biased viewpoint of one's academic training. Therefore, rest assured that you are just as qualified and capable as anyone else to study this phenomenon. There is one exception: *provided you have not made up your mind ahead of time that any and all strange sights in the skies represent an extraterrestrial invasion!*

For the investigator of all aerial phenomena the critical question is: Why is it whenever someone goes outside, looks up at the sky, and sees a very strange, unfamiliar flying object—why does he immediately adopt the ET (extraterrestrial) hypothesis instead of the NO (natural object) hypothesis, or the MM (manmade) hypothesis, especially in light of the fact that the NO and MM hypotheses are much more probable? Why the ET hypothesis first? The answer is easy: because we have been conditioned by the media and our culture to expect the miraculous in the form of extraterrestrial visitors. Not only has the idea of extraterrestrial life become scientifically respectable, it has now become an *expectation* and *the norm.* Nevertheless, as both John Keel and Allan Hendry have written, it has little in the way of support even among UFOlogists. In Keel's words, "All of the evidence, both historical and contemporary, indicates that the ET concept is completely erroneous" (Keel 1990). Hendry is equally blunt, "Adherence to the extraterrestrial hypothesis (ETH) has gained us nothing in thirty years, and outright contrivances are necessary to plug up the growing cracks. I find the ability of the 'twentieth-century mythology' model to account for the observations very satisfying. . . . I am prepared to accept some, or none, or all worthy UFOs as startling natural phenomena, vivid technological 'spirits', or complicated misperceptions . . . whichever answer is correct for each individual event" (Hendry 1979, p. 284). We seriously doubt that any skeptic familiar with the phenomena would disagree.

People do see things in the sky that they cannot explain. Ninety-five percent or more are misidentifications of natural or manmade objects. The most frequent offenders are aircraft, balloons, rockets and missiles, satellites, meteors, bolides, bright stars, planets, and plasma. Despite the arguments of UFOlogists that there are a number of cases that cannot be identified as either natural or manmade, there is little reason to believe that they could not be if more information were available and an intensive effort were made to identify them. This certainly proved to be the case in many of the so-called "inexplicable classic cases" which did cough up their secrets when diligent researchers such as Phil Klass, Robert Sheaffer, et al. applied themselves to the problem. Ian Ridpath has made a very crucial point that is often overlooked: the fact that there are simply *too many UFOs being seen* to support the ET hypothesis. In his words, "Imagine, for a moment, that there are one million other civilizations in the galaxy, all sending out starships. Since there must be something like 10 billion interesting places to visit (one-tenth of all stars in the galaxy), then each civilization must launch 10,000 spaceships annually for only one to reach here every year. If each civilization launches the more reasonable number of one starship annually, then we would expect to be visited once every 10,000 years. Alternatively, the higher number of reported UFOs might be taken as indicating that we are something special. If so, then life cannot be a very common phenomenon in the galaxy—and thus there would be fewer civilizations to send out starships, and we would expect a smaller number of UFOs" (Ridpath 1977).

Stymied in this regard, the UFOlogists are by no means dismayed. If the aliens are not coming from *outer* space, then they damn well must be coming from *hyper* space, i.e., from forward in time, from the future, or from another dimension. In other words, if one unlikely hypothesis doesn't work, then create one even more unlikely but one that will be much, much harder to disprove. This they have done with relish. Yet the fact remains that as of this date the UFOlogists have yet to produce one concrete bit of material evidence of an alien visitation from anywhere. What evidence we have been able to amass over the past forty years of searching all points to the fact that the aliens are coming from *inner* space, i.e., the space between the two ears of the human head. What aliens there are are the imaginary creations of the human mind.

Nevertheless, as a dedicated and conscientious investigator you should collect and record all of the available facts and you should not prejudge the outcome of your investigation. Even so, you should be aware that most of the available UFO literature is based upon hearsay and speculation, and a lot of the original eyewitness observations and testimony is distorted in the process of being retold and published. Therefore, no matter what is reported by the media, you should follow up any and all reports with your own independent investigation, obtaining your own interviews with the witnesses, and carrying out your own on-the-scene observations, inspections, and measurements. But how do we do this?

Investigating and Reporting UFO Sightings

Most of the sightings you will investigate will be ordinary, prosaic, and easily explained since they will be misinterpretations of astronomical and aeronautical events. This will take care of ninety percent or more. Remember, you will be studying only the *reports* of UFOs, not the UFOs themselves. These reports will fall into four categories: Unidentified Flying Objects (UFOs), Identified Flying Objects (IFOs), Hoaxes, and Fantasies. The reports also fall into six categories: Nocturnal Lights (NLs), Daylight Discs (DDs), Radar Visuals (RVs), Close Encounters I—sightings made from five hundred feet away or less (CEIs), Close Encounters II—sightings involving physical traces or electromagnetic effects (CEIIs), and Close Encounters III—sightings involving communication and contact with vehicle occupants or entities (CEIIIs). Most of your data will, of course, be anecdotal. The reports will come in an infinite variety and there will be few, if any, pattern or patterns to the reports you will receive. Many of the reported UFOs will violate the laws of physics. Do not be surprised if some of the reports are illogical and irrational.

In your interviews you need to consider several aspects of your witness and his or her behavior: their reliability, their accuracy, their emotional and psychological status, and their expectancies with regard to aerial phenomena.

As for their reliability and/or credibility, ask if they have made any previous sightings: When? Where? How many? What is their level of interest in the subject? Have they read anything concerning UFOs in the past? What did they read? How imaginative are they? Do they engage in much speculation about what they saw? What is their level of confidence as to what they witnessed? What was their emotional reaction? Fear? Joy? Excitement? Stress? Are they publicity seekers, insisting on immediate media contact? Is their story internally consistent? Is it consistent with the reports of other witnesses—if any? Is their story consistent with the prevailing weather and atmospheric conditions at the time of the sighting? Is there any confirming radar reports or reports from other witnesses in the area? Did they take any pictures?

With regard to the sighting per se: What was the object's apparent or angular size? A convenient scale you can use is: 1—a star, 2—a plane, 3—the full moon, or 4—larger than the full moon. What were its features? Lights? Color? Domes? Fins? Windows? Shape? What was its direction and what was its azimuth, i.e., its angle of elevation above the horizon? What was its speed and altitude? What were the prevailing weather conditions at the moment of sighting? You also need to obtain background information about the witness—age, sex, education, occupation, home address, phone number, visual acuity, eyeglasses, visual aids employed at sighting if any, type of area in which sighting was made, witness' location at time of sighting, and clarity of view, i.e., unobscured, through a window, etc. As for the object itself: Was it luminous? How bright? How big? When and where did it appear? Trajectory? Point of appearance—direction, angle, and manner? How long was it in view? What was its speed? What sort of path did it follow? Any surface or internal details? Did it pass behind or come close to any objects on the earth's surface? All of these questions can be put together in a questionnaire format and used repeatedly if you so desire.

But what do you do with this information once you have it? Who should you direct your reports to? This is a very good question because, other than the media and the UFOlogical organizations, no one else seems to be interested. As for the U.S. Air Force, their official stance is that they are no longer interested. If you call in a report to any Air Force agency, they will refer you to the Hynek Center, i.e., CUFOS, or MUFON. Airports? They aren't interested either, but they might be able to provide radar confirmation depending, of course, on the nature of your target and its immediacy. If you call them, they will most likely refer you to the nearest university or college. The police? If they come when you call, they will watch with you, but they can do little else except refer you to a UFO group. If you bother either NASA or NORAD (North American Air Defense Command), they will also refer you to CUFOS or MUFON. If you are brave enough to report it to the news media, be prepared for the fact that *you* will probably become the story, not the UFO.

Looking at the most commonly misidentified aerial objects—the UFOs—we find the nocturnal lights category to be the sort most frequently reported. Lights in the night sky are of many different kinds but, as of this writing, none of them are ET spaceships. Easily confused and misreported are bright stars and planets. Stars like Sirius, Vega, Capella, and Arcturus are very bright, and even brighter are the planets Venus, Jupiter, Mars, and, on occasions, Saturn. The fact that they are often mistaken for something else is legendary. During World War II, the U.S.S. Houston did its best to shoot down Venus, firing more than two hundred and fifty rounds at it while the gunnery officer kept shouting, "Lengthen your range,

lengthen your range!" Odder still is what an air traffic controller at Detroit Metropolitan Airport told Allan Hendry, "Do you know how many
times we've cleared Venus to land?" Stars change color and flash, and
seem to move when stared at against a dark black sky. This normal visual
phenomena is called *autokinesis,* and the scintillating and winking is due
to atmospheric refraction while the appearance and disappearance is due
to moving clouds. Watching stars and planets from a moving car gives
rise to the illusion of the light "keeping pace." When the vehicle stops,
the light stops. When the vehicle moves, the light moves. Time and time
again people have confused Venus and Jupiter as UFOs and because of
their lack of familiarity with the night sky will argue, "Well, it couldn't
have been Venus because Venus was over to the left!" They were, of course,
referring to Jupiter. Stars and planets can easily be confirmed via the use
of a *Star Chart* available from most any good local bookstore. Care should
be taken when a telescope or binocular is used for UFO observing. These
visual aids can often distort the appearance and cause further confusion.

The second largest contributors to misidentification are "advertising
planes." With their flashing lights, trailing banners, and slow air speed,
they have again and again been reported as UFOs. After flying parallel
to the observer for a while and then turning and flying toward him or
her, the light definitely appears to stop dead in the air and hover; similarly, when the light is moving away from the observer. With air speeds
as low as forty-five miles per hour, these planes do cause untold confusion
among those unfamiliar with them. Additionally, if the pilot turns off the
lights or turns the dark side of the banner toward the observer, the result is the appearance of sudden acceleration and an instant departure.
If the aircraft is moving toward you and the wind is blowing toward the
plane, frequently you do not hear the engine noise. This produces many
reports of "Well, it couldn't have been a plane because there was no noise."
Normally one does not see ad planes after midnight since their primary
use is for large gatherings of people on the ground at sports events,
exhibitions, fairs, carnivals, and so forth, To determine if this is what was
seen, you can check with your local airports and the "Aerial Advertisers"
listed in the Yellow Pages.

Airplanes and aircraft in general are another major source of UFO
reports. They all bear running lights and use very powerful landing lights
when coming in for a landing. When they are moving directly toward the
observer or directly away from him or her, they appear to be standing
still in midair. Remember also that helicopters can hover, and often do.
If you are not sure that what was seen was or was not an aircraft of
some sort, a call to the local FAA facility watch supervisor can sometimes
be helpful. As far as aircraft are concerned, you should also be aware

of the fact that all of the armed services are always engaged in developing new and radical types of aircraft. The Stealth progam with its radically new design for both fighters and bombers had to endure many reports of UFOs every time these planes left the earth; similarly for many of the Vertical Take Off (VTO) type of aircraft. As long ago as the Vietnam War, the Armed Services were employing remote-controlled, pilotless types of small reconnaissance aircraft with strange shapes and designs that were also frequently reported as UFOs. The problem here is that members of the Armed Services may be extremely reluctant to discuss these with you unless you have a good reason to know. Some of these types of newer craft are even more startling to observers who have never seen anything like them before. Even so, these vehicles are *not, repeat not,* from outer space nor do they pose a threat to our American citizenry.

Another frequently reported IFO are meteors and satellite reentries. These can be seen anytime, day or night, and they show up in every color of the spectrum. Most meteors last from five to ten seconds and are noiseless. Although most appear to be falling straight down, many can also travel horizontally as well. Their distance from the observer can also be quite illusory. Near can be far and vice versa. All satellite reentries are considerably slower than meteors. They also last longer than ten seconds and they have a flat—usually eastbound—trajectory. Satellites, usually seen as point sources of light moving slowly across the sky, may last as long as twenty minutes. They, too, may appear to stop, jump around, and move erratically because of the autokinetic effect. Plot their direction, azimuth, and trajectory carefully and then call NASA if you are not sure whether it is or is not a satellite.

Believe it or not, the moon has been reported as a UFO on countless occasions, especially when it is seen through a thin layer of clouds. It has been reported quite frequently as a large, orange, glowing ball that appeared and then disappeared instantly. True, indeed, if dark thick masses of clouds moved between you and the moon before the thin layers again permitted you to see the glow. Almost as commonly reported are the glowing circles of light reflected off of cloud layers that suddenly dart from one side of the horizon to the other at the speed of light. The reason that they do this is because *it is light,* i.e., searchlight beams reflecting off the surface of clouds. Time and again they have been mistaken for ET spaceships. Balloons are also commonly mistaken for ET spaceships, particularly because some of them—especially weather and high altitude balloons—have a completely circular and metallic appearance. They do expand to almost completely circular shape as they ascend to high altitudes. Borne slowly or swiftly by high altitude winds, they, too, may appear to hover, move quickly or slowly across the night sky.

In addition to these things there are birds, kites, flares, clouds, experimental test clouds of chemicals, airborne residue, mirages, sun-dogs and moon-dogs, as well as window reflections—all these things have been reported as UFOs with the ET assumption riding close behind. All of these things have also been seen and reported in the daytime as Daylight Discs. Especially popular in the reports of disc shapes are ordinary aircraft when seen on edge. Lenticular clouds, the planet Venus, mirages, and even— believe it or not—orange spheres on power lines that make them more visible to approaching aircraft have been reported as UFOs. On one occasion even the reflection of the sun off of kite wire was called in by a number of observers looking at it from the same vantage point. Most amusing of all were several reports made by people suffering from serious visual defects—deficiencies which caused the misinterpretations of birds and jet planes.

With regard to CEI reports, upon investigation most of these proved to be due to ad planes, stars and planets, aircraft and helicopters, prank balloons, missiles, meteors, and, on one occasion, a streetlight. For CEII sightings involving physical traces and/or electromagnetic effects, you may need to use a number of different sorts of tools, as well as some technical consultants. If it is some sort of electrical or electronic device that malfunctioned due to the presence of the UFO, you might want to call in a repairman or technician. If there was a power failure, you should call the supervisor at the local power company to determine the cause. If excessive radiation is claimed—which is highly unlikely since few UFO reports any longer involve reports of radiation—then you might want to borrow a Geiger-Mueller survey or scalar-rate meter and an expert to go with it. You need to know something about the type of radiation—Alpha, Gamma, Beta, and X-ray—as well as the background count in the area before measuring the specific place where the UFO allegedly landed. Moreover, just because you find some radioactivity at the site doesn't mean it has anything to do with a UFO.

As for the electromagnetic interference claims and the claim that a device has been magnetized due to a UFO presence, make sure you know everything there is to know about the device prior to the UFO's appearance. It could have misbehaved like this many times before, and don't forget to check the operation of other electrical devices in the area at the same time to see if they, too, were affected. Also check for any residual magnetism with a magnetometer. For both claims of EM interference and radiation you would be wise to consult experts—either an engineer or a certified Civil Defense radiologist.

For any and all physical trace cases and claims that the UFO visibly affected either a natural or manmade substance or structure, you need to inspect it in person and as soon as possible after the event occurred. In any event, a description of the shape, size, depth, and so forth is needed, as well as a description of the material affected. Was it discolored, depressed, melted, fused by heat, scarred, scratched, or broken? Measurements of the size of the depression or area affected is also needed. Was there anything left behind of a material nature? Solid, liquid, or gaseous material? Were there any bits and pieces of foreign residue? If you find anything you shouldn't, remove it until you have carefully marked its location, position, and orientation. You should also make a map of the trace site and its surrounding area, including the flight path of the UFO, and it should include a distance scale and the direction of true north. Photos of the trace and its features should also be made, and a twelve-inch ruler next to the trace should be added before filming.

Soil samples should also be taken of the allegedly affected area, as well as samples taken from the unaffected surrounding area as a control. As for the soil tests themselves, you should depend on experts from the U.S. Department of Agriculture since hundreds of different tests are possible. As Hendry notes, magnetometer surveys, soil compression, moisture measurements, and zeta potential tests are best handled at the site itself by trained geophysicists. Chemical, thermal, calorimetric, thermoluminescence, and zeta potential (effects on the edges of mineral grains) tests alone will not prove absolutely that the UFO was responsible. As Hendry states, "physical-trace analysis continues to be rooted in ambiguity. The successful interpretation of CEII traces continues at this time to pivot around the integrity and accuracy of human testimony, the testimony of the UFO witness" (p. 292). Hendry also has stated that, based on his own investigative experience, he would have to see the UFO causing ground damage with his own eyes before he would believe anything coming from trace analyses!

Most of the material you have read thus far in this section has been condensed from Allan Hendry's *The UFO Handbook* (Doubleday, 1979) and you are strongly advised to read this book carefully in the event you are called upon to undertake a detailed or intensive on-the-scene investigation. As an investigator, you should also read the Klass books and the Sheaffer volume for clues to how they approached and solved some of the classic UFO cases—cases such as the famed Socorro, New Mexico landing of 1964, which turned out to be nothing more than a publicity stunt by the local mayor, who, by odd chance, owns the land on which the alleged UFO settled down. Or the case of the famous MJ-12 papers in which the UFOlogists claimed President Harry Truman personally authenticated the capture and securing of alien spacecraft complete with crews. Diligent detective work by Klass and Nickell has shown that the documents were faked and the signatures forgeries (Klass 1987, Nickell 1990).

Just as is the case with all claimed photographs of ghosts, no photograph of any UFO can be regarded as authentic—no matter how clear or how many may be offered in evidence. As was the case with the famous or infamous Gulf Breeze photographs, not only were they shown to be photographs of a model, but one of the local investigative reporters, with the help of a photographer friend, was able not only to duplicate, but in some instances even improve upon the originals. Anyone with an older model Polaroid camera can photograph anything—model, lampshade, picture cut from a magazine, etc.—against a solid black backgound and, without advancing the film, go outside and photograph the sky. As a result of the double exposure, you will have your UFO floating merrily across the sky and no one will be able to tell you didn't photograph it *in* the sky originally. Even better pictures can be made if you go to just a little more trouble.

Neither should you place all of your trust and confidence in the results of radar reports and confirmations. Radar evidence is as complex and ambiguous as—and can be as easily misread and interpreted as—any other phenomena. For example, the famous case of the radar reports of UFOs over Washington, D.C. during the height of the UFO hysteria after lengthy investigation turned out to be a case of "temperature inversion" effects. Even the dedicated UFO believer Jenny Randles has stated that radar, unfortunately, "is no talisman for the UFOlogist." Interestingly enough, NORAD detects eight hundred to nine hundred radar unknowns every day. The majority of these are due to auroral effects: electromagnetic noise pulses, meteorionization trails, and re-entering satellites. While an automated file of unknowns is generated, it is not kept for very long because it is irrelevant to NORAD's mission. The intermittent nature of radar itself and the volume of airspace sampled by each radar site severely limit its usefulness in UFO identification. Even if it does appear on the scope, the image is difficult to distinguish from that of an airplane. Unless it is flying at high speed and carrying out impossible maneuvers, it cannot be discriminated from planes. It is merely one more dot on the tube. If you do find it worthwhile to consult with radar operators, you need to know where the objects were first seen and where they finally disappeared: time, range, azimuth, height, velocity, heading, image number and formation (if any), image quality and strength, maneuvering details. You need to know if the images appeared suddenly or slowly and the details of their disappearance from the scope. Was the operator watching the unknowns continuously or did he leave the scope at any time? Did other operators or the controller also watch them? How experienced was the operator? What kind of radar equipment was used? What were the weather conditions at the time of observation? Were there any unusual or anomalous propagations seen at the time the UFO was spotted, e.g., ghosts, superrefractions, angels, ground clutter, etc.? Were other aircraft, such as regularly scheduled jets, military flights, or birds on the screen at the time? Did any of these aircraft see it and report it? Was the UFO in the radar shadow area at any time? Such questions are essential if the information is to be of any value whatsoever because even at best it is unreliable.

Investigating CE IIIs—Contacts and Abductions[1]

The probability of your being the first human in history to interview the first human in history who was abducted by an alien from outer space is about the same as the probability that if you take a shovel and go out in your back yard and dig, that you will uncover the world's largest diamond. Both are equally unlikely. Yet, despite all of the abduction claims, none of them stand up under careful and intense scientific scrutiny. To fully understand the behavior of people claiming contact with and abduction by extraterrestrial or interdimensional (one of the latest UFOlogical theories) aliens, we need to look at a number of psychological concepts that need to be understood if we are to work effectively with all such claimants. We need to look at hypnosis and hypnotic regession, confabulation, cueing, fantasy-prone personalities and psychological needs, hypnopompic and hypnogogic hallucination, missing time, the psychology of hoaxsters and lying, cryptomnesia and screen memories, and public confusion about mental disorders.

HYPNOSIS AND HYPNOTIC REGRESSION

In France in the 1770s, when Mesmerism was in its heyday, the king appointed two commissions to investigate Mesmer's activities. The commissions included such eminent men as Benjamin Franklin, Lavoisier, and Jean-Sylvan Bailly, the French astronomer. After months of study the report of the commissioners concluded that it was *imagination,* not magnetism, that accounted for the swooning, trancelike rigidity of Mesmer's subjects. Surprisingly enough, this conclusion is still closer to the truth about hypnosis than most of the modern definitions found in today's textbooks.

So-called authorities still disagree about "hypnosis." But whether it is

---

Some of the material in this section is taken verbatim from the senior author's earlier work *They Call It Hypnosis* (Baker 1990).

or is not a "state," there is common and widespread agreement among all the major disputants that "hypnosis" is a situation in which people set aside critical judgment (without abandoning it entirely) and engage in make-believe and fantasy; that is, they use their imagination (Sarbin and Andersen 1967, Barber 1969, Gill and Brenman 1959, Hilgard 1977). As stated earlier, there are great individual differences in the ability to fantasize, and in recent years many authorities have made it a *requirement* for any successful "hypnotic" performance. Josephine Hilgard (1979) refers to hypnosis as "imaginative involvement," Sarbin and Coe (1972) term it "believed-in imaginings," Spanos and Barber (1974) call it "involvement in suggestion-related imaginings," and Sutcliffe (1961) has gone so far as to characterize the hypnotizable individual as someone who is "deluded in a descriptive, nonpejorative sense" and he sees the hypnotic situation as an arena in which people who are skilled at make-believe and fantasy are provided with the opportunity and the means to do what they enjoy doing and what they are able to do especially well. Even more recently Perry, Laurence, Nadon, and Labelle (1986) concluded that "abilities such as imagery/imagination, absorption, disassociation, and selective attention underlie high hypnotic responsivity in yet undetermined combinations." The same authors, in another context dealing with past-lives regression, also concluded that "it should be expected that any material provided in age regression (which is at the basis of reports of reincarnation) may be fact or fantasy, and it is most likely an admixture of both." The authors further report that such regression material is colored by issues of confabulation, memory creation, inadvertent cueing, and the regressee's current psychological needs.

CONFABULATION

Because of its universality, it is quite surprising that the phenomenon of confabulation is not better known. Confabulation, or the tendency of ordinary, sane individuals to confuse fact with fiction and to report fantasized events as actual occurrences, has surfaced in just about every situation in which a person has attempted to remember very specific details from the past. A classical and amusing example occurs in the movie *Gigi,* in the scene where Maurice Chevalier and Hermione Gingold compare memories of their courtship in the song "I Remember It Well." We remember things not the way they really were but the way we would have liked them to have been.

The work of Elizabeth Loftus and others over the past decade has demonstrated that the human memory works not like a tape recorder but more like the village storyteller, i.e., it is both creative and recreative. We can and we do easily forget. We blur, shape, erase, and change details of the events in our past. Many people walk around daily with heads full of "fake memories." Moreover, the unreliability of eyewitness testimony is not only legendary but well documented. When all of this is further complicated and compounded by the impact of suggestions provided by the hypnotist plus the social-demand characteristics of the typical hypnotic situation, little wonder that the resulting recall on the part of the regressee bears no resemblance to the truth. *In fact, the regressee often does not know what the truth is.*

An experiment by A. H. Lawson and W. C. McCall (1977) of California State University is relevant here. They hypnotically induced imaginary UFO abductions in a group of subjects, who were then questioned about their experience. Not only were these subjects able to tell plausible stories about what happened to them aboard their imaginary flying saucers, but their stories showed no substantive differences from tales in the UFO literature by persons who claimed to have actually experienced an abduction. In 1978 Lawson read a paper at an American Psychological Association meeting that contained a revised account of the experiment. He pointed out some differences between the findings of the experiment and the tales in the UFO literature, along with the many similarities. He also warned that it was important to be very cautious about using the results from hypnotic regressions, since a witness can lie and even believe his own lies, thus invalidating the investigation.

It is also common knowledge that hypnotized witnesses subtly confuse their own fantasies with reality, without either the witness or the hypnotist being aware of what is happening. Martin Orne has warned again and again of the dangers of using hypnosis as a means of getting at the truth. Not only do we translate beliefs into memories even when we are wide awake, but in the case of hypnotized witnesses with few specific memories, the hypnotist may unwittingly (or wittingly in some cases) suggest memories and create in the witness a number of crucial and vivid recollections of events that never happened, i.e., pseudomemories.

It is also important to recognize that deeply hypnotized subjects (i.e., those who are deeply involved in the game) may not only willfully lie, but may become expert at doing so. When we also consider that most psychologists and psychiatrists are not particularly skillful at detecting and recognizing deception, and certainly have not been trained to do so, it becomes even harder to determine whether a subject was or was not telling the truth.

Orne also has warned that hypnotic suggestions to relive a past event, particularly when accompanied by questions about specific details, put pressure on the subject to provide information for which few, if any, actual memories are available. While this situation may stimulate the subject's memory and produce some increased recall, it can also cause him to confabulate. Moreover, there is no way anyone can determine whether such information is from actual memory or is confabulation, unless somehow one is able to obtain an independent verification. Even more troubling is the fact that if the hypnotist has beliefs about what happened, it is almost impossible for him to prevent himself from inadvertently steering the subject's recall in such a way that the subject will remember what the hypnotist believes! Elizabeth Loftus also has warned that no one—not even the most sophisticated hypnotist—can tell the difference between a memory that is real and one that has been created (Loftus 1979). If a person who is highly suggestible is hypnotized and false information is implanted in his mind, he tends to believe it. And even polygraphs cannot distinguish between real and phony memory.

Confabulation shows up without fail in nearly every context in which hypnosis is employed, including the forensic area. Thus it is not surprising that most states have no legal precedents on the use of hypnotic testimony. Furthermore, many state courts have begun to limit testimony from hypnotized witnesses or to follow the guidelines laid down by the American Medical Association in 1985 to assure that witnesses' memories are not contaminated by the hypnosis itself. For not only do we translate beliefs into memories when we are wide awake, but in the case of hypnotized witnesses with few specific memories the hypnotist may unwittingly suggest memories and create a witness with a number of crucial and vivid recollections of events that never happened, i.e., pseudomemories. It may turn out that the recent Supreme Court decision allowing the individual states limited use of hypnotically aided testimony may not be in the best interests of those who seek the truth. Even in their decision the judges recognized that hypnosis may often produce incorrect recollections and unreliable testimony.

There have also been a number of clinical and experimental demonstrations of the creation of pseudomemories that have subsequently come to be believed as veridical. Ernest R. Hilgard (1981) implanted a false memory of an experience connected with a bank robbery that never occurred. His subject found the experience so vivid that he was able to select from a series of photographs a picture of the man he thought had committed the robbery. At another time, Hilgard deliberately assigned two concurrent —though spatially different—life experiences to the same person and regressed him at separate times to *that date*. The individual subsequently gave very accurate accounts of both experiences, so that anyone believing in reincarnation who reviewed the two accounts would conclude the man *really had* lived the two assigned lives.

In a number of other experiments designed to measure eyewitness reliability, Loftus (1979) found that details supplied by others invariably contaminated the memory of the eyewitness. People's hair changed color, stop signs became yield signs, yellow convertibles turned to red sedans, the left side of the street became the right-hand side, and so on. The results of these studies led her to conclude, "It may well be that the legal notion of an independent recollection is a psychological impossibility." As for hypnosis, she says: "There's no way even the most sophisticated hypnotist can tell the difference between a memory that is real and one that's created. If a person is hypnotized and highly suggestible and false information is implanted in his mind, it may get embedded even more strongly. One psychologist tried to use a polygraph to distinguish between real and phony memory, but it didn't work. Once someone has constructed a memory, he comes to believe it himself."

CUEING: INADVERTENT AND ADVERTENT

Without a doubt, inadvertent cueing also plays a major role in UFO-abduction fantasies. The hypnotist unintentionally gives away to the person being regressed exactly what response is wanted. This was most clearly shown in an experimental study of hypnotic age regression by R. M. True in 1949. He found that 92 percent of his subjects, regressed to the day of their tenth birthday, could accurately recall the day of the week on which it fell. He also found the same thing for 84 percent of his subjects for their fourth birthday. Other investigators, however, were unable to duplicate True's findings. When True was questioned by Martin Orne about his experiment, he discovered that the editors of *Science,* where his report had appeared, altered his procedure section without his prior consent. True, Orne discovered, had inadvertently cued his subjects by following the unusual technique of asking them, "Is it Monday? Is it Tuesday? Is it Wednesday?" etc., and he monitored their responses by using a perpetual desk calendar in full view of all his subjects. Further evidence of the prevalence and importance of such cueing came from a study by O'Connell, Shor, and Orne (1970). They found that in an existing group of four-year-olds, not a single one knew what day of the week it was. The reincarnation literature is also replete with examples of such inadvertent cueing. Ian Wilson (1981), for example, has shown that hypnotically elicited reports of being reincarnated vary as a direct function of the hypnotist's belief about reincarnation. Finally, Laurence, Nadon, Nogrady, and Perry (1986) have shown that pseudomemories were elicited also by inadvertent cueing in the use of hypnosis by the police.

As for advertent, or *deliberate,* cueing, one of my own studies offers a clear example. Sixty undergraduates, divided into three groups of twenty each, were hypnotized and age-regressed to previous lifetimes. Before each hypnosis session, however, suggestions very favorable to and supportive of past-life and reincarnation beliefs were given to one group; neutral and noncommittal statements about past lives were given to the second group; and skeptical and derogatory statements about past lives were given to the third group. The results clearly showed the effects of these cues and suggestions. Subjects in the first group showed the most past-life regressions and the most past-life productions; subjects in the third group showed the least (Baker 1982).

Regression subjects take cues as to how they are to respond from the person doing the regressions and asking the questions. If the hypnotist is a believer in UFO abductions, the odds are heavily in favor of him eliciting UFO-abductee stories from his volunteers.

Fantasy-Prone Personalities

"Assuming that all you have said thus far *is* true," the skeptical observer might ask, "why would hundreds of ordinary, mild-mannered, unassuming citizens suddenly go off the deep end and turn up with cases of amnesia and then, when under hypnosis, all report nearly identical experiences?" First, the abductees are not as numerous as we are led to believe; and, second, even though Strieber and Hopkins go to great lengths to emphasize the diversity of the people who report these events, they are much more alike than these taxonomists declare. In an afterword to Hopkins's *Missing Time,* a psychologist named Aphrodite Clamar raises exactly this question and then adds, "All of these people seem quite ordinary in the psychological sense—*although they have not been subjected to the kind of psychological testing that might provide a deeper understanding of their personalities"* (italics added). And herein lies the problem. If the abductees were given this sort of intensive diagnostic testing, it is highly likely that many similarities would emerge—particularly an unusual personality pattern that Wilson and Barber (1983) have categorized as "fantasy-prone." In an important but much neglected article, they report in some detail their discovery of a group of excellent hypnotic subjects with unusual fantasy abilities. In their words:

> Although this study provided a broader understanding of the kind of life experiences that may underlie the ability to be an excellent hypnotic subject, it has also led to a serendipitous finding that has wide implication for all of psychology—it has shown that there exists a small group

of individuals (possibly 4% of the population) who fantasize a large part of the time, who typically "see," "hear," "smell," and "touch" and fully experience what they fantasize; and who can be labeled *fantasy-prone personalities.*

Wilson and Barber also stress that such individuals experience a reduction in orientation to time, place, and person that is characteristic of hypnosis or trance during their daily lives whenever they are deeply involved in a fantasy. They also have experiences during their daily ongoing lives that resemble the classical hypnotic phenomena. In other words, the behavior we would normally call "hypnotic" is exhibited by these fantasy-prone types (FPs) all the time. In Wilson and Barber's words: "When we give them 'hypnotic suggestions,' such as suggestions for visual and auditory hallucinations, negative hallucinations, age regression, limb rigidity, anesthesia, and sensory hallucinations, we are asking them to do for us the kind of thing they can do independently of us in their daily lives."

The reason we do not run into these types more often is that they have learned long ago to be highly secretive and private about their fantasy lives. Whenever the FPs do encounter a hypnosis situation, it provides them with a social situation in which they are encouraged to do, and are rewarded for doing, what they usually do only in secrecy and in private. Wilson and Barber also emphasize that regression and the reliving of previous experiences is something that virtually all the FPs do naturally in their daily lives. When they recall the past, they relive it to a surprisingly vivid extent, and they all have vivid memories of their experiences extending back to their early years.

Fantasy-prone individuals also show up as mediums, psychics, and religious visionaries. They are also the ones who have many realistic "out of body" experiences and prototypic "near-death" experiences.

In spite of the fact that many such extreme types show FP characteristics, the overwhelming majority of FPs fall within the broad range of normal functioning. It is totally inappropriate to apply a psychiatric diagnosis to them. In Wilson and Barber's words:

> It needs to be strongly emphasized that our subjects with a propensity for hallucinations are as well adjusted as our comparison group or the average person. It appears that the life experiences and skill development that underlie the ability for hallucinatory fantasy are more or less independent of the kinds of life experience that leads to pathology.

In general, fantasy-prone personalities are "normal" people who function as well as others and who are as well-adjusted, competent, and content or discontent as everyone else. Anyone familiar with the fantasy-prone personality who reads Strieber's *Communion* will suffer an immediate shock of recogniton! Strieber is a classic example of the fantasy-prone type: easily hypnotized, amnesic, from a very religious background, with vivid memories of his early years and a very active fantasy life—a writer of occult and highly imaginative novels featuring unusually strong sensory experiences, particularly smells and sounds and vivid dreams.

Even more remarkable are the correspondences between Strieber's alien encounters and the typical hypnopompic hallucinations, which will be discussed later.

It is perfectly clear, therefore, why most of the UFO abductees, upon cursory examination by psychiatrists and psychologists, would turn out to be sane, ordinary, normal citizens. It is also evident why the elaborate fantasies on the now universally familiar UFO abduction theme would have so much in common. Any one of us, if asked to pretend that he had been kidnapped by aliens from outer space or another dimension, would make up a story that would vary little, either in details or in the supposed motives of the abductors, from the stories told by any and all of the kidnap victims reported by Hopkins. Our imaginative tale would be remarkably similar in plot, dialogue, description, and characterization to the close encounters of the third kind and conversations with little gray aliens described in *Communion* and *Intruders*. The means of transportation would be saucer-shaped; the aliens would be small, humanoid, two-eyed, and grey or white or green; and the purpose of their visits would be to: (1) save our planet, (2) find a better home for themselves, (3) end nuclear war and the threat we pose to the peaceful life in the rest of the galaxy, (4) bring us knowledge and enlightenment, and (5) increase the aliens' knowledge and understanding of other forms of intelligent life. In fact, the fantasy-prone abductees' stories would be much more credible if some of them, at least, reported the aliens as eight feet tall, red-striped octopeds riding bicycles, and intent upon eating us for dessert.

Finally, what could motivate even the fantasy-prone type to concoct such outlandish and absurd tales, tales that without fail draw much attention and notoriety? What sort of psychological motives and needs would underlie such fabrications? Perhaps the best answer to this question is provided by the author-photographer Douglas Curran. Traveling from British Columbia down the Pacific coast and circumscribing the contiguous United States along a counterclockwise route, Curran spent over two years questioning ordinary people about outer space. In Curran's words,

> On my travels across the continent I never had to wait too long for someone to tell me about his or her UFO experience, whether I was chatting

with a farmer in Kansas, Ruth Norman at the Unarius Foundation, or a cafe owner in Florida. What continually struck me in talking with these people was how positive and ultimately life-giving a force was their belief in outer space. Their belief reaffirmed the essential fact of human existence; the need for order and hope. It is this that establishes them—and me—in the continuity of human experience. It brought me to a greater understanding of Oscar Wilde's observation, "We are all lying in the gutter—but some of us are looking at the stars." (Curran 1985)

Psychologist Carl Jung, in his essay, *Flying Saucers: A Modern Myth of Things Seen in the Sky* (Jung 1969), argues that the saucer represents an archetype of order, wholeness, deliverance, and salvation—a symbol manifested in other cultures as a sun wheel or magic circle. Jung compares the spacemen aboard the flying saucers to the angelic messengers of earlier times who brought a message of hope and salvation—the theme emphasized in Strieber's *Communion*. Curran observes that the spiritual message conveyed by the aliens is, recognizably, our own. None of the aliens, Curran was told, advocated any moral or metaphysical belief that was not firmly rooted in the Judeo-Christian tradition. As Curran says, "Every single flying-saucer group I encountered in my travels incorporated Jesus Christ into the hierarchy of its belief system." Many theorists have noted that whenever world events prove too psychologically destabilizing, men turn to religion as their only hope. Jung wrote,

> In the threatening situation of the world today, when people are beginning to see that everything is at stake, the projection-creating fantasy soars beyond the realm of earthly organization and powers into the heavens, into interstellar space, where the rulers of human fate, the gods, once had their abode in the planets. (Jung 1969)

Psychological Needs

The beauty and power of Curran's portraits of hundreds of true UFO believers lies in his sympathetic understanding of their fears and frailties. As psychologists are well aware, our religions are not so much systems of objective truths about the universe as collections of subjective statements about humanity's hopes and fears. The true believers interviewed by Curran are all around us. Over the years I have encountered several. One particular memorable and poignant case was that of a federal prisoner who stated he could leave his body at will, and sincerely believed it. Every weekend he would go home to visit his family, while, physically, his body stayed behind in his cell. Then there was the female psychic from the planet

Xenon who could turn electric lights on and off at will, especially traffic signals. Proof of her powers? When she drove up to a red light, she would concentrate on it intently for thirty to forty seconds and invariably it would turn green.

Recently, Keith Basterfield and Robert Bartholomew have proposed that all persons who claim to have been abducted by UFOs are, with few or no exceptions, fantasy-prone personalities. Moreover, they have also noted that there is a strong correlation between being a UFO abductee or contactee and possession of paranormal ability, or at least claiming to possess it (Basterfield and Bartholomew 1988). In line with this hypothesis, Bartholomew carried out a biographical analysis of 154 people who reported temporary abductions or persistent contacts with UFO occupants. He found that in 132 of the cases these individuals had fantasy-prone personality characteristics. Though all were devoid of any history of mental illness and appeared to function as normal, healthy adults, they all had rich fantasy lives, showed high hypnotic susceptibility, claimed psychic abilities, healing powers, out-of-body experiences, automatic writing, religious visions, and apparitional experience.

Bartholomew has since expanded his study to cover 300 alleged communications or contacts with UFO entities throughout history. This larger study has shown the same pattern of sociological, psychological, and folkloric processes, "including amnesias and possession states, lucid dreams, out-of-body experiences, hypnotic fantasy, hypnopompic and hypnogogic imagery, road hypnosis, auto hypnosis, rumors, myths, legends, urban legends, fantasy-prone personalities, mental disturbance, multiple personalities, conversion hysteria/psychosomatic reactions, mass hysteria, automatic writing, hallucinations, etc." (Personal communication). The only exceptions to the hypothesis, in my opinion, are those individuals who are deliberately carrying out a hoax and claiming abduction in order to gain publicity, attention, and money.

Since Wilson and Barber's identification of the fantasy-prone personality in 1983, Myers and Austrin (1985) and Rhue and Lynn (1987) have confirmed their finding and identified fourteen personality characteristics not shared by any other population groups. These characteristics are:

1. They are excellent hypnotic subjects.
2. As children they lived in make-believe worlds most of the time.
3. They believed in fairies when they were children.
4. They had imaginary companions when they were children.
5. During their childhood they learned to be secretive about their fantasies.
6. As adults they spend a large amount of their time fantasizing.

7. They share their fantasy life with no one else.
8. They claim they are psychic and report telepathy and precognition.
9. They report out-of-body experiences at a higher rate than normal population groups.
10. They believe they have the power to heal others.
11. They report apparitions.
12. They frequently have hypnogogic and hypnopompic dreams.
13. They are normal, socially aware, healthy individuals.
14. They experience vivid realistic dreams.

HYPNOGOGIC AND HYPNOPOMPIC HALLUCINATIONS

Another common but little-publicized and rarely discussed phenomenon is that of hypnogogic (i.e., when falling asleep) and hypnopompic (i.e., when waking up) hallucinations. These phenomena, often referred to as "waking dreams," find the individual suddenly awake but paralyzed and unable to move, and most often also encountering a "ghost."

The typical report goes somewhat as follows: "I went to bed and went to sleep, and then sometime near morning something woke me up. I opened my eyes and found myself wide awake but unable to move. There, standing at the foot of my bed, was my mother, wearing her favorite dress—the one we buried her in. She stood there looking at me and smiling, and then she said, 'Don't worry about me, Doris. I'm at peace at last. I just want you and the children to be happy.' "

Well, what happened next? "Nothing, she slowly faded away." What did you do then? "Nothing, I just closed my eyes and went back to sleep."

There are a number of characteristic clues that tell you whether a perception is or is not a hypnogogic or hypnopompic hallucination. First, it always occurs before or after falling asleep; second, one is paralyzed or has difficulty in moving, or on the other hand, one may float out of one's body and have an out-of-body experience; third, the hallucination is unusually bizarre, i.e., one see ghosts, aliens, monsters, etc.; fourth, after the hallucination is over, the hallucinator typically goes back to sleep; and, fifth, the hallucinator is unalterably convinced of the reality of the entire experience.

Recently on a talk show I was discussing sleep and dreams when a female caller told of being awakened in the middle of the night by a ghostly, haloed man standing by her bed. She was certain she was wide awake, but she could not move. She felt she could scream if she wanted, but had no desire to do so. I asked her if she was afraid. "No," she replied. I then asked her what the man did. "Nothing, he just walked around, and then disappeared." I asked her what she did next. "Nothing. I just closed my eyes and went back to sleep." I then asked what did she think her friends would do if they were to awake in the middle of the night to find a strange man standing by their bed? "They'd scream bloody murder, I'm sure." Well, I told her, the mere fact that she didn't is positive proof that it was what we call a hypnopompic dream, not reality.

Strieber's *Communion* contains a classic, textbook description (pp. 172–175) of a hypnopompic hallucination, complete with the wakening from a sound sleep, the strong sense of reality and of being awake, the paralysis (due to the fact that the body's neural circuits keep our muscles relaxed to help preserve our sleep), and the encounter with strange beings. Following the encounter, instead of jumping out of bed and going in search of the strangers, Strieber, typically, goes back to sleep. He even reports that the burglar alarm had not gone off—proof again that the intruders were mental rather than physical. On another occasion Strieber reports awakening and believing that the roof of his house is on fire and that aliens are threatening his family. Yet his only response to this is to go peacefully back to sleep again, clear evidence of a hypnopompic dream.

Strieber, of course, is convinced of the reality of these experiences. This, too, is expected. If he were not convinced of their reality, the experience would not be hypnopompic nor hallucinatory. The point cannot be more strongly made that ordinary, perfectly sane and rational people have hallucinatory experiences, and such individuals are in no way mentally disturbed or psychotic. But neither are such experiences to be taken as incontrovertible proof of some sort of objective reality. Subjectively they may be real, but objectively they are nothing more than dreams and delusions. They are called "hallucinatory" because of their heightened subjective reality.

Leaving no rational explanation unspurned, Strieber is nevertheless forthright enough to suggest the possibility that his experiences could, indeed, be hypnopompic. Moreover, in a summary chapter he speculates, correctly, that the alien visitors could be "from within us" and/or "a side effect of a natural phenomenon . . . a certain hallucinatory wire in the mind causing many different people to have experiences so similar as to seem to be the result of encounters with the same physical phenomena." Interestingly, these hypnopompic and hypnogogic hallucinations show individual differences in content and character as well as a lot of similarity: ghosts, monsters, fairies, friends, lovers, neighbors, and even little gray men and golden-haired ladies from the Pleiades. Do such hallucinations appear more frequently to highly imaginative and fantasy-prone people than to other personality types? There is evidence that they do (Reed 1972, Wilson and Barber 1983), and there can certainly be no doubt that Strieber is a highly imaginative personality type.

Missing Time

As for the so-called "missing time" or lacunae experienced by all the UFO abductees, these experiences too are quite ordinary, common, and universal. Jerome Singer in his *Inner World of Daydreaming* (1975) comments:

> Are there ever any truly "blank periods" when we are awake? It certainly seems to be the case that under certain conditions of fatigue or great drowsiness or extreme concentration upon some physical act we may become aware that we cannot account for an interval of time and have no memory of what happened for seconds and sometime minutes. . . . Some people may say that their day-to-day experience is much more full of blank spots than I seem to be suggesting. Introspection tells me that may seem to be the case when a person is not actively attending to the fact that the stream of thought is running along and he has not developed a labeling system for the stream of thought. . . . All too often we do not have already developed labels for many of our emotional reactions in particular situations and without them we may be led to threatening or frightening interpretations of our own feelings and experiences.

Reed (1972) has also dealt with the "time-gap" experience at great length. Typically, motorists will report after a long drive that at some point in the journey they woke up to realize they had no awareness of a preceding period of time. With some justification, people will describe this as a "gap in time," a "lost half-hour," or a "piece out of my life." In Reed's words,

> The strangeness of the experience springs partly from "waking up" when one is already awake. But mainly it is due to the knowledge of a blank in one's temporal awareness. Doubtless the uneasiness associated with such a realization is largely culturally determined.
>
> For in our culture our everyday lives are sharply structured by time requirements. For most of us there are conventional times for commencing and finishing work, for taking breaks, for eating, sleeping, and enjoying leisure pursuits. We talk about "wasting time" as opposed to "spending time profitably." We are continually consulting our watches or turning on the radio to check our subjective estimates of the passage of time, and in many jobs "clock-watching" has a very real significance. Only when we are on holiday can most of us indulge in the luxury of ceasing to bother about clock time. But furthermore, our consciousness of self is closely related to the sense of continuity in the passage of time. To miss a period of time can be very disturbing; it has been used as the theme of several stories and films, as in the alcoholic's "lost weekend."
>
> A little reflection will suggest, however, that our experience of time

and its passage is determined by events, either external or internal. What the time-gapper is reporting is not that a slice of time has vanished, but that he has failed to register a series of events which would normally have functioned as his time-markers. If he is questioned closely he will admit that his "time-gap" experience did not involve his realization at, say, noon that he had somehow "lost" half an hour. Rather, the experience consists of "waking up" at, say, Florence and realizing that he remembers nothing since Bologna. . . . To understand the experience, however, it is best considered in terms of the absence of events. If the time-gapper had taken that particular day off, and spent the morning sitting in his garden undisturbed, he might have remembered just as little of the half-hour in question. He might still describe it in terms of lost time, but he would not find the experience unusual or disturbing. For he would point out that he could not remember what took place between eleven-thirty and twelve simply because nothing of note occurred.

In fact, there is nothing recounted in any of the abduction literature that cannot be easily explained in terms of normal, though somewhat unusual, psychological behavior we now term "anomalous." Different and unusual? Yes. Paranormal or otherworldly and requiring the presence of extraterrestrials? No.

One of the most recent and most fascinating developments among the abduction gurus is their belated recognition of the dangers of depending wholly upon hypnotic regression as proof of their pudding. In a recent issue of the periodical *UFO,* published by an organization called California UFO and devoted to the topic of "Hypnosis in UFO Research," both Strieber and Hopkins urged caution in the use of hypnosis and hypnotic regression. Strieber titles his article "Technique Out-of-Control," and for an individual who has in the past relied so heavily on hypnotic regression to prove his abduction claims, it is extraordinary indeed to hear him now make the following statement:

> Abduction research may not even be possible utilizing hypnosis: even highly trained hypnotists cannot use the technique reliably for retrieving basic factual information. Until there is a base of information gained from un-hypnotized subjects, it must properly remain a therapeutic tool, not an investigative one. The so-called "abduction narrative," which has been gained primarily from hypnotically induced recall, probably does not reflect actual experience, but rather the application of the subject's worst fears to their most enigmatic experiences. (Streiber 1989, p. 22)

And in another part of the article Strieber observes,

There is a tendency among abduction researchers—largely untrained in the scientific method and unrestrained by licensing—to be less-than-objective in their treatment of witnesses and to summarily dismiss evidence not consistent with their previous findings. I have come to believe that many techniques used by amateur investigators are not just suspect but disastrous. They amount to a form of unintentional but devastatingly effective brainwashing that denies witnesses access to the truth of their experience as they originally perceived them. (p. 23)

Finally, Strieber comes down firmly on the side of respectability with the recommendation that

nobody except a professionally trained hypnotist—preferably one with the credentials and ethical considerations of a mental health professional—should hypnotize any UFO witness for any reason, and then only for therapeutic purpose. Both free and regressed narrative should be interpreted by behavioral psychologists and other professionals skilled in the process. (p. 25)

Hopkins, too, has undergone a conversion, and while he still supports the use of hypnosis as an investigative tool, he is, he claims, extremely sensitive to the difficulties and dangers of using regressive hypnosis. In Hopkins's words in his article in *UFO,* titled "One UFOlogist's Methodology,"

Perhaps the most basic misconception about hypnosis holds that one's hypnotically-recalled memories and one's normal memories are somehow innately different. They are not. Normal recollection, obviously, can be inaccurate, so can hypnotic recall. *All testimony,* hypnotically elicited or otherwise, is affected to some extent by the questioner. In a court trial, a calm, non-leading judge can elicit one kind of information, a bullying prosecutor another. A lover sharing one's bed may inquire with a special kind of intimacy, eliciting yet another kind of recollection. All of this is self-evident with regard to hypnosis, but it is not so easily recognized that with normal recall exactly the same problems exist. (Hopkins 1989, p. 27)

Just a few paragraphs earlier Hopkins dramatically declares that it is not hypnosis that establishes the truth or falsity of the abduction, because the true believers nowadays proudly declare that many of the abduction tales are recounted while abductees are wide awake and prior to hypnosis. In Hopkins's words, "In roughly one-fourth of the abduction cases I've investigated, the subject has recalled virtually all of his or her basic abduction scenario prior to hypnosis" (p. 27).

SCREEN MEMORIES

Hopkins also wants us to know that he is aware of the existence of "screen memories," that is, memories that soften or cover up the horror of the true meaning of a person's recollection. An example would be recalling a beautiful deer with large soulful eyes instead of the horrible alien with his slanted eyes. But the fact of such screen memories clearly establishes the need for hypnosis if one is to ever know the whole truth about any abduction. Hopkins is also aware that the aliens probably use some form of "alien hypnotic suggestion" to block abductees' memories in the first place. And Hopkins also assures us that he is aware of the existence of fantasy-prone individuals—he ran into one once—but since he now has established contact with the proper professionals, everything is hunky-dory. In his words,

> The network of psychiatrists, psychologists, therapists, and investigators which I have slowly been assembling [very slowly, I'll bet!] now encompasses 22 circles in 14 states, Canada, and the District of Columbia. In addition to this network, three psychiatrists have come to me for hypnosis because of their own apparent abduction experiences, as well as four psychologists and a number of therapists. . . . Unfortunately, unqualified practitioners abound, with and without the necessary academic and medical degrees. (Hopkins 1989, p. 30)

Hopkins is indeed correct in this last regard!

Abductions As Folklore

By far the most scholarly and sober of the abduction gurus is Dr. Thomas Bullard, who has a Ph.D. in folklore from Indiana University. Bullard has gained considerable attention and has built up a following primarily on the basis of his attack upon the use of hypnosis in UFO abduction research, which he incidentally takes very, very seriously. He believes in the reality of abductions. According to Bullard, who has catalogued and compared over 300 reports of abductions or abduction-like events, 104 of his cases qualified high in both reliability and information content. A careful analysis on his part has led him to conclude:

> Weighed and found wanting time and again, hypnosis cannot shoulder nearly as much responsibility for abductions as the skeptics have proposed. None of their appeals to confabulation, influence by the hypnotist, and experiments with non-abductees stand up under a comparative examination. In light of these findings, the burden of proof now drops on the skeptics.

They can no longer report their old claims as meaningful answers. For any future rebuttals the skeptics must look deeper into the phenomenon itself rather than simply deduce the hazards of hypnotic testimony from scienific studies of hypnosis, or read theoretical interpretations into abduction reports from a safe distance. The skeptical argument needs rebuilding from the ground up. (Bullard 1989a, p. 36)

Bullard's efforts would be much more acceptable and credible were it not for several considerations. First, the database he used to arrive at his conclusions is certainly highly questionable, and much of it is based on hearsay. Maybe in folklore circles such data are acceptable and de rigeur. In the hard sciences they are not. Second, nothing he has said in his analysis contradicts the fact that all of the contactees and abductees are, more than likely, either fantasy-prone or perpetrators of a hoax. Third, with regard to differences he found between stories of experimental subjects and those of "real" abductees, Bullard failed to consider that the narratives themselves are quite different. One group of stories is told by normal, ordinary students, while the other group of stories is told by experienced fantasizers —the fantasy-prone. Fourth, most damaging to Bullard's cause are his own words:

> Contrary to popular belief, hypnosis cannot guarantee truthful testimony, and in that sense, hypnosis is a disappointment. . . . The potential for misuse of hypnosis is undeniable, yet an examination of abduction evidence points to a reassuring conclusion: what might happen according to theory seems not to have happened in fact. . . . Carefully worked out programs of abduction investigation now under development promise far tighter control over hypnotic procedures in the future, leading to even more reliable testimony. . . . One cloud still darkens this otherwise bright vista: the negative scientific reputation associated with hypnosis. . . . For UFOlogists hypnosis will remain an indispensable tool, but attention to conscious testimony, multiple-witness cases, and physic evidence holds out better hope than hypnosis for gathering the kind of evidence no one can ignore. (Bullard 1986b)

It certainly does not take a clinical psychologist to interpret the above remarks and conclude which side Dr. Bullard is on. He is a "true believer," and it is a dirty shame that people are still doubting the truth of the abductees' claims! Just you wait. Soon we will have the "kind of evidence no one can ignore," and then all of those skeptics will eat their words! With regard to hypnosis per se, it is high time indeed that the UFOlogists recognize its inherent limitations and that hypnosis is not a "truth serum." "Hypnosis no 'truth serum,' " incidentally, is the title of Bullard's essay (1989b).

At this point, many readers might feel compelled to ask, Well, what is so bad about people having fantasies anyway? What harm do they do? They are entertaining. And as far as psychiatric patients are concerned, whether the fantasies are true or false is of little matter—it's the patient's perception of reality that matters, and it is this that you have to treat.

True. If the client believes a thing is so, you have to deal with that belief. The only problem with this procedure lies in its potential for harm. Too many people's lives have been negatively affected and even ruined by well-meaning but tragically misdirected persons who believe the fantasies of children, the alienated, the fantasy-prone, and have charged innocent people with rape, child molestation, assault, Satanic practices, and other sorts of abusive crimes. Nearly every experienced clinician has encountered such claims and then later has discovered to his chagrin that none of the fantasized events ever happened.

Law enforcement officials are also quite familiar with the products of response expectancies and overactive imaginations of fantasy-prone persons who confess to murders that never happened or to murders that did happen but with which they have no connection. Other problems with the UFO and abduction literature is that it is false, misleading, rabble-rousing, sensationalistic, and opportunistically money-grubbing—taking advantage of people's hopes and fears and diverting them from more scientific studies and endeavors. Our journeys to the stars will be made on spaceships created by determined, hardworking scientists applying the principles and laws of science, not flying saucers piloted by little gray aliens from some other dimension.

Flying saucers and spaceships from beyond? Unlikely. Those lights in the sky are much more likely to be ball lightning, normal lightning, meteors, auroras, auroral meteors, weather balloons, experimental aircraft, phenomena related to the murky problems of human perception, or just plain hoaxes.

Need we be concerned about an invasion of little gray kidnappers? Amused, yes. Concerned, no.

Should we take Strieber, Hopkins, et al., seriously? Not really. They are a long way from furnishing reliable and replicable data, and their shaky hypotheses are miles from obtaining anything resembling proof.

In their way, though, the UFOnaut creations may be of some redeeming value. Besides their value as entertainment, they provide the useful albeit unintended service of directing our attention to the extremities of human belief and the perplexing and perennial problem of detecting deception. In spite of all our scientific accomplishments, we have today no absolutely certain, accurate, or reliable means for getting at the truth—for simply determining whether or not someone is lying. Not only are the polygraph and voice-stress analyzer notoriously unreliable and inaccurate, the professional interrogators, body language experts, and psychological testers are also the first to admit their lack of absolute predictive skill. If the abduction claims do no more than stimulate greater effort toward the development of better "truth detectors," they will have made an important contribution.

In the meantime, no matter how skillfully the fabulists present their case, it is important to remember that no authoritative news source has published detailed reports of contacts with aliens backed by proof in the form of nonfantasy-prone multiple witnesses initially freely reporting these contacts *without the benefit of regressive hypnosis.* When one man has a private conversation with an angel in the corner, we consider it hallucinatory; when twenty people simultaneously see and talk with this angel, then we would have good reason to suspect it might not be hallucinatory. When one man never sees an angel in the corner until and unless he is hypnotized and regessed, even then such reports are not hallucinatory. They are merely confabulations. Nor do we classify such a person as psychologically disturbed or even a liar. Most likely he is as normal and mentally healthy as any one of us, and if he has been properly primed with powerful suggestions, might sincerely believe in the truth of his confabulations. If fantasy-prone types tell us about their fantasies, again, we are justified in questioning the validity of their imaginings.

The Psychology of Hoaxters and Lying

For the paranormal investigator the question is sure to arise, "Why would anyone in his right mind want to claim they have been abducted by ET aliens?" The better question to ask is, "Why not?" The quickest way to attain fame, attention, and notoriety—especially from the media—is to claim an alien abduction. Moreover, with the media attention and notoriety comes financial gain in the form of paid appearances on TV talk shows, reimbursement for articles in magazines and journals, and even possible TV specials and movie contracts, and books about the experience. When we remember that every time a murder occurs that is well publicized, many innocent individuals will rush down to police headquarters and confess to the crime. Truly, it is better to be wanted for murder than not to be wanted at all! A policeman friend told us about a man who came by bus all the way from Kansas City, Missouri, to confess to a murder in Lexington, Kentucky—one he had read about in the newspaper. He was, of course, in Missouri at the time the murder was committed in Kentucky. Many individuals have a deep-seated need to create a stir, excitement, to set things into motion, or trigger large social reactions. Arsonists, for example, receive tremendous thrills from all of the uproar created by their inflammatory acts. The need to "be somebody," to "be important and significant" in the scheme of things is also a strong motivating force in many people. You will certainly be treated as important and significant if you associate with ET aliens in our UFO-mythologized culture today. Contact with aliens gives our lives power and meaning.

Since the UFO era began, there have been hoaxes galore. In fact, less than two weeks after Arnold made his sighting, two hoaxsters reported they had seen a saucer crash near Maury Island and even had recovered fragments of it three days before Arnold's sighting. The fragments proved to be pieces of lava rock and the entire story a fraud. The reasons why we have had so many UFO hoaxes from the one just mentioned to the MJ-12 and Gulf Breeze affairs is that they are necessary to keep the myth alive. Without them to continually stimulate and arouse public interest, the UFO phenomena would go the way of the yo-yo and the hula hoop —merely a passing fad. How do you determine whether any report is or is not the truth? This is far from simple or easy. The polygraph or lie detector and the voice stress analyzer are unreliable and easy to beat. A valium tablet fifteen minutes before the polygraph test will mess up the results. Felons know of several other ways to beat the system. As for psychopaths, they have no trouble at all beating the machine because of their lack of emotion. Torture is also equally ineffective in that people will say anything to stop the pain. Unfortunately, as Leonard Saxe and others have stressed (Saxe 1991), at present there is no reliable way of determining truth from falsehood and we currently live in a society in which lying is endemic. According to Ludwig in his book *The Importance of Lying* (1965):

> Who has not falsified, misstated, misquoted, misinterpreted, glossed over, disguised, colored, varnished, dressed up, embroidered, exaggerated, invented, trumped up, fudged, or doctored the truth? Who has not equivocated, quibbled, fenced, beat about the bush, dissembled, dissimulated, feigned, simulated, deceived, or malingered? Who has not been hypocritical, mendacious, artful, political, tricky, cunning, sly, or faithless? Show me a man who denies all of this behavior and you show me a liar! (p. 11)

We lie sometimes to achieve something positive because the truth will hurt or will do nothing good, as in the case of the physician telling the doomed person he will recover. We also tell defensive lies to keep ourselves out of trouble, as well as lies for some sort of financial, political, or social gain. Some people are compulsive liars and they may well lie because of motives deeply buried in their unconscious. In many cases people lie to deceive themselves because they want to believe something is true that isn't or to deny the truth of something unpleasant. Some UFO hoaxsters fall into this category. They so want ET aliens to exist and to contact them, thereby providing them with salvation and special status, that they first invent the tale and then persuade themselves that it is true. Among the UFO hoaxsters we will also find the psychopathic liar or the psychopath. Known also as people with a psychopathic personality, these individuals are in no way mentally abnormal or deficient, but what they do lack is the normal ability to abide by our social standards of honesty, truthfulness, and decency in dealings with others. They can be socially charming and persuasive and they are usually very bright. They can lie so convincingly that you will find it hard to believe they could not be telling the truth were not their tale so utterly incredible. These are the ones you need to take particular care with.

Although there is no sure way to determine if the alleged abductee is lying or not, you should interrogate him about his belief system and his familiarity with the UFO literature, whether or not he believes he is psychic, and whether or not he has had any paranormal experiences. Also ask about his mental and physical health, drug and alcohol consumption, educational background and experiences, employment and financial status, and social stability, i.e., friends, club memberships, etc. It is also advisable to have him repeat his abduction tale several times and make sure you tape each account so that you can compare them for reliability and details. Look for glaring discrepancies and similarities to other classical descriptions such as those reported in Strieber's and Hopkins's books. As Hilary Evans reminds us, while there are shared details in the *kind* of events reported, no two space ships are alike, no two crews of abductors are alike, and so on. Moreover, the existence of abducting spaceships has never been convincingly confirmed by an independent witness, and no one has ever seen an abductee in the process of being abducted. Abductees also have a penchant for exaggerating or elaborating and improving their tale as they go along. For this reason make sure that you get their story and then begin to show skepticism as you go back over the details with them. Give them enough rope to see if they improve and elaborate as you show skepticism and doubt. Continue this for a while and then have them repeat the entire tale from beginning to end. After this is done, then compare the *original* version of the story with the *final* version. This is an important technique because we have noted in a number of cases that someone will call in as did a young housewife to report that all of the pictures on her wall were removed one night and placed on the floor. She wanted us to come and investigate immediately. I told her it would be at least two weeks before I could get there. The next day she called to report her house was haunted, that she had seen the man doing it, and she wanted me to come immediately. I politely informed her it would be another ten days or more before I could make the trip. The following day she called again to report two ghosts, a man, and a woman whom she talked to, and would I please come that day? Again, I urged her to keep a daily record of the hauntings and told her I would be there the following week. A day later she called again to report that the ghosts were now four in number, were attacking her at night and disturbing her sleep, destroying her home, and would kill her if I didn't come and get rid of them for her. I did send her help, but the pattern is clear. If at first you don't get what you want, keep embellishing and elaborating until you *do* get what you want!

Cryptomnesia and Screen Memories

One of the more interesting psychological aspects of the UFO abduction claims is the frequent report by alleged abductees that it wasn't until after they were hypnotized that they began to recall the fact that they had encountered ET aliens on a number of occasions when they were much younger. Other claimants, after encountering a UFOlogical amateur psychotherapist who talks to them about aliens and abductions, suddenly recall that yes, they, too, now remember very clearly that the same thing happened to them. The existence of these "hidden memories" are all examples of cryptomnesia—a psychological experience much more common than is realized. Rather than being memories of actual events, most of the time these "hidden memories" are examples of the failure of recall. We find we have the memory but we can't remember how we got it or where the memories came from. Therefore, if we remember it, it must have happened to us but we just forgot it. The word refers to thoughts and ideas that seem new and original, but which are actually memories of things you've forgotten you knew. A typical example is the Bridey Murphy case. Upon being hypnotized, a Chicago housewife, Virginia Tighe, went back to a previous lifetime and became Bridey Murphy, a young Irish girl living back in nineteenth-century Ireland. The story, written up and published by Morey Bernstein, was taken by many as proof positive of reincarnation. Research by *Chicago American* reporters and by the skeptic Melvin Harris uncovered the source of Virginia's past-life memories. As a Chicago teenager, Virginia lived across the street from an Irish woman named Mrs. Anthony Corkell, who regaled her with tales about the old country. Moreover, Mrs. Corkell's maiden name was Bridey Murphy. Virginia had also been active in high school dramatics and had memorized several Irish monologues, which she learned to speak with a heavy Irish brogue. Also, Virginia heard stories about the Chicago Columbian Exposition that had an entire Irish village recreated. She put all this together to form the basis for her memories while growing up in Chicago in the 1920s. Nearly every case of so-called "past-life memory" that is carefully investigated follows the same pattern: the strange foreign memories seemingly alien to the subject's life experience turn out to be confabulations of something that happened to them in this lifetime, not something in the past.

Rather than assuming that the abductee claimants are mentally ill or deliberately lying, or that they actually were abducted, there is another possibility: that is, the memories are not actually real events in the lives of the claimants, and the amnesia, while it is a real response to a real trauma, is not caused by an abduction. Since our minds reconstruct the past and reorganize, repackage, and alter the memories we have stored, we do not remember very accurately. We fabricate and embellish, and when we can't remember something and have a gap to fill in, we do so with things that didn't occur or didn't happen as we imagine they did. People who experienced severe trauma are usually desperate to fill in the gaps, and to avoid being paralyzed by painful recall will doctor their memories, making them less terrible than they really were. On some occasions the event may take on an entirely different—and sometimes very strange— form in the person's memory. It may be that they remember being tortured by satanists in black masses or being abducted and abused by ET aliens. Rather than remember being abused by parents whom they love, they "screen off" these memories and see themselves as victims of otherworldly demons, aliens, or the devil. This reconstruction protects and *screens* them from the pain of knowing they were hurt by those they loved. There is every reason to believe something like this does happen in some cases of alleged abduction. This is something worthy of exploring in selected cases.

Confusion About Mental Disorders

Many investigators assume that normal, ordinary people do not experience vivid hallucinations. This is untrue; on rare occasions they do. Ronald Siegel of UCLA says that we all can expect to have one or two hallucinations every few years. Not only are all of us likely to misperceive at times, but on occasion—even though we are sane, sober, and free of drugs and mental aberrations—we also occasionally hallucinate (Asad 1990). This little publicized fact is far from new. In 1894 Edmund Parish, following up work undertaken earlier by Edmund Gurney, published a study called *Nature and Frequency of the Occurrences of Hallucinations in the Sane,* which was part of a larger study called the *International Census of Waking*

Hallucinations (Walter Scott 1897). Data for this census was gathered in America by William James, and data was also collected in France, Germany, England, and the Netherlands. One of the questions put to all participants was: "Have you ever, when believing yourself to be completely awake, had a vivid expression of seeing or being touched by a living being or inanimate object, or of hearing a voice; which impression, so far as you could discover, was not due to any external physical cause?" (p. 83).

In response to this question, 27,329 answers were received, of which 24,058 were negative and 3,271 (or 11.96 percent) affirmative. This is to say, that 3,271 people had experienced hallucinations. While a certain proportion could be explained away, most could not and followup investigations in a number of individuals clearly showed the validity of "waking hallucinations" in the sane, and established the fact they are much more common than one would expect. More recent surveys corroborate this finding (Stevenson 1983). The idea that normal, ordinary people do not hallucinate UFOs or suffer delusional fantasies regarding them and that only people with psychological problems do so is erroneous. Also erroneous is the idea that a "lay field investigator" with no psychiatric background or training can determine this by merely talking with the witness. Also erroneous is the UFOlogical argument frequently heard that the mentally ill, the mentally incompetent, the mentally disturbed, and what have you, never report UFO encounters, abductions, etc. In 1971 Dr. Berthold Schwartz made a big issue of the case of Stella Lansing—a paranoid schizophrenic —who saw and photographed UFOs, talked with aliens, visited with them, and so on. (*Flying Saucer Review,* 1971, 1972, 1973, vol. 20, nos. 4, 5, and 6; vol. 21, no. 1) Other therapists are well aware of the fact that aliens and UFOs are themata frequently encountered in the clinic, particularly in schizophrenic delusions and serious personality disturbances. When we also recognize that approximately one percent of the population suffers from schizophrenia, we still have a very large number of individual cases, e.g., over two million in the United States alone.

Recently, a number of UFOlogists with professional degrees have tried to convince the world that many people claiming alien abductions are also perfectly sound, sane, and free from psychological pathology. They have even created a psychological term to describe them: "experienced anomalous trauma," or EAT. There is, however, no such entity in the American Psychiatric Association's Diagnostic and Statistical Manual (DSM), the diagnostic bible for all psychotherapists. Moreover, not only is psychiatric diagnosis a difficult art, but equally experienced, well-trained, and qualified experts will disagree widely in their diagnosis of a specific patient's or client's disorder or illness. They will also disagree with regard to what constitutes the most efficacious treatment. Any court case involving expert psychiatric testimony for the plaintiff, and the defense dramatically exposes the problem. As Faust and Ziskin (1988) observed, "the expert will most likely move the jury further from the truth, not closer to it, given the common tendency to countervail actuarial conclusions and thereby decrease overall judgmental accuracy." Diagnosis is difficult enough when the patient is in front of you and time to administer lengthy test batteries and extensive and exhaustive interviews is available. Yet such prediagnostic procedures are carried out in but a few rare instances by harried and hurried clinicians.

Also of relevance in this connection is the famous (or infamous) Rosenhahn study reported in 1973 (and the subsequent replications), in which eight normal and sane individuals gained admission to twelve different and well-respected psychiatric hospitals by feigning mental illness. None of the eight had any difficulty being admitted and, with but one exception, all were diagnosed as "schizophrenic." Shortly after being admitted, despite their protestations that their symptoms were gone and they felt normal, their confinement lasted from seven to fifty-two days with an average stay of nineteen days. In none of the cases was the person's sanity discovered by either the staff or the physicians, and all were finally discharged only after the physician stated that, in his opinion, their illness was "in remission." The Rosenhahn study has been replicated a number of times with similar results. Some hospitals, when told that a similar study was going to be attempted during a certain time period, managed to identify forty-one out of one hundred ninety-three admissions during this period as "pseudopatients." Unfortunately, no pseudopatients tried to get in.

While it might be somewhat imprecise to call all of the abductees "crazy," they certainly are different from people who do not make such claims. If they are sincere and truly believe what they are saying, then they are deluded and are suffering from an *Unexperienced Anomalous Delusion* (UAD). If they do not believe what they are saying, then they are lying for a reason and are suffering from *Unexperienced Anomalous Prevarication* (UAP). With regard to "crazy" people, i.e., people with psychoses or mental derangements, there is a great misunderstanding generally about their psychopathology. People are not "crazy" all over; they are only crazy in spots. Nor do they hallucinate all day, day in and day out; they only hallucinate some of the time. As for delusions or false beliefs, you wouldn't know you were talking to someone who is disturbed as long as you avoid the subject matter of the person's delusion. Confine your conversation to the weather, baseball, or politics and you won't know there is anything amiss. If you bring up the subject of fire, however, to a delusional arsonist, *then* you would know: he tells you he wants to burn up the world and he has even tried to do it! If he had never set any buildings afire but still had the desire to, he would not be behind bars, and as long as he can resist and control these desires he has the right to run around loose. The dilemma the therapist has is obvious, and the difficulty of diagnosing these sorts of compulsions and delusions is well known to clinicians. It also explains why the Rosenhahn study and its several replications had such an impact on a public unaware of such diagnostic difficulties. A person with paranoid delusions can be particularly dangerous in that he can convince boards of experienced psychiatrists that he no longer believes his wife is trying to kill him. When he is then released by the board, his first action is to go home and kill the wife.

While we would not dare to suggest that the UFOlogical community as a whole or in part may be suffering from paranoid delusions, if some of their members truly believe what they have written, they are coming dangerously close to the territory. Jacques Vallee, for example, believes that miracles, UFOs, and religious revelations are all different aspects of a vast control system—some form of alien intelligence that is manifesting itself in different ways according to the current cultural expectations. In his book *Dimensions* (Contemporary Books, 1988) Vallee argues UFOs are an interdimensional phenomenon. John Keel's contribution to these bizarre ideas is even more strange and paranoid. He believes we are being controlled and manipulated by an intelligence that is out to trick, annoy, and harass us by confronting us with all sorts of bizarre and self-contradictory information and phenomena. He calls these "intelligences" the "mimics of man." Our world is, of course, "The Disneyland of the Gods," which is also the title of his book (Amok Press, 1988). Keel believes that all of our paranormal phenomena are "somehow being protected by unknown psychic forces." Also, according to Keel, the way that the UFOs have historically echoed normal technology is another good example of what Keel believes is this intelligence's way of harassing man. Charles Fort, of course, once exclaimed, "We are property!" Paranoia or truth? You decide.

To summarize this chapter we can do no worse than to present Phil Klass's ten principles of UFOlogy and, with his permission, we have also added an eleventh. We believe these succinctly and brilliantly encapsulate just about everything of any lasting value that we have learned about the UFO phenomenon over the past forty-four years, a phenomenon that the late Donald Menzel described as "the greatest nonsense of the 20th century." We wholeheartedly agree.

UFOlogical Principles

*UFO*logical Principle 1: Basically honest and intelligent persons who are suddenly exposed to a brief, unexpected event, especially one that involves an unfamiliar object, may be grossly inaccurate in trying to describe precisely what they have seen.

*UFO*logical Principle 2: Despite the intrinsic limitations of human perception when exposed to brief, unexpected and unusual events, some details recalled by the observer may be reasonably accurate. The problem facing the UFO investigator is to try to distinguish between those details that are accurate and those that are grossly inaccurate. This may be impossible until the true identity of the UFO can be determined; in some cases this poses an insoluble problem.

*UFO*logical Principle 3: If a person observing an unusual or unfamiliar object concludes that it is probably a spaceship from another world, he can readily adduce that the object is reacting to his presence or actions, when in reality there is absolutely no cause-effect relationship.

*UFO*logical Principle 4: News media that give great prominence to a UFO report when it is first received subsequently devote little, if any, space or time to reporting a prosaic explanation for the case after the facts are uncovered.

*UFO*logical Principle 5: No human observer, including experienced flight crews, can accurately estimate either the distance/altitude or the size of an unfamiliar object in the sky, unless it is in very close proximity to a familiar object whose size or altitude is known.

*UFO*logical Principle 6: Once news coverage leads the public to believe that UFOs may be in the vicinity, there are numerous natural and man-made objects which, especially when seen at night, can take on unusual characteristics in the minds of hopeful viewers. Their UFO reports in turn add to the mass excitement, which encourages still more observers to watch the UFOs. This situation feeds upon itself until such time as the media lose interest in the subject, and then the "flap" quickly runs out of steam.

*UFO*logical Principle 7: In attempting to determine whether a UFO report is a hoax, an investigator should rely on physical evidence, or the lack of it where evidence should exist, and should not depend on character endorsements of the principals involved.

*UFO*logical Principle 8: The inability of even experienced investigators to fully and positively explain a UFO report for lack of sufficient information, even after a rigorous effort, does not really provide evidence to support the hypothesis that spaceships from other worlds are visiting the earth.

*UFO*logical Principle 9: When a light is sighted in the night skies that is believed to be a UFO and this is reported to a radar operator, who is asked to search his scope for an unknown target, almost invariably an "unknown" target will be found. Conversely, if an unusual target is spotted on a radarscope at night that is suspected of being a UFO, and an observer is dispatched or asked to search for a light in the night sky, almost invariably a visual sighting will be made.

*UFO*logical Principle 10: Many UFO cases seem puzzling and unexplainable simply because case investigators have failed to devote a sufficiently rigorous effort to the investigation. (Klass 1983)

*UFO*logical Principle 11: Despite wide and varied claims of abductions, not one of the roughly two hundred "abductees" has returned with a single physical artifact that could confirm his or her story nor has any abductee returned with any new scientific data to substantiate his or her claims. Further, not a single claimant nor any UFOlogist has reported any alleged abduction to the FBI—the public agency responsible for investigating kidnapings. Finally, despite claims to the contrary, all abductee claimants are victims of their own hallucinations and delusions or fantasies lifted from their subconscious, or else they are victims of other misguided individuals using suggestion to convince the unwary and unsuspecting that their fantasies of abduction and violation were suppressed memories of actual occurrences. In the latter instance such behavior is a form of psychological rape worse than any claimed "alien abduction" and should be proscribed—especially by unskilled and untrained amateur psychotherapists.

7

Mysterious Objects and Nature's Enigmas

The works of both man and nature provide us with countless mysteries. Often, however, these are displaced by pseudo-mysteries of an allegedly paranormal cast. In this chapter we look at a variety of mysteries, focusing largely on the means investigators have used to sift fact from fantasy.

Ancient Astronauts

Extraterrestrials are not only making regular visits to planet Earth, some say, but have been doing so for centuries. Erich von Däniken put forth this notion in 1970 with his *Chariots of the Gods?*—a book as popular as it was ridiculous. In it von Däniken postulates that visiting extraterrestrials provided primitive peoples with the technology needed to produce the world's great wonders: the Egyptian pyramids, the massive statues on Easter Island, and the giant drawings on Peru's Nazca plain.

By starting with the "theory" and then casting about for evidence in favor of it, von Däniken imagines he finds such evidence everywhere. Worse, as Terence Hines notes:

> He fabricates and distorts the facts with the sole purpose of supporting his theories. Readers unaware of the detailed archaeological research on the various pseudo-mysteries that von Däniken makes up are tricked into thinking that the evidence for the ancient astronaut theory is much stronger than it really is. (Hines 1982, p. 212)

244

Consider, for example, how von Däniken treats the pyramids. He suggests the Egyptian civilization "appears suddenly and without transition with a fantastic ready-made civilization" (p. 95) complete with the remarkable pyramids that he is sure mere humans could not have produced.

Actually, archaeologists have traced the culture that settled along the Nile back more than a dozen millennia. The pyramids themselves evolved in a definite progression from earthen mounds placed over tombs, to small structures called *mastabas;* to larger stepped mastabas; to stepped pyramids; to the first attempt at a nonstepped pyramid with stone facing, built about 2800 B.C. at Meidum.

Von Däniken's notions about the large stone statues on Easter Island were demolished by research actually conducted years before any of his books were published. Thor Heyerdahl, in his *Aku-Aku* (1958), described how modern islanders accomplished what von Däniken presumed was impossible for their ancient forebears: half a dozen men fashioned a roughly hewn statue using only primitive tools, and a dozen men erected one of the ancient statues that weighed some thirty tons. Successful experiments in quarrying and transporting techniques were also conducted.

As to the Nazca drawings—great lines and huge pictures of birds and other figures that mark some thirty miles of Peruvian desert—von Däniken's treatment of them is revealing of his approach. First of all, the idea that they were created by ancient spacemen is not his own but one that Paul Kosok (1947) orignated in jest. Kosok, the first to study the Nazca markings, wrote: "When first viewed from the air, [the lines] were nicknamed prehistoric landing fields and jokingly compared with the so-called canals on Mars." In addition, a photo published by von Däniken (1970), which shows a Nazca configuration "very reminiscent of the aircraft parking areas in a modern airport," actually depicts a portion of one of the bird drawings, the picture having been cropped so as to disguise the configuration's true context (Woodman 1977, p. 37).

Von Däniken supposes that the Nazca lines represent an ancient "spaceport," with the large pictorials as "signals" and the longer, wider lines as "landing strips." Since the figures can only be properly viewed from the air, von Däniken envisions the UFOs hovering over the desert and broadcasting instructions to the awed Nazca Indians (von Däniken 1970, 1972).

One must wonder, of course, why the extraterrestrials would create signals for themselves in the form of monkeys and spiders, and why some of them would be comparatively small (less than eighty feet in some cases). In fact, the iconographic evidence—the unmistakable resemblances of the stylized ground figures to those produced by the Nazca Indians on their pottery—leaves little doubt as to their cultural origin. So does carbon-14 dating: one of the wooden stakes that mark the end of some of the long lines yielded a date of about A.D. 525, consistent with the Nazca culture that flourished there from about 200 B.C. to A.D. 600 (Isbell 1978, 1980).

Skeptics have provided much more plausible theories for why the drawings were made, for example, that they were offerings to the Indian gods (McIntyre 1975) or represented a giant astronomical calendar (Isbell 1978). They have also speculated as to *how* they were created. Woodman (1977) imagined that the Nazcas did fly over the desert, not in spaceships, but in hot-air balloons which they used for "ceremonial flights" that permitted them to "appreciate the great ground drawings on the *pampas.*" Woodman and his fellow members of the International Explorers Society actually constructed a balloon and gondola (using cloth, rope, and reeds) and made a daring flight complete with crash landing.

However, since proof is lacking that the Indians had such technology, the principle of Occam's razor (see chap. 3, "Rules of Evidence") effectively undercuts the adventurers' credibility. In fact, the Indians needed neither spacecraft nor balloons to insure that their method of enlargement was accurate. Some simpler, earlier figures are found on hill slopes where they can be seen easily. Once a technique was found that was successful for making such figures, it could be employed for larger images on the *pampas* (McIntyre 1975; Isbell 1978, 1980; Nickell 1983).

Maria Reiche (1968) has spent years studying the great drawings, the lines of which are made by removing the dark gravel that covers the *pampas* to expose the lighter-colored earth beneath. She discovered that the Nazca artists employed small, six-foot drawings as models for the larger figures. Somewhat vague on the method of enlargement, she has proposed that "Ancient Peruvians must have had instruments and equipment" together with "prehistoric engineering skills" that have remained hidden.

More specifically, Isbell (1978) suggested that the Indians used a grid system, adapted from their weaving designs, as a means of enlarging small drawings. However, he seems to have little or no experience in making large drawings, nor has he apparently consulted anyone who has; otherwise he would not ascribe the mismatched, asymmetrical features of, say, the giant "condor" to grid enlargement. Even less likely would be the use of surveying techniques that depend on the accurate measurement of angles, a capability the Nazcas are not known to have possessed (Nickell 1983).

As previously mentioned in chapter 2 (under investigative strategy number 2: "Attempt to recreate the 'impossible' "), one of us reproduced the giant condor by a means the Nazcas might have employed. Using a landfill area, a crew of six "Indians" used sticks and knotted cord to establish a center line and locate points on the drawing by plotting their coordinates. Lime was used to mark the resulting lines of the 440-foot duplicate (Nickell 1983). According to *Scientific American* ("Big Picture" 1983), it was "remarkable in its exactness" to the Nazca original.

Another ancient astronaut theorist, Robert Temple (1976), advances a specific theory of extraterrestrial visitation. His book *The Sirius Mystery* argues that beings from the Sirius solar system visited a West African tribe known as the Dogon over one thousand years ago. Temple's main argument is not new. It is that Dogon legends provide accurate astronomical information about a dwarf star in the Sirius system—a star, known as Sirius B, that was not discovered until 1862, although the Dogon legends are supposed much earlier.

As it happens, investigators discredited the claim on various grounds. Ridpath (1978), for example, demonstrated that the Sirius system is incapable of supporting life. Moreover, he and others have, by careful analysis of the claims (see investigative strategy no. 1 in chapter 2), shown that the Dogon's knowledge about Sirius B corresponded to astronomical thinking of the 1920s, a time when European missionaries had begun to visit them. Thus, it would appear that "When westerners in the early twentieth century learned of the Dogon's interest in Sirius, they told them of Sirius B and that information was incorporated into the legends" (Hines 1988, p. 218).

Both Temple and von Däniken—indeed, all who subscribe to the ancient astronaut notion—detract from mankind's genuine accomplishments and hinder, or worse, proper study of their meaning. An investigative approach to such notions is an excellent corrective.

Incredible Icons

Not unlike von Däniken, other zealots begin with a desired answer and work backward to the evidence. Certain religious zealots are a prime example. In chapter 3 we noted briefly how those who believe in the authenticity of the Shroud of Turin (the supposed burial cloth of Christ, bearing the frontal and dorsal images of an apparently crucified man) approach the evidence. They concoct separate rationalizations for the various pieces, which—in contrast—investigators fit together into a cohesive proof that the "shroud" is a fake.

While a detailed look at this evidence is not possible here, we can, quite profitably, briefly review some of the different investigative approaches (detailed in Nickell 1988, 1989b) that have been taken (noting how—despite their different perspectives—they point to a similar conclusion):

Historical Review. Research shows that no burial cloth in the history of the world is known to have borne the imprint of a person's body (albeit that fact is no deterrent to those who ascribe to the Shroud of Turin a miraculous origin). Although some forty cloths have been reputed over the centuries to be the true shroud, there is no record of the Turin cloth prior to the mid-fourteenth century. At that time comes the earliest document mentioning it, a bishop's report to Pope Clement that an artist had confessed to having "cunningly painted" the image. Clement judged the matter (then the subject of controversy) and determined the alleged relic was a mere "painting or picture made in the semblance or representation of the shroud."

Iconographic Approach. Although Christ's actual features are unknown, the "shroud" suddenly appeared in the fourteenth century bearing an image like the one artists had already arrived at by evolutionary development. Indeed, the figure strongly resembles those of French gothic art. Also the shroud combines two earlier traditions: by the eleventh century artists had begun to represent the Holy Shroud as a double-length cloth (like the Turin one), and by the thirteenth century there were ceremonial shrouds bearing full-length images of Jesus' dead body. From an iconographic point of view, the combination of these traditions in the Shroud of Turin suggests it is the work of an artist of the thirteenth century or later.

Physical and Anatomical Study. Simply by looking at the shroud image, one can see elements that are obviously not in accord with reality. For example, the hair hangs down on either side of the face as if the figure had been upright rather than recumbent. A bloody footprint on the dorsal image would have required the leg to have been drawn up, with the knee bent at a considerable angle, and not outstretched as on the shroud. The "blood" flows in a neat and picturelike manner (for example, failing to mat the hair and instead running in rivulets on the outside of the locks), and it has remained red, unlike real blood which darkens with age. On further reflection, one wonders how *dried* blood (as on the arms) could have transferred to the cloth at all.

Microscopic and Chemical Analyses. In 1973 the "blood" was tested by two internationally known forensic specialists. Microscopic examination failed to reveal corpuscles or other blood components. Routine chemical tests were likewise negative, as were more sophisticated analyses, including thin-layer chromatography and attempts to speciate the blood. In 1979 Walter McCrone, an internationally known microanalyst, discovered paint pigments on the shroud. In a "blind" study he found significant amounts of red ocher (iron oxide) on the image but not off-image areas. He later determined the "blood" to be tempera paint containing red ocher and vermilion.

Image Replication. Attempts to produce similar images are instructive. Simple contact between cloth and body yields wraparound distortions, and not all the areas that are imprinted on the shroud would have been touched by a draped cloth. Postulated "body vapors" and "radiant energy" are also incapable of producing shroudlike images (even putting aside the artistic-appearing "blood" flows). Artistic techniques meet with varying success. Ordinary painting seems unlikely given that the image stain (unlike the "blood") does not soak into the threads. However, a type of rubbing technique, using a bas-relief, does yield numerous shroudlike features including quasi-negativity (the image's darks and lights being approximately reversed), minimal depth of penetration, presence of pigments, and so on.

Carbon-14 Testing. Given the foregoing evidence, the age of the cloth seemed a foregone conclusion (although it remained possible that a forger had obtained an ancient cloth for the purpose). In 1988, using accelerator mass spectrometry to carbon-date the cloth, laboratories at Zurich, Oxford, and the University of Arizona obtained dates in close agreement, and their credibility was enhanced by correct dates obtained from several swatches of ancient cloth used for controls. A span of circa A.D. 1260-1390 was indicated, the mid-point date of 1325 being fully consistent with the cloth's first known appearance about 1355.

Immediately after the test, shroud advocates were attempting to rationalize—or discredit—the results. (For example, some thought that a burst of radiant energy at the moment of Christ's resurrection had altered the carbon ratio.) However, observe how each of the very different approaches yields results that demonstrate the "shroud" is the handiwork of a medieval artisan. Taken together, the results are impressive.

Another supposedly miraculous icon is Mexico's Image of Guadalupe, a sixteenth-century depiction of the Virgin Mary, which—according to pious legend—miraculously appeared as a "sign" to a skeptical bishop to cause him to build a shrine to her. "Yearly," according to Jody Bryant Smith's *The Image of Guadalupe,* "an estimated ten million bow down before the mysterious virgin, making the Mexico City church the most popular shrine in the Roman Catholic world next to the Vatican" (1983, p. 4).

The Image is so popular that:

> You will find every imaginable representation of her in the churches. . . .
> You may find her outlined in neon as part of a downtown spectacular,
> chalked into a hillside, on a throwaway advertising mouthwash, pricked
> out in flowers in public parks; clowns and hucksters will distribute booklets
> about her as a preliminary to hawking patent medicines. . . . Bullfighters
> have her image woven into their parade capes; she is a popular tattoo subject; almost everyone wears her medal. (Demarest and Taylor 1945, p. 2)

Because the cloth was accompanied by a supposedly contemporary account of the "miracle," and because the Image itself was amenable to analysis (if not made available for full scientific testing), a two-pronged investigation was conducted, as reported in full in Nickell and Fischer's "The Image of Guadalupe: A Folkloristic and Iconographic Investigation" (1985).

Briefly, a study of the Mexican tale revealed disturbing elements, including a striking similarity to an earlier Spanish legend. Whereas in the Mexican account the Virgin first appears to an Aztec peasant, in the Spanish one she appears to a shepherd. And just as in the Mexican story she caused her miraculous portrait to appear, in the Spanish tale she prompted a statue of her to be discovered. Such similar elements (folklorists call them *motifs*) have evidential value, particularly when they are used together in a particular combination (Thompson 1955). Even more striking is the fact that the Spanish locale was on a river known as *Guadalupe*!

The legend also links the Image of Guadalupe to a tradition of *Acheiropoietos* or "not-made-with-hands" images, a tradition ranging from the sixth-century "self-portrait" of Christ known as the Image of Edessa, to its later variant, Veronica's Veil, to, of course, the fourteenth-century Shroud of Turin—pious frauds all. There was even a special tradition of miraculous "dark madonnas" to which—even apart from the legend—the Virgin of Guadalupe is linked.

In addition to other elements, there is an especially telling factor, one suggesting the legend was deliberately manufactured for a specific purpose. The shrine that housed the Image as the legend directed was located approximately where an Indian temple had stood, one dedicated to the Aztec virgin goddess, Tonantzin. Thus (in a process folklorists term *syncretism*) the Christian tradition was grafted onto the Indian one with predictable results: The "miracle" helped hasten the conversion of the conquered Indians.

Turning from folkloristics to iconography, again there is considerable borrowing. The Image, first of all, matches the traditional portrait of Mary —the result of a purely artistic tradition. The image also has numerous, standard artistic motifs (such as gold fleur-de-lis designs that symbolize the Virgin Mother), but pro-authenticity writers maintain they are later additions. Indeed, they insist that so much is the product of a later hand that only the "original figure, including the rose robe, blue mantle, hands and face" are part of the supposedly miraculous original image (Callahan 1981, pp. 18, 20).

However, there is obvious cracking and flaking—indicative of paint —all along a vertical seam that extends through the "original" areas of mantle and robe, and there are many additional indications of artistry.

For instance, her eyes, including the irises, are *outlined* as they often are in paintings but not in nature; the part in her hair is off center; and the *contrapposto* stance and other elements are indicative of European Renaissance paintings. Moreover, infrared photography reveals what appear to be sketch lines beneath the paint.

The separate studies of legend and image both clearly point not to a miracle but to human artistry. Taken together, they are mutually corroborative, and that conclusion is underscored by the fact that, during a formal investigation of the cloth in the year 1556, a Franciscan priest testified that the Image was "a painting that the Indian painter Marcos had done" (Nickell and Fischer 1988).

Other incredible icons are the bleeding and weeping pictures and statues that are reported frequently by the news media. For example, in 1985 a two-foot-high statue of the Virgin owned by a Quebec railroad worker began to weep—first tears and then blood. Beginning on December 3, the feast of the Immaculate Conception, the phenomenon soon spread to other nearby statues and icons. In scarcely a week's time, the "miracle" had drawn as many as twelve thousand people, many lining up for hours in sub-zero temperatures to see the bleeding statue.

Not surprisingly, given the track record of such phenomena, the "miracle" was soon exposed as a pious hoax. In this case a mixture of blood and beef fat applied to the statue would flow whenever the room became heated ("Virgin Mary" 1986).

In another case, that of a weeping thirty-nine-inch wooden statue of the Madonna that purportedly wept periodically in a Catholic church in southwest Chicago, the local Archdiocese conducted an investigation during 1984–85. Lacking any direct evidence—no one had thought to collect specimens of the "tears"—the investigators reportedly analyzed the statue's paint and attendant atmospheric conditions and took depositions from those who claimed to have witnessed the flows (Clark 1984). Unfortunately for those who had sought special meaning from the alleged phenomenon, the archdiocesan committee concluded that no miracle had occurred ("Church" 1985).

In July 1989, a color photograph of a painting in a Tarpon Springs, Florida, Greek Orthodox church began to weep—until Dr. Gary Posner, a founder of the Tampa Bay Skeptics, investigated. He soon discovered that the "tears" were actually on the original painting that was depicted in the photo, a painting captioned, *The Guiding Mother of God Weeping Icon* (Posner 1990). In Chicago, where the original painting is located, church officials refused to allow the artwork to be analyzed (Kavvadias 1986, Dahl 1987).

According to an article in the *Wall Street Journal:*

Most weeping icons remain mysterious, though. Unless they involve leaky plumbing or obvious mischief, these icon happenings are rarely investigated by church officials, for fear of offending the faithful. And scientific studies have been inconclusive. The Eastern New Mexico Medical Center in Roswell, for example, once analyzed blood from a picture of Jesus Christ. The blood was human, but whose blood it was wasn't determined. (Dahl 1987)

One investigator, Shawn Carlson, a physicist at the Lawrence Berkeley Laboratory in California who has been studying weeping icons, laments that people cannot distinguish a real miracle from a hoax unless proper examination is permitted. In response to the Chicago weeping painting, he demonstrated how salt crystals could be used to make a reproduction of the Mona Lisa seem to weep, while keeping his exact method a secret. Thus far, he has discovered "six ways to gimmick a painting and make it cry," he told *Newsweek*. "We're not saying the Chicago icon is a fake," Carlson says, "but you'd think 'a sign from God' would not be so easily duplicated by natural means" ("The Scientist" 1987).

A rather different type of "miracle," a *swaying* statue of the Virgin, drew "hundreds of thousands of pilgrims" to a roadside grotto in Ballinspittle, Ireland, in 1985—that is, until three men smashed it while nuns and worshipers stood by, horror-stricken ("3 Accused" 1985). In the meantime, scientists from University College, Cork, had studied the phenomenon:

> But the effect is an illusion, they say. It is induced when people rock gently back and forth while looking at the statue. At dusk, when the sky is grey and landmarks are obscured, the eye has no point of reference except the halo of blue lights. Therefore, say the scientists, the eye is unable to detect the fact that one's head and body are unconsciously moving. The viewer who sways is likely to get the impression that not he but the statue is moving. "None of us is out to belittle anybody's beliefs," the scientists say. "It's simply that we believe there's a physical explanation." ("Those Who" 1985, p. 19)

Another supposedly animated statue was a life-sized crucifix of Christ that reportedly closed its eyes during a Good Friday service in 1989. Suspended fifteen feet above the altar of Holy Trinity Church in Ambridge, Pennsylvania, and backlighted by a stained-glass window, the crucifix had recently been moved from an eye-level position in a corner of the Roman Catholic church. In the interim it had been restored and the eyes touched up with acrylic paint. At that time they were definitely open, according to the artist who did the restoration work. Although no one ever claimed to see the eyelids moving, several Good Friday worshipers insisted that the eyes had closed during the service.

Thorough investigation by the Pittsburgh diocese, however, turned up before and after photographs that revealed the eye in the same state: about one-third open. The effects of light and shadow, different angles of viewing, and the expectations of the Easter season faithful probably produced the illusion (Memmott 1989, "Devout" 1989, "No Proof" 1989).

A more profoundly animated statue in a Thornton, California, church, representing Our Lady of Fatima, allegedly exhibited both weeping and extraordinary movement: from place to place within the church! Each time the statue was returned to its location, but on the thirteenth of each month (when the original Lady of Fatima had supposedly appeared to Portuguese children in 1917) the statue would be found again at the altar. Eventually it was bolted in place, but it returned to the altar, leaving the bolt in its stand. "That's when we were finally convinced," stated one parishioner (Magagnini 1984). A yearlong investigation by a panel of priests, however, labeled the events a probable hoax (Memmott 1989).

Another class of incredible icon is the image—usually of Mary or Jesus —that suddenly comes to light, often in an unlikely place. For example, an image of Christ was seen in rust stains on a soybean-oil storage tank in Ohio ("Image" 1986). Another likeness was seen in skillet burns on a tortilla in New Mexico (Memmott 1989). Each created a sensation. Random stains found anywhere can function as something of an inkblot test in which the viewer sees what is in his or her imagination—possibly prompted by the suggestion of others.

Occasionally, some unusual circumstance creates an "apparition"—like the one that appeared on the wall of a suburban Wilkes Barre, Pennsylvania, house in mid-1937. Hundreds turned out to see what many insisted was an image of the Virgin Mary. A sensible patrolman, however, realized that the image was simply a reflection of a street light bouncing off a nearby curved-glass window, and demonstrated the fact by using his hand to obstruct the beam. "You try to show them, but they won't believe it," he said. "They just believe it's a miracle or something." Finally, the image ceremoniously disappeared when, at the police chief's request, the offending window was opened ("Reflected" 1987).

Similarly, images in the shape of crosses appeared on the glass of a bathroom window in a Los Angeles area home, but police and Roman Catholic priests insisted the phenomenon was simply the result of light refracted through the textured glass. That explanation, though, did not deter the faithful who lined up by the hundreds to file through the small home. "I think it is something from God. A warning," stated a three-time visitor who had brought her children (Wilkinson 1990).

Curiously—if icon phenomena are to be taken seriously—such occurrences seem profoundly absent at places where religious paintings and statuary often proliferate: art museums. There, controlled climates help keep artworks from sweating or collecting moisture by condensation, good security systems with ever-present guards help prevent hoaxes, and the generally unemotional atmosphere mitigates against "swaying" statues and other misperceived or imagined phenomena.

Monsters Galore

If fuzzy photographs, plaster casts of tracks, and other dubious evidence are to be believed, apelike creatures populate not only remote mountains of Asia but the North American continent as well, sea serpents inhabit both oceans and freshwater lakes, and other strange creatures are afoot around the globe. But like unicorns and other creatures of yore, they are nothing if not elusive.

Yetis for example are said to be shy and so are rarely seen and never captured. Yet for more than three centuries the Sherpa people of the Himalayan Mountains have believed in the wild apelike creature who is said to be up to eight feet tall, with conical skull and large feet (MacDougall 1983). Through their contact with Sherpa guides, western explorers and mountaineers (including those seeking to climb Mt. Everest) brought back rumors of the giant creature dubbed "Abominable Snowman" (Heuvelmans 1972, pp. 76–84).

Some early reports of sightings and descriptions of large footprints are ambiguous, but a 1925 sighting by Greek photographer N. A. Tombazi has often been mentioned. As Tombazi is quoted by Heuvelmans (1972):

> The intense glare and brightness of the snow prevented me from seeing anything for the first few seconds; but I soon spotted the "object" referred to, about two to three hundred yards away down the valley to the East of our camp. Unquestionably, the figure in outline was exactly like a human being, walking upright and stopping occasionally to uproot or pull at some dwarf rhododendron bushes. It showed up dark against the snow and, as far as I could make out, wore no clothes. Within the next minute or so it had moved into some thick scrub and was lost to view. (pp. 78–79)

Given the fleeting glimpse and poor viewing conditions, it is uncertain what Tombazi actually saw. He characterized the opinions of the natives as "fantastic legends." He added:

Without in the least believing in these delicious fairy-tales myself, notwithstanding the plausible yarns told by the natives, and the references I have come across in many books, I am still at a loss to express any definite opinion on the subject. (p. 79)

However, many years later he offered a theory: that the "wild man" could have been simply a hermit or ascetic. Daniel Cohen comments in his *The Encyclopedia of Monsters*:

There are Buddhist and Hindu ascetics who seek out the desolation of high places. They can live at altitudes of fifteen thousand feet and can train themselves to endure cold and other hardships that would kill the average person. They can and do walk about naked or nearly so in the frigid mountain air. So Tombazi might really have seen a wandering ascetic, as he first thought.

That is a disappointing beginning to the Abominable Snowman story, but it is also quite typical, for the evidence that supports the existence of this creature has frequently been less solid than it first appears. (Cohen 1982, pp. 6–7)

Such was the case with a 1986 photograph by British physicist Anthony Wooldridge. Taken in the Himalayas near the India-Tibet border, the photo depicted what Wooldridge and many others believed was the first *yeti* ever photographed.

Alas, recent photogrammetric evidence (photogrammetry is the making of surveys by photographic means) demonstrated—by Wooldridge's own admission—"beyond a reasonable doubt that what I had believed to be a stationary, living creature was, in reality, a rock." Corroborating evidence came from a subsequent photo of the mountian slope that a local inhabitant took at Wooldridge's request. Absent the snow there was indeed a rock feature on the slope that the physicist conceded was clearly the object he had photographed (Dennett 1989a).

Equally disappointing have been Abominable Snowman tracks. Those photographed by Frank Smythe in 1937 reveal that the trail "was indisputedly a bear's" (Heuvelmans 1972, p. 81), and the celebrated photos of mountaineer Eric Shipton, taken in 1951, depicted the trail of a mountain goat (Cohen 1982, p. 7). Confusion can be caused by several factors, such as footprints melting, thereby enlarging and becoming distorted before refreezing.

Other alleged traces of the creature were "yeti scalps," curious objects treated as sacred relics in Tibetan monasteries. Having studied photographs of these "scalps," zoologist Bernard Heuvelmans considered the skepticism of others. As he said:

Now it is undoubtedly true that a flat piece of leather suitably moistened and stretched over a mold can be shaped into a miter. But if the hair tracts are to radiate outward, as they do on the supposed scalps, the piece of leather cannot be cut from any part of the skin. The crest of erect hair seemed to me to prove that the skin of the scalps must have been cut from somewhere along the medial line which runs along a mammal's back from its nose to the end of its tail. Moreover, I had to admit that on a neck or a back the hair always runs parallel to the medial line, whereas in these scalps most of it is at right angles to this line. This arrangement of the hair is found only on the crown of the head. And as a large primate is the only creature with a big cranium of the right shape, I thought this was a conclusive proof that the supposed scalps were genuine. (Heuvelmans 1972, p. 102)

But Heuvelmans soon changed his mind. When he was actually able to examine the scalp brought back by Hillary, it reminded him of the neck and mane of a serow (a chamois goat). Experiments by a fellow zoologist, Ivan T. Sanderson, showed that skin from an animal's neck, when stretched over a mold, could produce a "scalp" with hair pointing outward like that on a primate's head. A subsequent comparison of hair samples settled the matter: the "yeti's scalp" was a fake made from the pelt of a Nepalese serow (Heuvelmans 1972, pp. 102–103).

As an outcome of his expedition, Hillary denounced the whole concept of the Abominable Snowman as nonsense. Monster enthusiasts were angry, but Hillary's prestige and background gave him credibility. As a consequence, after 1960, according to Cohen, "interest shifted to other monsters, particularly Bigfoot in the United States and Canada" (1982, p. 9).

Like the Abominable Snowman, Bigfoot is a large, hairy, apelike creature. It is generally equated with the legendary Indian Sasquatch (or "hairy man") which is said to live in caves in British Columbia and the Pacific Northwest (Cavendish 1974, p. 219).

Questionable reports to the contrary, no credible capture of the alleged creature has been recorded (Bord and Bord 1982, p. 20), and skeptics are quick to point out that no carcasses or even partial skeletons have ever been recovered. "Surely the creatures die," insists Cohen (1982, p. 18).

The main evidence for the creature's existence, therefore, consists of sightings and footprints—neither able to provide conclusive proof that the animal exists. Interestingly, alleged Bigfoot tracks vary considerably in size and structure, even possessing anywhere from two toes to six—just the variety one would expect from independent hoaxers. Indeed, just how easy it is to perpetrate a hoax involving a set of Bigfoot tracks is illustrated by the following story.

In 1930 near Mount St. Helens, Washington, some people who had been picking huckleberries returned to their parked cars to discover huge, manlike tracks circling the area. Excitedly, they reported the tracks to rangers at a nearby Forest Service station. For more than half a century the tracks remained a mystery.

Then in 1982 a retired logger named Rent Mullins, who had been working for the Forest Service at the time the tracks appeared, confessed that he had been involved in faking the giant footprints. As a prank he had carved from a piece of wood a pair of 9-by-17-inch feet. A friend, Bill Lambert, had then strapped them on to his own feet and walked around the area where the huckleberry pickers' cars were parked (Dennett 1982).

Much more realistic footprints have appeared in recent years, curiously following extensive published descriptions of what genuine Bigfoot tracks should be like. In 1982, in the Mill Creek Watershed of Oregon's Blue Mountains, a new Forest Service patrolman discovered sets of humanlike but oversized footprints complete with dermal ridges (the ridges that on the hands produce fingerprints). Several experts thought the footprints could not have been faked, and they were hailed as startling new proof of Bigfoot's existence.

Investigation at the time by the U.S. Forest Service and later by skeptical investigator Michael Dennett (1989b) turned up numerous reasons for suspecting a hoax, which would make a useful checklist of procedures for investigators to follow in future such cases:

1. On-site biologist's inspection. Forest Service wildlife biologist Rodney L. Johnson visited the Mill Creek site the very next day and noted the following (summarized from Dennett 1989b):

a. *Surface condition.* According to Johnson, "It appeared that the fine forest litter (needles, etc.) had been brushed aside prior to making the track. It was obvious that the litter had been displaced sideways from the track area in an unusual manner."

b. *Depth of tracks.* Suspiciously, "the tracks at both sites were not to the bottom of the mud," whereas the investigators themselves "were sinking in deeper with boots on at the same locations." This suggests the creature who actually made the tracks was incongruously lightweight to have such large feet.

c. *Appearance of tracks.* Johnson also reported, "In several cases, it appeared that the foot may have been rocked from side to side to make the track." Also the "toes on some tracks appeared wider" from one print to another.

   d. Dermal ridges. Johnson (in contrast to a later dermatological specialist who examined a cast of the prints but not the original tracks)
   observed that dermal ridges "were very clear on the portions of
   the foot that should be worn smooth and calloused."

   e. Stride. Johnson found that the tracks' stride "did not change with
   slope," as would be expected, and that there was "no sign of heel
   or toe *slippage* on the steep gradient."

2. Tracker's proximity search. Professional tracker Joel Hardin, a U.S.
Border Patrol officer, was brought in on the case. With the lack of human
traffic, Hardin found that the conditions for the "observation and read-
ability of human sign" were "excellent." However, an exhaustive search
of the vicinity failed to reveal any continuity of the trail beyond the immediate impressions. Hardin stated that "the tracks appeared and disappeared
on the trail with no sign leading to or away from the area." He concluded
the tracks were a hoax (Dennett 1989b).

3. Background investigation. Investigators found that the new
patrolman who discovered the tracks, Paul Freeman, had an interesting
background in light of his discovery (again summarized from Dennett 1989b):

   a. Prior discoveries. Freeman had an astonishing propensity for making alleged Bigfoot discoveries: he has found handprints and several sets of footprints plus specimens of hair (identified by a police
   lab as "being exactly like human hair") and dung; he has tape-
   recorded the animal's screech, and has photographed the creature
   twice; and on at least two occasions, he has had face-to-face encounters with Bigfoot.

   b. Financial interest. Freeman is a talented amateur artist and sculp-
   tor who carves and sells small busts of Bigfoot and other Sasquatch
   memorabilia. He also had plans to establish a Bigfoot museum as
   a business endeavor.

   c. Previous fakery. Astonishingly, Freeman actually has admitted to
   having previously made false Sasquatch footprints.

   d. Previous employment. According to two reliable sources, Freeman
   at one time worked for an orthopedic-shoe business, where he could
   have learned the techniques of making molds of feet from casting
   material.

4. Track replication. Given the foregoing evidence that the tracks were a hoax and the possibility that Freeman could have faked them, Dennett (1989b) had a cobbler make him a set of fake Bigfoot feet, complete with dermal ridges, using as models a customer's size-16 feet. With these, Dennett made convincing Mill Creek-like impressions.

Like many other alleged Bigfoot traces before, the Mill Creek tracks were revealed as hoaxes. Although they were more cleverly done than previous hoaxed footprints, they were not done carefully enough to withstand a thorough investigation by competent, tough-minded investigators.

But what about several frames of 16mm color motion picture film of the creature? The film was taken in October 1967 by Roger Patterson who, like Paul Freeman, was a longtime Bigfoot enthusiast who had frequently "discovered" the creature's tracks. Accompanied by his friend Bob Gimlin, he encountered a female Sasquatch while the two Bigfoot buffs were riding horseback in the Bluff Creek, northern California area. As their frightened horses reared, the pair alleged, Patterson's horse fell, but he jumped clear and grabbed for the movie camera in his saddlebag. He managed to briefly film the creature that strode away, a few frames recording its hairy, pendulous breasts that identify it as a female of the legendary species (Bord and Bord 1982, p. 80).

Many who viewed the film have been skeptical. For example, the stride seemed exaggerated, as Cohen (1982, p. 17) states, "almost as if a bad actor were trying to simulate a monster's walk." Dr. John Napier of the Smithsonian Institution, an expert in primate biology and anatomy, seemed to sum up the opinion of many scientists when he quipped: "I couldn't see the zipper" (Cohen 1982, p. 17). In other words, all Patterson's film would have required was a monster costume, similar to one pictured in Janet and Colin Bord's *The Bigfoot Casebook* (1982, p. 128). The fur suit was used in a Bigfoot hoax in 1977 near Mission, British Columbia.

Showing the length hoaxers will go to provide "proof" of the mythical monster's existence is the case of the Minnesota Iceman, a Sasquatch-type creature encased in a block of ice and exhibited at fairs and carnivals. Viewing it through the ice's foggy surface in 1968, two famous "cryptozoologists" (as scientists who look for unknown animals term themselves), Ivan Sanderson and Bernard Heuvelmans, were impressed. Heuvelmans thought the creature was "most probably" a Neanderthal man who had been living fewer than five years before. Alas, the creature was only a rubber figure crafted by Howard Ball, a top Disneyland model-maker (Emery 1981–82; Cohen 1982, p. 25).

Quite a different-appearing monster from Bigfoot and the Abominable Snowman is a creature affectionately dubbed "Nessie." However, it has proven just as elusive in its own domain: Loch Ness, a twenty-two-mile-long Scottish lake (loch) which is the largest freshwater body in Great Britain.

Nessie has been variously described. It may be only six feet long or extend up to one hundred twenty-five feet. Sometimes it resembles a great eel, but on other occasions it has a large hump or humps, twelve by one count. At times it has also possessed either fins, flippers, a mane, horns, tusks, or any of various other features; then again it has had none of them. Its color has been described as brown or gray or blue-black or black or other shades of this or that (Gould 1934, Binns 1984).

One theory of this chameleonesque monster is that it is a prehistoric sea creature, perhaps a Pleisosaurus, that entered the lake by swimming up the River Ness from the sea. Of course, the long-necked Pleisosaurus became extinct millions of years ago.

Some alleged sightings of the creature—and some photographs—have been attributed to swimming deer, salmon, a group of otters swimming in a row, even floating logs and other objects. The most famous pictures are on a film taken by Tim Dinsdale in 1960. An analysis of the film was conducted by the Royal Air Force Joint Air Reconnaissance Intelligence Center, which concluded that the moving object shown in the film was likely an "animate object." Carefully read, however, the center's report shows that the object could be attributed to a motorboat, if it is assumed the boat was painted a dull color (Binns 1984; Hines 1988, p. 287).

A more recent photograph, taken underwater in 1972 by Robert Rines and a crew from his Academy of Applied Science, supposedly depicted a "flipper" from an unknown creature. As it happens, the original computer-enhanced pictures were subsequently discovered to have been "significantly altered to give the impression of the flipperlike objects that appear in the published version" (Razdan and Kielar 1984–85). The unretouched photos could depict virtually anything. In addition, expert review of the sonar evidence—which Rines claimed as support for his interpretation of the "flipper" photo—discredited the supposed proof of a sea creature's existence (Razdan and Kielar 1984–85).

Many other sightings have been outright hoaxes, as have other alleged traces of the monster. In one instance, for example, large tracks were discovered along the shore of the loch, but it turned out that they had been produced by a cast made from a hippopotamus's hoof (Gould 1934; Nickell 1989a, pp. 91–92)!

In short, no authentic trace of Nessie—no carcass floating to the surface of the loch or skeleton bleaching on the shore—has ever been discovered. As *Time* magazine once reported, "There is hardly enough food in the loch to support such leviathans" and, "in any case, there would have to be at least twenty animals in a breeding herd" in order for the species to have continued to reproduce over the centuries ("Myth" 1972).

Many other monsters could be discussed, such as the legendary werewolf, or "Jersey Devil," or other strange creatures (Fort 1974, pp. 608–24; Cohen 1982, passim), but with similarly unrewarding results—at this time, anyway. Still, one remains mindful that the existence of the largest known ape, the mountain gorilla, was not confirmed until 1901 (Heuvelmans 1972, p. 21) and that the coelacanth—a fish thought to have been long extinct—was discovered otherwise in 1938 (Binns 1984, p. 215). But these creatures' existence *was* confirmed; they were not merely the subject of endless "discoveries," speculation, and even outright silliness like that which has characterized the topic of monsters and provoked so many necessary—if ultimately fruitless—investigations.

Nature's Mysteries

Charles Fort (1874–1932) loved to challenge scientists with things they supposedly could not explain: fish falling from the sky, for example. After working briefly as a reporter, Fort came into an inheritance that permitted him to indulge his hobby. For his remaining twenty-six years he scoured old newspapers and magazines for instances of mysterious occurrences that he used to attack what he dubbed the scientific "priestcraft" (Gardner 1957, pp. 42–54). Fort did not investigate the occurrences; rather he gives the impression that he believed whatever was reported was true, or at least suitable to use in taunting scientists. Just before Fort's death, admirers formed the Fortean Society. A brochure boasted:

> The Society provides haven for lost causes, most of which—but for our sympathy—might become quite extinct. . . . A good many adherents of a flat earth are members, anti-vivisectionists, anti-vaccinationists, anti-Wasserman-testers and people who still believe disarmament of nations would be a good thing. (as quoted in Gardner 1957, p. 44)

Today, many students of the paranormal style themselves "Forteans," an unfortunate label when all too often it is used by those who seem primarily interested in fostering mysteries as a challenge to "orthodox" scientists.

A more appropriate and more mature stance is to recognize that nature does offer genuine mysteries, but to further recognize that—rather than deserving to be either promoted or dismissed—they are meant to be investigated and hopefully solved.

A case in point is the spine-tingling subject of "spontaneous human combustion" (SHC), an alleged phenomenon in which people are supposedly consumed by fire without external source for the ignition. If there is no such phenomenon—as, yes, "orthodox" science holds—then whatever happened to the Countess Bandi of Italy, who in 1731 was mysteriously reduced to "a heap of ashes"? Or—to consider more modern cases, fully documented with photos of the remains—what happened in 1951 to Mrs. Mary Reeser of St. Petersburg, Florida, a large woman whose body was nevertheless almost totally destroyed, although her apartment was virtually undamaged? Or, again, what befell Dr. J. Irving Bentley, a Coudersport, Pennsylvania, physician, who perished in 1966, little being left of him but his leg, burned off at the knee?

In the nineteenth century, the debate over spontaneous human combustion raged. Those who postulated the phenomenon came in for criticism from scientists like Liebig who wrote:

> The opinion that a man can burn of himself is not founded on a knowledge of the circumstances of the death, but on the reverse of knowledge —on complete ignorance of all the causes or conditions which preceded the accident and caused it. (Liebig 1851, letter 22)

In other words, the proponents were guilty of the fallacy of arguing *ad ignorantiam* (discussed earlier in chapter 3), that is, of arguing from ignorance.

Skeptics were not always willing—or in fairness to them, not always *able*—to conduct investigations of SHC, particularly since occurrences that might be attributed to the phenomenon are rare. However, in response to SHC theorists, including members of the temperance movement who had suggested alcohol-impregnated tissues were responsible for heightened combustibility, several scientists conducted experiments which disproved the notion. They also observed that one would die of alcohol toxicity long before consuming enough to affect the body's flammability (Lewes 1861).

But what about the cases cited above? A two-year investigation began with an historical overview—thirty alleged instances of the phenomenon, selected from a much larger number, that dated from the eighteenth to the twentieth century—then focused in more detail on the often cited Reeser case. This amounted to a reinvestigation of that death, which involved digging up the original police report, Mrs. Reeser's death certificate, contemporary news accounts, and the like (Nickell with Fisher 1988, pp. 149–57, 161–71).

For example, in the case of the Italian countesss, a source published in 1746 not only described the gruesome state in which her remains were discovered, but provided an obvious key for unlocking the supposed mystery: *On the floor was a lamp, empty of its oil and covered with ashes!* Quite probably the countess had fallen on the lamp, the flaming oil aiding in the burning of her body.

In the Reeser case, investigation revealed that when last seen, the widowed, sixty-seven-year-old Mrs. Reeser had been wearing flammable night clothes, sitting in a large stuffed chair, and smoking a cigarette after having taken between two and four sleeping pills! Why had the apartment been so little damaged? The floor and walls were of concrete and the chair was sitting in the center of the room. (An adjacent lamp and end-table *were* destroyed, along with the chair). As to the severe destruction of Mrs. Reeser's body, a clue comes from the fact that "grease" (obviously residue from her body) had been left where the chair had stood. Mrs. Reeser was a plump woman whose own body fat probably aided in the destruction. Absorbed into the stuffing of the chair, this would have fuelled the fire, destroying more of the body and releasing still more fat to continue the cycle. This is known in the forensic literature as the "candle effect."

In the case of Dr. Bentley, the ninety-two-year-old physician was a pipe-smoker who had a history of dropping ashes on his clothes. Burns on the bedroom rug indicate he had done this a final time. He made his way into the bathroom (by the aid of his aluminum walker) in a pathetic but vain attempt to extinguish his burning clothing. The fact that he had shed his robe—which was found smoldering in the bathtub—points to an external rather than internal source for the ignition. A hole was burned through the floor, demonstrating that a considerable amount of floor covering, flooring, and sub-flooring had contributed to the destruction.

The thirty cases studied demonstrate not only the need to treat instances of alleged spontaneous human combustion on a case-by-case basis, but they also permit a couple of generalizations that will be of use to other investigators. First, there did seem to be a correlation between instances of unusual burning deaths and drunkenness, but this was attributed to intoxicated individuals being more careless and less able to respond properly to an accident. A second correlation was the amount of the body's destruction with the utilization of fuel sources. That is, where destruction of the body was comparatively minimal, only the clothing seems to have been involved; but where the destruction was extreme, additional materials (such as chair stuffing or wooden flooring) augmented the combustion.

Occasionally SHC proponents—such as Larry Arnold, a Pennsylvania school bus driver—cite a case in which the body is burned but not the clothes. For example, Arnold (1982) cites the case of Jack Angel, "The Man Who Survived Spontaneous Combustion." Embarrassingly, Arnold's skimpy research, combined with his credulity in accepting whatever was told him by an obvious blowhard, caused him to overlook convincing legal evidence that would have been his for the asking. Angel admitted in a lawsuit against the manufacturers of his motor home that in an attempt to learn why there was no hot water, he had opened the safety valve on his water heater, thereby releasing a jet of scalding water (Nickell and Fischer 1989).

Even greater destructive forces than SHC are at work if we credit claims made of the dread "Bermuda Triangle." Also known as the Devil's Triangle and the Triangle of Death, it is an area of the Atlantic approximately bounded by imaginary lines drawn between Bermuda, Puerto Rico, and the tip of Florida.

This "triangle" has achieved legendary status for the disappearance of countless ships and airplanes, and even two nuclear submarines. "Theories" —or rather, fanciful notions offered to explain the mysterious vanishings —include "time warps," reverse gravitational fields, UFO kidnapings, and occult forces including witchcraft (Jordan 1981, Weiner 1974, Kusche 1975).

In 1975, however, investigator Lawrence David Kusche published his monumental The Bermuda Triangle Mystery—Solved, a classic example of paranormal investigation at its best. Rather than merely paasing along the legends published in secondary sources, or sources at even greater remove, Kusche—a librarian and experienced pilot—searched out and scrutinized original records.

Take, for example, the case of the vanished tanker. In early February 1963, the S.S. Marine Sulphur Queen, a 523-foot tanker on a voyage from Texas to Virginia, vanished. Its last message was a routine one on February 4 as it approached the Straits of Florida. Four days later, when it was a day overdue at Norfolk, officials launched a sea and air search, but found neither the tanker nor any of its crew of thirty-nine. Two life preservers were all that were found, according to Charles Berlitz in his bestselling The Bermuda Triangle Mystery (1974, pp. 56–57), who adds that "the weather was good" and a Coast Guard investigation offered "neither solution nor theory concerning this disaster."

In fact, as Kusche learned from the Coast Guard Board of Investigation report, there were "rough seas" and the ship had structural flaws caused by the removal of bulkheads to accommodate large storage vats. These held the ship's cargo, some fifteen thousand tons of molten sulphur, either the fumes or steam from which offered the possibility of an explosion. This possibility is underscored by the fact that during prior voyages tons of molten sulphur had leaked into the tanker's bilges. As to the life preservers, much "additional debris" was recovered, including part of a name board bearing the letters "ARINE SULPH" between its shattered ends. Thus, as Kusche's investigation demonstrated, the Marine Sulphur Queen's fate was not a mysterious disappearance, but obviously a tragic accident instead (Kusche 1975, pp. 205–16, illus pp. 166–167).

One by one, the other major "vanishings" of the Bermuda Triangle came under Kusche's scrutiny. The *Sandra,* a freighter which "disappeared" in "peaceful weather" (Gaddis 1965, p. 202), was actually lost at sea during hurricane-force winds. The *Freya,* which was supposedly found mysteriously abandoned in "The Triangle area" (Berlitz 1974, p. 50), was in fact abandoned (probably during a storm as indicated by its condition) *in the Pacific Ocean*! And so on, and on (Kusche 1975, passim).

Flight 19, a group of five U.S. Avenger aircraft, which allegedly disappeared under what Gaddis (1965, p. 191) termed "ideal flight conditions," was really a *training* mission plagued by malfunctioning compasses and weather that was " 'average to undesirable' for a training flight," as Kusche notes in a book devoted to this mystery, *The Disappearance of Flight 19* (1980). Kusche's investigation demonstrates the probability that the crew became disoriented, flew far out to sea, and were lost at night in rough water. A plane that was subsequently lost searching for the Avengers becomes less the mystery Triangle promoters make of it when we learn from Kusche that such Mariner planes were nicknamed "flying gas tanks" (due to a chronic problem with fumes) and that there occurred an explosion— just where the Mariner would have been—approximately twenty minutes after takeoff (Kusche 1980, p. 119).

As the U.S. Coast Guard states concerning the legendary Triangle: "there is nothing mysterious about disappearances in this particular section of the ocean. Weather conditions, equipment failure, and human error, not something from the supernatural, are what have caused these tragedies" (as quoted in Nickell 1989a, p. 44). One might add that it is also human error on the part of paranormalists that has helped perpetuate the pseudomystery.

Another mystery of the catastrophe genre has not failed to attract the attention of those who are ever-ready with a fanciful "theory," in this case that the so-called "Tunguska event" represented the explosion of a nuclear-powered flying saucer!

Whatever its cause, the event was indeed a massive explosion, equal to that of a hydrogen bomb. It occurred over the Tunguska River area of Siberia on the morning of June 30, 1908. Trees were flattened in a circular area many miles across, small villages were destroyed, and a "pillar of fire" shot into the air with smoke clouds rising several miles high. Eyewitnesses had seen a UFO approaching on a collision course with the earth, and radioactivity later detected at the site—say some flying-saucer buffs— proves the craft was nuclear-powered (von Däniken 1971, pp. 122–25).

In fact, the most common description of the UFO that eyewitnesses provided was of a spherical object with a fiery tail—a description which matches that of a meteor. In fact, some saucer theorists to the contrary, a group of craters was located at the site, consistent with the theory that a meteor exploded just before impact. Soil analysts seemed to support the meteor theory, although a strong case can also be made for the UFO having been a comet. As to the radiation, authorities say the amount of radioactivity at the site is small, easily having derived from a natural event (Ballantine 1981; Hines 1988, pp. 192–93; Oberg 1980).

Nature's skies offer many less catastrophic yet often intriguing mysteries, just the type Fort loved to use to taunt scientists whose educations and credentials he must have envied. Unusual rains, for example, such as showers of fish or frogs or other animate or inanimate objects, Fort attributed to a Super Sargasso Sea in which floated an island called Genesistrine. These regions yielded the various falling objects.

Take so-called "red rains" or "rains of blood," for example, of which there are several verified instances. Fort rejected (or pretended to reject) the conventional scientific explanation: that reddish sand or dust (e.g., iron oxide) that had been windswept into the air had mixed with the water (Gardner 1957, p. 47). Instead, he speculated (if somewhat tongue-in-cheek):

> Rivers of blood that vein albuminous seas, or an egg-like composition in the incubation of which this earth is a local center of development— that there are super-arteries of blood in Genesistrine: that sunsets are consciousness of them: that they flush the skies with northern lights sometimes: super-embryonic reservoirs from which life-forms emanate—
>
> Or that our whole solar system is a living thing: that showers of blood upon this earth are its internal hemorrhages—
>
> Or vast living things in the sky, as there are vast living things in the oceans—
>
> Or some one especial thing: an especial time; an especial place. A thing the size of the Brooklyn Bridge. It's alive in outer space—something the size of Central Park kills it—
>
> It drips. (Fort 1974, p. 304)

Many such phenomena (along with other mysteries) are described in the Reader's Digest Association's *Mysteries of the Unexplained* (Calkins 1982, pp. 184–206) as well as in William R. Corliss's interesting book, *The Unexplained: A Sourcebook of Strange Phenomena* (1976). The latter, for instance, discusses not only strange showers, but also ball lightning, earthquake lights, "dark days," the Brocken specter (an illusion of a giant figure seen in the mists of Germany's Brocken Mountain), and so on. Various oceanic mirages, atmospheric sounds, and other phenomena of earth, sea, and sky are treated (including toads in rocks, musical sands, etc.) sometimes with a proffered explanation, sometimes not.

In their *Arthur C. Clarke's Mysterious World* Welfare and Fairley (pp. 180, 33–49) discuss some of the same phenomena, including strange falls of frogs and other objects that are usually attributed to hoaxes or whirlwinds. Clarke himself observes that "Baby frogs can suddenly appear in such surprising number, when they have completed their metamorphosis from tadpoles, that they seem to have fallen from the skies" (p. 49). Here as in other cases, we see the wisdom of investigating on a case-by-case basis in order to discover which of several possible explanations may be responsible for a given phenomenon.

Another example of multiple explanations is provided by mysterious lights. Some may be due to the piezoelectric effect, wherein earthquake pressure upon rocks generates electricity in the form of luminous discharges (Corliss 1975, pp. 209–10). Other potential sources are automobile headlights on distant mountain roads and reflections. The latter proved responsible for the Colorado "ghost lights" that haunted an old cemetery near the tiny mining town of Silver Cliff. On-site investigation demonstrated that the phenomenon was caused by distant city lights (or on other occasions by the moon or bright stars) reflecting off the polished surfaces of marble tombstones (Bunch and White 1988).

Miscellaneous Paranormalities

Not all allegedly paranormal phenomena are readily pigeonholed. There are countless mysteries—both real and imagined—that evade our previous classifications but nevertheless offer features of interest.

For example, an ancient paranormal investigation is the subject of a legend concerning the prophet Daniel's encounter with Babylonian priests (recorded in the fourteenth chapter of the Book of Daniel in the Revised Standard Version Common Bible).

According to the legend, during the reign of Cyrus, the Persian king, the Babylonians had set up an idol of Bel in a temple devoted to him. Cyrus had been persuaded to worship Bel because of the idol's apparent ability to consume tremendous quantities of food placed before it. Each day the priests would place before the idol some forty sheep, twelve bushels of flour, and fifty gallons of wine, and then the temple doors would be closed. By the following morning the great meal would have been devoured.

Daniel, an advisor to Cyrus, was skeptical, and when the king asked him why he refused to worship the idol, Daniel voiced his doubts, adding that he believed in a *living* God. Cyrus retorted: "Do you not think that Bel is a living God? Do you not see how much he eats and drinks every day?" Daniel laughed and then said: "Do not be deceived, O King, for this is but clay inside and brass outside, and it never ate or drank anything."

An angry Cyrus proposed a test. Summoning the seventy priests of Bel he announced that whoever lost would be put to death. The king had the food and wine placed before the idol as before, but then sealed the temple doors to prevent anyone from entering without betraying the fact.

The following morning the royal seals were found unbroken, yet the food had disappeared. However, Daniel had set a trap (a harbinger of modern ones used to reveal the true nature of certain "ghosts" and "poltergeists"). According to the legend, before the temple was sealed, Daniel had his servants sift ashes upon the temple floor. Come morning when the door was opened, Daniel kept the king from entering, saying, "Look at the floor, and notice whose footprints these are." King Cyrus replied, "I see the footsteps of men and women and children," whereupon the Babylonians confessed and revealed the secret doors by which they had been accustomed to enter.

Although the story may be apocryphal and intended to prompt Jews to eschew idolatry (Asimov 1968, pp. 621–22), Daniel's approach still deserves the characterization of the *New Catholic Encyclopedia* as "clever detective work" ("Bel" 1967). Certainly it has many elements that the modern paranormal investigator can appreciate.

Another manmade effigy that is reputed to have magical powers is the so-called "Skull of Doom," more recently known simply as "The Crystal Skull." It is a life-sized human skull carved from quartz crystal and weighing eleven pounds, seven ounces.

At one time the skull was alleged to hold the power of death over anyone who would scoff at it, but investigation revealed no basis for such a claim. More recently, the skull has been reported to have less fearful properties: those in its presence have supposedly heard silver bells; have observed an "aura" surrounding the skull; and, peering into its surface as one does a crystal ball, have observed shadowy shapes. All such properties, however, seem to be subjective. (For instance, the "aura" could only be represented in a "simulated photograph.") Its current owner, alleging it has beneficial powers, told one of us, "the skull has been used for healing a number of times, and I hope one day it will go to an institution where it will be used by mathematicians [sic], weather people, surgeons, etc., etc." (Nickell with Fischer 1988, pp. 29–46).

The owner, Anna Mitchell-Hedges, is the adopted daughter of F. A. Mitchell-Hedges, the sometime-adventurer and inveterate raconteur. He claimed the "sinister Skull of Doom" was "at least 3,600 years old and according to legend was used by the High Priest of the Maya when performing esoteric rites." Of its provenance, he said only that "How it came into my possession I have reason for not revealing" (Mitchell-Hedges 1954,

p. 243). Actually he bought the skull in 1944 from an art dealer named Sydney Burney, as shown by documentary evidence. Now, however, Miss Mitchell-Hedges has begun to claim—without a shred of proof and in contradictory accounts—that she was on an expedition with her father in the 1920s when she herself discovered the skull at the lost Mayan city of Lubaantun in British Honduras.

Erich von Däniken cited the skull in his *Chariots of the Gods?* (1971) as an example of fabulous ancient technology: "Nowhere on the skull is there a clue showing that a tool known to us was used!" he claimed, and his assertion is repeated by others. Actually, however, polishing has removed most tool marks, but even so, traces of "mechanical grinding" are evident on the faces of the teeth. In addition, there are peg-holes in the bottom of the skull (obviously intended as a means of supporting the skull) that undoubtedly result from drilling with metal, and Miss Mitchell-Hedges has stated they were there when she "found" the skull (Nickell with Fischer 1988, pp. 32–33).

The only real mystery about the skull is its origin. It might have been possible to indicate the date of manufacture by measuring fluorine diffusion into the crystal, but Miss Mitchell-Hedges refused to permit any analyses beyond some earlier ones (which merely showed the traces of grinding and revealed that the skull had been carved from a single block of crystal). Nevertheless, the artifact's similarity to other rock-crystal skulls suggests it may have originated in Mexico (where, in contrast to the Maya culture, there were frequent skull depictions) no earlier than the Colonial period, i.e., 1519–1821 (Nickell with Fischer 1988, pp. 33–34, 42).

Journeying now to Mars for our next flight of fantasy, we find the "Great Stone Face"—a rock feature one mile across photographed by the Viking 1 orbiter in 1976. Shadows resemble eyes, nose, and mouth, leading some extraterrestrial theorists to suspect it was made—along with a nearby "pyramid" and possible "lost city"—by an advanced civilization.

Alas, planetary geologists ascribe the formations to nature, and skeptics observe that the "pyramid" is even cruder than similar rock formations in Arizona. Wags have also discovered on the Martian surface a great Happy Face (a five-mile-wide crater formation) and a giant Kermit the Frog (a lava flow complete with "eye" (a small impact crater) (Gardner 1985).

All this is reminiscent, of course, of the earlier "canals" on Mars that some astronomers thought they could see through their telescopes in the late nineteenth and early twentieth centuries, or the supposedly manmade "bridges" and spires later seen on the moon. (Were the latter rocket ships or perhaps radio beacons?) As it happens, the bridges vanished when subsequent space photographs were taken, and the spires were revealed as boulders, their lengthy shadows merely having been the result of low-angle sunlight (Gardner 1955; Hines 1986, p. 170).

Returning to Earth, it is not canals but mystical "lines of force" that paranormalists in Britain claim to have evidence of. (See Cohen 1985, pp. 26–28). In 1921 an amateur archaeologist named Alfred Watkins intuited a network of crisscrossing lines that passed through ancient structures, including stone monuments, earthworks, castles, and cathedrals. Since many of the place names involved ended in -ley (or -ly or -leigh), Watkins named the lines "ley" lines. Today his work is carried on by "ley hunters" who suppose the perceived lines have mystical or cosmic significance. Some believe the lines represent "forces" that can actually be followed by dowsing rods. But according to Daniel Cohen (1985, p. 27), "What orthodox archaeologists and prehistorians think of such theories should not be difficult to imagine; they have derided leys as 'lunatic fabrications.' "

Such skeptics point out that the ley hunters permit themselves great latitude in their work. They allow a wide variety of features to be used, including modern monuments, claiming the more recent ones had replaced earlier monuments. In addition, they permit the imagined lines to run *near* a site, not necessarily through it. With countless sites being postulated, it would be amazing if some of them did not—purely by chance—fall into approximate alignment. According to one critic, "There are no university professors of ley science to quibble about methods, or tiresome paper qualifications to hold the novice hunter back. All you need is a map, a straight edge, and sufficient patience" (As quoted in Cohen 1985, p. 28).

Quite a different type of mystic power is supposedly represented by the so-called "mummy's curse" reportedly carved above the door of King Tutankhamen's tomb and responsible for the mysterious deaths of those who disturbed the young pharaoh's peace. In fact, however, there was no curse carved above the entrance or anywhere else, either on or in the tomb. The alleged "victims" of the "curse" actually died of a variety of causes, and those who would have been the most likely targets lived full lives. For example, Howard Carter, who opened the tomb, lived an additional seventeen years to the age of sixty-six, and Dr. Douglas Derry, who actually dissected the mummy, lived to be over eighty! In 1980 the expedition's security officer stated that the "curse" tale was launched to deter would-be tomb plunderers (Hines pp. 188, 215–16; Nickell 1989a, pp. 55–57).

Numerous other mysteries—as well as nonmysteries and curiosities—could be discussed, but the examples given in this and earlier chapters should be sufficient to acquaint the serious student with the possibilities. After all, it has not been our intention to propose solutions for all paranormal mysteries, but rather to facilitate serious, conscientious investigative work by those willing to devote their time, efforts, and resources to possible solutions.

Part 3

Dealing with Others

8

Public and Private Relations

The Media

Throughout this book we have made reference time and again to the important role that the media plays in aiding and abetting the cause of the paranormal. Beyond all doubt paranormal events are newsworthy because of public interest. No matter what the event—a UFO sighting, a haunted house, or a busy poltergeist—it will receive publicity. And publicity, as everyone in public relations knows, can effectively promote or acutely damage a cause or organization depending upon the messages communicated, the way they are communicated, and the way the public receives and understands them. Publicity should have something to offer and have a receptive audience. Most audiences today are media-wise, so there is no guarantee that you will get the attention you desire or that you will be able to get your point across. Nowadays, publicity is a game of seconds, and targeting the information effectively is not a game for amateurs or the faint-hearted. We are beseiged with hundreds of messages daily from TV, radio, newspapers, magazines, billboards, sides of subways and buses, and in the daily mail. They link each of us to the rest of society and the larger world. If we have something important to say, we are forced to use an established medium, otherwise we will have little or no credibility. And credibility is something that, as a psi-cop and a paranormal investigator, you *must have* to get the results and findings of your investigation across.

As this book must have made you realize, science and sanity are rapidly being overcome and drowned out by the sensationalistic claims of the psi-cophants. Sadly enough, it is much easier to get TV time and newspaper space for most any paranormal claim than it is to get the same amount of time and space for a story reporting "the truth" about a claimed paranormal or psychic event. In general, the media considers the first newsworthy and the latter commonplace. Why? Let's listen to what Marilyn Schultz, an expert in mass communication, has to say about this problem.

According to Schultz, since the 1970s the media—particularly radio and television—has attempted to cover the "unreal" world, as well as the "real" one. To fill in the news hole, often referred to as "the black hole," you do what you can to keep the audience's attention. In her own words, "The medium of television has changed and, if you wanted to remain a part of it, you had to go with the flow, particularly if you were a woman. As more years passed, and I became a producer, to stay in the business was to participate in sensationalism, hoaxes, entertainment instead of journalism—to cover anything to fill the news hole, often referred to as the 'black hole.' The ratings race allowed no barriers to our coverage. Finally I had enough and left" (Skeptical Briefs, 1988).

Ms. Schultz's sentiments are echoed by Bill Thompson, a syndicated columnist for the *Fort Worth Star-Telegram,* who argues that in the news business he was taught that if you did not have both sides of a news story, you don't have any story at all. Thompson argues also that in the past the act of pursuing news used to be a noble quest for the truth, but now it seems that the "idea of reporting is to collect unfounded accusations about public figures and private individuals and mindlessly foist them upon the public under the guise of 'investigative reporting.' Too often, our idea of editing is to insert the word 'alleged.' " Thompson also feels that "TV is an arrogant pretentious medium that lays claim to seriousness even as it sets new standards for shallowness, for superficiality." He also feels that newspapers are at fault for allowing TV to define what is and isn't news. Thompson strongly objects to the arrogance of reporters and TV news personnel who destroy reputations with no more justification than "it makes a good story" and their failure to evaluate the information, consider the consequences of passing it along to the public, and the ethical issues involved. Now, he argues, the rule is: If one knows it, he has to tell it! True or false, good consequence or bad, no one seems to care anymore. Although more time and attention is given to paranormal issues than to the presentation of scientific ones, television no longer has to account to the Fairness Doctrine, and many programs such as "Unknown Mysteries" and other pseudodocumentary programs about the occult and pseudoscience no longer use either disclaimers or anything in the way of scientific rebuttal. Were it not for the efforts of CSICOP and other skeptics, any nonsense—no matter how blatant or offensive—would go unchallenged.

And it most definitely does need to be challenged. In 1979 William

S. Bainbridge stated why, in unmistakable terms, "the prevalence of pseu-dodocumentary programs about the occult and pseudo-science has become a serious social issue. Such shows may spread false and dangerous notions among the viewing public, both encouraging faith in costly frauds and diminishing popular acceptance of real scientific findings." Bainbridge also studied how viewers see and remember such programs as "In Search Of" and "Project UFO" and found that the viewers saw them as part of a wish-fulfillment fantasy and were not able to clearly distinguish between what was fact and what was fiction (*The Skeptical Inquirer,* Fall 1979).

David Slavsky has also remarked about the progress of bogus science. In his words, "For many of us watching television and listening to the radio have become painful experiences. In what might be one of the most brutal ironies of our day, broadcasting—the synthesis of some of the most elegant scientific and technological advances of the last century—has become a major stomping ground for the proponents of pseudoscience." Slavsky, however, went one step further and gained access to a radio show. When people called in to ask about pseudoscience, Slavsky talked to them about real science (*The Skeptical Inquirer,* 1983).

While we are well aware of the fact that most skeptics and scientists are quite modest and self-effacing individuals, character traits that go along with honesty and humility and the other things that make for a good scientist, there are times and occasions when all of these need to be laid aside and, like Slavsky, the skeptical investigator needs to don the accoutrements of the public relations professional and go forth to do battle with the forces of ignorance and superstition. It is, perhaps, excessive humility and an unwillingness to fight on the part of scientists and skeptics in the past that has led to the present successes of the popularizers of the paranormal. John C. Burnham at least, in his superb *How Superstition Won and Science Lost* (Rutgers University Press, 1987), seems sure that this is why it happened. To avoid all such future mistakes the paranormal investigator must become an advocate of the cause of skepticism and a booster of, and the publicist for, the results of his own investigations. In this day and age every cause needs publicity—especially the CSICOP cause and the results of your own investigations.

How to Beat Your Own Drum: Public Relations

Although it is easy to fool people and there are, to be sure, a lot of fools in the world, not everyone is a fool. In fact, there are actually a lot of editors, journalists, TV newspeople, reporters, and writers who are eager to see and hear skeptics stick pins in the psychic's overinflated balloons.

Merely telling people that you are in the "ghostbusting" business draws media interest like sugar draws flies. Believe it or not, there are still many old-style cynical and skeptical people in the media business who take a very jaundiced view of all paranormal claims. Since the stuff is so popular and newsworthy, anyone challenging or rebutting or disproving supernatural claims also becomes "news" because of his/her opposition, and are equally deserving of time and space. Therefore, make sure that media people know you exist. If they know you exist, at least you have a chance for rebuttal. If they don't know you exist, you have no chance at all.

If you have carried out an investigation and have learned something worth reporting as a result, then you should go public with it, i.e., publicize it. Maybe, however, you think what you have done isn't worth publicizing. How do you determine it is or it isn't? Simple. If, for example, you have investigated a haunted house because the house was widely reported to being so by several newspapers in the area—and this is why you launched your investigation—then you are fully justified in publicizing the fact that you found the house was *not haunted* but *only occupied* by a family of friendly raccoons. A simple rule is: *If the thing you investigated has received any publicity, then your investigation and its outcome should also receive publicity.* A more general and equally important rule is: *If what you are doing is worth doing, then it is worth reporting.* This goes for groups and organizations as well. Most groups and organizations exist for a reason and if this reason is important enough to justify the existence of an organization, then the public needs to know it exists, e.g., if you don't survive, then your cause isn't worth supporting anyway.

In our case publicity is very important in that it can inform people about the services we provide and motivate them to use them. If you are a member of a skeptical organization or group, then publicity can also attract new members, increase financial support, encourage volunteers, and stimulate the present group members to become more active. Favorable publicity can also counteract any negative attention or misunderstanding about you and your group's claims, intentions, and motives. Good publicity can draw attention to serious problems, issues, injustices that need attention, and it certainly can serve the many important and badly needed educational and conscious-raising functions within the community at large.

If public interest is high on your subject, then editors and reporters will be interested in what you have to say—especially if you have information, data, results, etc. that is more than mere opinion. The more people are affected by your information, the more newsworthy the story will be and the greater will be the media's interest. Story value? If it has entertainment value, educational value, human interest, or is of historical significance, then it has story value.

As for your own story you could, of course, buy air time or space in the paper, i.e., advertise, but there is a catch here. In addition to the drawback of cost, there is the problem of credibility. The public is skeptical of ads and much more trusting of news stories. For these reasons it is not wise to pay for your publicity. Your job anyway is to inform and educate, and ninety-nine times out of one hundred the media representative will recognize this and give you—if your cause is just—all the time and space you need.

As far as publicity is concerned, newspapers are your best bet. You have a better chance of landing a news item here and having it reach the largest number of people for the least cost than any other medium. Just about every community in America has its own newspaper—daily, weekly, monthly, or quarterly. Most of them—especially the smaller ones—depend on nonpartisan sources for their stories. You can find out what newspaper sources are available to you by looking in the yellow pages of the phone book or going to your local library and talking with the librarian. When you find copies of the newspapers, look at the kind of audiences they cater to and the kind of stories they print. This will help you find out who will be receiving your information, when they might want to publish it, and if and when they do publish it who will be reading it. To give yourself maximum coverage, don't hesitate to make a list of all the papers in your area and try to spread the word over the entire geographic region.

Once you have located the papers, your next step is to make personal contact with the appropriate editors, reporters, and feature editors. This is particularly important for large newspapers with hundreds of employees. Take the trouble to find out the names and phone numbers of all the personnel on the paper who can help you get your story into print. Getting your story in the right and proper hands is ninety percent of the battle. Large newspapers have many specialized departments or sections, e.g., Religion, Sports, Travel, Style, TV, Books, etc., so if your report fits into any one of these, then this is the editor you contact. A few telephone calls will get you to the right desk and to the person who can help you the most. Many smaller and medium-sized papers have a much smaller staff, and you can get the help you want by sending your stories to the news editor, assistant editor, feature editor, or one or two reporters who have covered similar things in the past.

If you want to put your story in magazines, you should contact the editor or an associate editor in the proper area, e.g., nonfiction, special projects, etc. Many magazines often use freelance writers and if what you report is well-written, they may have you do the story yourself. You should contact them ahead of time if you want to do this. They may prefer to put one of their own writers on the project and send them down for pictures and an in-depth interview. The editors will, of course, want to clear all story ideas. If you know of specific reporters who have written on similar topics for the magazine, you may want to contact them directly and let them persuade their editor.

As far as most newspapers are concerned, the most frequently used and abused method of publicizing an event is the press release. The format is very simple. It can be anywhere from one to five pages, but one page is preferable. Your purpose is not to tell the story in detail but to capture the reporter's or the editor's attention. Use standard white 8½ by 11 inch paper with a letterhead (if your organization has one) or your name and address and phone number where you can be reached (if you don't). Type either the name and address of your organization at the top of the page, centered, or your name. Skip several lines and then on the left hand side of the page type a contact's name and phone number where additional information and details can be had. On the right hand side opposite the contact's name type FOR IMMEDIATE RELEASE, and the mailing date, or FOR ADVANCE RELEASE ONLY with the earliest date on which the article should be printed. Skip a few more lines and then type a short descriptive title—a one-line statement of what you have to tell. Follow this with the body of the release: a typed, double-spaced set of three or four short, five- or six-line paragraphs summarizing your story. Set margins for lines no more than sixty characters, including spaces between words. If you use a second page, type MORE at the bottom of the first, centered. At the top of the second, type CONTINUED in parentheses. Be clear and succinct and use quotes if you have them. Type END, centered, after skipping two lines when you are through. If photos are good and help with the story, send them along. Protect the picture at all costs. Don't bend, staple, or paper clip it, and never draw crop marks on it. Don't crop or trim it yourself. Put tissue paper over it and write on the tissue paper. When you send it along with the press release, enclose it between two pieces of corrugated cardboard and write PHOTO ENCLOSED on the envelope so the post office won't damage it.

It is also a good idea to watch the newspapers closely. When you come across a story about the paranormal or in an area of your immediate interest, you can always contact the reporter writing the story and offer your congratulations and suggest another story or a rebuttal. In other words, identify yourself with the issue and let the reporter know you have something to add. If you have a skeptic's group, invite the reporter to your next meeting. Also send him information he might be interested in writing about. Call him and suggest that he cover upcoming events. Also make him aware of your various areas of expertise and let him know you are an information source available to him in case he needs help in this area in the future. Don't be overly solicitous, but be helpful and available.

If you find that a story about you or your work or your group is grossly misleading or in error, call or write the reporter and point it out. Be careful and tactful, however, and keep your temper. You don't want to make an enemy—you want to win him over to your side so the damage won't happen again. Tell him it didn't reflect the entire picture, it was unbalanced and gave only one side or one point of view. Point out specific inaccuracies and suggest how they can be clarified. Show your open-mindedness. Convince him you are calling not to retaliate, but to set the record straight. Make your criticism gentle. Praise something before finding fault. If he proves to be stubborn and unyielding, then call the editor or ombudsman. Here, again, be gentle and politic.

On Being Interviewed

Sooner or later you will find yourself standing in front of a reporter or on a phone talking to someone who wants to interview you. When this happens you should keep in mind that you want two things to happen: (1) you want to create a good or positive impression; and (2) you want to communicate your ideas clearly and effectively. If someone asks you for an interview and you agree, and if time permits, try to find out exactly what the interviewer wants. Does he want a news story, a feature article, or just your comment on a current topic? Who else will be interviewed along with you? When will the story appear? You should know exactly what the reporter is up to and how he or she intends to use your input. You can be made to look utterly foolish if he quotes you out of context or only quotes some of the information, allowing your position to appear naive because only part of it is cited. Another ploy is to allow opposing "experts" to ridicule your position and not allow you time or space for rebuttal. Even worse is the reporter's failure to understand what he or she is being told and then reporting not what you said, but what he or she thought was said. Because of deadlines, most stories are not written and sent to you first for editing before they are printed. Most go directly from your lips through the reporter's ears to his typewriter and directly into the morning or evening edition. This is the way it has to be on many occasions, so you should take extra pains and precautions to make sure you communicate clearly.

If the reporter agrees to come to your home or office for the interview and you have some time to prepare, you might jot down some of the questions he or she is sure to ask or, even better, some of the points you want to communicate and emphasize. Prepare ahead of time what you want to say and what you want to reply when he asks certain questions you can almost guarantee will be asked. For example, "Have you ever run into any ghostly phenomena that you couldn't explain?" or, "Do you really believe that UFOs are extraterrestrial?" or, "Have you ever met a psychic that could do things you couldn't explain?" You can be sure that questions such as these are bound to arise. Anticipate questions even for which the answers seem obvious. Such questions will give you a chance to provide background material and set the stage for getting your larger message across. When answering the reporter's questions be direct and honest and avoid rambling. If you don't know, don't hesitate to say so. If you have forgotten some small details, tell him you can look it up for him and let him know later if it is important. Remember that reporters like detail, so try to have facts and figures at hand ahead of time if possible. Be wary of those reporters who like to get you emotionally aroused or even make you feel threatened. Learn to stay calm and unruffled and refuse to be angered. This will stymie even the most hostile reporter. Since most of the time you will be much better informed than the reporter, don't be afraid to take charge of the interview and talk about what you want to communicate. Whether he likes it or not, he'll have to go along.

If the reporter or his editor wants your picture, let them have it. A photogenic room, an office, or your den or study, complete with lots of books, is a good place to have your picture taken. As many publicists have noted, books lend weight to your words and give them an air of authority. A background of books is definitely recommended if you want to create a serious image.

Another excellent source of publicity is the local radio station or stations. Radio is an extremely effective medium with regard to local news and information. Remember, people listen to the radio all the time while they are working, walking, playing, riding, and doing just about anything and everything—except watching TV. In fact, radio has just about taken over as the major source from which people receive news and information. It is, nowadays, the portable medium, and daytime radio is by far more influential than daytime television. Most radio stations run a lot of public service programs because they are required by law to do so. In order to maintain its license with the Federal Communications Commission (FCC), the station must serve its community by providing air time for nonprofit public interest groups, as well as political, educational, and public affairs programs. Although competition for air time may be heavy and you may have to wait your turn, you will be surprised at how easy it is to get your message on the air. You should look for the type of station that appeals to the audience you want to attract. Rock music stations will have mostly young teenagers as an audience, so you probably don't want to put your message on this station with its limited audience. AM (amplitude modulated) stations do, of course, reach a larger audience than FM (frequency modulated) stations, but the FM stations are clearer with much less static. The more power a station has, i.e., watts, the larger the audience. If a station has as much as 50,000 watts, then their transmissions can reach several states, whereas smaller stations with only 200 to 500 watts are usually restricted to a small community. Large cities can have as many as thirty or more stations, so you usually should not have any difficulty finding an outlet for your message.

You should try to contact the program director, the news director, or the public affairs director at the station. They can be the most help. If the station has a regular talk show program, a local affairs show with a regular host, or a weekly public affairs show, then the producer or host of this show is the one to phone. These regular scheduled shows are always on the lookout for new material and something they haven't done before. These are excellent outlets for any and all psi-cop programs. Don't forget to send the directors and the hosts copies of your press releases as well. They can get all sorts of ideas from these materials and can also suggest other publicity outlets. It is always a good idea to cultivate these people, even though they may be booked up for weeks at the time you establish contact. They will keep you in mind and call on you later. Another sure-fire trick is the public service announcement (PSA). If you or your group is holding a meeting and you have a guest lecturer who is fairly well known, then you can get wonderful free publicity by preparing a PSA which is a short, simple, concise announcement usually taking up about thirty to sixty seconds of air time. Remember, it has to be short and sweet if it is going to be broadcast. It will go over much better if it is written like announcers talk, i.e., in the active voice, short terse sentences, stating only the facts. Don't be surprised if after you have done your best, you find the station has pared your thirty or sixty seconds down to ten or twenty. That's the way the game is played.

Radio and Television Interviews

Occasionally you will be asked to appear in person on a radio or TV talk show and you might be a little nervous if this is the first time it has ever happened. Don't be. In fact, you should volunteer and take advantage of every opportunity to get your message across. Learn the program format and how the host behaves and what he or she expects. Begin by outlining what you want to talk about, and make sure you bone up on the facts and figures about your group or organization, as well as its purpose and plans. Your job is to be friendly, personable, and as articulate as you can be. If time is limited, concentrate on three or four major points or topics. If it's a question and answer type format, try to think of the kinds of questions people are sure to ask and have your answers ready. Refine any answers that seem inadequate or evasive. You also must assume that people are not very familiar with you or your group and may have little or no interest. Your job is to interest them. Don't whine, rasp, or stutter. Don't argue. Be friendly and personable, and remember that even though the person you're talking to is miles away and invisible, assume he or she is right before you and talk to them in the same way. If the format is a panel discussion, make sure you participate but don't hog the conversation. Use other participants' first names as well as the host's. Remain alert and listen to what is being said even though it doesn't concern you at the moment. Don't be caught off guard if the subject does suddenly change. Never get angry or shout, stay cool and calm, and never forget to smile—even though the audience can't see it, it helps calm you down. For call-in shows you will often get some very hostile or even insulting calls. Don't let them throw you; remain calm and cool and answer simply and directly with "I'm sorry, I don't agree," "I'm afraid you misunderstand what we are saying and doing," "That isn't relevant, but it reminds me of something that is," and *you* change the subject. Use their challenge to get across informational points you haven't made before. You can always make your caller rephrase or clarify his question, and gradually gain control of the situation. If nothing else works, ask the host to deal with it.

TV is, of course, a wonderful medium for persuasion. Stations are bound by the same rules as radio, but getting TV time is much more difficult. As you may have heard, even sixty seconds of TV time can cost thousands of dollars. Nevertheless, you go about getting TV time the same way you approached radio. Contact the news director, station director, talk show hosts, reporters, and so forth. Find out about the station's policies regarding public service and how they handle information spots and PSAs. The news and public affairs divisions are your best bets and their heads should be your first contacts. For TV PSAs you should also send along one or two color slides—35 mm and glass mounted (cardboard warps). Word slides can also be helpful, but make sure they are made so they can be seen and read.

Television interviews can be a little anxiety arousing, especially if they are sudden and unexpected. Even when they are scheduled well in advance they can require some quick thinking on one's feet. TV does not lend itself to complex issues and answers most of the time. We have agreed to TV interviews a number of times and have been in front of the cameras for over an hour and then, when the program appeared, we found ourselves on the tube for less than a minute. In fact, it is perhaps more important when preparing for a TV interview to consider what you shouldn't say more than what you should. Your job is to make a relevant statement about something important in a limited amount of time while at the same time appearing confident and persuasive. This is not easy while staring into a bank of lights and having a reporter firing questions at you. Old hands advise forgetting the camera and microphone and talk to the reporter as if he's the only one there. Just remember that you are having a personal chat with another person. Use a conversational tone and speech, simple words and sentences, and be as direct as possible. Look and act natural, remain friendly and calm, and never show anger or hostility. Laugh off anything personal. Make sure you speak slowly, distinctly, and clearly. If you're asked a question you can't answer, simply say "I don't know." This is much better than trying to fake it and babbling incoherently. On TV your appearance is important, so dress conservatively, neatly, and cleanly. In other words, dress to suit the occasion—don't wear a tux on the golf course. To make a good impression on your audience, skeptics should look credible, neat, honest, and intelligent. No shorts and sandals! Since the viewer has only a few seconds in which to form his opinion of you, it will, like it or not, be based on how you look. If you are unsure about how you should behave, watch other people on TV interview and talk shows and take your cues. Most of all, try to relax and enjoy yourself. If you seem to be (or actually are) having fun, your audience will too.

Public Speaking

Speaking in public is a real chore and a pain to many people, but it is something that everyone who has something to say that is worth saying should learn to master. Talking to someone directly is the best way to win them over or to persuade them. There is simpy no substitute for personal contact. Meetings, seminars, workshops, lectures with audience feedback, and such are the best ways to handle complex and difficult issues and to fully clarify one's convictions and beliefs. To be an effective speaker is, perhaps more than anything else, to simply be yourself and to allow your passions and convictions (we assume that you *do* have them) to come across naturally. Although effective public speaking is a personal skill and one can develop it through courses in high school, college, and at Dale Carnegie offices, there is no guarantee that you will be listened to or believed. No matter how good you are, there will still be people who will refuse to listen. Nevertheless, there are some general guidelines that, if followed, can make your presentations more effective. Called the Ten

Commandments of public speaking by writers like David Tedone in his superb book *Practical Publicity* (Harvard Common Press, 1983), they are as follows:

1. Be human—Use humor, make yourself approachable.
2. Be prepared—Know where your talk is going and steer it there.
3. Be enthusiastic—Show life and energy, enjoyment, don't drone.
4. Be confident—Convince people you're an authority on your topic.
5. Be specific—Use statistics, real information, quotes, visual aids.
6. Be accurate—Make sure the information you present is all true.
7. Be entertaining—Add personal interest, tell stories and anecdotes.
8. Be alert—Watch your audience, answer questions, clarify.
9. Be relevant—Make your speech topical, relate to local affairs.
10. Be calm—Avoid nervousness, be open, friendly, smile, and laugh.

Another seldom mentioned aspect of speaking in public is that of personal comfort. You should be both mentally and *physically* comfortable when delivering your speech. One definite detractor to your private comfort is the need to use the bathroom. If you are feeling the urge to relieve yourself while you are delivering your talk, your audience may also feel that you are rushing things and will be very uncomfortable with what you are saying. Make sure that before you start your delivery you visit the restroom. While many people seated at the speaker's table are hesitant to leave their place with hundreds of eyes upon them, do it anyway. This is a minor embarrassment compared to the impression you make with a talk delivered while you are in physical pain. Getting up and leaving while another speaker is talking is a relatively minor disturbance for which you will be quickly forgiven by most attendees. If, however, your talk is delivered while you are distressed, your audience will be even more mystified and much less forgiving.

If you really feel that you just aren't up to public speaking, then a sure-fire way to do it is with a slide show. As the speaker you can control the slides while you are reading from a prepared script, standing either in front or at the rear and controlling the projector with an extension switch. This is a very effective technique, especially if you are unusually nervous or totally inexperienced. No one is looking at you; they are all looking at the slides. Another advantage is that just about any member of your group can also give the same presentation since the slides and the script are prepared ahead of time and don't depend on who is presenting them. Once the show is prepared, you don't have to follow the script word for word. You can always deviate and bring in rhetorical questions and get the audience involved. Flexibility can also be further increased by substituting other slides and even series of slides to fit certain particular groups and audiences, e.g., children or science majors. Many public speaking authorities feel that a properly designed slide show can bring out the best in most any speaker.

Writing and publishing is, of course, one of the best publicity techniques of all. Every skeptical group should have its own newsletter and, if their finances allow, should circulate it as widely as possible. This is one of the best ways to recruit new members and to publicize the group's activities. Good quality, professional-looking newsletters should be printed if possible and should contain illustrations and photographs as well. Publications like this are definitely expensive and you should not overlook either the printing or the distribution costs. Unless your organization has a minimum of a hundred or so active, dues-paying members, an attractive, high-quality newsletter is almost out of the question and you will be restricted to stencils and a mimeographed format with limited circulation. One particularly effective form of writing that should not be overlooked in seeking publicity for one's cause is the conventional letter to the editor. Nearly every newspaper and magazine and journal in existence will have a letters to the editor section. This is a sure-fire way to call the public's attention to your cause and to field objections to paranormal claims published earlier. Your letter can run to as many as three pages or more, but be prepared for some cutting and trimming on the paper's part. Of course, this can be circumvented by writing a series of letters and having each letter take up another aspect of the issue—particularly if the issue is one involving considerable controversy. You are required, of course, to sign your name, and you should always include the name of your organization if it meets with their approval. This is an excellent way to break into print and gain the attention you want and need. If your organization is fairly large, having a number of members firing off letters to all the papers and journals in your area can be a very effective way to gain both the papers' and the public's attention. In fact, this is another means of getting a feature story done by one of the paper's investigative reporters. As long as your letter is not libelous or obscene you can say just about anything you want to without fear of censorship. Just make sure that what you have to say is correct and fully expresses your point of view. It is very important that paranormal investigators learn to speak out whenever they encounter unusually credulous newspaper stories, magazine articles, and television shows. Your letters have a better chance of being printed if they are brief and specific, and if the main point is in the first paragraph. Space for these letters is limited and a hard-hitting, succinct, and pointed letter will be accepted over a long, rambling, and verbose one. Don't waste space in your letter by restating what was said to trigger your response. Referring to the original story by name and date is enough. Also don't delay. If you wait until the issue is dead, then the editor will throw your comment away. Readers will no longer be interested. Don't let your anger seep through. A calm, rational tone is much more persuasive than angry invective. Be firm, and if you can be witty, do so. A good laugh is unusually effective. Don't forget to sign it; anonymous letters will not be printed. In fact, before printing, the paper will usually call to confirm that you did write it.

As for replying to TV and radio broadcasts, you should write to the station's public affairs director with copies also sent to the program's producer, writer, and reporter. A phone call to the station will supply their names. For network shows you can write to the network's audience service department. The addresses for the three major networks are: Columbia Broadcasting System (CBS), Audience Services, 51 West 52nd Street, New York, N.Y. 10019; American Broadcasting Company (ABC), Audience Services, 1330 Avenue of the Americas, New York, N.Y. 10019; and National Broadcasting Company (NBC), Audience Services, 30 Rockefeller Plaza, New York, N.Y. 10020. In your letters always indicate the particular show or program you are commenting on and the date and time in which it was aired in your area. Another very effective trick is to contact the sponsors of the show you wish to criticize or praise. Sponsors are usually very responsive to audience opinions and you can get the sponsor's addresses from the reference section of your local library if they are not given on the program itself.

Proper and Improper Criticism

Several years ago the noted psychologist and skeptic Ray Hyman published a wise and helpful article titled "Proper Criticism" (*Skeptical Briefs,* May 1987) in which he outlined the steps necessary to make the skeptic's criticism of paranormal claims both effective and responsible. Unfortunately, many times in the years past zealous skeptics have often displayed more emotion than logic, made sweeping charges that the evidence failed to support, failed to document their assertions, and generally did not do what was necessary to make their challenges credible. Such ill-considered criticism can do much more harm than good. Hyman also pointed out that as a member of the CSICOP Executive Council he often found himself and other Council members devoting most of their time to undoing the damage done by thoughtless and ill-considered statements of the skeptical community. Over the years CSICOP has had to fend off quite a number of lawsuits filed because some one or other member had made public statements of a slanderous or near-slanderous nature and had published statements of a libelous or near-libelous nature. Such lawsuits are tremendously costly in terms of both time and money and whether true or false still must be dealt with by all concerned. It is therefore of great importance that the skeptical investigator learn what he can and cannot say and should and should not publish in dealing with the purveyors of paranormal poppycock. Hyman notes that we must be very careful not to violate our own standards—standards that the paranormalists violate with impunity—in our eagerness to challenge their irrationalities. If we champion science, logic, precision, and rationality, then we should demonstrate these virtues in the criticisms we make. Hyman warns that if we go beyond the facts we have and we fail to communicate exactly what we intend, we not only confuse the public, but we unwittingly put the paranormalists in the position of underdogs and create sympathy for them. To insure that this doesn't happen, Hyman offers a few suggestions. First, we should *always be prepared* to explain why skeptical activity is important, why false beliefs are harmful, and why people should listen. Also, learn the principles of critical thinking, effective writing, and argumentation. Second, *clarify your objectives.* Before attempting to cope with a paranormal claim, determine what you are trying to accomplish. Are you trying to belittle your opponent? Releasing pent-up resentment? Gaining publicity for your views? Show the claim is false? Educate the public about adequate evidence? Make sure you discriminate between long range and short range objectives. Don't sacrifice the long-range educational goal for the short range one of vindictiveness. Make sure you know who your audience is and make it clear you are attacking the argument and the claim, not the claimant. Make sure you aren't interfering with anyone's civil liberties. Don't advocate censorship. Don't try to get anyone fired. Make sure you do not oppose academic freedom or civil liberties. Third, make sure you *do your homework.* Make sure you get all of the relevant facts in countering a paranormal claim and document your sources when you do. Don't depend on the media or a secondary source for what is being claimed —go directly to the horse's mouth, i.e., the claimant, himself or herself. Fourth, *don't go beyond your level of competence.* No one is an expert on all subjects, so whenever possible consult appropriate experts. We are critical of paranormalists who make assertions beyond their competence, so make sure you don't commit the same offense. Make sure you really have something to say. It is better to remain silent than to speak out of turn and talk nonsense. Don't be afraid to say I don't know. Fifth, *let the facts speak for themselves.* If you have the facts, let the audience draw their own conclusions. If a psychic claims she located a missing child and the police tell you otherwise, it is counterproductive to claim the psychic "lied" or made a fraudulent claim. Maybe she really thought she helped. If you're too hard on her, the public might sympathize with her. If you just stick to the facts, the public will draw their own correct conclusions. Sixth, *be precise*. In challenging psychic or paranormal claims we must be as honest and accurate in our own statements as we can. Don't make assertions about psychic claims you cannot back up with hard evidence. Be especially careful when talking with the media and make sure the media rep knows exactly what you are and are not saying. Seventh, *use the principle of charity*. This may be the hardest of Hyman's principles to apply because of our zeal to defeat the enemy. Although it is hard to lean over backward and give them the benefit of the doubt, in the long run this is the best attitude. Make sure you distinguish between being wrong and being dishonest. You can challenge the validity of a paranormal claim without accusing the claimant of dishonesty or deliberate lying. Many people honestly believe and are merely deceived. When you have a choice as to how to interpret or represent your opponent's arguments, try to see it in a fair, objective, and non-emotional light and deal with it in these terms. You will get farther and win more friends in the long run. Don't stoop to your opponent's level if he resorts to these things. Rather than being a matter of turning the other cheek, it is more important to gain credibility for your cause. While emotional charges and sensational challenges might make headlines, think of the long term mission: to persuade the public that we have a serious message to convey and that we want to gain their trust as a credible and reliable source of information. We want the public to see us as respectable people with personal integrity and as serious rational scientists. If one follows Hyman's principles of criticism, it is highly unlikely that you or anyone else will find himself facing charges of either slander or libel. Unfortunately, whether we do or don't we still may find ourselves on the receiving end of a lawsuit, so it is worth our while to fully understand what does and does not constitute libel and slander.

Libel and Slander

Everyone who writes and publishes and who gives interviews should be aware of what libel and slander are and how to avoid them. Generally, in writing or speaking about other human beings you should do everything in your power to be accurate and fair. Approximately ninety-five out of every one hundred libel suits result from public charges of crime, immorality, incompetence, or inefficiency. Libel is, simply, an injury to a person's reputation. Words, pictures, or cartoons that expose a person to public hatred, shame, disgrace or ridicule, or induce an ill opinion of a person are libelous. Actions for civil libel result primarily from published stories that allege crime, fraud, dishonesty, immoral or dishonorable conduct, or stories that defame the individual professionally, and cause financial loss either personally or to a business. There is only one complete and unconditional defense to a civil action for libel and that is that the facts stated are *provably true.* The critical word here is "provably." Quoting someone correctly is not sufficient. You must be able to satisfy a jury that the libelous statement is substantially correct. A second important defense is *privilege.* Privilege comes in two kinds: *absolute* and *qualified.* Absolute means that certain persons in some circumstances can state, without fear of being sued, material which may be false, malicious, and damaging. These circumstances include judicial, legislative, public and official proceedings, and the contents of most public records. The doctrine of absolute privilege is founded on the fact that on certain occasions the public interest requires that some individuals be exempted from legal liability for what they say. The interests of society require that judicial, legislative, and similar official proceedings be subject to public discussion and, to that extent, the rights of the individual about whom damaging statements may be made are subordinated to what are deemed to be the interests of the community. With regard to the press, the courts have generally held that privilege is not absolute, but rather is *qualified,* which means it can be lost or diluted according to how the writer handles the material. Privilege can be lost if there are errors in the report of the hearing, or if the plaintiff can show malice on the part of the publication or broadcast outlet. There is an exception with regard to the statements of political candidates who are given air time under the equal opportunity rule. Legislators do have absolute privilege and they cannot, for example, be sued for anything said on the floor of the legislature. Writers are not as well protected, but the press can report freely on items of public interest. For example, they have the qualified privilege to report that John Smith has been arrested for bank robbery, and if the report is fair and accurate, there is no problem. While official proceedings such as trials, legislative sessions, and hearings, etc., are obvious, conventions of private organizations, however, are *not public* even though they may discuss public questions. Therefore, statements made on the floor of convention sessions or from speaker's platforms may not be privileged.

There is, however, such a thing as *fair comment and criticism.* This says that the publication of defamatory matter that consists of comment and opinion as distinguished from fact, with reference to matters of public interest or importance, is covered by the defense of fair comment. Certainly, whatever facts that are stated must be true and/or protected by a privilege. The right of fair comment has been summarized as follows:

> Everyone has a right to comment on matters of public interest and con-
> cern, provided they do so fairly and with an honest purpose. Such com-
> ments or criticism are not libelous, however severe in their terms, unless
> they are written maliciously. Thus it has been held that books, prints,
> pictures, and statuary publicly exhibited, and the architecture of public
> buildings, and actors and exhibitors are all the legitimate subjects of
> newspapers' criticism, and such criticism fairly and honestly made is not
> libelous, however strong the terms of censure may be. (*Hoeppner* v. *Dun-
> kirk Pr. Co.* 254 N.Y. 95)

Legally, the publication of a libelous statement is seen as a breach of peace.
For this reason it may constitute a criminal offense and thus it can give
rise to a civil action for damages.

According to some legal experts, there are five typical charges that
are usually leveled against private citizens and organizations who exercise
their First Amendment right of free speech against those believed to be
acting contrary to the public interest. The five, which normally are unsuccessful and without any legal merit, are: (1) Defamation, (2) Business wrongs,
(3) Judicial wrongs or abuse of process, (4) Civil rights violations, and
(5) Conspiracy. For our purposes we will only look at the first one, which
skeptics are most likely to encounter.

Defamation covers both libel and slander and is defined as: "a statement or other communication is defamatory of a person if it: (1) holds
him or her up to contempt, ridicule, disgrace or hatred; or (2) tends to
injure him or her in their office, trade, business or profession." *Slander*
is defined as defamation conveyed to another person orally, by gestures,
by mocking imitation, and so forth. *Libel,* defined earlier, generally refers
to defamation communicated in a permanent form. One should also be
careful about *invasion of privacy* since the law considers that some matters
are of such a personal nature that even if they happen to be true, they
are nobody else's business. If one is convicted of defamation and the jury
decides in favor of the plaintiff, three kinds of damages may be assessed.
First, there are *general damages,* which are awarded by juries on the basis
of what they consider to be fair compensation for your wrongful act. The
jury may also award *punitive damages,* which is extra compensation for
the injured party in order to punish you and to set an example for others.
It is, usually, based upon your ability to pay. Finally, there are *special
damages,* which are above and beyond the ordinary and not the usual
consequences of the wrongful act. In cases of slander (excluding libel) all
such special damages must be specified by the plaintiff in the pleading
of the case if they are to be recovered.

Recently, The National Council Against Health Fraud published a short brochure providing some general guidelines for activists who are fighting quackery and health fraud. The guidelines are most useful for anyone who is opposing the psi-cophants. Some of their most cogent and useful points are worth repeating here. First, remember that it is not libelous to attack an idea, to list the characteristic signs of quackery, or to say that something is "questionable." Remember also that one cannot libel a large group of individuals or an entire industry. One can, however, libel an individual or an organization by name-calling. You are on safe legal grounds if you mention adverse facts about someone who places himself in the public spotlight by claiming to have expert knowledge. You should be careful, however, and avoid all statements about the person's motivation (e.g., "He's only in it for the money!"), since such statements may be impossible to prove. If you are involved in a sensitive interview, make sure you have your own tape recorder operating.

To avoid defamation charges do not aim your remarks at any one specific entity. Refrain from singling out specific individuals, organizations, products, companies, and such. Keep your statements general and concentrate on generic formula types of practitioners, methods of practice, and so forth. If you feel it necessary to call someone a "quack" or to label something "quackery," make sure that you supply a clear definition of what you mean, and always preface your remarks with "in my opinion" or some comparable statement. By prefacing your remarks with the statement that what you say is your opinion, it automatically becomes a true statement! Be careful, however, if you say "In my opinion John Smith is a dangerous quack." While it is a true statement of your opinion, it is not necessarily a true description of John Smith. This statement is not only inflammatory, but it is likely to invite a lawsuit by John Smith. In general, it is not a good idea to call anyone a liar, a quack, dishonest, etc., unless you are willing to go to court. It is better to call the practice "quackery" without directing charges at specific individuals. Don't ever go off half-cocked. Instead, make sure you are well informed and know what you are talking about. When criticizing or abusing a person, be aware of the nature of your accusation. Know whether you are making an accusation of criminal behavior, incompetence, or anything that could injure him or her in their business, trade, or profession. Make very sure that your evidence will support such a charge. It is also very important that you be accurate when describing people's actions. Get a clear picture of what they are doing and describe it in proper terms. Use standard terminology from recognized authoritative sources. Another rule is to focus primarily upon obtaining a clear, accurate, and thorough description of the product, service, book, practitioner, company organization, theory, belief, or whatever. If possible, get it in writing and make sure you understand it in detail.

If you're not sure you understand it, get a clarification.

Although you may be tempted, it is not necessary or a good idea to exaggerate or to embellish the bare facts. All you need to do is to point out the adverse truths about the entity in question. If a "quack's" doctorate is from an unaccredited school or "degree mill," simply point this out. If he or she has a criminal record, cite it accurately. If the claim is ungodly and outrageous, merely provide the accurate counterinformation or possibly some aid in logic or insight. Remember, understatement is better in the long run. Though it is tempting to attack fraud and quackery and nonsense at the top of your voice, such strident approaches to public issues often fail in the long run because of the "Chicken Little" phenomenon. Credibility and persistence are the skeptic's most effective weapons, and an objective, unemotional, well-informed statement given with tolerance and understanding—and with some humor when appropriate—is the best way to win. Many times quacks and true believers themselves are victims who unwittingly victimize others in their misguided efforts. While it is true that some psi-cophants are greedy con men and women, others may be deranged, incompetent, or zealots who sincerely believe in what they are saying and are motivated by good will, love, and altruism. From the public's and consumers's point of view, in the last analysis, motivation doesn't matter.

In your attack focus on the critical and important issues and on the present and potential harm that is being done. From one point of view, what the quack and charlatan is doing is small potatoes compared to the drug use, child molestation, and murder the public is made aware of every day. If you are going to be effective, you had better have some good arguments up your sleeve. Some of the categories of harm that the quacks and psi-cophants fall into include: (1) Economic harm; (2) Direct harm by commission, e.g., poisoning, malnutrition, injuries; (3) Indirect harm by omission, e.g., avoiding or delaying proper care; (4) Psychological harm, e.g., causing mental anguish by leading someone to a false belief or creating false hope or creating distrust of science and medicine; (5) Social harm, e.g., widespread misbeliefs can lead to misguided policy, undermining of sound consumer laws, waste resources, deflect research from sound pursuits, and so forth. Once you have the facts in hand and know where you stand, be firm in your resolve. Do not allow threats of lawsuits or lawsuits filed against you to cause you any panic. Most threats never materialize and even lawsuits that have been filed are often not pursued when it becomes clear you know what you are doing and have a good case for your claims.

Before leaving the topic of defamation, some definitions might be helpful. The requirements for an actionable defamation suit require that there must be a specific entity or "entity under the law," i.e., a person, an organization, or class of persons recognized by law must be involved. For example, the statement "All medical doctors are quacks" would not be actionable because it does not involve an entity that is specific enough. The statement is too general to be applied to any specific medical doctor. There must also be a third party, that is, someone other than the entity that is the object of the communication must hear or see it and this witness must be able to understand the communication in the case of slander. As for libel, no third party is required because the communication is in a permanent form. Also, it is defamatory to accuse someone of *impotence* or unchastity, having a loathesome disease, criminal acts, or incompetence in his or her trade, business, or profession. Defamation need not be intentional. For example, if a personal or private letter that is not so marked is opened and read by a secretary, the secretary constitutes the third party and defamation can be claimed. If, however, a third party reads a private communication by mistake, the defendant cannot be held responsible if the mistake was not caused by him or her. If the defendant caused the reading even by mistake, then he or she is held to be responsible.

As for your defenses against defamation in any civil action for libel or slander, it is always a complete defense that the defamatory charge is true. It is immaterial whether or not the defendant believed it was true at the time he or she made it or what the motive was for making it. In criminal cases, the defendant must have believed the charge was true and the defendant has the burden of proof of the truth of the charge. Repetition of a defamation with sufficient exactness and citation may be used as a defense, but because great injury may accrue from the wrongful repetition of defamation, the person repeating the charge can be held liable. Therefore, potentially defamatory information should be checked out before it is repeated. Remember, however, that anything placed before the public, such as a book or play, or the conduct of public persons, may be commented upon and criticized provided such comment is fair, without malice, and not an invasion of privacy. There is also such a thing as "leave and license," which means that if the plaintiff consented to the publication of a defamation, then he or she cannot afterwards make a complaint of it. Remember also what was said earlier about absolute privilege, that is, that under certain circumstances specified individuals are exempted from charges of defamation, e.g., the President, legislators, judges, et al. Even here, however, these individuals have to be aware that privilege does not follow them from the hearing room. If they make a statement to the press outside of the hearing room, such statements are not protected by privilege.

Make sure that you also remember the above statements are guidelines only and in the event that you do find yourself on the receiving end of a lawsuit—either justly or unjustly inspired—you should immediately seek wise and professional legal counsel.

Psychic and Health Frauds

A few months ago Michael Botts, the Secretary of CSICOP's Legal and Consumer Protection Sub-Committee, sent a memo to all the skeptical groups dealing with consumer protection for psychic fraud. Botts's major points were that all of the normal consumer protection laws also apply to psychic and health frauds. Even though consumers in general are reluctant to seek redress when they have been victimized because of the costs of litigation in time and money, as well as the subsequent fear and embarrassment, and usually because of the small amount of money involved, exposure of such frauds and the sanctions of the courts are the only weapons we have. We should use them.

In discussing the remedies available to consumers, Botts points out that contract law remedies are generally inadequate in consumer fraud cases because the underlying contract is usually fraudulently induced and only in rare circumstances are punitive damages available. Tort law is useful only if personal injuries are involved and statutory laws are not usually applicable to psychic and health frauds. The primary individual remedies for actual frauds are the state consumer fraud statutes, commonly known as the UDAP statutes, an acronym for Uniform Deceptive Acts and Practices. Common law fraud requires proof of a false representation, usually fact; a "scienter," i.e., the speaker's knowledge that the fact is false; the speaker's intent that the victim rely on the false representation; the victim's reliance on the false representation; and damage to the victim as a result of the reliance. Common law fraud usually must be proven by "clear and convincing evidence," which is a little higher standard of proof than the normal civil standard of a "preponderance of the evidence."

Contrary to common law fraud, "deception" under the Federal Trade Commission Act (FTC) does not require a showing of intent, scienter, etc. Even actual deceptions are unnecessary. A deception can be established if one can prove that the practice will deceive even a minority of consumers. The standard of proof is the lower "preponderance" standard. The FTC act is the model for many states' UDAP rulings. Statutory fraud under the states' UDAP laws is also classified as deception and it can be found even where there is no breach of contract or warranty, and even where there is no negligence. Simply being misled by a seller's statement or actions is sufficient. "Unfairness" is still recognized by most states also, and for this the courts ask: (1) whether the practice offends public policy;

(2) whether the practice is immoral, unethical, oppressive, or unscrupulous; and (3) whether the practice causes substantial injury to consumers. Similarly, the FTC test is: (1) the injury must be substantial, (2) the injury must not be outweighed by any countervailing benefits to consumers or competition that the practice promotes, and (3) the injury must be one that the consumers themselves could not reasonably have avoided. In finding unfairness, emotional or other subjective harm will not ordinarily be considered an injury.

For the particular section of the various states' codes and statutes that cover consumer protection you should consult an attorney or call the state attorney general's office. The important thing here is that when you encounter cases of psychic fraud, you do not allow the psychic to get away with his bilking the public. Do not hesitate to work with the client who has been deceived to expose the fraud and take advantage of the sanctions of the courts.

Copyrights and Fair Use Doctrine

One of the trickiest issues of all that faces every paranormal investigator and writer is the question of quoting from the works of others. Whenever we have need to quote from the works of others, and the work is copyrighted—or although unpublished is copyrightable—we must either gain specific permission or use the material in such a way that it falls within the "fair use" provision of Title 17 of the United States Code. The word "copyright" itself means what it says, i.e., *the right to make copies*. The purpose of the copyright is to protect the rights of the author, and it applies to work that not only has been published, but to work that has not been published. Interestingly enough, in general no person may make use of the unpublished materials and writings of another for any purpose. According to statute, U.S. Code 17, Sec. 301 and Sec. 302, if the work was created before 1 January 1978, the duration of the copyright (the protection under the statute) is for the life of the author plus fifty years, with renewal provisions provided, further, that in no event and no matter how long ago the writing may have been accomplished will such protection end before 1 December 2002. As for writings created after 1 January 1978, the protection extends from the moment of creation through the same time period, i.e., the life of the author plus fifty years, plus such renewals as may be permitted. The law further states that even though a proposed use might be considered fair if the material had been published, the fairness does not provide an excuse for the use of unpublished works. Unless and until a writer or his legal heirs either grant permission to use the unpublished material, publish it, or "freely set those thoughts and words adrift in the great ocean of intellectual scrutiny by introducing the material into the public domain," that author is entitled to maintain his peculiar rendering of thoughts for a very long period indeed.

While the law clearly recognizes that all knowledge is cumulative and that there is a need to cite the work of others, it also recognizes that this need requires not only protection of the author, but also faithfulness to the original writing. Recognition of the need to place limitations on the exclusivity of the copyrights Congress has called "the fair use doctrine." Fair use provisions are found in Title 17 of the U.S. Code and specifically in Section 107, where it states: "Notwithstanding [the prohibitions herein] the fair use of a copyrighted work, including such use by reproduction in copies . . . for purposes such as criticism, comment, . . . teaching (including multiple copies for classroom use), scholarship, or research, is not an infringement of copyright. In determining whether the use made of a work in any particular case is a fair use the factors to be considered shall include: (1) the *purpose and character* of the use, including whether such use is of a commercial nature or is for nonprofit educational purposes; (2) the *nature* of the copyrighted work; (3) the *amount and substantiality* of the portion used in relation to the copyrighted work as a whole; and (4) the *effect* of the use upon the potential market for or value of the copyrighted work."

It is important to note that Section 107 completely omits reference to any intent to do harm. Significantly, malicious intent and criminal intent on the part of the infringer are conspicuous by their absence. Whereas in other areas of the law where a breach invokes restriction, punishment, or fines, Congress does not regard infringers as willfully undertaking breach. It is sufficient ·to show that the infringer—knowingly or not—engages in conduct that by using the work of others might bring profit his way.

If one is teaching, being critical of, or confirming what another has said, he may legitimately use the expressions. On the other hand, if the *purpose and character* of the use, rather than being of an intellectual nature, is designed to either directly or indirectly gain profit, then he cannot legitimately use the words of another. No one is allowed to profit off the time, labor, and thoughts of someone else and to pretend that the borrowed material is his own. The single most important element in any consideration of the "fair use" doctrine is the effect of an illegal use upon the potential market for or the value of the copyrighted work. To win his case the copyright owner has only to show that *if* the challenged use should become widespread, it would adversely affect the *potential* market for the copyrighted work. This means that the court must also consider not only the harm to the market for the original work, but also any harm which *might* come to the market for derivative works.

In general, the courts define fair use quite broadly within the area of intellectual activities but define it quite narrowly when moving into the commercial area. Based on prior court cases, it seems that each and every commercial use is regarded as unfair. Any evidence of sale or intent to sell almost surely precludes "fair use." Thanking the author or giving him credit after borrowing is not regarded as sufficient according to the statute; neither are regarded as substitutes for express permission. Neither is an infringement upon the work of another excused merely because the amount of material borrowed was small. If the quantity borrowed had great interest or novelty, then the original author has been injured. While the number of words or pages borrowed have been determinative in previous cases, the courts have usually looked for and found other reasons as well for determining the presence or absence of infringement.

Another question that is bound to arise has to do with rewriting and paraphrasing. The courts once again have uniformly decided that it makes no difference whether the plagiarizer changes the arrangement of the original words or not—rewriting the material is not sufficient to aid the charge of infringement. In one case, even though the accuracy of the material copied was checked extensively by the infringer and many changes were made, the court found that the starting material was the key to determining infringement. Merely modifying an original effort is not sufficient to deprive the author of protection, and neither will extensive paraphrasing. One court, in fact, stated that in the absence of justifying circumstances, an act of paraphrasing in and of itself constituted infringement. More importantly, even if the use of the words and statements of another is totally honest, unintentional, or subconscious, it is still prohibited. Neither forgetfulness nor ignorance is regarded as a legitimate excuse. If, however, it was an honest and unintentional mistake, and no intent to plagiarize was in mind, the infringer usually gets off with a lesser punishment.

In general and as a rule of thumb, in any case where the work of someone else is to be copied or used, even if you think your use of it is fair, you should obtain the original author's written permission. A nonprofit purpose for quotation will strengthen your case for fair use. The First Amendment protection of free speech can be a defense against infringement, especially if there is great public interest in the material. Remember, criticism, comment, teaching, scholarship, and research is never an infringement of copyright.

Some Ethical Issues

A few months ago a psychiatrist friend of ours was brought before the
State Medical Board by another psychiatrist on a violation of medical ethics
charge. Our psychiatrist friend had been accused by his fellow practitioner
of engaging in fraud. What our medical friend did was to treat one of
his patients who required hospitalization by sprinkling voodoo dust all
around the hospital room to keep the evil spirits away. Despite the fact
that the treatment was successful, i.e., the patient's anxieties were relieved
and he now felt safe and secure in his hospital room, the complaining
physician was outraged that our friend would not only engage in primitive
medicine, but that he also would deceive his patient and encourage his
irrational beliefs. In our opinion the complaining physician is not only
in error, but is also trapped in his own shortsightedness and biases and
also lacks the insight needed to properly deal with his clients. Was our
friend being unethical in his treatment with voodoo dust? We do not think
so and neither did the medical board, which dismissed the charges as friv-
olous. They were. In fact, our psychiatrist friend was practicing an old
and very ancient medical art: the art of reassurance. The power of belief
and suggestion can be very powerful tools indeed and there is nothing
wrong in using these to help one's client solve a pressing problem. Utter-
ing a few magical words over a child's warts or sprinkling them with "magic
water" can also, via the power of suggestion, cause them to gradually
disappear. Certainly, in the long run, if time and money permit, the physician
could embark on a long-term educational program in which his eighty-
year-old deeply religious client can be brought into the twentieth century
and fully re-educated to the point that not only has he changed his religious views, but that he also fully understands all of the nuances and subtle-
ties of psychosomatic medicine and the latest developments in effective
psychoneuroimmunological practice. Once accomplished, our psychiatrist
friend could then dispense with the voodoo dust and treat him effectively
with long-term psychoanalytical therapy. We, of course, exaggerated because only a fool would do this. Ethics, after all, is more a matter of
commonsense than anything else and, as far as practitioners of therapy
are concerned, their first commandment is: *Do no harm!* You can avoid
ethical dilemmas most of the time by using your good old common sense
and good judgment. If you would do more harm to people by ridicul-
ing their religious beliefs than by allowing them to keep them and yet
helping them solve their immediate problem, you let their beliefs alone
and help them solve their pressing problem. This is the *only* ethical thing
to do. Zealotry, whether on the part of a skeptic or on the part of a
psychic, is equally deplorable. Intense uncritical devotion, i.e., fanaticism,

is equally ugly no matter where it is encountered. It is the hallmark of the irrational, and what we must avoid at all cost. Even science, as a friend once remarked, has a mighty, *not an almighty,* mission.

Our use of loud, raucous music and flashing strobe lights to drive away ghosts, or the use of holy water and the powdered bones of saints might also be considered as "unethical" in that these ghost-busting tools require the practice of deception and trickery on one's part. We have learned long ago that people who believe in ghosts and apparitions also believe in other powers: the powers of sacred objects to repel the demons and the powers of ghost busters to drive spirits away. Persons familiar with the psychology of belief are well aware that it is easier to change or modify a belief system by introducing the believer to new and credible people and to new experiences on a gradual basis rather than through direct and abrupt confrontation. For these reasons you will be more effective in your long range goals if you approach the modification of the belief system slowly and gradually rather than by way of challenge or ridicule. Despite your eagerness to change the world and to bring an immediate end to the New Age and to the wave of superstition and irrationality now sweeping the land, it cannot be done overnight and you cannot do it alone. We must be patient, persistent, resolute, and work to strengthen the cause of science and sanity wherever we can. This is a formidable task and there will be times when a sense of frustration and futility will cause you to doubt the value of your efforts. If and when such occasions arise, recognize that you are probably suffering from what old skeptical hands call "skeptical burnout" and "temptations to fatalism." A few years ago, the brilliant psychologist and skeptic, Dr. Steven Cody, put together some words of advice and wisdom which we feel will help all of us maintain our energy and enthusiasm. With Dr. Cody's permission a slightly edited version of his paper follows.

Skeptical Burnout and How to Resist It

In the decade since the establishment of the Committee for Scientific Investigation of Claims of the Paranormal, the "skeptical movement" has flourished, developing into a significant force for promoting critical inquiry and confronting pseudoscience, irrationality, and chicanery. The inside back cover of *Skeptical Inquirer* currently lists some sixteen local associate organizations and ten international committees sharing the goals and aims of CSICOP, and several others are in the process of forming, illustrating the growth of the skeptical enterprise into a broadly based, grass-roots phenomenon. We are justified in feeling a considerable measure of gratification over these circumstances, for they reflect the energy and commitment of a growing pool of talented scientists, educators, and other concerned citizens. As the participants in our common endeavor work to develop ever more sophisticated educational resources, to challenge ever more assertively the unjustified claims and twisted reasoning of pseudoscience, and to reach an ever wider public, there is also much cause for optimism about the future.

At the same time, there is no shortage of cause for feelings of frustration and even futility when dealing with the seemingly endless array of silliness encompassed by the domain of pseudoscience, or the apparent ease with which people are seduced by what Paul Kurtz (1986) has called the "transcendental temptation." Benassi and Singer (1981) have provided an excellent review of the factors involved in the intransigence of paranormal and pseudoscientific beliefs, not the least of which is the fact that such beliefs can provide meaningful psychological benefits without significant cost to the believer.

Based first of all on the principle that "forewarned is forearmed," it is my purpose in this paper to consider several factors that tend to promote the feelings of discouragement and disillusionment to which I refer when I use the term *skeptical burnout*. Identifying those factors is the first step in preparing ourselves to deal with the feelings involved; in addition, I believe that a forthright discussion of the sources of disillusionment with the skeptical enterprise can lead to more explicit and practical means for coping with it.

In this article I will examine ten aspects of our endeavor that I believe tempt us to give up in frustration, and I will conclude with some ideas about how to respond in such a way as to maintain our energy and enthusiasm for a task that, however difficult, involves stakes too high to make withdrawal an acceptable outcome. The central theme underlying all of these "temptations" is the added burden to the skeptic's energies and the perception that effort does not lead to progress, both of which are fundamental determinants of burnout.

Ten Temptations to Fatalism

1. *The persistence of long-standing nonsense.* Astrology furnishes probably the best example of a pseudoscientific phenomenon that has persisted, in this case for centuries, in spite of the absence of either a cogent rationale or empirical justification. Even when its most ludicrous manifestation—the newspaper horoscope—is dismissed, as it frequently is by devotees, there is the insistence that "serious" or "scientific" astrology is different, somehow more credible.

2. *The abundance of new nonsense.* If anything positive is to be said about pseudoscience, it is that the enterprise is a creative one, with new items being added to the catalog on a regular basis. Some are actually rehashings of old foolishness, as in the case of the recent firewalking craze (Leikind and McCarthy 1985) or the numerology reincarnation of bio-rhythms (Bainbridge 1978, Hines 1979). Some are more novel; in my own locale, there is a creature known as Ko-Laim-Ni, which its adherents trans-late as "Connected With Light" and promote as the latest step "forward" in alternative health care. It supposedly involves massage of the "etheric body" and its adherents tell me it was communicated to them by former denizens of Atlantis via psychic channeling. In the face of such develop-ments, it is easy to feel that we are losing ground. From this point, it is a very short step to concluding that the enterprise is not worth the effort.

3. *Reactions of resentment and hostility.* Most of us are involved in the skeptical endeavor at least in part because we believe it to be a socially valuable enterprise, and it is thus understandable that we should experience some dismay and discouragement when our efforts to protect the public by exposing fraud and foolishness are greeted with hostility. People do not like to view themselves as credulous or gullible, and often-times overestimate their own ability to detect deception and evaluate doubt-ful claims. We should not expect them to enjoy being told that we've been duped, but we are nevertheless often ill-prepared for the degree of resent-ment that our well-intended efforts can generate. People seem to find paranormal phenomena exciting and fascinating, and our response also tends to take the fun out of it all.

4. *Public incomprehension of scientific fact and method.* In many cases, such as in the instance of creationism, understanding pseudoscience for what it is requires a rudimentary understanding of the facts as well as an appreciation for what terms like *theory* mean to the scientist. Having participated in public debates on creationism, I recall very vividly how fidgety an audience can get when the scientist tries to explain why the creationist is guilty of distortion in describing evolution as "just a theory." The pseudoscientist is not constrained by complexity, and his or her dis-tortions and simplifications present the scientist with a morass of nonsense to wade through for a public that does not share the fundamentals of knowledge and method that are the basic tools of scientific analysis. Scien-tific knowledge does not in itself provide an immunity to pseudoscience, but in its absence the task of refuting pseudoscientific propositions is immeasurably more difficult.

5. *The inability to argue from evidence.* When we can restrict the argument to issues of substantive evidence, the task of responding to irra-tional belief is much easier, but commitment to pseudoscientific ideas often

persists without reference to meaningful standards of evidence. In part, this is because people (including scientists; cf. Tversky and Kahneman 1974) are often more impressed by anecdotal evidence, testimonials, and personal experience than the scientifically sophisticated would prefer, and because part of the public incomprehension of scientific method involves ignorance of what constitutes substantive evidence. We can thus find ourselves armed to the teeth with what is to us an irrefutable body of data, only to find that it virtually bounces off our audience.

6. *Anti-intellectualism and name-calling.* It is doubtful that any of us engaged in the skeptical enterprise have escaped some exposure to the ad hominem argument. "Negative," "close-minded," "earthbound" (I rather like this one; it was used by a local devotee of things paranormal to describe me to two of my students at a recent "craft fair" for psychics, healers, and astrologers, "communist" (yes, that too), "dogmatic" and "rigid" are only a few of the (kinder) characteristics that are supposed to account for our views, and responding in the face of that puts an added burden on one's energies for the task. Some of the more unpleasant things come about when the pseudoscientist appeals to the ambivalence people can feel toward those involved in intellectual pursuits: the writers, teachers, scientists, and philosophers who populate the skeptical ranks. Starr (1984) speaks of this ambivalence, particularly with regard to medicine, as a reluctance to grant to others a special status based on a skill or understanding that "ordinary people" do not possess, and as a rejection of elitism. There is a resistance to the sense of dependency this creates; witness the persistence of folk remedies and lay healers. It adds another layer of resistance to the effort to make the skeptic's message heard.

By the way, there's no implication here that skeptics are sinless when it comes to ad hominem arguments and arguments by authority. In fact, finding ourselves increasingly prone to such things is a common symptom of burning out.

7. *Preaching to the converted.* There is of course a part of the audience the skeptic tries to reach that is open to clearly presented evidence and well-reasoned argument, but there are also times when that fact can be obscured by the zealotry on both sides of the issues. The sense that we are only talking to each other, which is in part a potential symptom of being ineffective and of circumscribing our audiences ourselves, is also occasionally to be expected in light of the dichotomous nature of the position people sometimes tend to adopt.

8. *Lack of interest and disapproval from colleagues.* It is not only believers who question the worthiness of the skeptic's efforts. Questions about the value of devoting resources and time to evaluating and responding to unlikely claims come from our colleagues as well, typically in the

form of "Why do you waste your time on that stuff, anyway?" Sagan (1980) and Scott (1985) have eloquently expressed the responsibility of scientists to see that pseudoscience does not go unexamined or unchallenged, but it is still not uncommon to find that our colleagues do not share our enthusiasm or our appreciation of the need to confront the claims of fringe science. As human beings, skeptics have the same needs as anyone else for the approval of their peers, to feel that their efforts are valued and respected by those with whom they work, and discouraging responses from those people are certainly not among the rewards of skeptical activism.

9. *Colorful competition.* The wonders of our universe and the curiosities of our own behavior offer no end of opportunity and stimulation for the inquiring mind, but reaping the rewards requires two things that involve a disadvantage in competing with pseudoscience and the paranormal. One is that appreciation of scientific topics often requires rather more effort (and knowledge and training) than is demanded by pseudoscience, and is more dependent on the person's fund of information. The other is that science does not offer the same possibility for people in the general population to be personal participants in accomplishing the wonderful. Anyone, on the other hand, can apparently be psychic (see Targ and Harary 1984), and anyone can learn in a few short weeks to heal illness and relieve pain through reflexology (see Carter 1969). At another level, pseudoscientific and paranormal phenomena appeal to the desires for personal control and a sense of predictability about the world, and in the health fields can sometimes involve the promise of help, however illusory, with conditions for which traditional medicine has limited value.

10. *Organizational failings.* Starting and running organizations is not a prominent subject in graduate science education, just to choose one area in which skeptics commonly have some expertise. That can make organizational mechanics onerous and sometimes intimidating. In addition, skeptical pursuits don't pay our bills, and like everyone else we have families, careers, and other personal interests competing for our time and energy. These circumstances conspire to concentrate the bulk of the work in the hands of the few who are both willing and able to take it on, and I suspect this is familiar phenomenon to many of those helping to run the local affiliate around the country. In a separate issue, we aren't always very good at the level of organization required for handling the tasks of securing facilities, publicizing meetings and programs, identifying and utilizing resources in various disciplines, and so on. It adds up to further burdens on the energies of the more active skeptics, and increases the possibility of burning out.

Strategies for Energy and Enthusiasm

The first step in coping with the challenges of our energy and enthusiasm is to recognize them and to be aware that feeling them from time to time is expected. People burning out will find themselves apathetic, irritable, more prone than usual to ad hominem argument and impatient dismissal of critics, and disinclined to discuss the issues with those outside a circle of like-minded folks, with an attendant insularity. Detecting those signs can alert us to the need for changes, and the sooner that happens the better the chance that changes will be effective in bringing back our zest for the task.

Realism is an essential component in accomplishing this, and it covers a variety of issues. First of all, you can't win them all in anything. Second, you can't do everything that might be worth doing, and ignoring the need to take care of the rest of our lives is unhealthy. Third, it is risky to start things before you identify who is going to do the work, since you might find out a bit late in the game that you aren't drawing the support you need, so it pays to be realistic about developing an organization and its programs. Doing this in no way implies pessimism; in fact, it is as essential to success and optimism as boldness.

Good organizing includes mobilizing and utilizing the support you will need, and delegating tasks and duties is an absolute necessity. The healthier the organization, the better the work is distributed, and the more likely that those most active will be able to enjoy what they're doing. Aside from getting the business done, support means people who share the commitment, affirm mutual goals, and provide each other with stimulation. It helps to begin with a core of people whose support and interest can be counted on, and to make contact with other organizations whose experience can be immensely helpful. Communication and interaction among representatives of local CSICOP affiliates, on a regular basis, would be an important step in the right direction.

A final point involves making a distinction between the "hard" and the "soft" goals of the skeptical enterprise. The hard goals are those with clearly identifiable outcomes, such as getting the local newspaper to run a disclaimer with the daily horoscope. The soft goals involve outcomes more difficult to specify and measure, as in "promoting a more critical perspective toward pseudoscientific claims, where it can simply be hard to know whether you're winning or not. We need to be conscious of the difference, and of the value of mixing the goals in order to maintain everyone's interest, including our own. Vague and general and abstract goals will not on their own maintain interest for long.

Final Comments

Participation in the skeptical response to pseudoscience and claims of the paranormal can be both gratifying and stimulating. Moreover, there is immense value to it, since important social decisions depend on the participation of an informed public, and the continued growth and development of science depends to some extent on the consent of the entire body politic. If we don't defend good science and good sense, no one will.

At the same time, we need very much to be conscious of what we need in order to preserve our own energies. In the long run, it's in our best interests and in the best interests of the enterprise as well. (Cody 1986)

References

Introduction

Abbott Magic Company, Colon, MI 49040.

Abell, George, and Barry Singer, eds. 1981. *Science and the Paranormal.* New York: Charles Scribner's Sons.

Alcock, James. 1981. *Parapsychology: Science Or Magic?* New York: Permagon Press.

Asaad, Ghazi. 1990. *Hallucinations in Clinical Psychiatry.* New York: Brunner Mazel Publishers.

Barrett, Stephen. 1991. *Health Schemes, Scams, and Frauds.* New York: Consumer Reports Books.

Beam, Maurice. 1962. *It's a Racket.* New York: MacFadden Books.

Brandon, Ruth. 1983. *The Spiritualists.* New York: Alfred A. Knopf.

Bronowski, Jacob. 1978. *The Common Sense of Science.* Cambridge, Mass.: Harvard University Press.

Christopher, Milbourne. 1970. *ESP, Seers, and Pyschics.* New York: Thomas Crowell.

――――. 1972. *Mediums, Mystics, and the Occult.* New York: Thomas Crowell.

――――. 1973. *The Illustrated History of Magic.* New York: Thomas Crowell.

Diedrich, Paul B. 1967. "Components of the Scientific Attitude." *The Science Teacher,* vol. 20: 23–24.

Drake, James L. 1989. *Private Intelligence Secrets.* Sharon Center, Ohio: Alpha Publications.

Dunninger, Joseph. 1967. *Dunninger's Complete Encyclopedia of Magic.* New York: Lyle Stuart.

Evans, Bergen. 1954. *The Spoor of Spooks.* New York: Alfred A. Knopf.

Factsheet Five. Mike Gunderloy, 6 Arizona Avenue, Rensselaer, NY: 12144–4502.

Fallis, Greg, and Ruth Greenberg. 1989. *Be Your Own Detective.* New York: M. Evans & Co.

Frazier, Ken. 1981. *Paranormal Borderlines of Science.* Buffalo, N.Y.: Prometheus Books.

———. 1986. *Science Confronts the Paranormal.* Buffalo, N.Y.: Prometheus Books.

Ferraro, Edward. 1989. *You Can Find Anyone.* Santa Ana, Calif.: Marathon Press.

French, Scott, and Paul Van Houten. 1987. *Never Say Lie.* Port Townsend, Wash.: Loompanics.

Gallup, George H., and Frank Newport. 1991. "Belief in Paranormal Phenomena Among Adult Americans." *Skeptical Inquirer,* Winter 1991, vol. 15, no. 2: 137–146.

Gardner, Martin. 1957. *Fads and Fallacies in the Name of Science.* New York: Dover Books.

———. 1981. *Science: Good, Bad and Bogus.* Buffalo, N.Y.: Prometheus Books.

Gibson, Walter B. 1986. *The Bunco Book.* Secaucus, N.J.: Citadel Press.

Gruenberger, Fred. 1964. "A Measure for Crackpots." *Science* 25 (Sept. 1964): 1413.

Harris, Melvin. 1986. *Investigating the Unexplained.* Buffalo, N.Y.: Prometheus Books.

Hay, Henry. 1987. *The Amateur Magician's Handbook,* 4th ed. New York: New American Library.

Hines, Terence. 1988. *Pseudoscience and the Paranormal.* Buffalo, N.Y.: Prometheus Books.

Henderson, M. Allen. 1989. *Flim-Flam Man.* Fountain Valley, Calif.: Eden Press.

———. 1989. *Money for Nothing.* Fountain Valley, Calif.: Eden Press.

Hopkins, A. A. 1977. *Magic: Scientific Diversions and Stage Illusions.* New York: Arno Press.

Houdini, Harry. 1924. *A Magician Among the Spirits.* New York: Harper & Row.

Inbau, Fred E., John E. Reed, and Joseph Buckley. 1986. *Criminal Interrogation and Confessions,* 3rd ed. Baltimore, Md.: Williams and Williams Publishing Co.

Jastrow, Joseph. 1935. *Error and Eccentricity in Human Belief.* New York: Dover Books.

Kaye, Marvin. 1973. *The Handbook of Magic.* New York: Dorset Press, Stein & Day.

———. 1975. *Handbook of Mental Magic.* New York: Stein & Day.

Keene, M. Lamar. 1976. *The Psychic Mafia.* New York: St. Martin's Press.

Klass, Philip J. 1974. *UFOs Identified.* New York: Random House.

———. 1975. *UFOs Explained.* New York: Vintage (Random House).

———. 1983. *UFOs: The Public Deceived.* Buffalo, N.Y.: Prometheus Books.

———. 1988. *UFO Abductions: A Dangerous Game.* Buffalo, N.Y.: Prometheus Books.

Korem, Dan. 1988. *Powers: Testing the Psychic and the Supernatural.* Downers Grove, Ill.: InterVarsity Press.

Kurtz, Paul. 1985. *A Skeptic's Handbook of Parapsychology.* Buffalo, N.Y.: Prometheus Books.

Kusche, Lawrence D. 1975. *The Bermuda Triangle Mystery: Solved.* New York: Harper & Row.

Lapin, Lee. 1983. *How to Get Anything on Anybody*. San Francisco: Auburn Wolfe Publishing Co.

Macdonald, John, and David Michaud. 1987. *Interrogation and Criminal Profiles for Police Officers*. Denver, Colo.: Apache Press.

MacDougall, Curtis. 1958. *Hoaxes*. New York: Dover Publishing Co.

MacKay, Charles. 1841 (1980). *Extraordinary Popular Delusions and the Madness of Crowds*. London: Richard Bentley; New York: Bonanza Books.

Marks, David, and Richard Kammann. 1980. *The Psychology of the Psychic*. Buffalo, N.Y.: Prometheus Books.

Maslow, Abraham. 1970. *Motivation and Personality*, 2d ed. New York: Harper & Row.

Maurer, David. 1962. *The Big Con*. New York: New American Library.

Neher, Andrew. 1980. *The Psychology of Transcendence*. Englewood Cliffs, N.J.: ·Prentice-Hall.

Nelms, Henning. 1969. *Magic and Showmanship: A Handbook for Conjurors*. New York: Dover Publishing Co.

Nickell, Joe. 1983. *Inquest on the Shroud of Turin*. Buffalo, N.Y.: Prometheus Books.

Nickell Joe, and John Fischer. 1988. *Secrets of the Supernatural*. Buffalo, N.Y.: Prometheus Books.

Nickerson, R. S. 1986. *Reflections on Reasoning*. Hillsdale, N.J.: Erlbaum & Associates Publishers.

———. 1987. "Why Teach Thinking?" in *Teaching Thinking Skills*, edited by J. B. Baron and R. J. Sternberg. New York: W. H. Freeman Co.

Palmiotto, R., ed. 1990. *Critical Issues in Criminal Investigation*. Cincinnati, Ohio: Anderson Publishing Co.

Pool, Robert. 1991. "Science Literacy: The Enemy Is Us." *Science* 251 (18 January 1991): 266–267.

Randi, James. 1975. *The Magic of Uri Geller*. New York: Ballantine Books.

———. 1980. *Flim-Flam!* New York: Lippincott & Crowell.

———. 1987. *The Faith Healers*. Buffalo, N.Y.: Prometheus Books.

Rapp, Bert. 1987. *Interrogation: A Complete Manual*. Port Townsend, Wash.: Loompanics.

Rawcliffe, D. H. 1959. *Illusions and Delusions of the Supernatural and the Occult*. New York: Dover Books.

Reed, Graham. 1988. *The Psychology of Anomalous Experience*. Buffalo, N.Y.: Prometheus Books.

Santoro, Victor. 1984. *The Rip-Off Book*. Port Townsend, Wash.: Loompanics.

Saunders, Richard. 1980. *The World's Greatest Hoaxes*. New York: Playboy Press.

Sheaffer, Robert. 1981. *The UFO Verdict*. Buffalo, N.Y.: Prometheus Books.

Smith, Edward R. 1989. *Practical Guide for Private Investigators*. Sharon Center, Ohio: Alpha Publications.

Stang, Ivan. 1988. *High Weirdness By Mail*. New York: Simon & Schuster.

Steiner, Robert A. 1989. *Don't Get Taken*. El Cerrito, Calif.: Wide Awake Books.

Sidgwick, Henry, et al. 1894. "Report on the Census of Hallucinations." *Proceedings of Society for Psychical Research*, vol. 10: 25–422.

West, D. J. 1948. "A Mass Observation Questionnaire on Hallucinations." *Journal of Society for Psychical Research,* vol. 34: 187–196.

Whaley, Donald L., and Sharon L. Surrat. 1967. *Attitudes of Science,* 3rd ed. Kalamazoo, Mich.: Behaviordella.

Williams, Ben, and Jean Williams (with John B. Shoemaker). 1991. *The Black Hope Horror.* New York: William Morrow Publishers.

Wilson, Mark. 1988. *Mark Wilson's Complete Course in Magic.* Philadelphia, Pa.: Courage Books.

Zusne, L., and W. Jones. 1982. *Anomalistic Psychology.* Hillsdale, N.J.: Lawrence Erlbaum Associates.

Chapter 1: The World of the Paranormal

Alcock, James. 1990. *Science and Supernatural: A Critical Appraisal of Parapsychology.* Buffalo, N.Y.: Prometheus Books.

Auerbach, Loyd. 1986. *ESP, Hauntings and Poltergeists.* New York: Warner Books.

Baker, Robert A. 1990. *They Call It Hypnosis.* Buffalo, N.Y.: Prometheus Books.

Bartlett, Laile. 1981. *Psi Trek.* New York: McGraw-Hill.

Beloff, John. 1978. "The Limits of Parapsychology." *European Journal of Parapsychology,* 2, no. 3: 291–303.

————. 1990. *The Relentless Question: Reflections on the Paranormal.* Jefferson, N.C.: McFarland & Co.

Broughton, Richard S. 1991. *Parapsychology: The Controversial Science.* New York: Ballantine Books, Random House.

Cohen, Daniel. 1982. *Encyclopedia of Monsters.* New York: Dodd, Mead & Co.

Gittelson, Bernard, and Laura Torbet. 1987. *Intangible Evidence.* New York: Fireside Books, Simon & Schuster.

Gurney, Edmund, F. W. H. Myers, and Frank Podmore. 1886. *Phantasms of the Living.* London, England: Richard Bentley.

Haught, James A. 1990. *Holy Horrors.* Buffalo, N.Y.: Prometheus Books.

Hyman, Ray. 1977. "Cold Reading." *The Zetetic,* Spring-Summer, 1, no. 2: 18–37.

————. 1989. *The Elusive Quarry: A Scientific Appraisal of Psychic Research.* Buffalo, N.Y.: Prometheus Books.

Jahn, Robert G. 1982. "The Persistent Paradox of Psychic Phenomena: An Engineering Perspective." *Proceedings of the IEEE,* 70, no. 2, February 1982.

————. 1989. *Margins of Reality.* New York: Harcourt, Brace, Jovanovich, Inc.

Klimo, Jon. 1987. *Channeling: Investigations on Receiving Information from Paranormal Sources.* Los Angeles: J. P. Tarcher Co.

Knight, J. Z. 1986. *I Am Ramtha.* Portland, Ore.: Beyond Words Publishing Co.

Kurtz, Paul, ed. 1985. *A Skeptic's Handbook of Parapsychology.* Buffalo, N.Y.: Prometheus Books.

Maclaine, Shirley, 1970. *Don't Fall Off the Mountain.* New York: W. W. Norton.

————. 1975. *You Can Get There From Here.* New York: W. W. Norton.

————. 1983. *Out On a Limb.* New York: Bantam Books.

————. 1985. *Dancing in the Light.* New York: Bantam Books.

————. 1987. *It's All in the Playing.* New York: Bantam Books.

Mishlove, Jeffrey. 1988. *Psi Development Systems.* New York: Ballantine Books.

Myers, F. W. H. 1903. *Human Personality and Its Survival of Bodily Death,* 2 vols. London, England: Routledge & Co.

Randles, Jenny. 1985. *Beyond Explanation.* Manchester, N.H.: Salem House.

Roberts, Jane. 1979. *The Further Education of Oversoul Seven.* New York: Pocket Books, Simon & Schuster.

Schmidt, Helmut. 1971. "Mental Influences on Random Events." *New Scientist,* 24 June 1971: 757–758.

———. 1975. "Toward a Mathematical Theory of Psi." *Journal of American Psychical Research,* volume 69: 267–292.

Schucman, Helen. 1975. *A Course in Miracles.* Tiburon, Calif.: Foundation for Inner Peace.

Shepard, Leslie. 1984. *The Encyclopedia of Occultism and Parapsychology,* 2d ed. Detroit, Mich.: Gale Research.

Sorokin, Pitrim A. 1957. *Social and Cultural Dynamics.* Boston: Porter Sargent Publishing Co.

Stewart, Louis. 1980. *Life Forces: A Contemporary Guide to the Cult and Occult.* Kansas City, Kans.: Andrews & McMeel Inc., Universal Press Syndicate.

Tabori, Paul. 1972. *Pioneers of the Unseen.* New York: Taplinger Publishing Co.

Targ, Russell, and Harold Putoff. 1977. *Mind Reach.* New York: Dell Publishing Co.

Targ, Russell, and Keith Harary. 1984. *The Mind Race: Understanding and Using Psychic Abilities.* New York: Ballantine Books.

Tyrell, G. N. M. 1953. *Apparitions.* London: Gerald Duckworth & Co. Ltd.; New York: Collier Books, Crowell Collier.

Ullman, Montague, Stanley Krippner, and Alan Vaughan. 1973. *Dream Telepathy: Experiments in Nocturnal ESP.* New York: Macmillan Publishing Co.

Vessey. 1983. Cited by J. Mishlove in *Psi Development Sytems.* New York: Ballantine Books. Citation on pages 30–31, no additional references given.

Wolman, Benjamin B., ed. 1977. *The Handbook of Parapsychology.* New York: Van Nostrand Reinhold.

Zollaschan, G. K., J. F. Shumaker, and G. F. Walsh. 1989. *Exploring the Paranormal: Perspectives on Belief and Experience.* Garden City Park, N.Y.: Avery Publishing Group.

Chapter 2: Investigatory Tactics and Techniques

Anson, J. 1978. *The Amityville Horror: A True Story.* New York: Bantam.

Beveridge, W. I. B. 1950. *The Art of Scientific Investigation.* New York: Vintage.

"The Big Picture." *Scientific American* (June 1983): 84.

Binder, D., and P. Bergman. 1984. *Fact Investigation: From Hypothesis to Proof.* St. Paul: West.

Blassingame, W. 1975. *Science Catches the Criminal.* New York: Dodd, Mead.

Broad, W., and N. Wade. 1982. *Betrayers of the Truth: Fraud and Deceit in the Halls of Science.* New York: Simon & Schuster.

Christopher, M. 1970. *ESP, Seers & Psychics.* New York: Crowell.

Delgado, P., and C. Andrews. 1989. *Circular Evidence: A Detailed Investigation of the Flattened Swirled Crops Phenomenon.* London: Bloomsbury.

Fairley, J., and S. Welfare. 1987. *Arthur C. Clarke's Chronicles of the Strange and Mysterious.* London: Collins.

Feder, K. 1990. "Piltdown, Paradigms, and the Paranormal." *The Skeptical Inquirer* 24 (4): 397–402.

Fletcher, W. 1986. *Recording Your Family History.* New York: Dodd, Mead.

Gardner, M. 1957. *Fads and Fallacies in the Name of Science.* New York: Dover.

———. 1981. *Science: Good, Bad and Bogus.* Buffalo, N.Y.: Prometheus Books.

Heyerdahl, T. 1958. *Aku-Aku.* New York: Rand McNally.

Holloway, A. 1981. *The Handbook of Photographic Equipment.* New York: Knopf.

Houp, K. W., and T. E. Pearsall. 1988. *Reporting Technical Information,* 6th ed. New York: Macmillan.

Jones, M. 1990. *Fake? The Art of Deception.* London: British Museum Publications.

Korem, Dan. 1988. *Powers: Testing the Psychic & Supernatural.* Downers Grove, Ill.: InterVarsity Press.

Lester, P. 1979. "Beyond the Amityville Hogwash . . ." *People* (Sept. 17): 90–94.

Moran, R., and P. Jordan. 1978. "The Amityville Horror Hoax." *Fate* (May): 43–47.

Morris, R. L. 1977–78. Review of *The Amityville Horror. The Skeptical Inquirer* 2 (2): 95–102.

Myers, D. G. 1989. *Psychology,* 2d edition. New York: Worth.

Nickell, J. 1983. "The Nazca Drawings Revisited." *The Skeptical Inquirer* 7(3): 36–44.

———. 1988. *Inquest on the Shroud of Turin.,* 2d updated ed. Buffalo, N.Y.: Prometheus Books.

Nickell, J., with J. F. Fischer. 1988. *Secrets of the Supernatural.* Buffalo, N.Y.: Prometheus Books.

Quinn, G. 1986. *Getting the Most Out of Your Video Gear.* Blue Ridge Summit, Pa.: Tab Books.

Randi, J. 1985. "The Columbus Poltergeist Case: Part I." *The Skeptical Inquirer* 9(3): 221–35.

———. 1987. *The Faith-Healers.* Buffalo, N.Y.: Prometheus Books.

Ronan, C. A. 1982. *Science: Its History and Development Among the World's Cultures.* New York: Facts on File.

Smith, J. 1983. *The Image of Guadalupe.* Garden City, N.Y.: Doubleday.

Thomason, S. 1987. "Past Tongues Remembered." *The Skeptical Inquirer* 11 (4): 367–75.

Thomason, S., and T. Kaufman. 1989. Personal communication to Robert A. Baker. January 16.

Thorwald. J. 1964. *The Century of the Detective.* New York: Harcourt.

Tierney, P. 1983. "The Arts." *Omni* (Sept.): 174, 190.

Tompkins, P., and C. Bird. 1973. *The Secret Life of Plants.* New York: Harper & Row.

"Twenty 'Scientific' Attitudes." 1989. *The Kansas School Naturalist;* reprinted in *The Great Lakes Skeptic* 1 (2): 4–5.

Von Däniken, Erich. 1970. *Chariots of the Gods?* New York: Putnam.

Wade, C., and C. Farris. 1990. "Thinking Critically and Creatively." *The Skeptical Inquirer* 14(4): 372–77.

Weiner, J. S. 1955. *The Piltdown Forgery.* London: Oxford University Press.

Winslow, J. H., and A. Meyer. 1983. "The Perpetrator at Piltdown." *Science 83* 4 (September): 33–43.

Zim, H. R. Burnett, and W. Brummitt. 1964. *Photography: The Amateur's Guide to Better Pictures.* New York: Golden Press.

Chapter 3: Getting at the Truth

ABA Journal. 1978. Feb. 2. Quoted in Loftus 1980, 58–59.

Bailey, F. G. 1988. *Humbuggery and Manipulation: The Art of Leadership.* Ithaca: Cornell University Press.

Baker, R. A. 1990. *They Call It Hypnosis.* Buffalo, N.Y.: Prometheus Books.

Beveridge, W. 1950. *The Art of Scientific Investigation.* Reprinted New York: Vintage, n.d.

Beyerstein, B. L., and D. F. Beyerstein, eds. 1992. *The Write Stuff.* Buffalo, N.Y.: Prometheus Books.

Binder, D., and P. Bergman. 1984. *Fact Investigation: From Hypothesis to Proof.* New York: Dover.

Blassingame, W. 1975. *Science Catches the Criminal.* New York: Dodd, Mead.

"Evidence." 1960. *Encyclopedia Britannica,* 8: 905–15.

Gardner, M. 1957. *Fads & Fallacies in the Name of Science.* New York: Dover.

Gibson, W. B., and M. N. Young. 1953. *Houdini on Magic.* New York: Dover.

Greenberg, D. S. 1988. Quoted in "The Commentators Comment. . . ." *The Skeptical Inquirer* 13(1) Fall: 12.

Hansel, C. E. M. 1966. *ESP: A Scientific Evaluation.* New York: Scribner.

Harre, R., and R. Lamb. 1983. "Contagion." *Encyclopedic Dictionary of Psychology.* Cambridge, Mass.: MIT Press.

Hay, H., ed. 1949. *Cyclopedia of Magic.* Philadelphia: David McKay.

Hill, J., Jr.; H. Rossen, and W. Sogg. 1978. *Evidence.* St. Paul: West.

Hines, T. 1988. *Pseudoscience and the Paranormal.* Buffalo, N.Y.: Prometheus Books.

"House Measure to Restrict Use of Lie Detectors." 1985. *Courier-Journal* (Louisville, Ky.): October 24.

Inbau, F. E., A. A. Moenssens, and L. R. Vitullo. 1972. *Scientific Police Investigation.* Philadelphia: Chilton.

Klass, P. 1976. *UFOs Explained.* New York: Vintage.

———. 1980. "Beware of the 'Truth Evaluator.' " *The Skeptical Inquirer* 14 (4): 44–51.

———. 1981. "UFOs." In G. Abel and B. Singer (eds.), *Science and the Paranormal.* New York: Scribner's, 310–28.

Kytle, R. 1987. *Clear Thinking for Composition,* 5th ed. New York: Random House.

Loftus, E. 1980. *Memory: Surprising New Insights into How We Remember and Why We Forget.* Reading, Mass.: Addison-Wesley.

Loftus, E., and J. Palmer. 1974. "Reconstruction of Automobile Destruction: An Example of the Interaction Between Language and Memory." *Journal of Verbal Learning and Verbal Behavior* 13: 585–89.

Mabery, D. 1985. *Tell Me About Yourself: How to Interview Anyone from Your Friends to Famous People.* Minneapolis: Lerner Publications.

Mackay, C. 1841. *Memoirs of Extraordinary Popular Delusions and the Madness of Crowds.* Reprint of 1852 edition. Toronto: Coles, 1980.

Mark, V. 1990. "Why We Forget." *Modern Maturity* (August-September): 70–75.

Mulholland, J. 1938. *Beware Familiar Spirits.* Reprinted. New York: Scribner's, 1979.

Nickell, Joe. 1989. "Unshrouding a Mystery: Science, Pseudoscience, and the Cloth of Turin." *The Skeptical Inquirer* 13 (3) Spring: 296–98.

O'Hara, C. 1973. *Fundamentals of Criminal Investigation,* third edition. Springfield, Ill.: Charles C. Thomas.

O'Leary, L. 1976. *Interviewing for the Decisionmaker.* Chicago: Nelson-Hall.

Randi, J. 1977. " 'Levitation' for Fun and Profit." *The Zetetic* 2 (1) Fall/Winter: 7–9.

———. 1979. "The Sounds of Silence." *The Skeptical Inquirer* 3 (3) Spring: 78.

———. 1982. *Flim-Flam!: The Truth About Unicorns, Parapsychology, and Other Delusions.* Buffalo, N.Y.: Prometheus Books.

———. 1987. *The Faith Healers.* Buffalo, N.Y.: Prometheus Books.

Shneour, E. 1986. "Occam's Razor." *The Skeptical Inquirer* 10: 310–13.

Spraggett, A. [1971.] *Probing the Unexplained.* New York: World.

Van Kampen, H. 1979. "The Case of the Lost Panda." *The Skeptical Inquirer* 4(1) Fall: 48–50.

Weber, M. 1978. *Economy and Society.* G. Roth and C. Wittich, eds. Berkeley: University of California Press.

Wells ,G., and E. Loftus, eds. 1984. *Eyewitness Testimony: Psychological Perspectives.* Cambridge: Cambridge University Press.

Woodward, S., with F. Graham, Jr. 1967. *Sportswriter.* Garden City, N.Y.: Doubleday.

Yarmen, A. D. 1984. "Age as a Factor in Eyewitness Memory." Chapter 7 of Wells and Loftus, 142–54.

Chapter 4: Investigating Ghosts, Haunted Places and Things, Poltergeists, and Other Nonentities

Auerbach, Loyd. 1986. *ESP, Hauntings and Poltergeists: A Parapsychologist's Handbook.* New York: Warner Books.

Baker, Robert A. 1986. "How to Bust a Ghost: Two Quick But Effective Cures." *The Skeptical Inquirer,* vol. 11 (Fall 1986): 84–90.

Basowitz, H. H. Persky, S. J. Korchin, and R. R. Grinker. 1955. *Anxiety and Stress.* New York: Blakiston Division, McGraw-Hill.

Cochran, Tracy. 1988. "The Real Ghost Busters." *OMNI,* August 1988, vol. 10, no. 11: 35, 78–83.

Doyle, Arthur Conan. 1930. *The Edge of the Unknown.* New York: G. P. Putnam's Sons.

Finucane, R. C. 1984. *Appearances of the Dead.* Buffalo, N.Y.: Prometheus Books.

Fodor, Nandor. 1951. *Haunted People.* New York: E. P. Dutton.

———. 1958. *On the Trail of the Poltergeist.* New York: Citadel Press.

Fodor, Nandor, 1964. *Between Two Worlds.* West Nyack, N.Y.: Parker Publishing Co.

———. 1968. *The Unaccountable.* New York: Award Books.

———. 1968. *The Haunted Mind.* New York: New American Library.

Grinker, Roy R., and John P. Spiegel. 1945. *Men Under Stress.* Philadelphia: Blakiston Co.

Haining, Peter. 1988. *Ghosts: The Illustrated History.* Secaucus, N.J.: Chatwell Books Inc.

Harrington, John W. 1983. *Dance of the Continents.* Los Angeles: Jeremy P. Tarcher.

Holzer, Hans. 1971. *Hans Holzer's Haunted Houses.* New York: Crown Publishers Inc.

Kaczmarek, Dale. 1987. "In Search of the Elusive Ghost." *National New Ages Yellow Pages.* Fullerton, Calif.: NNAYP.

Klawans, Howard. 1988. *Toscanini's Fumble and Other Tales of Clinical Neurology.* New York: Contemporary Books.

Lidden, S. C. 1967. "Sleep Paralysis and Hypnogogic Hallucinations." *Archives of General Psychology,* vol. 17: 88–96.

Maher, Michaleen. Cited in Cochran, Tracy, 1988.

McKay, Charles. 1841 (1980). *Extraordinary Popular Delusions and the Madness of Crowds.* London, England: Richard Bentley; New York: Farrar, Straus & Giroux.

Moody, Raymond. 1987. *Elvis After Life: Unusual Psychic Experiences Surrounding the Death of a Superstar.* Atlanta, Ga.: Peachtree Publishers; New York: Bantam Books, 1988.

Peach, Emily. 1991. *Things That Go Bump in the Night.* London, England: The Aquarian Press.

Randles, Jenny. 1985. *Beyond Explanation.* Manchester, N.H.: Salem House.

Roll, William. 1972. *The Poltergeist.* New York: Nelson Doubleday.

Sacks, M. H. 1988. "Folie à deux." *Comprehensive Psychiatry,* vol. 29: 270–277.

Scott, Beth, and Michael Norman. 1986. *Haunted Heartland.* New York: Warner Books.

Strieber, Whitley. 1987. *Communion.* New York: Nelson & Neff, Inc. (Avon Books, 1988.)

Tyrrell, G. M. 1963. *Apparitions.* New York: Collier Books, Crowell Collier Publishing Co.

Valente, Gianni. 1991. "The Great Catholic Ghost Hunt." *30 Days,* Feb. 1991: 10–11.

Williams, Ben, and Jean Williams, with John B. Shoemaker. 1991. *The Black Hole Horror.* New York: William Morrow and Co.

Chapter 5: Investigating Amazing Powers

Abbott's Magic Manufacturing Company Catalog 23. 1987. Colon, Mich.: Abbott.

Adams, E. 1942. *Astrology for Everyone.* New York: New Home Library.

Aitken, M. J. 1959. "Test for Correlation between Dowsing Response and Magnetic Disturbance." *Archaeometry* 2: 58–59; cited in Feder 1990, pp. 167–68.

Annemann, T. 1938. "Was Prof. J. B. Rhine Hoodwinked?" *The Jinx*. August: 1ff; cited in Christopher 1970, 23.

Behe, G. M. 1990. "The Titanic: A Disaster Foreseen?" *Fate* (June): 44–50.

Bird, C. 1979. *The Divining Hand*. New York: Dutton.

Brown, M. 1988. "Happiness Is a Secret Stored Up Your Sleeve." London *Sunday Times*, Oct. 2.

Cavendish, R., ed. 1974. *Encyclopedia of the Unexplained*. London: Routledge & Kegan Paul.

Christopher, M. 1962. *Panorama of Magic*. New York: Dover.

———. 1970. *ESP, Seers & Psychics*. New York: Thomas Y. Crowell.

———. 1975. *Mediums, Mystics and the Occult*. New York: Thomas Y. Crowell.

Cohen, Daniel. 1985. *The Encyclopedia of the Strange*. New York: Dorset.

"CSICOP Challenges Mrs. Reagan's Astrologer to a Scientific Test." 1988. *The Skeptical Inquirer* 13(1) Fall: 9.

Dale, L. A., et al. "Dowsing: A Field Experiment in Water Divining." *Journal of American Society for Psychical Resarch* 45: 3–16; cited in Vogt and Hyman, 1979, pp. 72–73.

Dennett, M. R. 1985. "Firewalking: Reality or Illusion?" *The Skeptical Inquirer* 10(1) Fall: 36–40.

Dexter, W. 1958. *This Is Magic: Secrets of the Conjurer's Craft*. New York: Bell.

Eisendrath, D., and Reynolds, C. 1967. "An Amazing Weekend with Ted Serios," Parts I and II. *Popular Photography* (October): 81–87, 131–40, 158.

Feder, K. L. 1990. *Frauds, Myths, and Mysteries: Science and Pseudoscience in Archaeology*. Mountain View, Calif.: Mayfield.

Frazier, K. 1983. "Exposure of Psychic's Envelope Trick Ignored by Columnist." *The Skeptical Inquirer* 8(2) Winter: 101–105.

Frazier, K., and J. Randi. 1981. "Prediction After the Fact: Lessons of the Tamara Rand Hoax." *The Skeptical Inquirer* 6(1) Fall: 4–7.

Gardner, M. 1957. *Fads and Fallacies in the Name of Science*. New York: Dover.

———. 1981. *Science: Good, Bad and Bogus*. Buffalo, N.Y.: Prometheus Books.

Gibson, W. 1967. *Secrets of Magic: Ancient and Modern*. New York: Grosset & Dunlap.

Gibson, W. B., and M. N. Young. 1953. *Houdini on Magic*. New York: Dover.

Gorman, T. 1973. " 'Man with the Magic Eyes' Can Stop Machines—Just by Looking at Them." *Midnight*. January 22.

Hansel, C. E. M. 1966. *ESP: A Scientific Evaluation*. New York: Scribner's.

Hay, H., ed. 1949. *Cyclopedia of Magic*. Philadelphia: David McKay.

Hines, T. 1988. *Pseudoscience and the Paranormal*. Buffalo, N.Y.: Prometheus Books.

Hyman, R. 1977. " 'Cold Reading': How to Convince Strangers That You Know All About Them." *The Skeptical Inquirer* (*The Zetetic*) 1 (2) Spring/Summer: 18–37.

———. 1985. "The Ganzfeld Psi Experiment: A Critical Appraisal." *Journal of Parapsychology* 49: 3–49.

Kilner, W. J. 1911. *The Human Atmosphere;* reprinted as *The Aura*, York Beach, Maine: Samuel Weiser, 1973.

Kurtz, P., and A. Fraknoi. 1985."Tests of Astrology Do Not Support Its Claims." *The Skeptical Inquirer* 9(3) Spring: 210–11.

Leikind, B. J., and W. J. McCarthy. 1985. "An Investigation of Firewalking." *The Skeptical Inquirer* 10(1) Fall: 23–24.

LeVert, L. E. (Everett Bleiler). 1979. *The Prophecies and Enigmas of Nostradamus.* Glen Rock, N.J.: Fireball Books: quoted in Randi 1982b.

Loftin, R. W. 1990."Auras: Searching for the Light." *The Skeptical Inquirer* 14(4) Summer: 403–409.

Marks, D. F. 1982. "Remote Viewing Revisited." *The Skeptical Inquirer* 6(4) Summer: 18–29.

McGervey, J. D. 1977. "A Statistical Test of Sun-Sign Astrology." *The Skeptical Inquirer* 1(2) Spring/Summer: 49–54.

Mulholland, T. 1938. *Beware Familiar Spirits.* Reprinted New York: Scribner's, 1979.

Mulholland, J. 1944. *Magic for Entertaining.* New York: Grosset & Dunlap.

Nickell, J. 1976. "The Authenticity of Mr. Henry." *The Yukon News,* Sept. 22.

———. 1987. *Literary Investigation.* Doctoral dissertation, University of Kentucky.

———, with J. F. Fischer. 1988. *Secrets of the Supernatural.* Buffalo, N.Y.: Prometheus Books.

Nostradamus (Michele de Notre Dame). 1655. *Centuries.* Lyon, France: Mace Bonhomme.

Phillips, P., ed. 1978. *Out of This World: The Illustrated Library of the Bizarre and Extraordinary,* vols. 7 and 9. England: Phoebus.

"Psychic Vibrations." 1978. *The Skeptical Inquirer* 2(2) Spring/Summer: 19–20.

Rachleff, O. S. 1971. *The Occult Conceit.* Chicago: Cowles.

Randi, J. 1979. "Edgar Cayce: The Slipping Prophet." *The Skeptical Inquirer* 4(1) Fall: 51–57.

———. 1982a. *Flim-Flam! Psychics, ESP, Unicorns and Other Delusions.* Buffalo, N.Y.: Prometheus Books.

———. 1982b. "Nostradamus: The Prophet for All Seasons." *The Skeptical Inquirer* 7(1) Fall 1982: 30–37.

———. 1983. "The Project Alpha Experiment," Parts I and II. *The Skeptical Inquirer* 7(4) Summer: 24–33 and 8 (1) Fall: 36–45.

———. 1987. *The Faith-Healers.* Buffalo, N.Y.: Prometheus Books.

Regan, D. 1988. Quoted in "Donald Regan's In-House View" (excerpted from Regan's book *For the Record*). *The Skeptical Inquirer* 13(1) Fall: 10.

Scot, R. 1584. *The Discoverie of Witchcraft.* Reprinted New York: Dover, 1972.

Smith, D. 1982. "Two Tests of Divining in Australia." *The Skeptical Inquirer* (4) Summer: 34–37.

Stein, G. 1989. "The Lore of Levitation." *The Skeptical Inquirer* 13 (3) Spring: 277–88.

Steiner, R. A. 1986. "Exposing the Faith-Healers." *The Skeptical Inquirer* 11 (1) Fall: 28–31.

Steiner, R. 1989. "Live TV Special Explores, Tests Psychic Powers." *The Skeptical Inqurier* 14(1) Fall: 3.

Votg, W. Z., and R. Hyman. 1979. *Water Witching U.S.A.,* 2d ed. Chicago: University of Chicago Press.

Watkins, A. J., and W. S. Bickel. 1986. "A Study of the Kirlian Effect." *The Skeptical Inquirer* 10(3) Spring: 244–57.

Chapter 6: Investigating Things in the Sky and Alleged Abductions

Adamski, George, and Leslie Desmond. 1952. *Flying Saucers Have Landed.* New York: British Book Center.

Adamski, George. 1955. *Inside the Space Ships.* New York: Abelard-Schuman.

Arnold, Kenneth, and Ray Palmer. 1952. *The Coming of the Saucers.* Amherst, Wis.: Amherst Press. (Privately published by the authors).

Angelucci, Orfeo. 1955. *Secret of the Saucers.* Amherst, Wis.: Amherst Press.

Assad, Ghazi. 1990. *Hallucinations in Clinical Psychiatry.* New York: Brunner-Mazel Publishing Inc.

Baker, Robert A. 1982. "The Effect of Suggestion on Past-Lives Regression." *American Journal of Clinical Hypnosis,* vol. 25, no. 1: 71–76.

———. 1987. "The Aliens Among Us: Hypnotic Regression Revisited." *Skeptical Inquirer,* vol. 12 (2) Winter 1987–1988.

———. 1990. *They Call It Hypnosis.* Buffalo, N.Y.: Prometheus Books.

Barber, Theodore X. 1969. *Hypnosis: A Scientific Approach.* New York: Van Nostrand Co.

Basterfield, Keith, and Robert Bartholomew. 1988. "Abductions: The Fantasy-Prone Personal Hypothesis." *International UFO Reporter,* vol. 13, no.3 (May–June 1988), 9–11.

Bernstein, Morey. 1956. *The Search for Bridey Murphy.* New York: Doubleday and Co., Inc.

Bethrun, Truman. 1954. *Aboard a Flying Saucer.* Los Angeles: DeVorss & Co. Inc.

Blum, Howard. 1990. *Out There.* New York: Simon & Schuster.

Blumrich, Joseph F. 1974. *The Spaceships of Ezekiel.* New York: Bantam Books.

Bullard, Thomas. 1989a. "Hypnosis and UFO Abductions: A Troubled Relationship." *Journal of UFO Studies,* vol. 1, no. 1: 3–40.

———. 1989b. "Hypnosis Is No Truth Serum." *UFO,* vol. 4, no. 2: 31–35.

Condon, Edward U., and Daniel S. Gillmor, ed. 1969. *Final Report of the Scientific Study of Unidentified Flying Objects.* New York: Bantam Books.

Corliss, William R. 1983. *Handbook of Unusual Natural Phenomena.* New York: Arlington House, Inc.

Curran, Douglas. 1985. *In Advance of the Landing: Folk Concepts of Outer Space.* New York: Abbeville Press.

Faust, David, and Jay Ziskin. 1988. "The Expert Witness in Psychology and Psychiatry." *Science,* vol. 241: 31–35.

Fawcett, Lawrence, and Barry J. Greenwood. 1984. *The UFO Coverup.* Englewood Cliffs, N.J.: Prentice-Hall.

Fiore, Edith. 1989. *Encounters: A Psychologist Reveals Case Studies of Abductions by Extraterrestrials.* New York: Doubleday & Co.

Flournoy, Theodore. 1901 (1963). *From India to the Planet Mars.* New York: University Books.

Fowler, Raymond E. 1979. *The Andreasson Affair: The Documented Investigation of a Woman's Abduction Aboard a UFO.* Englewood Cliffs, N.J.: Prentice-Hall (Bantam Books 1980).

———. 1990. *The Watchers: The Secret Design Behind UFO Abductions.* New York: Bantam Books.

Fry, Daniel. 1954. *The White Sands Incident.* Los Angeles: New Age Publishing Co.

Fuller, John G. 1966. *The Interrupted Journey.* New York: Dial Press.

Gill, M. M., and M. Brenman. 1959. *Hypnosis and Related States.* New York: International Universities Press.

Good, Timothy. 1988. *Above Top Secret: The Worldwide UFO Coverup.* New York: Quill Books, William Morrow.

Hartman, William K. 1978. *Astronomy: The Cosmic Journey.* Belmont, Calif.: Wadsworth Publishing Co.

Hendry, Allan. 1979. *The UFO Handbook.* New York: Doubleday.

Hilgard, Ernest R. 1977. *Divided Consciousness: Multiple Controls in Human Thought and Action.* New York: John Wiley & Sons.

———. 1981. "Hypnosis Gives Rise to Fantasy and Is Not a Truth Serum," *The Skeptical Inquirer,* vol. 5, no. 3 (Spring 1981): 25.

Hilgard, Josephine. 1979. *Personality and Hypnosis: A Study of Imaginative Involvement.* Chicago: University of Chicago Press.

Hopkins, Budd. 1981. *Missing Time.* New York: G. P. Putnam's Sons.

———. 1987. *Intruders: The Incredible Visitations at Copley Woods.* New York: Random House.

Hynek, J. Allen. 1972. *The UFO Experience: A Scientific Inquiry.* New York: Henry Regnery Co.

———. 1977. *The Hynek UFO Report.* New York: Dell Books.

Jacobs, David. 1976. *The UFO Controversy in America.* New York: Signet Books, NAL.

Jung, Carl. 1969. *Flying Saucers: A Modern Myth of Things Seen in the Sky.* New York: Signet Books, NAL.

Keel, John. 1988. *The Disneyland of the Gods.* New York: Amok Press.

———. 1990. "Investigating UFOs." *Strange Magazine,* no. 6: 12–15.

Keyhoe, Donald. 1950. *Flying Saucers Are Real.* New York: Gold Medal Books, Fawcett Publishing Co.

———. 1955. *The Flying Saucer Conspiracy.* New York: Henry Holt.

Kinder, Gary. 1987. *Light Years: An Investigation into the Extraterrestrial Experiences of Edward Meier.* Boston: Atlantic Monthly Press.

Klass, Philip J. 1974. *UFOs Explained.* New York: Random House.

———. 1981. "Hypnosis and UFO Abductions." *The Skeptical Inquirer,* vol. 5, no. 3 (Spring 1981): 16–24.

———. 1983. *UFOs: The Public Deceived.* Buffalo, N.Y.: Prometheus Books.

———. 1987. "The MJ-12 Crashed Saucer Documents." *The Skeptical Inquirer,* vol. 12 (2) Winter 1987–88: 137–146.

———. 1988. *UFO Abductions: A Dangerous Game.* Buffalo, N.Y.: Prometheus Books.

Lawson, A. H., and W. C. McCall. 1977. "What Can We Learn from the Hypnosis of Imaginary Abductees?" MUFON UFO Symposium Proceedings. Seguin, Tex.: Mutual UFO Network.

Loftus, Elizabeth. 1979. *Eyewitness Testimony.* Cambridge, Mass.: Harvard University Press.

Ludwig, Arnold. 1965. *The Importance of Lying.* Springfield, Ill.: C. C. Thomas.

Menger, Howard. 1959. *From Outer Space to You.* Clarksburg, W. Va.: Saucerian Books.

Menzel, Donald H. 1953. *Flying Saucers.* Cambridge, Mass.: Harvard University Press.

Menzel, Donald H., and Lyle G. Boyd. 1963. *The World of Flying Saucers.* New York: Doubleday & Co.

Menzel, Donald H., and Ernest H. Taves. 1977. *The UFO Enigma.* New York: Doubleday & Co.

Myers, S. A., and H. R. Austrin. 1985. "Distal Eidetic Technology: Further Characteristics of the Fantasy-Prone Personality." *Journal of Mental Imagery,* vol. 9, no. 3: 57–66.

Nickell, Joe, and John F. Fischer. 1990. "The Crashed Saucer Forgeries." *International UFO Reporter,* March/April 1990: 4–12.

O'Connell, D. N., R. E. Shor, and M. T. Orne. 1970. "Hypnotic Age Regression: An Empirical and Methodological Analysis." *Journal of Abnormal Psychology,* Monograph 76, no. 3, Part 2: 1–32.

Parish, Edmund. 1897. "The International Census of Waking Hallucinations," in *Hallucinations and Illusions: A Study of the Fallacies of Perception.* London, England: Walter Scott Publishers.

Perry, C., J. R. Lawrence, R. Nadon, and Louise Labelle. 1986. "Past Lives Regression," in *Hypnosis: Questions and Answers,* edited by B. Zilbergeld, M. G. Edelstein, and D. L. Araoz. New York: W. W. Norton Co.

Randles, Jenny. 1983. *UFO Reality.* London, England: Hale Publishers.

———. 1985. *Beyond Explanation.* Manchester, N.H.: Salem House.

Reed, Graham. 1972. *The Psychology of Anomalous Experience.* Boston: Houghton-Mifflin.

Rhue, J. W., and S. J. Lynn. 1987. "Fantasy Proneness: Developmental Antecedents." *Journal of Personality,* vol. 55, no. 1: 121–137.

Ridpath, Ian. 1977. "Flying Saucers Thirty Years On." *New Scientist* (14 July 1977): 77–79.

Rosenhahn, D. L. 1973. "On Being Sane in Insane Places." *Science,* vol. 179: 250–58.

Sarbin, T. R., and M. L. Andersen. 1967. "Role Theoretical Analysis of Hypnotic Behavior," in *Handbook of Clinical and Experimental Hypnosis,* edited by Jesse E. Gordon. New York: Macmillan Co.

Sarbin, T. R., and W. C. Coe. 1972. *Hypnosis: A Social Psychological Analysis of Influence Communication.* New York: Holt, Rinehart, & Winston.

Saxe, Leonard. 1991. "Lying: Thoughts of an Applied Social Psychologist." *American Psychologist,* vol. 46, no. 4: 409–415.

Scully, Frank. 1950. *Behind the Flying Saucers.* New York: Henry Holt & Co.

Sheaffer, Robert. 1981. *The UFO Verdict: Examining the Evidence.* Buffalo, N.Y.: Prometheus Books.

Sidgwick, H. A., et al. 1894. "Report of the Census of Hallucinating." *Proceedings of Society of Psychical Research,* vol. 26: 259–394.

Singer, Jerome. 1975. *The Inner World of Daydreaming.* New York: Harper & Row.

Spanos, Nicholas, and T. X. Barber. 1974. "Toward a Convergence in Hypnotic Research." *American Psychologist,* vol. 29, no. 3: 500–511.

Spencer, John, and Hilary Evans, eds. 1989. *Phenomenon: Forty Years of Flying Saucers.* New York: Avon Books.

Steiger, Brad. 1976. *Project Blue Book.* New York: Ballantine Books.

Stevenson, Ian. 1983. "Do We Need a New Word to Supplement 'Hallucination'?" *American Journal of Psychiatry,* vol. 140, no. 12: 1609–1611.

Strieber, Whitley. 1987. *Communion: A True Story.* New York: William Morrow Co.

Sutcliffe, J. P. 1961. " 'Credulous' and 'Skeptical' View of Hypnotic Phenomena." *J. Ab. Soc. Psychology,* volume 62, no. 2: 189–200.

Swedenborg, Immanuel. 1970. *The Essential Swedenborg.* New York: The Swedenborg Foundation.

Vallee, Jacques. 1988. *Dimensions.* New York: Contemporary Books.

Walters, Ed, and Frances Walters. 1990. *The Gulf Breeze Sightings.* New York: William Morrow Publishing Co.

Wilson, Ian. 1981. *Mind Out of Time.* London, England: Gollancz Publishing Co.

Wilson, Shirley C., and T. X. Barber. 1983. "The Fantasy-Prone Personality," in *Imagery: Current Theory, Research and Application,* edited by A. A. Sheikh. New York: John Wiley & Sons.

Chapter 7: Mysterious Objects and Nature's Enigmas

Arnold, L. 1982. "The Man Who Survived Spontaneous Combustion." *Fate,* September: 60–65.

Asimov, I. 1968. *Asimov's Guide to the Bible,* Vol. II: The Old Testament. New York: Equinox.

Ballantine, M. 1981. "It Came from Outer Space," in Martin Ebon, ed., *The World's Great Unsolved Mysteries.* New York: Signet, 19–39.

"Bel and the Dragon." 1967. *New Catholic Encyclopedia,* 2: 235–6.

Berlitz, C. 1974. *The Bermuda Triangle Mystery.* Garden City, N.Y.: Doubleday.

"The Big Picture." 1983. *Scientific American* (June): 84.

Binns, R. 1984. *The Loch Ness Mystery Solved.* Buffalo, N.Y.: Prometheus Books.

Bord, J., and C. Bord. 1982. *The Bigfoot Casebook.* Harrisburg, Pa.: Stackpole.

Bunch, K., and M. White. 1988. "The Riddle of the Colorado Ghost Lights." *The Skeptical Inquirer* 12 (3): 306–309.

Calkins, C., ed. 1982. *Mysteries of the Unexplained.* Pleasantville, N.Y.: Reader's Digest.

Callahan, P. 1981. *The Tilma Under Infra-red Radiation.* Washington, D.C.: Center for Applied Research in the Apostolate.

Cavendish, R. 1974. *Encyclopedia of the Unexplained.* London: Routledge & Kegan Paul.

"Church Says 'Weeping' of Statue Not a Miracle." 1985. *The Courier Journal* (Louisville, Ky.), Sept. 19.

Clark, J. 1984. "Chicago's Virgin Weeps." *Fate,* December: 84–89.

Cohen, D. 1982. *The Encyclopedia of Monsters.* New York: Dodd, Mead & Co.

———. 1985. *The Encyclopedia of the Strange.* New York: Dorset.

Corliss, W. 1976. *The Unexplained: A Sourcebook of Strange Phenomena.* New York: Bantam.

Dahl, Jonathan. 1987. "Icons Shedding Tears Are a Mixed Blessing to Congregations." *The Wall Street Journal,* January 30.

Demarest, D., and C. Taylor, eds. 1956. *The Dark Virgin.* N.p.: Academy Guild Press.

Dennett, M. 1982. "Bigfoot Jokester Reveals Punchline—Finally." *The Skeptical Inquirer* 7(1): 8–9.

———. 1989a. "Abominable Snowman Photo Comes to Rocky End." *The Skeptical Inquirer* 13(2): 118–19.

———. 1989b. "Evidence for Bigfoot? An Investigation of the Mill Creek 'Sasquatch Prints.' " *The Skeptical Inquirer* 13(3): 264–72.

"Devout Flocking to Crucifix." 1989. *Courier-News,* April 2.

Emery, E. 1981–82. "Sasquatchsickle: The Monster, the Model, and the Myth." *The Skeptical Inquirer* 6(2): 2–4.

Feder, Kenneth L. 1990. *Frauds, Myths, and Mysteries: Science and Pseudoscience in Archaeology.* Mountain View, Calif.: Mayfield.

Fort, C. 1974. *The Complete Books of Charles Fort.* New York: Dover.

Gaddis, V. 1965. *Invisible Horizons.* Philadelphia: Chilton.

Gardner, M. 1957. *Fads and Fallacies in the Name of Science.* New York: Dover.

———. 1985. "The Great Stone Face and Other Nonmysteries." *The Skeptical Inquirer* 10(1): 14–18.

Gentleman's Magazine. 1746. 16: 368.

Gould, R. 1934. *The Loch Ness Monster.* London: Geoffrey Bles.

Heyerdahl, T. 1958. *Aku-Aku.* New York: Rand McNally.

Heuvelmans, B. 1972. *On the Track of Unknown Animals.* Cambridge, Mass.: MIT Press.

Hines, R. 1988. *Pseudoscience and the Paranormal.* Buffalo, N.Y.: Prometheus Books.

Isbell, W. 1978. "The Prehistoric Ground Drawings of Peru." *Scientific American* 239 (October): 140–53.

———. 1980. "Solving the Mystery of Nazca." *Fate* (October): 36–48.

"Image of Christ on Oil Tank Causes Traffic Jams." 1986. *The Cedar Rapids Gazette,* August 22.

Jordan, K. 1981. "Bermuda Triangle Mystery," in Martin Ebon, ed. *The World's Great Unsolved Mysteries.* New York: Signet, 50–57.

Kavvadias, T. 1986. "Icon's 'Miraculous Sign' Draws Multitude." *Chicago Tribune,* Dec. 15.

Kosok, P. (in collaboration with M. Reiche). 1947. "The Markings of Nazca." *Natural History* 56: 20–38.

Kusche, L. 1975. *The Bermuda Triangle Mystery—Solved.* New York: Warner.

———. 1980. *The Disappearance of Flight 19.* New York: Harper & Row.

Lewes, G. 1861. "Spontaneous Combustion." *Blackwood's Edinburgh Magazine* 89 (April): 385–402.

Liebig, J. von. 1851. *Familiar Letters on Chemistry,* letter no. 22. London: Taylor, Walton, & Maberly.

McIntyre, L. 1975. "Mystery of the Ancient Nazca Lines." *National Geographic,* May: 716–28.

MacDougall, C. 1983. *Superstition and the Press.* Buffalo, N.Y.: Prometheus Books.

Magagnini, S. 1984. "When the Madonna Wept." *Fate* (March): 42–46.

Memmott, C. 1989. " 'Miracles' Many, but Proof Hard to Come By." *USA Today,* April 12.

Mitchell-Hedges, F. A. 1954. *Danger My Ally.* London: Elek Books.

"Myth or Monster?" 1972. *Time,* November 20: 66.

Nickell, J. 1983. "The Nazca Drawings Revisited: Creation of a Full-Sized Duplicate." *The Skeptical Inquirer* 7(3): 36–44.

———. 1988. *Inquest on the Shroud of Turin,* 2d updated ed. Buffalo, N.Y.: Prometheus Books.

———. 1989a. *The Magic Detectives.* Buffalo, N.Y.: Prometheus Books.

———. 1989b. "Unshrouding a Mystery: Science, Pseudoscience, and the Cloth of Turin." *The Skeptical Inquirer* 13(3): 296–99.

Nickell, J., and J. Fischer. 1985. "The Image of Guadalupe: A Folkloristic and Iconographic Investigation." *The Skeptical Inquirer* 8(4): 243–55.

———. 1988. *Secrets of the Supernatural.* Buffalo, N.Y.: Prometheus Books.

———. 1989. "Did Jack Angel Survive Spontaneous Combustion?" *Fate,* May: 80–84.

"No Proof of a Miracle Found at Pittsburgh Church." 1989. *Washington Post,* July 8.

Oberg, J. 1980. "Tunguska (Russia) Event," in Ronald D. Story, ed. *The Encyclopedia of UFOs.* Garden City, N.Y.: Doubleday, 371–73.

Posner, G. 1990. "Tampa Bay's Weeping Icon Fiasco." *The Skeptical Inquirer* 14(4): 349–50.

Razdan, R., and A. Kielar. 1984–85. "Sonar and Photographic Searches for the Loch Ness Monster: A Reassessment." *The Skeptical Inquirer* 9(2): 147–58.

"Reflected Glory." 1987. *Courier-News,* June 4.

Reiche, M. 1968. *Mystery on the Desert,* rev. ed. Stuttgart: Privately printed.

Ridpath, I. 1978. *Messages from the Stars.* New York: Harper & Row.

"The Scientist Who Makes Icons Weep." 1987. *Newsweek,* October 26: 19.

Smith, J. 1983. *The Image of Guadalupe.* Garden City, N.Y.: Doubleday.

Thompson, S. 1955. *Motif-Index of Folk Literature,* rev. ed. (6 vols). Bloomington: Indiana University Press.

"Those Who Sway Together Pray Together." 1985. *Discover,* October: 19.

"Three Accused of Smashing Statue of Virgin Mary." 1985. *Lexington* (Ky.) *Herald-Leader,* November 2.

"Virgin Mary 'Miracle' that Drew Thousands Is Exposed As a Hoax." 1986. *The Courier-Journal* (Louisville, Ky.), January 18.

Von Däniken, E. 1970. *Chariots of the Gods?* New York: Bantam.

———. 1972. *Gods from Outer Space.* New York: Bantam.

Welfare, S., and J. Fairley. 1980. *Arthur C. Clarke's Mysterious World.* New York: A & W Visual Library.

Wilkinson, T. 1990. "Despite Skeptics, Faithful Line Up to View Cross Images in Window." *Los Angeles Times,* August 17.

Winer, R. 1974. *The Devil's Triangle.* New York: Bantam.

Woodman, J. 1977. *Nazca: Journey to the Sun.* New York: Pocket Books.

Chapter 8: Professional and Personal Relations

Bainbridge, William S. 1978. "Biorhythms: Evaluating a Pseudoscience." *The Skeptical Inquirer,* vol. 2, no. 2: 40–56.

———. 1979. "In Search of Delusion: Television Pseudo-Documentaries," *The Skeptical Inquirer,* vol. 14, no. 1 (Fall 1979): 25–32.

Benassi, V., and B. Singer. 1981. "Occult Beliefs." *American Scientist,* vol. 69: 49–55.

Botts, Michael. 1986. "Consumer Protection for Psychic Fraud." *Private Communication,* Kansas City, Mo.

Burnham, John C. 1987. *How Superstition Won and Science Lost.* Rutgers, Pa.: Rutgers University Press.

Carter, M. 1969. *Helping Yourself with Foot Reflexology.* Nyack, N.Y.: Parker Publishing Co.

Cody, Steven. 1986. "Skeptical Burnout and Temptations to Fatalism," *Skeptical Briefs,* CSICOP, December 1986, vol. 2, no. 4: 4–6.

French, C. W., Eileen A. Powell, and H. Anginone, eds. 1980. *The Associated Press Stylebook and Libel Manual.* Reading, Mass.: Addison-Wesley Publishing Co.

Hines, Terence M. 1979. "Biorhythm Theory: A Critical Review." *The Skeptical Inquirer,* vol. 3, no. 4: 26–36.

Hyman, Ray. 1987. "Proper Criticism," *Skeptical Briefs,* CSICOP, May 1987, vol. 3, no. 2: 4–5.

Kurtz, Paul. 1986. "CSICOP After Ten Years: Reflections on the 'Transcendental Temptation'." *The Skeptical Inquirer,* vol. 10, no. 4: 229–234.

Leikind, B. J., and W. J. McCarthy. 1985. "An Investigation of Firewalking." *The Skeptical Inquirer,* vol. 10, no. 1: 23–35.

National Council Against Health Fraud. 1986. *Avoiding Legal Problems.* NCAHF Resource Center, Kansas City, Mo.

Sagan, Carl. 1980. "Nightwalkers and Mystery Mongers: Sense and Nonsense at the Edge of Science," in *Broca's Brain.* New York: Ballantine Publishing Co., 51–76.

Schultz, Marilyn. 1988. "An Insider's Look at the Media and the Paranormal." *Skeptical Briefs,* CSICOP, March 1988, vol. 14, no. 1: 4–6.

Scott, C. 1985. "Why Parapsychology Demands a Critical Response," in *A Skeptic's Handbook of Parapsychology,* Paul Kurtz, ed. Buffalo, N.Y.: Prometheus Books.

Slavsky, David. 1983. "Battling on the Airwaves." *The Skeptical Inquirer,* vol.7, no. 4 (Summer 1983): 188–192.

Starr, P. 1984. *The Social Transformation of American Medicine.* New York: Basic Books.

Targ, Russell, and Keith Harary. 1984. *The Mind Race.* New York: Ballantine Books.

Tedone, David. 1983. *Practical Publicity.* Boston: Harvard Common Press.

Tversky, A., and D. Kahneman. 1974. "Judgment Under Uncertainty: Heuristics and Biases." *Science,* vol. 185: 1124–1131.

Bibliography

Part 1: Some Books that Find and Expose the Missing Pieces

The books listed below are particularly useful in solving many of the paranormal mysteries and claims and exposing, wherever necessary, the many fraudulent practices and schemes used by so-called psychics and mediums to hoodwink and bedazzle an unsuspecting public. While some of the work listed herein may have been referred to earlier in the preceding chapters, every attempt has been made to avoid any unnecessary duplication. In a few of the references listed below, while they willingly admit that many of the reputedly supernatural phenomena were fraudulent, they still insist that there were other *truly* psychic and/or paranormal events. In such instances it should be remembered the burden of proof rests upon their shoulders.

RAB

Abbott, David P. 1907. *Behind the Scenes with the Medium.* Chicago: Open Court Publishing Co.

Abell, George, and Barry Singer, eds. 1981. *Science and the Paranormal.* New York: Charles Scribner's Sons.

Acquistapace, Fred. 1991. *Miracles that Never Were: Natural Explanations of the Bible's Supernatural Stories.* Santa Rosa, Calif.: Eye-Opener Books.

Anderson, George. 1963. *It Must Be Mind-Reading.* Chicago: Ireland Magic Company.

Annemann, Theodore. 1944. *Practical Mental Effects.* New York: Holden's Magic Shop.

Bach, Marcus. 1955. *The Will to Believe.* Englewood Cliffs, N.J.: Prentice-Hall.

Baggally, W. W. 1920. *Telepathy: Genuine and Fraudulent.* London, England: Methuen.

Baker, Robert A. 1992. *Hidden Memories.* Buffalo, N.Y.: Prometheus Books.

Bayless, Raymond. 1972. *Experiences of a Psychical Researcher.* New York: University Books.

Baldwin, Gordon. 1971. *Schemers, Dreamers and Medicine Men.* New York: Four Winds Publishers.

Blackmore, Simon A. 1924. *Spiritism Facts and Frauds.* New York: Benzinger Brothers.

Blackmore, Susan. 1986. *Adventures of a Parapsychologist.* Buffalo, N.Y.: Prometheus Books.

Blackstone, Harry, Jr. 1985. *The Blackstone Book of Magic and Illusion.* New York: Newmarket Press.

Bok, Bart, and Lawrence Jerome. 1975. *Objections to Astrology.* Buffalo, N.Y.: Prometheus Books.

Bowers, Edwin F. 1936. *Spiritualism's Challenge.* New York: National Library Press.

Brunvand, Jan Harold. 1981. *The Vanishing Hitchchiker.* New York: W. W. Norton Co.

———. 1984. *The Choking Doberman.* New York: W. W. Norton Co.

———. 1986. *The Mexican Pet.* New York: W. W. Norton Co.

———. 1989. *Curses! Broiled Again!* New York: W. W. Norton Co.

Cannell, J. C. 1973. *The Secrets of Houdini.* New York: Dover Publications.

Carrington, Hereward. 1920. *The Physical Phenomena of Spiritualism.* New York: American Universities Press.

———. 1973. *Sideshow and Animal Tricks.* Atlanta, Ga.: Pinchpenny Press.

Cavendish, Richard. 1968. *The Black Arts.* New York: Capricorn Books.

Cazeau, Charles, and Stuart Scott. 1980. *Exploring the Unknown.* New York: DeCapo Books.

Cohen, Daniel. 1965. *Myths of the Space Age.* New York: Dodd-Mead & Co.

———. 1971. *Masters of the Occult.* New York: Dodd-Mead & Co.

———. 1982. *The Encyclopedia of Monsters.* New York: Dodd-Mead & Co.

Christopher, Milbourne. 1962. *Panorama of Magic.* New York: Dover Publications.

———. 1970. *ESP, Seers, and Psychics.* New York: Thomas Y. Crowell.

———. 1973. *The Illustrated History of Magic.* New York: Thomas Y. Crowell.

———. 1975. *Mediums, Mystics and the Occult.* New York: Thomas Y. Crowell.

Curry, Paul. 1965. *Magician's Magic.* New York: Franklin Watts, Publishers.

Dawes, Edwin A., and Arthur Setterington. 1986. *The Encyclopedia of Magic.* New York: Gallery Books, W. H. Smith Publishers.

DeCamp, L. Sprague. 1980. *The Ragged Edge of Science.* Philadelphia: Owlswick Press.

———. 1983. *The Fringe of the Unknown.* Buffalo, N.Y.: Prometheus Books.

Dexter, Will. 1948. *This Is Magic: Secrets of the Conjurer's Craft.* New York: Bell Publishing Co.

Dingwall, E. J., and Harry Price. 1925. *Revelations of a Spirit Medium.* London, England: Kegan Paul.

Dunninger, Joseph. 1928. *Houdini's Spirit Exposé.* New York: Experimenter Press.

———. 1935. *Inside the Medium's Cabinet.* New York: David Kemp.

Dunninger, Joseph, as told to Walter B. Gibson. 1974. *Dunninger's Secrets.* New York: Lyle Stuart Inc.

Edmunds, Simeon. 1966. *Spiritualism: A Critical Survey.* London: Aquarian Press.

Evans, Bergen. 1946. *The Natural History of Nonsense.* New York: Alfred A. Knopf.

———. 1954. *The Spoor of Spooks and Other Nonsense.* New York: Alfred A. Knopf.

Evans, Christopher. 1973. *Cults of Unreason.* New York: Delta Books, Dell Publishing Co., Inc.

Evans, Henry Ridgley. 1897. *The Spirit World Unmasked.* Chicago: Laird and Lee.

Fair, Charles. 1974. *The New Nonsense.* New York: Simon & Schuster.

Fisher, John. 1980. *Body Magic.* New York: Scarborough Books, Stein & Day Publishers.

Fodor, Nandor. 1959. *The Haunted Mind.* New York: Garrett Publications.

———. 1966. *Encyclopedia of Psychic Science.* New Hyde Park, N.Y.: University Books.

Frazier, Kendrick, ed. 1991. *The Hundredth Monkey and Other Paradigms of the Paranormal.* Buffalo, N.Y.: Prometheus Books.

Gardner, Martin. 1990. *The New Age: Notes of a Fringe Watcher.* Buffalo, N.Y.: Prometheus Books.

———. *How Not to Test a Psychic.* Buffalo, N.Y.: Prometheus Books.

Gibson, Walter B. 1967. *Secrets of Magic.* New York: Grosset & Dunlap.

———. 1986. *The Bunco Book.* New York: Citadel Press.

Goldsmith, D., ed. 1977. *Scientists Confront Velikovsky.* New York: W. W. Norton & Co.

Hall, Trevor H. 1962. *The Spiritualists.* New York: Helix Press, Garrett Publishers.

Hansel, C. E. M. 1980. *ESP: A Scientific Evaluation.* Buffalo, N.Y.: Prometheus Books.

Hardinge, Emma. 1970. *Modern American Spiritualism.* New York: University Books.

Harris, Melvin. 1986. *Investigating the Unexplained.* Buffalo, N.Y.: Prometheus Books.

Hicks, Robert D. 1991. *In Pursuit of Satan.* Buffalo, N.Y.: Prometheus Books.

Hopkins, Albert A. 1977. *Magic: Scientific Diversions and Stage Illusions.* New York: Arno Press.

Houdini, Harry. 1972. *A Magician Among the Spirits.* New York: Arno Press.

Houdini, Harry, and Joseph Dunninger. 1968. *Magic and Mystery.* New York: Tower Publications.

Hyman, Ray. 1989. *The Elusive Quarry: A Scientific Appraisal of Psychical Research.* Buffalo, N.Y.: Prometheus Books.

Jastrow, Joseph. 1935. *Error and Eccentricity in Human Belief.* New York: Dover Publishing Co.

———, ed. 1936. *The Story of Human Error.* New York: D. Appleton Century Co.

Jerome, L. 1977. *Astrology Disproved.* Buffalo, N.Y.: Prometheus Books.

Kaye, Marvin. 1973. *The Handbook of Magic.* New York: Dorsett Press.

———. 1975. *The Handbook of Mental Magic.* New York: Stein & Day.

Keene, M. Lamar. 1976. *The Psychic Mafia.* New York: St. Martin's Press.

Korem, Dan. 1988. *Powers: Testing the Psychic and Supernatural.* Downer's Grove, Ill.: Intervarsity Press.

Kreskin, 1973. *The Amazing World of Kreskin.* New York: Random House.
———. 1984. *Kreskin's Fun Way to Mind Expansion.* New York: Doubleday & Co.
———. 1991. *Secrets of the Amazing Kreskin.* Buffalo, N.Y.: Prometheus Books.
Kusche, Lawrence. 1975. *The Bermuda Triangle Mystery—Solved.* New York: Warner Books.
MacDougall, Curtis D. 1958. *Hoaxes.* New York: Dover Publishing Inc.
McHargue, Georgess. 1972. *Facts, Frauds, and Phantasms: A Survey of the Spiritualist Movement.* New York: Doubleday & Co.
MacKay, Charles, LL. D. 1970. *Extraordinary Popular Delusions and the Madness of Crowds.* New York: Farrar, Straus & Giroux.
Moore, Patrick. 1976. *Can You Speak Venusian?* London: Star Books, Wyndham Publishers.
Mulholland, John. 1938. *Beware Familiar Spirits.* New York: Charles Scribner's Sons.
Nickell, Joe. 1991. *Secrets of the Supernatural.* Buffalo, N.Y.: Prometheus Books.
———. 1992. *Ambrose Bierce Is Missing.* Lexington: University Press of Kentucky.
O'Donnell, Eliot. 1920. *The Menace of Spiritualism.* New York: Frederick A. Stokes.
Ord-Hume, Arthur. 1977. *Perpetual Motion: The History of An Obsession.* New York: St. Martin's Press.
Pearsall, Ronald. 1972. *The Table Rappers.* New York: St. Martin's Press.
Price, Harry. 1974. *Confessions of a Ghost Hunter.* New York: Causeway Books.
Proskauer, Julien. 1932. *Spook Crooks!* New York: A. L. Burton.
———. 1946. *The Dead Do Not Talk.* New York: Harper Brothers.
Randi, James. 1975. *The Magic of Uri Geller.* New York: Ballantine Books, Random House.
———. 1980. *Flim-Flam: The Truth About Unicorns, Parapsychology and Other Delusions.* New York: Lippincott & Crowell.
———. 1989. *The Faith Healers.* Buffalo, N.Y.: Prometheus Books.
———. 1990. *The Mask of Nostradamus.* New York: Charles Scribner's.
Rawcliffe, D. H. 1959. *Illusions and Delusions of the Supernatural and the Occult.* New York: Dover Publications.
Ridpath, Ian. 1978. *Messages from the Stars.* New York: Harper & Row.
Rinn, Joseph. 1950. *Sixty Years of Psychical Research.* New York: Truth Seekers Publishing Co.
Rydell, Wendy, with George Gilbert. *The Great Book of Magic.* New York: Harry N. Abrams Inc. Publishers.
Sagan Carl. 1973. *The Cosmic Connection.* New York: Doubleday.
———. 1977. *The Dragons of Eden.* New York: Random House.
———. 1979. *Broca's Brain.* New York: Random House.
Smith, Lindsay E., and Bruce A. Walstad. 1989. *Sting Shift: The Street-Smart Cop's Handbook of Cons and Swindles.* Littleton, Colo.: Street-Smart Communications.
Steiner, Robert A. 1989. *Don't Get Taken.* El Cerrito, Calif.: Wide Awake Books.
Stemman, Roy. 1976. *Spirits and the Spirit Worlds.* New York: Doubleday & Co.
Taylor, John. 1980. *Science and the Supernatural.* New York: E. P. Dutton.

Vogt, E. Z., and Ray Hyman. 1979. *Water Witching USA*. Chicago: University of Chicago Press.

Wilhelm, John L. 1976. *The Search for Superman*. New York: Pocket Books, Simon & Schuster.

Part 2: Reference Sources for the Investigator

The following are major reference works representing important information sources for the investigator. Many others could be listed. Consult your reference librarian for assistance: he or she can be a major ally involving your research problems. (Compiled by Joe Nickell and Rob Aken, Librarian at the University of Kentucky)

People

American Men and Women of Science. Current edition. New York: R. R. Bowker. A biographical directory of notables in the physical, biological, and related sciences.

Biography and Genealogy Master Index: Current annual edition. A first-look source for locating brief biographies in such reference works as *Dictionary of American Biography, Contemporary Authors,* various who's whos, etc.; should be found in any sizable library's reference section.

Biography Index. 1946–present. New York: H. W. Wilson. Index to currently published biographies in numerous periodicals and books. Also includes an index by *profession.*

Contemporary Authors. Current series. Detroit: Gale Research. A biographical guide to current writers and their works.

Dial An Expert: The Consumer's Sourcebook of Free and Low-Cost Expertise Available by Phone, by Susan Osborn. 1986. New York: McGraw-Hill. Aid to locating experts in such fields as appraisals, collectibles, education, health, law, travel, etc.

Faculty White Pages. Current edition. Detroit: Gale Research. Directory of faculty members at colleges, universities, and similar institutions, *arranged by subject.*

National Faculty Directory. Current edition. Detroit: Gale Research. Alphabetical list of faculty members of colleges and universities in the United States (and selected Canadian institutions).

The New York Times Obituaries Index. 1858–most recent issue. New York: The New York Times. Index to obituaries in a major newspaper. Vol. I covers 1858–1968 and Vol. II 1969–1978.

Personal Name Index to the New York Times Index. 1851–1984. Succasunna, N.J.: Roxbury Data Interface. A single alphabetized, multivolume index to the millions of names in the *New York Times Index.*

Associations, Corporations, and Institutions

Directory of Archives and Manuscript Repositories in the United States. Second edition, 1988. Phoenix: Oryx Press. Organized by state and city (but with subject index), a guide to locating repositories of archival materials.

Directory of Historical Agencies in North America. Current edition. Nashville: American Association for State and Local History. Directory of historical, genealogical, folklore, oral history, and archival societies.

The Directory of Museums & Living Displays, 3d edition, by Kenneth Hudson and Ann Nicholls. 1985. New York: Stockton Press. Revised edition of the *Directory of World Museums.* Arranged geographically.

Dun & Bradstreet, Inc., Million Dollar Directory. Current edition. New York: Dun & Bradstreet Corp. Lists thousands of U.S. companies by their net worth. Includes such data as goods and services, approximate sales, names of officers and directors, and number of employees. Alphabetically arranged with geographic and SIC classification access.

Encyclopedia of Associations. Current edition. Detroit: Gale Research. Issued annually, with supplements. Guide to more than 30,000 organizations of every variety, including national and international organizations. Focus on U.S. and Canada; there is also an international edition.

The Foundation Directory. Current edition. New York: The Foundation Center. Provides information about the largest private and community grantmaking foundations in the United States.

The Official Museum Directory. Current edition. Wilmette, Ill.: National Register Publishing Co. State-by-state and city-by-city listing of American museums; also contains alphabetized directory of the museums' personnel and categorized subject index.

Research Center Directory. Current edition. Detroit: Gale Research. Guide to thousands of university-related and other nonprofit organizations carrying on continuing research in numerous fields. Subject access.

Standard & Poor's Register of Corporations, Directors and Executives. Current edition. New York: Standard & Poor's Corp. A guide to the business community and its executives. Alphabetically arranged by company with geographic and SIC classification access.

Thomas Register of American Manufacturers. Current edition. New York: Thomas Publishing Co. Comprehensive guide to United States manufacturers, indexed by company name and product.

World Guide to Abbreviations of Organizations. Current edition. Detroit: Grand River Books. Identifies organizations from their acronyms.

Yearbook of International Organizations. Current edition. New York: Union of International Associations. Attempts to cover all international organizations/associations according to broad criteria. Keyword access.

Periodicals

Note: Many indexes to periodicals are available in computer form and can therefore be searched in a greater variety of ways than can a paper index; check with your reference librarian.

Applied Science and Technology Index. 1917–present. New York: H. W. Wilson Co. Similar to *Reader's Guide to Periodical Literature,* but indexing scientific and technical periodicals rather than popular ones. Previous to 1958 the series was known as *The Industrial Arts Index* and included business publications.

CBS News Index. 1975–present. Ann Arbor, Mich.: UMI. Comprehensive index to microfiche transcripts of CBS News television broadcasts.

DATATIMES. Current database. Oklahoma City, Okla.: Data Times Corporation. Computerized access to full text of national and regional newspapers. Updated daily.

General Science Index. 1978–present. New York: H. W. Wilson. Subject index to scientific periodicals published in English.

InfoTrac: General Periodicals Index. Current database. Foster City, Calif.: Information Access Co. Computerized database giving references to articles in hundreds of business, technical, and general interest periodicals. Updated monthly.

Legal Resource Index. Current database. Foster City, Calif.: Information Access Co. Computerized database giving references to articles in hundreds of legal journals and related sources.

Newpapers in Microfilm: United States 1948–72. Washington, D.C.: Library of Congress, 1973; Supplemental edition 1978. Invaluable guide for locating copies of old newspapers; lists dates that they commenced and (if applicable) ceased publishing, the issues (by dates) that are available on microfilm, and libraries having copies.

The New York Times Index. 1851–present. New York: The New York Times Company. Index to a major newspaper, organized under subject, geographic, organization, and personal name headings. (Note: Similar indexes are available for many others including *The Times* [London], Los Angeles Times, Washington Post.)

Poole's Index to Periodical Literature. Peter Smith, 1963. Guide to nineteenth-century periodicals arranged by subject; includes book reviews.

Psychological Abstracts. 1927–present. Arlington, Va.: American Psychological Association. Summaries on articles on psychology and related disciplines; arranged by major content classifications, and has subject index.

Reader's Guide to Periodical Literature. 1900–present. New York: H. W. Wilson Co. A comprehensive list of articles in popular magazines divided into volumes according to time period and arranged according to topic.

Ulrich's International Periodicals Directory. Current edition. New York: R. R. Bowker. Standard guide to identifying and locating periodicals, arranged by title and subject; provides description, circulation, publishers' address, and subscription price. Also tells *where* publication is *indexed.*

VU/TEXT Information Services. Current database. Philadelphia: VU/TEXT Information Services, Inc. Computerized information retrieval service providing access to the *full text* of national and regional newspapers and wire services, as well as business and financial publications in the United States. Updated daily.

Books

Book Review Digest. 1905–present. New York: H. W. Wilson. Annual index to book reviews, including brief excerpts. A quick reference guide to learning how critics have evaluated a particular book.

Book Review Index. 1965–present. Detroit: Gale Research. Provides broad coverage of book reviews from a wide range of periodicals, such as *Publishers Weekly, New York Times,* etc.

Books in Print. Current edition. New York: R. R. Bowker. Produced annually from a bibliographic database (begun in 1948). In sets of volumes listing Authors, Titles, and Subjects, the series shows what books may currently be purchased, together with publisher and price; thus enables one's bookstore to order a copy. Updated bimonthly by *Forthcoming Books.*

The British Library General Catalogue of Printed Books. 1983. London: K. G. Saur. Guide to published texts held in the British Library; listed alphabetically by authors.

Cumulative Book Index. 1928–present. New York: H. W. Wilson. Provides broad listing of books printed in the English language. Previously known as *The United States Catalog* (1902–1928).

The National Union Catalog: Pre-1956 Imprints. 1981. London: Mansell. In more than seven hundred fifty volumes, a catalog of the books contained in libraries in the U.S. and Canada. Identifies libraries having copies which facilitates obtaining copies on interlibrary loan. (For books after 1956 see OCLC.)

Subject Collections, 6th edition, compiled by Lee Ash and William G. Miller, 1985. New York: R. R. Bowker. A guide to special collections of books and other materials as reported by libraries and museums in the U.S. and Canada; arranged by subject (e.g., Phrenology).

Miscellaneous

Acronyms, Initialisms & Abbreviations Dictionary. Current edition. Detroit: Gale Research. Extremely broad in scope, including such diverse fields as education, the sciences, government, etc.

Directories in Print. Current edition. Detroit: Gale Research. Annotated guide to specialized directories published in the U.S. (or having national or regional interest). Also available: *International Directories in Print.*

Dissertation Abstracts International. 1938–present. Ann Arbor, Mich.: University Microfilms International. Provides abstracts of doctoral dissertations submitted from hundreds of participating institutions. Covers dissertations back to 1861. (Before 1952 was titled *Microfilm Abstracts.*)

Encyclopedia of Information Systems and Services. Current edition. Detroit: Gale Research. Guide to electronic information industry, i.e., to organizations and services using computers and related technologies to provide access to data.

Facts on File Yearbook. 1941–present. New York: Facts on File. An annual index to world news, consisting of fifty-two news digests and an annual index. Weekly updates.

Finding the Source: A Thesaurus-Index to the Reference Collection, by Benjamin F. Shearer and Barbara Smith Shearer. 1981. Westport, Conn.: Greenwood Press. Specifically designed for use by those who lack experience in using reference collections.

First Stop: The Master Index to Subject Encyclopedias. 1989. Phoenix: Oryx Press. *Specialized* encyclopedic reference works, arranged by subject and keywords.

Guide to Reference Books, by Eugene P. Sheehy. Current edition. Chicago: American Library Assn. A reference work that identifies other reference works: encyclopedias, periodicals, general reference books on countless subjects, etc.

Monthly Catalog of United States Government Publications. 1895–present. Washington: U.S. Government Printing Office. Wide-ranging index to U.S. government publications.

Motif-Index of Folk-Literature, rev. ed., by Stith Thompson. 1955–1957. Bloomington: Indiana University. Classifies "motifs" (narrative elements) in folktales, myths, fables, local legends, etc.

OCLC Online Union Catalog. Current database. Dublin, Ohio: OCLC Online Computer Library Center. Computerized database for locating books, journals, manuscripts, maps, music scores, sound recordings, films and machine-readable data files; identifies libraries having copies. Over twenty-two million titles.

The Oxford English Dictionary, 2d edition. 1989. Oxford: Clarendon Press. The definitive dictionary of the English language, in fifteen large volumes. Includes the etymology and history of words, indicating their origin or earliest known use.

Rand McNally Commercial Atlas & Marketing Guide. Current annual edition. Chicago: Rand McNally. Brings together current economic and geographic information; includes United States maps and indexes by state, U.S. and Canadian metropolitan area maps, U.S. transportation and communication data, and economic and population data.

The Reporter's Handbook: An Investigator's Guide to Documents and Techniques, ed. by John Ullmann and Steve Honeyman. 1983. New York: St. Martin's Press. Guide and sourcebook for investigative reporting, organized by the most common areas that reporters cover, including "Following the Paper Trail," "Using Publications," "The Freedom of Information Act," "Backgrounding Individuals," "Using Tax Records," "Finding Out About Licensed Professionals," "Health Care," etc.

Source: A Guidebook of American Genealogy, by Arlene H. Eakle and Johni Cerny, eds. 1984. Salt Lake City: Ancestry. Compendium of resources for genealogists and local and family historians; tells how to locate and use courthouse records, gravestones, obituaries, military files, etc.

Statistical Abstract of the United States. 1878–present. Washington: U.S. Government Printing Office. Convenient annual compilation of important United States economic, political, social, and industrial statistics. References more detailed sources.

The Video Source Book. Current edition. Detroit: Gale Research. Guide to thousands of movies, instructional programs, and the like that are currently available on video.

United States Government Manual. Current edition. Washington: General Services Administration. Annual directory of governmental agencies and their key personnel; includes addresses and telephone numbers.

Walford's Guide to Reference Material. Current edition. London: The Library Association. Provides help in finding various reference books and bibliographies.

Where's What: Sources of Information for Federal Investigators, by Harry J. Murphy. 1976. New York: Warner Books. Comprehensive list of such sources as educational records, motor vehicle records, credit record sources, etc.; compiled by Office of Security, Central Intelligence Agency.

Where to Find What: A Handbook to Reference Service. Revised edition, 1984. Metuchen, N.J.: Scarecrow Press. Useful guide to finding specific reference materials from Abbreviations to Zoos.

The World Almanac and Book of Facts. 1868–present. New York: World Almanac. Annually published reference to such diverse facts as population of cities, table of atomic weights, chronology of year's events, astronomical data, associations, colleges and universities, outlines of U.S. and world history, zip and area codes, etc.

Index